# Europeanisation, National Identities and Migration

The last decade has seen the progressive, but in many ways difficult, reconnection of a divided Europe. *Europeanisation, National Identities and Migration* concentrates on the changes in collective identities resulting from European integration and the Eastern enlargement of the EU. This overall process particularly includes the restoration and reorganisation of the European system of nation-states, alongside the redefinition and intensification of national identities and reciprocal boundary constructions.

Such contemporary reconstruction and restructuration of nation-states does not simply continue the thread of the pre-Second World War and pre-Cold War era of the modern nation state. Major social forces are now at work in contemporary Europe, namely the dynamics of European integration and the growing consequences of international migration, and with them the transformation of national identities.

This collection provides an invaluable overview of the theoretical and historical framework which will enable the reader to analyse identity, collective identities, geo-political borders and alternative views of nations and migrants. These essays cover specific case studies in Western and Central Eastern European countries, with particular reference to East–West migration, and the countries along the current Eastern border of the European Union, in particular Germany, Poland and Hungary.

**Willfried Spohn** is Adjunct Professor at the Free University of Berlin and Research Fellow, European University Viadrina, Frankfurt a.O.

**Anna Triandafyllidou** is Project Coordinator and Research Fellow at the European University Institute, Florence.

# Routledge advances in sociology

This series aims to present cutting-edge developments and debates within the field of sociology. It will provide a broad range of case studies and the latest theoretical perspectives, while covering a variety of topics, theories and issues from around the world. It is not confined to any particular school of thought.

# Europeanisation, National Identities and Migration

Changes in boundary constructions
between Western and Eastern Europe

**Edited by
Willfried Spohn and
Anna Triandafyllidou**

Routledge
Taylor & Francis Group

LONDON AND NEW YORK

First published 2003
by Routledge
11 New Fetter Lane, London EC4P 4EE

Simultaneously published in the USA and Canada
by Routledge
29 West 35th Street, New York, NY 10001

*Routledge is an imprint of the Taylor & Francis Group*

Typeset in Baskerville by
Keystroke, Jacaranda Lodge, Wolverhampton
Printed and bound in Great Britain by
St Edmundsbury Press, Bury St Edmunds, Suffolk

*British Library Cataloguing in Publication Data*
A catalogue record for this book is available from the British Library

*Library of Congress Cataloging in Publication Data*
Europeanisation, national identities, and migration : changes in boundary
constructions between Western and Eastern Europe / edited by Willfried
Spohn and Anna Triandafyllidou.
    p. cm.
  Includes bibliographical references and index.
  (alk. paper)
  1. Europe, Western–Ethnic relations. 2. Europe, Eastern–Ethnic relations.
  3. National characteristics, East European. 4. National characteristics,
  West European. 5. Europe, Western–Boundaries. 6. Europe, Eastern–Boundaries.
  I. Spohn, Willfried, 1944– . II. Triandafyllidou, Anna.

  D1056.E9654 2003
  321′.05′094–dc21                                          2002032637

ISBN 0–415–29667–6

**To Evgenios and Dionisio**

# Contents

# Notes on contributors

**Norbert Cyrus** obtained his PhD in ethnology from the European University Viadrina, Frankfurt (Oder). His research examines the cultural dimension of the formation and functioning of the Polish–German border and the related informal labour markets. He is author of several reports for the Commissioner of Foreigners in Berlin, for the labour and social affairs Committee of the Bundestag, and for trade unions.

**Andrew Geddes** is Professor in the Political Science Department at the University of Liverpool. His major research area is migration and citizenship in Europe. Recent publications include: *Immigration and European Integration: Towards Fortress Europe?* (1999); *Immigration and Welfare: Challenging the Boundaries of the Welfare State* (ed. with Michael Bommes) (2000); and *The Politics of Belonging: Migrants and Minorities in Contemporary Europe* (ed. with Adrian Favell) (1999).

**Bernhard Giesen** studied sociology, philosophy and history at the University of Heidelberg, Germany and obtained his PhD and Habilitation at the universities of Augsburg and Münster. He was professor of sociology at the University of Giessen and is now Professor of Sociology at the University of Konstanz and external professor at the European University Institute, Florence. His publications include: *Die Intellektuellen und die Nation. Eine deutsche Achsenzeit* (1993); and *Kollektive Identität: Die Intellektuellen und die Nation* (1999).

**John Hutchinson** teaches in the European Institute, London School of Economics. He is the author of *The Dynamics of Cultural Nationalism* (1987), and *Modern Nationalism* (1994). He has co-edited with Professor Anthony D. Smith *Nationalism* (1996), *Ethnicity* (1996), and *Nationalism* in five vols (2000), and is co-editing *Understanding Nationalism* (forthcoming). He is an editor of the leading journal *Nations and Nationalism* and is currently working on a third monograph, *Nations as Zones of Conflict*.

**Miroslava Marody** is Professor of Sociology and Social Psychology in the Institute of Sociology at the University of Warsaw and the Head of the Centre for Political Studies in the Institute for Social Studies. Her recent work focuses on transformation processes in post-communist Poland. She has published eighteen books, including *Co nam zostało z tych lat . . . Społeczeństwo polskie na progu* *zmiany systemowej* (What's Left of All Those Years . . . Polish Society at the Threshold of Systemic Change) (1991), *Między rynkiem a etatem. Społeczne negocjowanie polskiej rzeczywistości* (Between Market and State. Negotiating Polish Reality) (2000).

**Ewa Morawska** received her masters degree in history from Warsaw University and her PhD in sociology from Boston University, Cambridge. She has published widely on comparative historical sociology and the history and sociology of (im)migration to both the US and Western Europe. Her major books are: *Bread and Butter* (1985) and *Insecure Prosperity. Jews in Johnstown 1880–1940* (1996). Forthcoming publications include *Reflections on Migration Research: Promises of Inter-disciplinarity* (ed. with Michael Bommes) and *Toward Assimilation and Citizenship in Liberal Nation-States*, (ed. with Christian Joppke).

**Richard Münch** is Professor of Sociology at the University of Bamberg. He studied sociology, philosophy, psychology and political sciences at Heidelberg University and has been Professor of Sociology at Cologne University, Professor of Social Sciences at Heinrich-Heine University, Düsseldorf and a visiting professor at UCLA, USA. His publications include: *Das Projekt Europa: Zwischen Nationalstaat, regionaler Autonomie und Weltgesellschaft* (1993); *Sociological Theory* (1994); *Dynamik der Kommunikationsgesellschaft* (1995); *Risikopolitik* (1996); *Globale Dynamik, lokale Lebenswelten* (1998).

**Krystyna Romaniszyn** is Associate Professor at the Jagiellonian University in Krakow. She received her PhD from the University of Warsaw and her Habilitation from the Jagiellonian University. She has held visiting positions at Cambridge University, UK, the Free University in Berlin, the Institute of Human Sciences in Vienna and Panteion University in Athens. She is author of two books in Polish on migration and economic anthropology. She has written extensively on contemporary labour migration from the East to the West and on cultural pluralism.

**Endre Sik** is Professor at the Department of Human Resources at the University of Economics and affiliated to the Tarski Institute for Social Research, both in Budapest, Hungary. He has published widely (mostly in Hungarian) in the fields of post-communist transformation, social inequality, labour markets, migration and ethnic minorities.

**Willfried Spohn** studied and received his PhD and Habilitation at the Free University of Berlin. He was an assistant professor and is now Adjunct Professor at the same institution, has been a visiting professor at several universities in the United States and Senior Jean Monnet Fellow at the European University Institute. He has published widely in the areas of comparative historical sociology and social history. His major publications include: *Can Europe Work? Germany and the Reconstruction of Postcommunist Societies* (ed. with S. Hanson) (1995); and *Modernization, Religion and Collective Identities: Germany Between Western and Eastern Europe* (forthcoming).

**Erhard Stölting** studied and received his PhD from the Free University of Berlin, and his Habilitation from the University Erlangen/Nürnberg. He has been a professor of sociology at the Free University of Berlin and is currently professor of sociology at the University of Potsdam. His major publications include: *Academic Sociology in the Weimar Republic* (1986); and *A World Power Disintegrates: Nationalities and Religions in the Soviet Union* (1990). His current research is on borders and boundary construction in Central and Eastern Europe.

**Judit Tóth** is an assistant professor in the Department of Human Resources at the University of Economics, Budapest, Hungary. Her major research and publication area is on migrants, refugees and ethnic minorities. A recent publication is *Refugees and Migrants: Hungary at a Cross-Road* (ed. with Maryellen Fullerton and Endre Sik) (1997).

**Anna Triandafyllidou** is Project Coordinator and Research Fellow at the Robert Schuman Centre for Advanced Studies, European University Institute in Florence. She currently works on two international research projects in the field of European integration and migration. Her recent publications include *Immigrants and National Identity in Europe* (2001) and *Negotiating Nationhood in a Changing Europe: Views from the Press* (2002).

# Acknowledgements

Most of the contributions included in this volume were initially presented at a workshop on 'European Integration and Changes in European Boundary Constructions. Collective Identities, Citizenship and Europeanness in Western and Eastern Europe' organised by Willfried Spohn and Anna Triandafyllidou and hosted by the Robert Schuman Centre for Advanced Studies of the European University Institute, in Florence, Italy on 8–9 April 2000. The workshop took place in the context of a two-year Thematic Network on Europeanisation, Collective Identities and Public Discourses (IDNET) funded by the European Commission, Research Directorate General, Key Action Improving the Socio-Economic Knowledge Base (contract no. HPSE-CT-1999-00034). We would also like to acknowledge the financial contribution of the European Commission Research DG through the IDNET grant in covering the language-editing and copy-preparing expenses for the manuscript of the book.

Our warm thanks go to Diamond Ashiagbor who patiently and carefully edited the manuscript, even though she at the same time had to prepare for the defence of her PhD thesis. The Routledge editorial team and Yeliz Ali in particular, were as always careful, punctual and understanding in dealing with all the small issues arising during the finalisation and preparation of a manuscript and we would like to thank them for that.

# 1  Introduction

*Anna Triandafyllidou and Willfried Spohn*

## Introduction

The decade following the European revolution of 1989–91 has witnessed a progressive, although in many ways difficult, reconnection of the divided Europe. With this development, the basic structural and cultural pluralism of a common 'European civilisation' (Eisenstadt 1987) – damaged by the Second World War and torn apart by the Cold War system – is in the process of restoration. This overall process includes particularly the restoration and re-organisation of the European system of nation-states and with them the redefinition and often intensification of national identities and reciprocal boundary constructions. The contemporary reconstruction and restructuration of nation-states in Europe, however, does not simply continue the thread of the pre-Second World War and pre-Cold War era of the modern nation-state. Rather, two major social forces are at work in contemporary Europe: the dynamics of European integration and the growing consequences of international migration and with them the transformation of national identities.

The European integration process, on the one hand, has developed in deepening and widening movements in Western Europe since 1945, pooling and mediating the sovereignty of the participating member states. The imminent Eastern enlargement of the European Union will have similar impacts on the post-communist nation-states of Central and Eastern Europe. As a consequence, the classical model of the nation-state as a sovereign entity of political-territorial centre-formation is to an increasing degree in the process of modification. International migration, on the other hand, has for several decades had an impact on the most developed nation-states in Western Europe, yet in the last decade it has not only been intensifying, but its impact has also been increasingly felt in Southern and Central Eastern Europe (see the chapters by Romaniszyn and Morawska in this volume). With it, the notion of cultural homogeneity as the basis of the politically-centralised nation-state is to a growing measure modified by ethnic minorities and immigrant communities. Both of these processes of transnational modification of states and nations in Europe also manifest themselves – at least as a tendency – in a stronger weight of European and multicultural elements in collective identities.

The contributions assembled in this volume address these two major social forces of transnational modifications of nation-states and collective identities in contemporary Europe in a Western and Eastern comparative perspective. Most of these contributions have been presented at a workshop held at the European University Institute in Florence and as part of a two-year Thematic Network on Europeanisation, Collective Identities and Public Discourses (IDNET) funded by the European Commission, Research DG. The contributions are divided into three parts.

The five chapters of Part I present different theoretical approaches to the Europeanisation and multicultural transformation of nation-states and national identities. The focus, here, is on the theoretical conceptualisation and comparative analysis of the relationships between national, European and multicultural components of collective identities. Bernhard Giesen, Richard Münch and John Hutchinson discuss the (non-)emergence of a European identity in the context of the European Union. The debate is complemented by two chapters (by Krystyna Romaniszyn and Andrew Geddes) that concentrate on immigration and European integration.

This first part of the book does not aim to provide a definite answer to sociological and political dilemmas such as: Will the European Union prove a viable political project? Has a sense of belonging to Europe developed? or What is the nature of the European demos today and how will it develop in the decade to come? Rather our aim is to cast new light on the debate by highlighting different aspects of a dynamic and quickly-evolving process of European integration that includes many tensions, discrepancies and inconsistencies. Through the different viewpoints adopted by the contributors to this volume, we seek to provide a fuller picture of the complex process of redefining a collective identity that takes place today in Europe.

The three chapters of Part II (by Miroslava Marody, Erhard Stölting and Willfried Spohn) look at the redefinition of national identities as a consequence of the reconnection of Europe and the eastward expansion of the European integration project. The case studies chosen include Germany, Poland and Russia, as these countries demarcate the territorial and symbolic boundaries (and their current re-organisation) of Europe between its Eastern and Western components.

The contributions included in Part III (by Ewa Morawska, Norbert Cyrus, Judith Tóth and Endre Sik) also refer to both Western and Central-Eastern European countries and concentrate on the transformation of collective identities in relation to European integration, the Eastern enlargement and contemporary migration processes. The case studies presented in this part cover three of the countries located along the current Eastern border of the EU, namely Germany, Hungary and Poland and provide for comparative insights on migration processes in the context of EU integration and Eastern enlargement.

Through these two sets of case studies presented in Parts II and III of the book, our aim is to examine the concrete sociological processes of collective identity transformation that take place in the context of European integration and in relation to neighbouring countries (be they fellow member states or accession countries) and immigrant groups. We seek thus to highlight that collective identity change takes place in a complex and fluid societal environment where nations and dominant discourses on nationhood are confronted with supra-national political entities like the European Union and an emerging awareness of 'being European' among their constituencies as well as sub-national challenges activated by immigration flows between Eastern and Western Europe in particular.

In the sections that follow we will present the thematic axes around which this volume is organised and the theoretical debates with which they are associated. We shall also briefly underline how the contributions included in this volume address such debates and cast new light on important conceptual and sociological issues.

Regarding the relationships between European and national identities and boundary constructions, within the reconstruction of Europe and the expansion of the European integration project to the East, four issues are fundamental: (1) the historical processes of and current changes in state formation and nation-building in Western and Eastern Europe; (2) the impact of the European integration process and its extension to the East on states and nations in Western and Eastern Europe; (3) within this context the changing relationships between national and European identities and boundary constructions; and last but not least (4) the 'multicultural' impact of growing international migration and immigration on the historically-formed nations, national identities and boundary constructions in the context of European integration.

## State formation and nation-building in Western and Eastern Europe

The implosion of the Soviet communist system has enabled the restoration and reconstruction of independent nation-states in Central-Eastern Europe. These processes were accompanied by political transitions to democratic regimes and social transformations towards capitalist market societies. The 'great transformation' in the post-communist societies in Central and Eastern Europe has been pre-dominantly seen by social and political scientists as a bundle of catching-up processes of modernisation, emulating the Western European model of a modern, democratic and capitalist nation-state. To be sure, the processes of political and economic transformation in post-communist Central and Eastern Europe have displayed considerable variations (Beyme 1996; Linz and Stepan 1996). The evolution of political regimes ranges from the consolidation of liberal-constitutional democracies, to the development of mixed democratic/authoritarian structures or the reversal of authoritarian political systems. The transformation to capitalist market societies varies from relatively successful evolution to crisis-prone development and continuous decline. The processes of state formation and political/legal institution-building have generally been weak and, inversely, the tendency to create ethnically homogeneous nations generally strong. But despite these variations, the Western European capitalist and democratic nation-state has served as a forceful model for the Eastern European transformations. In this sense the modern nation-state has been developing, diversifying, not dying (Mann 1993) and, with it, the European structural pluralism of independent nation-states in Western as well as in post-communist Central and Eastern Europe has been reconstituted.

Under the impression of the enormous changes brought about by the implosion of the Soviet Empire, there emerged in the social and political sciences a renewed interest in the nature of the modern nation-state, the processes of state formation and nation-building and related political movements and identities. For many in a valid way, Ernest Gellner has defined the modern nation-state as the congruence between the state as a territorial–political unity of centre-formation and the nation as a shared culture of a political community (Gellner 1983). The socio-historical foundations of the formation of the modern nation-state and related national movements and identities, according to his modernisation theory, are the development of a capitalist–industrial economy, the standardisation of a common high culture and political democratic participation. At the same time, it has remained unclear whether this model of the modern nation-state constitutes an ideal-type in Max Weber's sense of social-action orienting idea or a real-type in the sense of a historically-materialising formation (Balakrishnan 1996; Hall 1997). As an ideal-type, this model seems to be a valid vision particularly for modernising national movements and political elites but has come under mounting criticism by alternative, post-nationalistic and multicultural ideas of political organisation. As a real-type, this model has been questioned regarding its teleological–evolutionary assumptions in view of the different historical preconditions, varying developmental trajectories and multiple modern types of the nation-state.

From this perspective, the contemporary reconnection of Europe is not simply reconstituting a pan-European system of converging modern nation-states. Rather, there have developed and are continuing to develop varying forms of modern nation-states on the basis of their differing historical trajectories in the various European regions. As particularly Stein Rokkan (see the recent reconstruction by Peter Flora, Stein Kühnle and Derek Urwin 1999) proposed and also Ernest Gellner suggested, it makes sense to distinguish between at least four major European time zones of state-formation and nation-building. The first Western European state formation zone has been characterised by early processes of political-territorial centralisation and corresponding high cultures; here, aristocratic incorporation enabled the inclusion of different ethnic groups very early on. The second Western Central European time zone has for a long time remained under the influence of the declining Western Roman Empire and was characterised by political fragmentation on the basis of cities and regions combined with two major high cultures; here, aristocratic inclusion remained territorially dispersed, contributing to the endurance of ethnically mixed populations. The third East Central European time-zone at the intersection between Western and Eastern Christianity has become until recently the victim of Empire-building; political centralisation here was predominantly part of imperial state-building in opposition to peripheral forms of nation-building. And the fourth time zone of nation-state formation has been created by the core regions of the Eastern Empires with imperial bureaucracies on the top of segmented ethno-religious groups; here, nation-state formation has involved the dismantling of Empires and subsequent ethnic nation-building.

In a parallel comparative perspective, there have developed attempts to construct typologies of nationalism and national identity in the European geographical and historical context. Hans Kohn (1964) and later Anthony Smith (1991) as well as John Hutchinson (1994) have proposed to distinguish between the Western state-led civic-territorial model and the Eastern state-seeking ethnic model of nationalism and national identity formation. In the recent debate, this binary opposition has been criticised as too categorical and a-historical. As Rogers Brubaker (1999) has recently proposed, it is more appropriate to see the ethnic and civic elements as two general, but in their combination varying and historically changing, components of nationalism and national identity. Accordingly, it makes sense to relate – more systematically than has been done so far – the varying forms of nationalism and national identity in the present to the different time zones of state formation and nation-building in Europe as well as to the historical development and expanding waves of democratisation during the nineteenth and twentieth centuries. Regarding the different time zones of nation-state formation, there are crucial differences between the French and British rather political nationalism (first Western European zone), the German or Swiss more federal nationalism (second city-belt zone), the Polish and Hungarian peripheral nationalism (third continental interface zone), or the Russian imperial nationalism (fourth continental Empire-building zone). Regarding the historical waves of democratisation, the early nineteenth-century dividing line between civic-territorial and ethnic types of nationalism at the Rhine moved during the late nineteenth and early twentieth centuries further eastward, retreated again with the rise of fascism, Soviet communism and the European Cold-War divide, but was after 1945 moving again to Western Central Europe and is now expanding further eastward. In a parallel, the institutional components of citizenship and the civic elements of nationalism or national identity are not fixed entities, but historically changing in their weight and scope.

## European integration and its expansion toward the East

The reconstruction of the pluralistic system of sovereign modern nation-states, whatever their individual configuration of statehood and civic or ethnic nationhood, in Western and Eastern Europe is, however, only one basic feature of the contemporary bridging of the Cold War European divide. Another feature is the deepening and widening process of European integration that started after the Second World War in the core of Western Europe, and which then included in several enlargement waves most parts of North Western, Southern and Northern Europe, intensified in cyclical and concentric movements, and is now on the move to expand to the East. Although bound to the basic pluralism of the European state system and perhaps even an important rescuer of the European nation-state (Milward 1992), the European integration process has developed into a European system of transnational governance that essentially modifies the model of the modern nation-state. One crucial feature is the pooling of the member states' national sovereignty into the transnational European Community/Union level that, although with the basic consent of each member, nevertheless restricts and mediates the independent power of each individual nation-state. Another crucial feature is the functional integration of particular political, economic or social issues that were traditionally in the hands of an individual state or society and are now merged into transnational institutions and policies. At the same time, the degrees of sovereignty transfers and functional integration vary according to national preferences. As a result, there has developed a multi-level system of European governance with a variable geometry of different speeds and scopes of integration.

In the public and scholarly debate, European integration as both a complex socio-economic process and the resulting type of European political system in relation to the member states, has been quite a controversial issue. The perception and conceptualisation of the European Communities/Union range from a mere intergovernmental framework leaving the nation-state basically intact, to an evolving federal state fundamentally changing the traditional sovereign nation-state. These contrasting perceptions and conceptualisations reflect, on the one hand, public attitudes in the different EU member states to what the European Union in the end should be (see the recent debate on a European constitution, V.A. 2001). On the other hand, they also reflect the scientific difficulties to determine the nature of a continually developing process that is neither predetermined nor finalised. Despite these contrasting perspectives, however, there has crystallised a scholarly consensus that the European Union should be viewed as a transnational regime *sui generis* in between a confederation of states and a federal state. Accordingly, the originally antithetic positions of realism (starting from the individual nation-state) and of functionalism (starting from the integration logic) have moved towards a neo-realist, neo-functionalist and liberal–intergovernmentalist synthesis. Within this synthesis, the crucial *problematique* is focusing on the modes and degrees of the Europeanisation of nation-states and their change over time. This volume is particularly concerned with the Europeanisation of collective identities – rather than that of public policies, a subject that is dealt with by political scientists and international relation theorists – to the extent that the existence of a collective identity is seen by many scholars (see the chapters by Giesen and Hutchinson in this volume) as a prerequisite for the functioning of a democratic polity. An alternative line of argument, however, would have it (see the chapter by Münch in this volume and Habermas 1994) that a sense of community can be built through active participation in a polity. Thus, Münch argues that the European polity may be based on a society of individuals enmeshed in a dense set of networks that keep them together.

The imminent Eastern enlargement of the European Union continues, in terms of a set of institutional and procedural mechanisms, the former enlargement waves of the European Community/EU to North Western, Southern and Northern Europe. As such, the Eastern enlargement will also mean a similar process of growing incorporation of the post-communist nation-states in Central and Eastern Europe into the transnational governance regime of the European Union. As a concrete socio-economic and political process, however, the Eastern enlargement is much more challenging than any former enlargement waves. From the perspective of the European Union, the Eastern enlargement means the inclusion of a large number of future members, which will (potentially) alter the power equilibrium between current members and require crucial reforms of the existing governance institutions and decision-making procedures. The still ongoing social and economic transition of post-communist applicant states to liberal capitalist market societies poses a challenge to the financial and political cohesion within the European Union. Moreover, a considerable shift in the financial resources of the European Union's budget from the less-favoured regions of Western Europe to the new Eastern European members is envisaged to speed up their economic adaptation to the single market. The differences in political institutions and cultural mentalities challenge the political coherence and cultural convergence of the European Union.

Not least, the Eastern enlargement raises the thorny issue of the Eastern borders of the European Union: the Europeanness of Russia (see the chapter by Stölting in this volume) or Turkey remains under question. Taken together, the Eastern enlargement considerably strengthens the centrifugal and potentially fragmenting forces within an extended European governance regime while, at the same time, it strengthens the legitimacy of the European Union as a political project that promotes democracy and Western liberalism. Overall, the course of the Eastern enlargement process in its timing, spatial scope and final outcome still remains contested in both member states and accession countries (see Spohn on Germany and Poland in this volume, and also Euronat Project Reports 2002, www.iue.it/RSC/Euronat).

From the Central and Eastern European applicants' perspective and particularly in the view of large parts of the post-communist elites, the hesitant development of the Eastern enlargement is rather disappointing. As compared to the original high hopes for the return to Europe, the impression is growing that Western Europe is rather reluctant to include Eastern Europe. With it, the hoped-for geopolitical protection against the potentially renewing Russian power is only partially settled, the expected acceleration of the crisis-prone economic transformation processes is postponed and the stabilising support for the consolidation of the still young democratic regimes remains weak. At the same time, the more the processes of the Eastern enlargement are actually underway, the more the potential critical effects of the European Union on the post-communist societies in Central and Eastern Europe are feared. These fears concern particularly the loss of the recently attained national sovereignty by the incorporation into the Western European governance regime and the renewed peripheral status vis-à-vis Western Europe. There are also fears concerning the critical impact of the superior Western economy on the potentially weakened sectors of the post-communist economies and the imagined threats to the national cultures and identities by the secular and materialist culture of Western Europe. In essence, these concerns and fears in the Central and Eastern European applicant states crystallise around the fear that the European Union will limit the model of the sovereign nation-state that has been at the core of the Eastern European revolutions and post-communist transformations. Thus, while in the actual member states' public discourses, Central and Eastern Europeans are perceived as distant brethren or indeed as distant aliens (Triandafyllidou 2002a), the populations in accession countries – Poland is the most obvious case in point (see the chapter by Marody in this volume) – grow increasingly disenchanted with the prospect of becoming part of the European Union.

## European and national identities and boundary constructions

In the social, political, cultural and historical sciences the predominant approaches conceive of collective identities as constituted by the collective group which individuals belong to and identify with. Accordingly, national identities are analysed as derivatives or prerequisites of nation-state formation and, translated to Europe, a European identity is seen as an attachment to the evolving European transnational governance regime. Within this perspective, in parallel to the opposition between the nation-state and an evolving European super-state, two opposite theoretical approaches define the methodological options for analysing the relationship between national identities and a potentially emerging European identity. The first position, starting from the conceptualisation of the European Community/ Union as a transnational layer above the constituting nation-state members, views the emerging 'Europeanness' as an additional layer to the basic national identity (Lepsius 1998). The premise here is that the emerging European identity is secondary or additional and therefore weak as compared to the primary and strong national identity. The opposite position, conceptualising the European Union as a system of governance which absorbs elements of national governance, assumes that a trans- or post-national European identity is increasingly replacing the pre-existing national identities (Eder 1998). The opposite premise here is that national identities are progressively declining against a strengthening European identity.

However, these approaches tend to neglect the interaction between nations and the EU and more generally the link between collective identity development and boundary constructions (Triandafyllidou 2001). Each national identity is constructed and continually reconstructed as a collective sentiment, self-awareness, self-definition and boundary setting of a national group, but at the same time in continued interaction with the surrounding national groups in the cultural and geopolitical context of Europe. The post-Second World War European integration project has been developing in interaction with the matrix of national groups and the web of national identities involved in it and has been influenced by a set of interwoven national and European elements. From this relational perspective, the European element in national identities is not simply an emerging property of or an identification with the formation of transnational European institutions, rather it is constituted in continual interaction between nationally formed European orientations and the developing transnational European framework. In this sense, the image of the intertwining of European and national components in collective identities is more appropriate than the alternative models of superimposition or replacement. The methodological task we are confronted with here is thus to analyse the amalgamation of European and national elements in the formation and development or change of collective identities over time and in their relationship with minorities and immigrants (see the chapters by Romaniszyn, Morawska, Tóth and Sik, and Cyrus in this volume).

From this relational perspective, the reconfiguration of collective identities in their national and European components with the implosion of Soviet communism, the opening and bridging of the East–West divide and the progressing reconnection of the European civilisation is crucial. On the Western European side, the opening of the Eastern European space means a geopolitical as well as a cultural reconfiguration of collective identities and redefinition of boundary constructions as cultural bases of the Eastern enlargement of the European Union. In geopolitical terms, it presents an opportunity to export and enlarge the Western European model of liberal-democratic welfare capitalism and create a military, political and social welfare zone. In cultural terms, a reconstruction of a Western 'mission' towards the East from defensive anti-communism to a cautious expansion of Western values is under way. This includes, dependent on the respective geopolitical location within Europe, different uses of 'the East' in Western European discourse (Neumann 1999). This also includes the geopolitical relocation and cultural reconstruction of national identities, particularly of those countries at the border of the former East–West divide and now again in-between East and West.

The Eastern enlargement changes the cultural and political baricentre of the EU and requires the re-positioning of each nation and national state within it. Ethnic, cultural and religious traditions that characterised the Eastern part of Europe are now integrated into the European project. Thus, countries such as Greece, which were deemed to represent the Eastern border of the Union in not only geopolitical but also cultural and religious terms, may find themselves closer to the centre. In contrast, countries such as the UK or France that represented the civic, democratic core of European identity may be pushed towards the political periphery. Even though nationalism theory has sought to categorise national identities in Eastern-ethnic and Western-civic types, in reality there are 'Eastern' and 'Western' elements in all national identities. Thus, the change in the context may lead to a re-evaluation of such elements within each national identity and a change in their relative importance.

European integration varies among nations depending on their own cultural traditions, history and geopolitical position. Thus, German national identity is imbued with Europeanness, but in historically changing cultural and political modes of self-definition between Western and Eastern Europe. United Germany now seems to be firmly anchored in a Western European civic identity, strongly supporting the Eastern enlargement of the European Union as a *mission civilisatrice* vis-à-vis Eastern Europe (see the chapter by Spohn in this volume). Italy is also one of the most enthusiastic supporters of the EU project even though it struggles to define its own role within it (Triandafyllidou 2002a). The case of Greece, which is also a border country, is different yet again because of its janus-faced, Eastern-and Western-looking identity and history. Despite the fact that classical Greek heritage, highly cherished by modern Greeks, is seen as the cradle of European civilisation, modern Greeks often feel alienated culturally and politically from the EU (see Triandafyllidou 2002b).

On the Eastern European side, in a mirror-inverted sense, the opening of the Western European space also goes hand in hand with a major geopolitical and cultural reconfiguration of collective identities. In geopolitical terms, it opens the possibility of a 'return to Europe', to join Western Europe, to become part of the

Western European community and at the same time to be protected and shielded against renewed threats from the East, Russia and Asia. This is the general motivational basis for the wish to become, as soon as possible, member states of the European Union. In cultural terms, the West, not only Western Europe, but also America represents a model to be emulated as a direction for societal, economic and political progress. At the same time, it is also a model to defend oneself from, because it is more powerful, expansive and undermining of traditional cultures, lifestyles, values and identities. Again, these cultural re-definitions of collective identities depend on the geopolitical location within the European space. In this volume, we seek to cast light on these processes through the study of the Hungarian, Polish and Russian cases. Hungary presents an important challenge because of its imperial historical experience and the current division of the Hungarian nation into one mother country and many diasporic communities, to be segregated in the near future by the Schengen border zone (see the chapter by Tóth and Sik in this volume). Poland plays a pivotal role in its location between the united Germany and its historical imperial neighbours from Lithuania to the Ukraine (see the chapters by Marody and Spohn in this volume), while Russia and its self-definitions towards its neighbouring Others sets a symbolic and geopolitical borderline between Europe and Asia (see the chapter by Stölting in this volume). Moreover, in the aftermath of 11 September, the representation of Russia by itself and other countries as part of 'the West' has acquired new emphasis. Its role as the symbolic and geopolitical border between 'the West' and 'the Islamic world' – where either are seen as homogenous and compact – has been cast with renewed emphasis. Other interesting examples of social and territorial boundary (re-)constructions are the Baltic countries between northern Europe and Russia and the Balkan countries and Turkey in the southeastern corner of the European continent.

## Immigrants as Others

Within the overall process of European integration and Eastern enlargement and the related reconfiguration of national and European identities, immigration remains a largely unsettled issue. It is our aim in this book to highlight the ingroup–outgroup dynamics that condition the relationship between the nation and the immigrant(s) both in general and with particular reference to the process of European integration. 'Othering' the immigrant is functional to the development of national identity and to achieving or enhancing national cohesion. The immigrant is a potential threatening Other because s/he crosses the national boundaries challenging, thus, the ingroup identification with a specific culture, territory or ethnic origin as well as the overall categorisation of people into nationals and others. In other words, the immigrant poses a challenge to the ingroup's presumed unity and authenticity, which it threatens to 'contaminate'.

Most European countries conceive of themselves as national states, where the state is the political expression of the dominant nation. This idea implies a static view of culture and ethnic descent: these are seen as homogeneous and unique. The presumed purity and authenticity has to be protected from the intrusions of foreigners. Thus, pluralism is accepted only (and not always) to the extent that a nation or ethnic minority is a constitutive element of the country, namely made part of the state from its very moment of creation and is in some way integrated into the national narrative. Even in these cases, of course, the potential of conflict between the dominant nation and minorities is high. A plurality of identities and cultures is not easily accommodated within national states.

In some countries immigrant communities are integrated into the national history and the cultural, territorial, civic and genealogical links between these populations and the nation are officially recognised. Thus, as it happens in France and the UK, the links between the 'mother country' and its former colonies are deemed to justify, under certain conditions, the conferral of citizenship on people of immigrant origin. Nonetheless, the status of citizenship often does not suffice to guarantee the social integration of these people. As a matter of fact, it is not unusual for individuals of immigrant origin, who have acquired the citizenship of the 'host' country by birth or residence, to continue to be subject to discrimination in practice. Discriminatory behaviour or practices are predominantly related to race, namely skin complexion and phenotypic characteristics, culture or a combination of both. Even though having access to the status of permanent resident or, indeed, the citizenship of that country constitutes a major step towards immigrant integration, a study of the process of Othering the immigrant must pay particular attention to more subtle mechanisms of discrimination and ingroup–outgroup construction (see Tóth and Sik's contribution in this volume).

It is worth noting that not all immigrants are perceived as Others and, in particular, as threatening Others. With regard to the European Union, for instance, citizens of fellow member states are endowed with the same rights and duties as the host country nationals, because they are citizens of the Union. Moreover, these people do not generally suffer from discrimination in the social sphere. Similarly, North Americans and citizens from other industrialised countries may be foreigners in Europe but do not come within the negative stereotype usually associated with immigration. In other words, the process of Othering the immigrant is activated towards specific groups.

The common feature that characterises such outgroups is their *subordinate* position in society and the existence of ethnic, cultural, religious or racial *markers* that distinguish them from the dominant group. Such markers are not the reason for which these groups are perceived as threatening outgroups. On the contrary, difference is context-bound: in one case, religious markers may be prevalent (for instance, anti-Muslim racism in Britain) while in another situation ethnic categorisation may be emphasised (e.g. prejudice against Albanians in Greece). The Othering of specific immigrant groups serves the interests and identity of the dominant nation. Immigrants become the negative Other in contrast to whom a positive ingroup identity is constructed and/or reinforced. Moreover, they provide flexible, dispensable and disenfranchised labour in an increasingly globalised post-industrial economy.

The process of European integration affects immigrant communities and minorities living in Europe. This happens both directly and through the channels of national states. First and foremost, even though member states are reluctant to concede any of their powers in matters of citizenship or migration to European institutions, a common European migration and asylum regime has emerged through intergovernmental cooperation. Most recently, immigration and asylum matters have been incorporated into the areas of EU competence and a common EU policy is envisaged to become effective in May 2004. Moreover, the decrease in internal border controls makes EU partners inter-dependent. Inefficient border-policing in Greece or Spain, for instance, may lead to undocumented immigration towards Germany or France.

Apart from policy effects, the relationship between European integration and immigration also has an impact on identity categorisations. Member state nationals acquire equal rights to citizens of member states by means of their common European citizenship. Immigrants from southern Europe residing in northern European countries are thus fully integrated into the host society and distinguished from third-country nationals, the famous '*extracomunitari*'. The role of the immigrant Other is delegated to labourers coming from outside the EU, notably Asia, Africa and Latin America. Moreover, the cultural, religious and physical difference of these groups makes them a suitable target population for racialisation.

However, matters become more complicated by East–West migration within Europe. The post-1989 period has been characterised by a dramatic population influx from the former communist countries to Western Europe, including southern European countries that had no previous experience as hosts. Hundreds of thousands of Albanians, Poles, Romanians or Ukrainians, just to name some of the most 'mobile' nationalities, have entered, with or without adequate documentation, a number of EU countries in search of work and/or better life chances. Xenophobic and racist reactions towards these people have been registered in a number of EU countries especially in southern Europe (European Commission 1997). National stereotyped images have developed towards specific nationalities (Palidda 1996; Triandafyllidou 2001) and immigrants have been subjected to a process of inferiorisation and subordination (dal Lago 1999).

The identity dynamics involved in the Othering of immigrants have to be seen within their international context, namely the end of the Cold War and the Eastern enlargement of the Union. Othering the immigrant has a double function for national identity: it provides a means for affirming the unity and superiority of the ingroup while, at the same time, it allows for and justifies the exploitation of immigrant labour in conditions that would be unacceptable for fellow nationals. This type of dynamic acquires new impetus after the disappearance of Western Europe's main threatening Other, namely the 'Eastern bloc'. Immigrants from non-EU countries provide the new threatening, internal Other: the negative image against which the ingroup identity is constructed.

The situation of immigrants coming from Central and Eastern European countries has however become ambivalent after the most recent opening of the EU towards further enlargement. The example of Polish immigrants, for instance, is particularly interesting, for Poles are subject to exploitation and inferiorisation in a number of countries of northern and southern Europe (e.g. Germany, Greece or

Italy) despite the imminent accession of Poland to the EU. These people play a pivotal role between a sense of cultural commonality and Europeanness, national identity and immigrants as outsiders. It is expected that as the Eastern enlargement is becoming a social and political reality, gradually the boundary between immigrants from EU countries and Others will be reorganised, so that certain Central and Eastern European nationalities will be integrated into the European 'we' (see the chapters by Cyrus and Geddes in this volume). The perception of threat will then concentrate on immigrants from Asia and Africa or on people originating from Eastern European or Balkan countries who did not meet the criteria for membership, such as Albania, Bulgaria or Romania for instance.

The cultural, religious or phenotypic features used to distinguish immigrants from the ingroup are the markers of difference between the dominant group and peripheral nations or minorities too. These minorities may be historical minorities that have participated in the nation-state formation (e.g. the Britons in France, the Turks in Greece or the Basque, Catalans and Roma in Spain) or of immigrant origin (such as the Moroccans in Belgium, the Algerians in France or the West Indian and Pakistani communities in the UK). Overall, relations between the dominant ingroup and minorities may be analysed within the same logic of subordination and racialisation that characterise the nation–immigrant relation. Even though members of the minorities are formally integrated into the host society, cultural, ethnic and religious boundaries remain. The fundamental opposition between the nationalist ideal of a homogeneous and 'pure' national culture and population and the existence of minorities is, however, challenged by the process of Europeanisation. The ever closer Union involves the re-organisation of national identity so as to accommodate political and cultural loyalties parallel to the nation. The European dimension may thus open identity and institutional space for minorities and provide alternative dimensions for inclusion. This inclusive process will in all likelihood be dominated by the Western European political and cultural framework. In this volume, Geddes gives a challenging account of how existing legal traditions and market-related concerns may shape immigrant policies in a united Europe. Even though the EU society and polity is characterised by internal diversity, its immigration and asylum policies may discriminate against specific Others because of historical or contextual reasons. The events of 11 September 2001 and their aftermath have painfully shown how 'the West' and with it the European Union, readily define themselves in opposition to Muslim countries across the world as well as the Muslim populations that are part of their societies, who are represented as their most important threatening Others.

## The contents of this book

Having thus outlined the theoretical and comparative framework of this volume, we shall now present in some more detail the chapters of this volume and their individual contributions to it.

The chapters included in Part I of the book offer different theoretical approaches to the study of collective identity change and multicultural transformation of the nation-state in Europe. The first three contributions in this part offer three different theoretical perspectives from which to approach the emergence of a common European identity within the EU and the related transformation of national identities. Bernhard Giesen in his study of *The collective identity of Europe: constitutional practice or community of memory?* dismisses the idea of constitutional patriotism as the bond that will bring together a European demos and highlights instead the role of collective memory and past experiences. He analyses the forms of constitutional regimes that have characterised European history as possible answers to the question of the political organisation of a united Europe. While Giesen identifies important cultural or political elements that could resonate well with contemporary European reality and experience, he eventually finds no single model that would provide the answer to the question. He therefore turns to the role of history and most importantly of collective memory. Giesen argues that the discursive repertoire of collective guilt and redemption exemplified in the German post-war experience in relation to the Nazi regime and the Holocaust resonates with a more general European-Christian tradition of sin, repenting and forgiveness. This common discursive repertoire may provide, according to Giesen, for a basis on which a common sense of Europeanness can develop in the EU.

Richard Münch in his chapter on *Democracy without demos: European integration as a process of the change of institutions and cultures,* studies the European integration process and its transformative impact on nation-states and national identities, focusing on the emerging form of a European society. Quite interestingly, Münch dismisses the idea of a cohesive European demos. He argues that European integration is leading towards a pluralistic multi-level democracy that is not based on a uniform demos but rather on a society of individuals interlinked by a complex web of networks. This emerging European society is, according to Münch, characterised by a pluralism of interests, life concepts and cultural traditions, in which politics and social justice are guaranteed by procedural rules rather than a common culture or identity.

In contrast to Giesen and Münch, John Hutchinson in his contribution on *Enduring nations and the illusions of European integration* defends the resilient weight of nation-states and national identities. He is highly sceptical of the process of European integration which he sees as lacking the necessary appeal to community and belonging that is necessary for a European society and polity to prove viable. Hutchinson argues that nations, as communities of fate, and nation-states, as political entities are both enduring and flexible. Their appeal to belonging and solidarity is difficult to resist and/or is unlikely to be substituted by a Europe with an 'empty heart' even though the political form and areas of competence of the nation-state may vary, as his historical analysis shows.

Thus, regarding the emergence of a European identity and the related re-organisation of national identities and boundary constructions, Hutchinson defends the enduring nature of the latter, Münch points to the overall fading away of collective identities and their replacement by multiple and dense connecting networks, whereas Giesen argues for the emergence of a common sense of Europeanness through collective memory repertoires.

Part I of this volume is complemented by the contributions of Krystyna Romaniszyn and Andrew Geddes who discuss the issue of Europeanisation of identities and the reshuffling of symbolic and territorial boundaries through the lens of migration. Krystyna Romaniszyn in her contribution *Migration, cultural diversification and Europeanisation* adopts a sociological bottom-up approach. She analyses the cultural diversification processes engendered through transnational population movements, exploring cultural and social change in various spheres of social life including consumer patterns, economic behaviour, social norms, ethnic stereotypes and interethnic relations. Regarding the European integration process, Romaniszyn argues that these processes of cultural and social diversification may facilitate the Europeanisation of cultural identities, but at the same time may also create problems, both at the national and EU level, concerning the management of cultural pluralism.

From a political-scientific top-down perspective, Andrew Geddes in his contribution on *Integrating immigrants and minorities in a wider and deeper Europe* investigates recent developments in immigration policy design at the European Union level. He shows how supra-national governance may override concerns with national sovereignty if the issue at stake is related to existing legal and economic repertories such as anti-discrimination policy or market-related provisions. Both papers thus indirectly sustain the view that although a European identity may not be easily distinguishable in contemporary European societies and politics, there are important cultural and policy transformations that point to different levels of Europeanisation of national identity and the re-shuffling of cultural and territorial boundaries.

Part II of the book discusses the transformation of collective identities and boundaries with particular reference to the Eastern Enlargement of the European Union. The three contributions included in this part study three pivotal cases, Germany, Poland and Russia, located along the territorial and symbolic divide of 'Eastern' and 'Western' Europe. These case studies approach from an empirical perspective the conceptual issues raised by the contributions in Part I.

In the chapter on *European East–West integration, nation-building and national identities: the reconstruction of German–Polish relations*, Willfried Spohn analyses, against the background of the burdened history between Germany and Poland, the evolving impact of the Eastern Enlargement process on the relations between the two societies, cultures and national identities. Despite the continuing historical asymmetries between Germany and Poland, Spohn argues – in agreement with the perspective presented by Giesen in the first chapter – that collective memory represents a cultural repertoire for a transformation of German–Polish relations that could support the Eastern Enlargement process.

In her study on *Polish identity in the process of Europeanisation*, Miroslava Marody discusses how the ongoing economic and cultural processes related to European integration influence Polish national identity. Through an extensive analysis of survey data, Marody shows that Poles' perceptions of their own nation and nation-state as well as of the European Union have changed through the past decade. She highlights particularly the cultural ambiguities in public attitudes towards

Poland's integration into the EU. Support for European integration as a modernisation strategy for Polish society coexists with concerns and even fears regarding the preservation of Polish national identity.

Erhard Stölting in his chapter on *Russian perspectives on German and Russian self-definitions* explores the historical relations between the Russian national-imperial identity and its embedded European components by reference to Germany. His argument is that for Russia Germany represented and still represents a model for Western modernisation to be emulated, but also to be rejected as a threat to Russian identity. Stölting's study shows the importance of Russia, its self-definition as European and its specific perceptions of Germany as significant Others to European integration and the Eastern enlargement of the EU.

Part III of the book includes three case studies that explore the transformation of nation-states and national identities from the perspective of international migration and thus take up the theoretical issues introduced by Geddes and Romaniszyn in Part I. The chapters by Morawska and Cyrus present two sociological ethnographic studies of Polish migration to Berlin and analyse the multi-faceted process of national identity re-definition in relation to European integration and the re-organisation of territorial and symbolic boundaries between Germany and Poland.

Ewa Morawska in her chapter on *National identities of Polish (im)migrants in Berlin* finds a multiple and ambiguous reaction of Polish migrants to German society. She identifies four types of cultural and identity reactions to the experience of migration. More specifically, she highlights how the latter shapes identifications with the nation of origin, strengthening a defensive attitude in some migrants while creating a perceived cultural distance between the migrant and her/his fellow nationals back home in other individuals. Morawska relates her analysis of identity issues to the different types of migration and varied socio-demographic features of the migrants showing thus, in accordance with Romaniszyn's arguments presented in Part I, that cultural and identity diversification through migration is a highly dynamic and multi-faceted process.

Norbert Cyrus in his study on *Changing rhetoric and narratives: German trade unions and Polish migrant workers* examines the reaction of German trade unions in Berlin to Polish migrants. As he demonstrates, the German trade unions representing Berlin construction workers also react in an ambiguous way to the opening of borders imposed by the Eastern enlargement and European integration process. Although they develop a European rhetoric in response to the hegemonic European attitude of the German elite, they also defend their interests, adopting welfare-nationalistic arguments against Polish immigrant workers and re-construct the 'national' boundary between insiders and outsiders.

The contribution by Judit Tóth and Endre Sik on *Joining an EU Identity: integration of Hungary or the Hungarians?* analyses the complex and delicate issue of Hungary and its diasporas. The forthcoming integration of Hungary into the EU raises a number of identity and policy issues related to the relationship between the Hungarian nation and nation-state and its minorities living in neighbouring countries. Tóth and Sik argue that the process of European integration gives priority to the security and well-being of the Hungarian nation-state over the perceived national and cultural unity of the Hungarian nation writ large. The boundaries between Hungarians in the 'mother country' and those living abroad have been shifting in relation to past and present experience, while the stakes for a future policy and politics concerning Hungarian diasporas remain a challenge not only for Hungary but also for the Eastern enlargement process. This argument supports John Hutchinson's viewpoint that national identities persist as the vital elements that hold societies together. However, Tóth and Sik's contribution does not preclude that Hungary's integration into the EU may strengthen the European components of Hungarian national identity and further re-define the relations between the mother nation and its diasporic communities.

## Conclusions

The contributions assembled in this volume present different theoretical and comparative approaches to and empirical case studies on the transformation of national states, societies and identities in the context of European integration, Eastern enlargement and international migration. They also give, therefore, different answers to the debates on the Europeanisation of collective identities and the re-organisation of symbolic and territorial boundaries between nations and (multi-)national states. In this sense, neither the theoretical arguments nor the empirical findings presented here aim to be conclusive or to provide generalised answers to questions such as will the European Union prove a viable political project? Has a sense of belonging to Europe developed? Or has the nation died? However, as we hope, they indicate innovative directions for comparative, theoretical and empirical work on the Europeanisation of nations and national identities, particularly in an East–West European comparative perspective. As Eastern enlargement gradually takes place, integrating Central-Eastern European countries to the EU and raising new social, cultural and economic challenges for European integration, such innovative directions in theoretical and empirical research seem to us very timely and at the same time indispensable.

## References

Balakrishnan, G. (1996) *Mapping the Nation*, London: Verso.

Beyme, K. v. (1994, English edition 1996) *Systemwechsel in Osteuropa*, Frankfurt am Main: Suhrkamp.

Brubaker, Rogers (1999) 'The Manichean myth: rethinking the distinction between "civic" and "ethnic" nationalism', in H. Kriesi, K. Armingeon, H. Siegrist and A. Wimmer (eds) *Nation and National Identity: The European Experience in Perspective*, Chur/Zürich: Verlag Ruegger.

dal Lago, A. (1999) *Non persone*, Milano: Feltrinelli.

Eder, K. (1998) 'Integration durch Kultur? Das Paradox der Suche nach einer europäischen Identität', in R. Viehoff and R. Seghers (eds) *Kultur, Identität, Europa: Über die Schwierigkeiten und Möglichkeiten einer Konstruktion*, Frankfurt am Main: Suhrkamp.

Eisenstadt, S.N. (1987) *European Civilization in Comparative Perspective*, Oslo: Norwegian University Press.

European Commission (1997) *Eurobarometer: Racism and Xenophobia in Europe*, Luxembourg: Office for Official Publications of the European Communities.

Flora, P and Kühnle, S. and Urwin, D. (1999) *State Formation, Nation-building and Mass-Politics in Europe: The Theory of Stein Rokkan*, Oxford: Oxford University Press.

Gellner, E. (1983) *Nations and Nationalism*, Oxford: Blackwell.

Habermas, J. (1994) 'Citizenship and national identity', in B. van Steenbergen (ed.) *The Condition of Citizenship*, London: Sage.

Hall, J. (1998) (ed.) *The State of the Nation: Ernest Gellner and the Theory of Nationalism*, New York: Cambridge University Press.

Hutchinson, J. (1994) *Modern Nationalism*, London: Fontana.

Kohn, H. (1964) *The Idea of Nationalism*, New York: Collier-Macmillan.

Lepsius, R. (1998) 'Die Europäische Union. Ökonomisch – politische Integration und Kulturelle Pluralität', in R. Vichoff and R. Seghers (eds) *Kultur, Identität, Europa: Über die Schwierigkeiten und Möglichkeiten einer Konstruktion*, Frankfurt am Main: Suhrkamp.

Linz, J. and Stepan, A. (1996) *Problems of Democratic Transition and Consolidation: Southern Europe, South America, and Post-Communist Europe*, Baltimore, MA: The Johns Hopkins University Press.

Mann, M. (1993) 'Nation-states in Europe and other continents: diversifying, developing, not dying', *Daedalus* 122, 3: 115–40.

Milward, A. (1992) *The European Rescue of the Nation-State*, London: Routledge.

Neumann, I. (1996) *Russia and the Idea of Europe*, London: Routledge.

—— (1999) *Uses of the Other: The 'East' in European Identity Formation*, Minneapolis, MN: University of Minnesota Press.

Palidda, S. (1996) (ed.) *La construction sociale de la déviance et de la criminalité parmis les immigrés en Europe*, Bruxelles: COST Communauté Européenne.

Smith, A. (1991) *National Identity*, Harmondsworth: Penguin.

Triandafyllidou, A. (2001), *Immigrants and National Identity in Europe*, London: Routledge.

—— (2002a) *Negotiating Nationhood in a Changing Europe: Views from the Press*, Ceredigion and Washington DC: Edwin Mellen Press.

—— (2002b) 'We belong to the West? Representations of Eastern and Western Europe in the Greek press and the positioning of the "we"', in V. Roudometof, G. Kourvetaris, A. Kourvetaris and K. Koutsoukis (eds) *The New Balkans*, Boulder, CO: East European Monographs.

V.A. (2001) European Community Studies Association, Review Forum: Analyzing the Treaty of Nice, European Community Studies Association (ECSA) Review 14, 2: 1–11.

# Part I

# Theoretical approaches and comparative perspectives

# 2 The collective identity of Europe

## Constitutional practice or community of memory?

*Bernhard Giesen*

## Introduction

Today Europe has to reflect on its collective identity more than ever before. It can no longer assume a self-assured superiority with respect to other civilizations: the age of a triumphant Europe ruling and teaching the world is undoubtedly gone. But neither can Europe retreat into an isolationist position. In a global context she has to face and to interact with significant others – political powers, civilizations, hegemonic regimes, etc. – and, as common in the encounters with outsiders, Europe has to reflect on her own identity in distinction to others.

In addition to this decline of her hegemonial position and demise of her missionary zeal, Europe has changed its structural foundations. In contrast to the last millennium, today's Europe is less a cultural discourse than a political organisation, carried less by intellectuals than by politicians, corporate executives and the European administration. But even on this political level, Europe cannot – at least not while claiming democratic foundations – dispense with a conception of collective identity. Only if we presuppose the collective identity of the demos can we then account for responsibility and historical continuity, decide about membership and citizenship, assume the sovereignty of the people and imagine the unity of collective decisions – in short: conceive of a body politic beyond the volatile coalition of strategic interests (Giesen 2001).

This categorical assumption of collective identity, however, has to be separated from its particular representations, imaginations and organisational forms. In contrast to the first that transcends any particular situation, the second depends on and varies with respect to social relations and historical situations, it is constructed and contested, it can be challenged and exchanged. Constitutions may change and histories may be debated, symbols may be transformed and monuments may be destroyed, but this variation in the level of representation does not affect the continuous existence and identity of the nation or of another collectivity without which we cannot imagine either sovereignty or history.

In the following we will explore this a priori of collective identity with respect to Europe. We will start by reversing the relationship between identity and constitution and ask whether Europe can be constructed on the basis of a constitutional practice or procedural form. Following Habermas' famous idea of *Verfassungspatriotismus* it is not a primordially given collective identity, but the identification with a constitution and the participation in its political practice that defines citizenship and not vice versa. In order to explore the degree to which collective identity can be substituted by a constitution instead of being presupposed by it, the first section will outline a repertory of constitutional regimes provided by European history. It will raise the question of whether the European Union revives the tradition of early modern city leagues or of hegemonial empires, whether it is a regime of enlightened absolutism or an emerging supernation-state – comparable to the United States of America.

The third section will present Europe as a cultural movement and distinguish between three different conceptions of this movement: Europe as translation, Europe as missionary universalism and Europe as a community of memory.

With respect to the last conception we will, in the last section, outline a major turn in the collective memory of contemporary Western societies – the turn from triumph to trauma, from the memory of heroes to the memory of victims and perpetrators. This turn towards a moral construction of a European identity was politically activated in the joint European ban on Austria after Jörg Haider's right wing FPÖ party entered the Austrian government in 2000.

The concluding remarks will briefly address the question of whether this turn towards the collective memory of the trauma of victims and the guilt of perpetrators appears to be a European or Western peculiarity.

## What is the nature of the beast? European identity as a constitutional regime

Sovereign political organisations like the European Union may conceive of their collective identity in terms of their basic constitutional practices, their patterns of legitimacy and their demarcation of citizenship. This refers to a procedural model of collective identity – as it has been suggested by Jürgen Habermas in his famous idea of *Verfassungspatriotismus*, i.e. constitutional patriotism.[1] Instead of imagining a collective identity, i.e. a demos that precedes the constitution, the procedural model of collective identity assumes that the long-term practice of citizenship, the routines of coping with cultural diversity and the firmly established patterns of legitimacy and sovereignty will provide an integrative tie of belonging and collective self-understanding. This attempt to ground the body politic in the practice of political traditions lends salience to the well-established paradigms of statehood and sovereignty provided by European history. In the following we will distinguish between four of these paradigms in an ideally typical way.

The European city-state, as it emerged in late medieval times, is – according to Max Weber – regarded as a particularly European institution. The European Union, as a confederation of sovereign states, can in this respect be well compared to former European city leagues like the *Hanse*, the Flemish cities of the fifteenth century, or the *Lega Lombarda*. Monetary and banking institutions, the protection of property and the legal supervision of contracts, treaties of cooperation and association between different cities and even a trend towards a unified jurisdiction and constitutional frame, opened up large spaces of safe and accountable commercial exchange, but never resulted in a new centralised political sovereignty on top of the city governments. The political order of these city leagues and associations was a polycentric network within a vast rural periphery that with increasing distance from the cities allowed for independent local forms of political authority. Migration and economic exchange between the urban centres and the rural periphery was common, the cities opened their gates to a multitude of immigrants and foreigners thus producing a vast range of internal cultural heterogeneity.

Contemporary inter-governmentalists occasionally present these early modern city constitutions as a promising paradigm for a liberal avenue to European integration (Majone 1996). There are, of course, some striking similarities between the early modern city leagues and the contemporary European community: the dissociation between a fragmented and multi-layered political order on the one hand and expansive and unifying market dynamics on the other, or the diversity of languages within the community and the elitist nature of governance.

But there are also strong barriers impeding an easy transfer of the city league model to the supranational administration level of contemporary Europe. Most important among them is the thrust toward inclusive and egalitarian citizenship that has ascended to the status of a trope for modern political discourse. Citizenship in the early modern city leagues was, however, a special privilege granted to a relatively small part of the populations of these cities. Although not entirely inaccessible for outsiders, the status of full political citizenship was highly exclusive and contrasted clearly to the open and inclusive nature of the city as a marketplace that aimed at attracting as many merchants and traders, buyers and labourers as possible. This conception of citizenship as a republican corporation mirrored in a certain way the exclusivity of the aristocratic world outside of the city walls.

Another structural difference results from the increasingly strong centre of modern European governance in Brussels. The new sovereignty of the European government with respect to the national governments as well as the sheer size of the centralised bureaucracy contrasts strikingly with the polycentrism of the early modern city leagues. These city leagues were confederations at the most and had no central authority of their own. Instead they relied formally on the supreme authority of the emperor or of a prince – but they could also occasionally support his adversaries, turn against the ruler and defeat him.

In distinction to the city league model the second historical paradigm – the traditional empire – was provided with exactly this feature: a strong centre embodied in the person of the emperor, administered by a large bureaucracy and carried by a dominant ethnic or national group. Around the centre extended a graded and stratified belt of various nations that accepted the authority of the ruler more or less voluntarily. We may call this political order the Habsburg model, but the ancient Roman empire, pre-Revolutionary Russia, the Ottoman empire, the Napoleonic empire and the British colonial empire may as well serve as illustrations.[2] Empires have, by definition, changing and insecure frontiers, in contrast to the sharply demarcated and stable boundaries that are typical for the modern nation-state. After a period of expansion or conquest this frontier is protected against invasions of unruly barbarians by a zone of military fortresses or fortifications like the Great

Wall of China or the Limes built by the Roman Empire. In most cases the degree of political control decreases in relation to the spatial distance from the centre. The political system of empires therefore has to allow for the coexistence of various national groups, ethnic and religious communities, languages and cultures. In direct consequence, the basic rights of citizenship in empires have to be inclusive and decoupled from ethnic or religious ties. In the mature Roman, in the British or Habsburg empires, citizenship could no longer be confined to a tiny elite of the core nation.

This constitutive multiculturalism of empires comes, however, at a price: it is not the ruled, but the person of the ruler who is the sovereign political subject. The integrative bond of the empire is provided by the sacredness of the emperor's personal or dynastic authority, and not by a public debate about the common good or by the constitutional rules, which the citizens have agreed upon. This does not prevent a close relationship between the ruler and the people: the emperor represents the people and the people can conceive of their collective identity only by referring to the all-embracing authority of their ruler.

Again, there are some structural similarities between the traditional European empires and the new European Community: the stratification between core nations and peripheral nations, the expansive and shifting frontiers and the fortification of the boundaries to protect against immigration of unwanted outsiders – more for economic than military reasons today. But one major difference remains: the idea of sovereignty in traditional empires was based on the personal rule of the emperor, on the sacredness of his descendants or his personal charisma, whereas in contemporary Europe, sovereignty is tied to democratic foundations and the legitimacy of the administration in Brussels is almost entirely of a bureaucratic or legal type. Charismatic leadership today rarely appears on the European level; instead it remains tied to the national arena. The political centre in Brussels has no face, no founding myth, no heroic narrative. The reasons for this are easy to discover if we consider the Weberian concept of charisma. Charisma results from the belief of followers and there is no common European public sphere that could provide an arena of communication in which a transnational charismatic community could emerge.

In contrast to the traditional empires that were based on the diversity of nations, the European enlightened absolutism of the modern territorial state aimed at the construction of a uniform internal space and a uniform citizenry.[3] Here, too, the political sovereign was the prince and not the people, citizens were imagined as passive subjects of the ruler and here too, the centre was regarded as the source of identity, authenticity and innovation. But the mission of the ruler was not just to establish and to expand a realm of peace for his subjects. Instead, he had to extend the rule of law, to modernise the state and its institutions and to get as much tax as possible out of a limited population that should be sedentary, accountable and comparable.

The citizens in enlightened absolutist states were, however, not only objects of accounting, taxation and policing matters, but also subjects that had to be educated and enlightened in order to respect the law, to engage in the development of science and technology, and to stimulate trade and crafts and the production of goods. Law and education became the core arenas of citizenship in enlightened absolutism. The people were transformed from a bunch of locally varying peasants and crafts-men into uniform and equal citizens of a state (Scott 1998). Enlightened absolutism discarded not only local and regional differences, but also disregarded the religious and ethnic diversity of the citizens – these differences were banned from the public sphere of the state and enclosed in the privacy of the citizens. Thus the distinction between 'public' and 'private' became the core institutional device for coping with cultural diversity.

Again, there are strong institutional similarities between the political order of enlightened absolutism and the current state of the European Union: the strong bureaucratic centre that claims to represent reason and rationality; the missionary rhetoric of progress and modernisation; the attempt to stimulate economic growth as the prime motive of political integration; the institutional protection of a large internal market against imports; the bureaucratic standardisation of products and services; the thrust to overcome the diversity of national and local identities and to turn the people of different nations into European citizens; and finally the sense of competition with respect to 'outside organisations' like the US or Japan.

But although the model of enlightened absolutism seems to come closest to the constitutional practice of the European Union, it is still incompatible with the central trope of modern political discourse – the idea of a sovereign demos. Even if EU politics actually operated according to the model of enlightened absolutism it would have to face the challenge of the deficit of democracy.

This idea of the sovereign demos is at the core of the modern nation-state. Although the idea of the nation is not a modern invention, the nation as the ultimate sovereign actor of politics is, indeed, a decisively modern, Western and European idea. It emerged in the seventeenth century and ascended to the position of an undisputed master-narrative of history and state formation in the first half of the nineteenth century (Giesen 1998). In the 'spring of nations' these were seen as naturally given collectivities, that – like sleeping giants – could awake, rise, break the chains of foreign domination and determine their fate by themselves. Thus the revolutionary uprising against the monarch or against foreign rule became the most important foundation myth of the modern democratic nation. Revolutions are, by their very definition, ruptures in the continuity of constitution and legal rule, a relapse into the state of nature, that can be conceived of as Hobbesian violence or as Rousseauian paradise (Koselleck, Meier, Fisch and Bulst 1984). Only if we presuppose that the demos, the people, the nation 'exists' in this state of nature, i.e. independently from and prior to any constitution, legal system and public sphere, only then can we account for the idea of democratic sovereignty as distinct from the idea of justice that was already at the core of the constitutional paradigms outlined above.

We have to assume this collective identity of the nation and to represent it in the discourse of political culture in order to decide about the question of who is to vote about the constitution, about citizenship rights, etc. and who is not. The phrase 'we, the people' in its most elementary sense implies boundaries against outsiders, against strangers, even against alleged 'enemies of the people'. Thus the a priori of collective identity seems to be indispensable for the idea of democratic sovereignty. If European politics is to be grounded on a democratic conception of sovereignty it cannot escape the question as to what is demos (Eder and Giesen 2001).

## Cultural heritage as the foundation of the European demos

Referring to a past revolution is, however, not the only way of constructing the pre-constitutional demos. It can also be grounded in culture and communication, in language and religion. National identities have been successfully built on the assumption of a pre-politically given cultural unity, on the assumption of a common language and common folkways. And – despite its internal diversity of languages and religious confessions, of regional folkways and national traditions – Europe, too, can claim such a common cultural heritage carried by intellectuals, by monks and artists, by philosophers and scholars, who, in periods of internal conflicts and crisis, appealed to an embracing unity of Europe in contrast to the scattered political map. This cultural construction of Europe was always a matter of relatively small intellectual elites the members of which communicated in a non-vernacular language – mostly Latin – across the boundaries of political territories. Since Augustinus' famous distinction between the two cities, the tension between the mundane realm of politics and the otherworldly realm of religion and culture has been a distinctive mark of European culture. The distinction between imperium and sacerdocium, between earthly power and heavenly salvation, between mundane reasoning and the transcendental order were among the core oppositions that shaped and structured the European discourse about politics and history and were embodied in the conflict between pope and emperor. Neither realm was conceived as independent from the other. Instead the transcendental order claimed to transform politics and history and the political order claimed to be grounded in eternal and sacred foundations. The cultural construction of Europe, too, was patterned by this axial age tension between history and transcendence: it was carried by intellectuals and grounded in spheres that transcended mundane politics, but it challenged the existing political order or justified claims to power (Eisenstadt 1986). Thus, the cultural construction of Europe tended to exceed the range of political authority and to reach out for a universal mission.

But the cultural idea of Europe did not only embrace the fractioned and divided realm of politics. It also claimed the unity and continuity of a heritage that by itself was based on ruptures and discontinuity. Historically, the power of the European cultural movement emerged mainly from its ability to absorb and to include, to assimilate and to merge seemingly inconsistent symbolic elements into an embracing unity. While the intellectuals' call to unity was rarely able to overcome political feuds and cleavages, it was rather successful in blending cultural diversity and ruptures into the unity and continuity of a tradition.

### Europe as translation

The famous concept of *translatio* referred to this continuity between past and present as the transfer of a cultural heritage from Greek antiquity to the contemporary Western civilization, as an assumed continuity in contrast to a history of political conflict. This cultural heritage was embodied in particular objects, places and territories. The European movement tried to control these places and objects that were to be considered its sacred core – here the term 'movement' can still be used in its original spatial meaning.

The first centre of Europe (a Greek term) was the eastern part of the Mediterranean Sea. Its constitutive boundary ran between the Greek culture and barbarian outsiders (Baldry 1965). Although the term 'Europe' was rarely used by Greek authors before Alexander the Great, the fractioned Greek principalities and republics considered their commonality – in distinction to barbarians – to be grounded mainly in culture. This cultural identity was seen as an aesthetics embodied in objects, in statues, buildings and even human bodies. The masterpieces of Greek art were replicated and translated and, in many cases, survived only as Roman copies of the lost Greek originals. Especially after Augustus and during the so-called Hadrianic renaissance, Greek art and literature was considered to be the undisputed aesthetic ideal.

But translation occurred not only in art and aesthetics. Roman culture in particular was also a field of deliberate religious hybridisation and syncretism. The gods of the classical world were not omnipresent; instead, their sacred presence was concentrated in particular places and objects, in temples and statues. This allowed for coexistence and multiculturalism. The statues of Latin deities were sent as gifts to the temples in the newly conquered colonies and the statues of foreign gods, in return, were venerated in Roman temples.

Later on, aesthetic movements of classicism and renaissance venerated the heritage of antiquity that was – until the famous 'Querelle des anciens et des modernes' in the seventeenth century – seen as the insurmountable summit of aesthetics. This aesthetic foundation of Europe was carried by an international community of artists who were united not only by a common reference to the classical heritage but also by a European-wide commonality of style that reflected the communication of artists across the confines of political boundaries. In European art, literature and music differences between epochs and styles matter more than regional traditions. This aesthetic imagination of Europe extended not only to the artists but also to collectors and the educated public that admired the classical masterpieces and recognised a commonality of taste and erudition. In contrast, those who were not able to relate to the heritage of the classics were considered as uneducated outsiders even if they belonged to the same political authority.

The second major translation occurred in the appropriation of the Roman imperial tradition by Frankish and, later on, Saxonian chiefs (Ullmann 1969). Again the European culture was conceived in spatial terms. After the coronation of Charlemagne by the pope in 800, Europe moved westwards. Its constitutive frontier now ran between Latin Christianity and the Muslim empires that controlled most of the southern and eastern coasts of the Mediterranean (Delanty 1995; Pirenne 1987). Until the sixteenth century and the conflict with the expanding Ottoman Empire, this eastern frontier was the focal point of reference for Christianity. Instead of merging Greek and Roman traditions in a common civilization of late antiquity, both were now separated by the great schism.

The political transfer of the imperial tradition from Byzantium to the West was backed by the cultural appropriation of the Christian heritage as embodied in the relics of the Christian martyrs that were traded or stolen in Byzantine or Muslim cities in the East and in the crusaders' attempt to conquer the holy places in Palestine (Geary 1978). Here, too, the translation of culture was closely connected with material objects and localities – the sacred was not everywhere, but concentrated in particular objects, in statues and churches, in relics and sacred sites.

The translation of an imperial heritage was not only embodied in movements of conquest and transfer but also supported by a discourse about the unity of Europe 'avant la lettre'. This discourse was carried by monks and scholars such as Widukind of Corvey and Lupold von Babenburg, Dante Alighieri and Marsilius of Padua, who advocated the imperial cause – frequently in opposition to the papal claim of supremacy (Gollwitzer 1964; Leyser 1992; Reuter 1992; Wallach 1972). The hegemonial claim of the Holy Roman Empire was not just a matter of political power but it had to be grounded in a spiritual unity of Latin Christianity and the papal claim to represent the invisible god in the visible world had to be respected by the power holders. Thus imperium and ecclesia embodied in pope and emperor clashed in the claim to cultural as well as political leadership. Their claims were supported and challenged, debated and denied by intellectuals, by scholars, jurists and theologians.

These intellectuals referred to each other by a transnational network of communication. Monks travelling between the centres of medieval scholarship, knights on a crusade or on a pilgrimage, bishops convening on a papal council or humanist scholars debating at a princely court discovered not only regional differences of origin but experienced also a strong commonality of Latin-speaking Christians in contrast to the local commoners and their vernacular tongue on the one hand, and to the non-European foreigners on the other. Europe appeared not only as a translation of imperial authority but also as a transnational community of Latin-speaking monks and scholars, noblemen and office holders, clergymen and artists.

The third major translation of Europe can be seen as a turn towards a western frontier brought about by Portuguese and Spanish conquistadors a well as by Dutch and English traders who crossed the Atlantic for the lure of the New World's treasures or the pursuit of religious perfection. Here, the constitutive boundary did run between the savages of the New World and the Christian conquerors who ventured out from the Western shores of the Old World and – despite their internal competition – kept an awareness of their common European identity (Bitterli 1993; Chiapelli 1976; Gollwitzer 1964). Religious mission and trade capitalism transformed the Atlantic Ocean into an Inland Sea of the European colonial empires. Here too, the movement of European culture was originally seen as a spatial expansion, as the transfer of statues and architectural styles, and as the conquest of territories in the name of god. The gold of Peru and the silver of Mexico, the slaves from Africa and the cotton from the New World provided the material bases for the undisputed claim of a European hegemony over the Old and New World.

## Europe as a missionary movement

This idea of translation contrasts to the idea of a European mission, which is based on discontinuity between past and present and assumes an invisible and categorical unity instead of an embodied, visible and tangible heritage.

The idea of a European mission is strongly represented in reformatory Protestantism, in its iconoclasm and abstention from splendour and personal mediation. Cromwell had still proclaimed 'the western project' as a missionary conquest of the Caribbean, but in the missionary conception Europe was gradually decoupled from its territorial ties and gained a temporal connotation. The *res publica christiana* could and should finally include every human being. European Christendom was turned into a universal community in relation to a god who was invisible and omnipresent, inaccessible and beyond description. The sacred core of European culture could no longer be seen as embodied in particular places and objects. It became a missionary project that referred to all human beings and to all global regions. Europe was still a cultural movement but instead of moving cultural objects it moved persons from outside into the community.

The universal claim of the missionary movement allowed, however, for internal diversity. In contrast to the discourse of pre-reformatory Christianity that communicated on the basis of a single language, reformatory Protestantism allowed for a variation of vernacular languages – the universal message of salvation was taught in many tongues.

Protestant missionary zeal and the counterreformation, however, also divided Europe into three religious camps that fought each other in devastating wars. As a response to these confessional wars, intellectuals engaged in a new discourse about the unity of Europe. This demanding discourse about Europe was, though, still a matter of relatively small elites of noblemen, scholars, officeholders and merchant capitalists. Pufendorf or Erasmus, Leibniz or Bodin, Comenius or Spinoza did not yet address a large public and they did not yet imagine their readership in national contours. They travelled between the princely courts and changed their commitments, communicated in several European languages and wrote for a small educated readership.

This missionary universalism of the European culture also shaped the process of modernisation and rationalisation that is commonly associated with the Enlightenment of the eighteenth century. The movement of enlightenment was borne by intellectuals who travelled between the centres of scholarship in Europe and frequently published abroad to escape censorship. New publications by famous authors were quickly translated and available to a European-wide readership. Although Paris and Leyden, London and Königsberg, Edinburgh and Göttingen had their own intellectual climate the Enlightenment was a decisively transnational movement (Darnton 1982; Gay 1977; Giesen 1998).

It gave rise to the idea of a universal human nature and reason, as well as to the conception of a natural world to be described by empirical science, and to the conception of progress as the guiding principle of history. The constitutive boundary between Europe and the other was even more temporalised and decoupled from the ties of descent and territory. It did run between the European vanguard of history and the backward 'races' of outsiders, but could also occasionally hint at the backwardness and decadence of the European centre and the natural innocence of the periphery. The noble savage could be closer to human perfection than the European – in particular in times when the Europeans seemed to oppose the rule of reason and natural order. The Enlightenment was a European movement that transcended the territorial boundaries and aimed at a universal community of mankind. Everybody's true identity was European – and it was the task of education and emancipation to further the awareness of this identity. Thus what started as a genuine European movement dissolved into a free-floating discourse that appealed to by every human being, everywhere and in every time.

Contemporary criticism frequently accuses the Enlightenment of being insensitive to cultural differences. The contrary is true. The Enlightenment was strongly interested in all variations of human society. More than ever before it gave rise to a comparative perspective on human civilizations and, possibly for the first time, it tried to take the position of the Other in order to focus on the peculiarities of the European culture. In its refined forms it still remains the most complex intellectual endeavour to account for differences between the others outside of one's own community.

The third version of the missionary movement of European culture can be seen in the thrust towards civil and human rights that, starting in the nineteenth century, has ascended to the status of a global ethic of international responsibility and intervention. This movement responded to the historical experience of the French Revolution and created a unity of discourse, which fuelled political movements against the *anciens régimes* throughout Europe.

The politicised intelligentsia of the nineteenth century created networks with equal nodes in Paris, London and St Petersburg.[4] Their cause was the defence of human rights and the call for civil rights. Censorship and state persecution have been the answer of the European powers. Such networks created a counter-unity to the *Metternich* system, which tried to restore the old European order. Their success was limited, but taken as a model by the European workers' movement, which, though it started as an international movement, was essentially a European movement.

The idea of human rights provided the meta-narrative for a better Europe, the 'post-war consensus', underlying the restructuring of Europe after the Second World War. More important, however, than its impact on the reconstruction of post-war Europe was the complete decoupling of the cultural movement from its place of origin. Human rights are by their very definition universal and unalienable rights that transcend not only territorial boundaries, but also the frontiers of civilization and culture. Consequently the human rights movement responds to violations all over the globe.

### Europe as a community of memory

If neither the idea of *translatio* and embodied heritage nor the idea of Europe as a vanguard of universal history can provide a distinct European identity any more, Europe can return to its particular historical past and conceive of its identity in terms of collective memory (Assmann 1999; Connerton 1989; Giesen 1999; Nora 1984–86). We have already mentioned the revolution as founding myth of the modern demos. In the heroic uprising against the princely rule or foreign domination the people relapse into a state of nature and constitute themselves as the ultimate political sovereign. In this respect the collective identity of the demos precedes analytically the constitution and the political practice of citizenship. In the memories of triumphant or tragically failed revolutions this democratic sovereignty is re-narrated, re-presented and re-enacted. But it is exactly this memory of a revolutionary birth of the demos that is lacking in the European case – there is no common memory of a heroic uprising that includes all European nations. The memory of a triumphant uprising is almost exclusively tied to single nations, i.e. it systematically undercuts the level of an embracing European identity. Even the memory of a tragically failed revolutionary uprising is related to a particular nation that rebelled against an oppressor, i.e. mostly against another European nation. Whether triumphant or tragic, the memory of past revolutions can hardly unite all European nations.

But the reference to triumphant foundations, to heroes and revolutions is not the only path of collective memory that could give rise to a European identity. In modern Western nations the triumphant founding myth is increasingly replaced by the reference to a traumatic past, to the collective memory of victims and perpetrators. New national memorials and museums rarely remember triumphant victories, but recall the victims of the past. The monument of the anonymous soldier rephrases the once victorious hero who had a face, name and story as the nameless victim among other depersonalised victims of ethnic cleansing and genocide (Koselleck 1997). The new national memorial of the reunited Germany in Berlin is such a memorial to anonymous victims, a memorial constructed by the nation and for the nation of perpetrators. In remembering a collective trauma it includes victims as well as perpetrators and it can do so because it represents the collective memory of the German nation instead of hinting at the personal guilt of individual perpetrators, very few of whom are still alive. Individual suffering and guilt on the one hand and collective trauma and responsibility on the other are decoupled here.

The turn from the memory of heroes to victims and perpetrators, from triumphant to traumatic foundations of collective identity is also reflected by official rituals performed by representatives of the state. The famous kneeling gesture, performed by the former German chancellor Willy Brandt in front of the Warsaw Ghetto memorial thirty years ago, engendered a political culture of ritual apologies with respect to the victims of the past (Cunningham 1999). So, in a strange way, the figure of the perpetrator becomes an archetype of collective identity – not only in Germany (Giesen 2002). Today many representatives of different European nations officially confess their nation's involvement in the *Shoah*. France is more concerned with issues of collaboration than with the myth of resistance, Norway's President Bruntland admitted that more young Norwegians died in the ranks of the *Waffen-SS* than as victims of the German occupation, Poland discovers its own genocidal involvement in Jedbabwne, the Pope apologises for the non-intervention of the Roman Catholic Church, and even the Italian neo-fascist leader Fini laid down flowers at the site of the murders of the *Fossi Adratici*, etc. Compared to these solemn confessions of guilt and its representation in monuments, museums and public debates, the traditional celebrations of triumphant memorial days are increasingly reduced to the status of local folklore.

The spread of a new culture of ritual confessions of guilt on the part of the perpetrators centres around the Nazi genocide of the European Jews not only as an exclusive German issue but as a collective European trauma, that relates to many nations as victims and collaborators and even includes the allied forces, because they did not prevent or stop the genocide by bombing the railroads to the death camps. This secular shift from triumphant to traumatic foundations of collective memory contrasts sharply with the post-war attempts to purify one's own community by shifting the guilt to one nation and within this nation to a limited group of criminal if not demonic perpetrators. A new traumatic memory of perpetrators now unites the European nations and provides for a tacitly assumed moral consensus: a European collective identity based on the horror of the past. Today, the burden of collective trauma is accepted by European nations because most of the individual perpetrators are already dead and therefore out of the range of jurisdiction. By decoupling collective identity from the sum of individual identities, the present of the European Union has been separated from the European past of war and genocide. Of course, one can observe right-wing extremism in most European societies today, but this is treated as political deviance that could never succeed in entering a national government.

That is why this new European identity based on a collective trauma of Nazism was challenged when the right wing FPÖ party, led by Jörg Haider, entered the Austrian government in 2000. The reason for sharp critique was not the mere existence of right-wing extremism, but the official representation of a member state by a party that is considered to be ridden with Nazism. We may consider the European response to the new Austrian government to be grossly exaggerated – Haider is a right-wing populist not much different from the French LePen or the Italian Fini – but the Austrian case provided an excellent opportunity to emphasise the new collective identity of European nations by staging the deviant case and marking her as an outsider. Stigmatising the Austrian government also demarcated the European boundary with respect to future candidates for membership of the European Union. Thus for the first time it phrased an encompassing identity of the European Union in moral terms without falling back into a missionary triumphalism.

## A European heritage?

At the end of these remarks we may raise the question why this secular shift from triumphant to traumatic memories occurred in Europe, what conditions fostered it, and in particular why this memory of a collective trauma should be considered as a European peculiarity? Indeed the trauma of genocide and the collective responsibility of the perpetrators are by no means a unique European feature. But the official response of Turkey to the Armenian genocide or the Japanese reaction to the international pressure to apologise for the Nanjing massacres differ in great respect from the European response to the *Shoah*. The Turkish and Japanese reluctance even to admit the crimes can hardly be explained by a phase of latency in which a nation is ridden with haunting individual memories and cannot stand to face the brutal conversion of her triumphant heroes into criminal perpetrators. In Europe as well as in Japan or in Turkey the perpetrators are dead and out of the reach of jurisdiction. Also the rise of international media networks that increases the sensitivity with respect to triumphant manifestations of national identity between neighbour states extends to Japan as well as to Europe.

But neither is it simple chauvinism that prevents these nations from admitting their genocidal crimes. Instead their reluctance or refusal hints at different religious foundations of collective identity. In the Judeo-Christian tradition the confession of guilt not only relieves the confessor from the burden of guilt but it even uplifts him to a purified position. If in addition to this, the confessing individual even proves to be innocent, but nevertheless takes the burden of collective guilt, he sanctifies his own mundane individuality, he performs *Christomimesis*. Christ represents the ultimate innocent individual, the son of God who sacrificed his life in order to relieve the burden of collective guilt from his people.[5] Thus the European ritual of confessing the guilt of the past relies on a mythology that continues even if the political representatives performing this ritual are utterly secularised individuals who ignore the cultural origin of their actions.

In contrast, Japanese confessions of guilt are limited to individuals, who are blamed for having put shame on the collectivity, the nation, the family (Benedict 1974). Here, the relation between individual and collective identity is reversed: it is only the individual who can be guilty, humiliated and ashamed, whereas the embracing collectivity cannot be imagined other than as innocent. The reason for this remarkable difference can be found in the axial contrast between the worldly deed and otherworldly salvation in the European case, whereas in the Japanese perspective the confession of guilt cannot be alleviated by the promise of salvation (Eisenstadt 1996; Eisenstadt and Giesen 1995). Furthermore, the European heritage of moral universalism also transfers its moral perspective to the level of international relations, while from a Japanese or Chinese point of view these are totally different spheres.

Even with respect to the spread of rituals of mourning and confessions of collective guilt, European identity relies on a cultural heritage that continues – in many transformations – even if the Europeans are no longer aware of it. Of course, the Christian myth of the redeeming sacrifice of the innocent is not the only possible foundation of European identity. Others – the Enlightenment, the idea of civil equality and civil rights, the individual as the source of creativity and carrier of rights in contrast to the authority of the state, the separation of state and religion, the constitutional nation-state – are of similar importance and have been exported to other areas of the globe – mostly even without keeping a mark of their European origin. But confessing the collective guilt of the past may provide a European identity that can neither be accused of missionary triumphalism, nor be regarded as darkening the future of Europe.

## Notes

1   This concept is largely borrowed from the US paradigm of national identity.
2   Even the rule of the Staufian emperor Frederic II come close to this model for the political system of empires see Eisenstadt (1993) and Mann (1986).
3   For a critical perspective on the modernising efforts of absolutist states see Scott (1998).
4   It is less easy to find such nodes in Germany or Italy where networks of small university towns did fulfil the same function.
5   The myth of the divine king sacrificing himself was quite common in African kingdoms too. See Mircea Eliade (1963).

## References

Assmann, J. (1999) *Das kulturelle Gedächtnis: Schrift, Erinnerung und politische Identität in frühen Hochkulturen*, Munich: Beck.

Baldry, H.C. (1965) *The Unity of Mankind in Greek Thought*, Cambridge: Cambridge University Press.

Benedict, R. (1974) *The Chrysanthemum and the Sword: Patterns of Japanese Culture*, New York: New American Library.

Bitterli, U. (1993) *Cultures in Conflict: Encounters between European and Non-European Cultures 1492–1800*, Cambridge: Polity Press.

Chiapelli, F. (1976) *First Images of America*, Berkeley: University of California Press.

Connerton, P. (1989) *How Societies Remember*, Cambridge: Cambridge University Press.

Cunningham, M. (1999) 'Saying sorry: the politics of apology', *The Political Quarterly* 70, 3: 285–93.

Darnton, R. (1982) *The Literary Underground of the Old Regime*, Cambridge, MA: Harvard University Press.

Delanty, G. (1995) *Inventing Europe: Idea, Identity, Reality*, Basingstoke: Macmillan.

Eder, K. and Giesen, B. (2001) *European Citizenship*, Oxford: Oxford University Press.

Eisenstadt, S.N. (1986) *The Origins and Diversity of Axial Age Civilizations*, Albany: State University of New York Press.

—— (1993) *The Political Systems of Empires*, New Brunswick: Transaction Publishers.

—— (1996) *Japanese Civilization*, Chicago, University of Chicago Press.

Eisenstadt, S.N. and Giesen, B. (1995) 'The Construction of Collective Identity', *European Journal of Sociology* 36: 72–102.

Eliade, M. (1963) *Aspects du mythe*, Paris: Gallimard.

Gay, P. (1977) *The Enlightenment: An Interpretation*, New York: Norton, 2 vols.

Geary, P. (1978) *Furta Sacra: Thefts of Relics in the Central Middle Ages*, Princeton, NJ: Princeton University Press.

Giesen, B. (1998). *Intellectuals and the Nation: Collective Memory in an Axial Age*, Cambridge: Cambridge University Press.

—— (1999) *Kollektive Identität. Die Intellektuellen und die Nation*, Frankfurt am Main: Suhrkamp.

—— (2000) 'National identity as trauma: the German case', in B. Stråth (ed.) *Myth and Memory in the Construction of Community: Historical Patterns in Europe and Beyond*, Brussels: PIE-Peter Lang.

—— (2001) 'Voraussetzung und Konstruktion: Überlegungen zum Begriff der kollektiven Identität', in C. Bohn and H. Willems (eds) *Sinngeneratoren: Fremd- und Selbstthematisierung in soziologisch–historischer Perspektive*, Konstanz: Universitätsverlag Konstanz.

—— (2002) 'The trauma of perpetrators', in N.J. Smelser, J.C. Alexander, R. Eyerman, B. Giesen, and P. Sztompka (eds) *Cultural Trauma*, Berkeley, CA: University of California Press.

Gollwitzer, H. (1964) *Europabild und Europagedanke: Beiträge zur deutschen Geistesgeschichte des 18. und 19. Jahrhundert*, Munich: Beck.

Koselleck, R. (1997) *Zur politischen Ikonologie des gewaltsamen Todes: Ein deutsch–französischer Vergleich*, Basle: Schwabe.

Koselleck, R., Meier, C., Fisch, J. and Bulst, N. (1984) 'Revolution', in O. Brunner, W. Conze and R. Koselleck (eds) *Geschichtliche Grundbegriffe*, Stuttgart: Klett-Cotta.

Leyser, K. (1992) 'Concepts of Europe in the Early and High Middle Ages', *Past and Present* 137: 25–47.

Majone, G. (1996) *Regulating Europe*, London/New York: Routledge.

Mann, M. (1986) *The Sources of Social Power. Vol I: A History of Power from the Beginning to AD 1760*, Cambridge: Cambridge University Press.

Nora, P. (1984–86) *Les lieux de mémoire*, Paris: Gallimard.

Pirenne, H. (1987) *Mohammed und Karl der Grosse: Die Geburt des Abendlandes*, Stuttgart: Belser.

Reuter, T. (1992), 'Medieval ideas on Europe and their modern historians', *History Workshop Journal* 33: 176–80.

Scott, J. (1998) *Seeing like a State*, New Haven, CT: Yale University Press.

Ullmann, W. (1969) *The Carolingian Renaissance and the Idea of Kingship*, London: Methuen.

Wallach, R. (1972) *Das abendländische Gemeinschaftsbewusstsein im Mittelalter*, Hildesheim: Gerstenberg.

# 3   Enduring nations and the illusions of European integration

*John Hutchinson*

## Introduction

By the Treaty of Maastricht (1992) the nation-states of the European Community bound themselves to a Union that reaches into many of the core functions of the nation-state: control of borders and territory, the policing of citizens and immigration, currency and taxation, management of the economy, and foreign policy and defence (Wallace 1997: 33). The nation-state was born in Europe and became through European imperial expansion the global norm. Is Europe now pioneering a new political form, embodying the principle of multiple sovereignties, that will supersede the nation-state and fit humanity for its postmodern future? Does Maastricht represent an 'irreversible move towards real federation' (Anderson 1997: 126)? Or is it a doomed experiment, likely to intensify the very thing it is designed to forestall – the resurgence of nationalism at the very heart of the Union?

My subject is the future of nations as political actors in the new Europe. I will argue that the enduring power of nations is misunderstood because commentators conflate nation with nation-state, and equate the potency of the political nation with its modernising rather than with its identity functions. Most analysts exaggerate the contemporary Europeanisation of nations, failing to note that being 'European' has always been enmeshed with national agendas. The concept of 'Europe' is largely indeterminate, given a common definition only when imposed by the 'great nation-states', and as such is unable to inspire a directive and solidaristic response in crises when national interests conflict. What is in doubt is the medium-term viability of the European Union, not of its constituent nation-states, for the historical record reveals federations, like empires, have a poor record in the modern world.

The chapter falls into two parts. The first is historical. This examines three aspects of nations: the basis and functions of national identities; the manner in which European nation-states have tried to regulate political, economic, cultural and military processes; and how such nations have conceived of their relationships to Europe. The second part discusses how far the formation of the European Community represents a fundamental break with the Europe of nation-*states*, and the likely future of nations in the new contexts of monetary union and eastwards expansion.

# The enduring character of nations

For many, the rise of the European Union arises from the inadequacy of the nation-state in the new era of globalisation, defined here as an intensification of interconnectedness between the populations of the world. The nation-state has been until recently the primary political unit of modern humanity and exercised a monopoly of political, juridical, cultural, economic, and military control over bounded territories. However, for many scholars (Giddens 1990; Albrow 1996; Castells 1996) because of the increasing global connectedness between populations, nation-states cannot hope to resolve such contemporary issues as nuclear prolifer- ation, instabilities of world trade and finance, the power of multinational firms, international economic migrations and refugee flows, area conflicts and threats to the ecosystem. Only regional associations of states such as the European Union can attend to the increased scale of problems. In the post-war period we see nation- states pool sovereignty and a growing identification (at least at elite level) with a European ideal. The unitary character of nation-states has given way as minority nationalities and regions have demanded measures of territorial autonomy, and their claims to cultural homogeneity have been undermined by large-scale immi- gration, fuelling demands for their reconstruction as multicultural communities (on this see, Guibernau 2001).

Many of the claims about the decline of national before European loyalties are predicated on three assumptions. First, nation is conflated with nation-state, and there is a presumption that a collective identification with nation-states arises because they deliver economic and social progress. Second, the idea of a crisis of the nation-state rests on a contrast with an alleged period in which nation-states were unitary and bounded societies. Third, the intermeshing of national and European loyalties, evident particularly at the elite level, is assumed to be unprecedented.

I reject all three propositions. First, national identities often predate the era of the modern state, and the persistence or intensity of national identities cannot be explained by the success of state-led modernisation, because the modern period is also one of disruption to state authority. Second, the pooling of sovereignty is not a revolutionary new development since nations have continually varied in strength and in the degree to which they wish to regulate the sectors of social life. Third, many, if not most, European national identities have been developed either alongside or in relation to a sense of Europeanness, and most conceptions of 'Europe' arise out of prior national views of the world.

## *Nations as communities of fate*

Scholars of the European Community, whether they believe that national loyalties have been enhanced or weakened by membership of the EU, tend to equate nation with nation-state. Alan Milward (1992) argues that membership 'rescued' the European nation-states, since mass loyalty was deepened by high levels of economic growth, employment, welfare provision, and of education that were unknown in the nineteenth and earlier twentieth centuries. William Wallace, although agreeing that this was true up to the 1960s, claims that since the 1980s recognition of the incapacity of individual nation-states to deliver such benefits has led to a surrender of core powers (see above), and to a loosening of their authority (Wallace 1997). Each views national identifications as at best the psychological underpinnings of a collective unit (the state) whose justification is the achievement of economic and social progress.

Such interpretations share the perspective of scholars such as Benedict Anderson (1991), Ernest Gellner (1983), and Eric Hobsbawm (1990) who regard the nation as a construct, even an invention, of the modern bureaucratic state and industrial capitalism. The nation is essentially a political project focused on autonomy and citizenship that resonates with modern necessities. 'Modernist' scholars are right to distinguish nations from earlier ethnic communities as entities based on notions of popular sovereignty and a consolidated territory and economy. But this perspective, I argue, is one-dimensional and cannot explain the persistence of nations in the modern world. Nations are a form of ethnic group, and as such are quasi-kinship groups, regulated by myths of common descent, a sense of shared history, and a distinctive culture. They are communities of fate. Through identifying with an historic community embodied in myths, symbols and culture, which has survived disaster in the past, individuals combine in a society to overcome contingency and find a unique meaning and purpose. At the core of national identity is a concern for identity, and meaning.

Of course, modern state-formation and industrialisation are significant factors in the rise of nations. But, as John Armstrong (1982) and Anthony Smith (1986) have argued, the ethnic building blocks of nations formed out of processes that began well before the modern period and included: administrative centralisation round a state capital; recurring interstate warfare; a sense of religious election; and experiences of colonisation and settlement. The rise of Paris and London as capitals facilitated the growth of strong administrations and the diffusion of a unifying culture through the kingdoms of France and England. Protracted conflicts such as the Hundred Years War between France and England created the lineaments of later national identities – historical legends and heroes, territorial identifications and canonical literatures. The differentiation of Christianity first into Latin Catholicism and Orthodoxy, and again with the Reformation, resulted in the Serbs, Dutch, Poles and Russians claiming a distinctive ethno-religious mission. Large-scale colonisation and settlement created an ethnic consciousness among the Spanish engaged in *Reconquista* against the Moors and the Irish against the English. It is out of such experiences that the ethnic components of the nation emerged: a sense of unique origins, an identification with a bounded territory as the homeland, a repertoire of historical periods and heroic models by which to guide change, a sense of cultural individuality through possession of distinctive religious, vernacular-cultural or legal institutions, and an identification with political constitutions.

Modernists argue that a new world has formed from a combination of the administrative, ideological and economic revolutions of the late eighteenth century, and that modern nations legitimate themselves as vehicles of mass economic and social progress, central to which is the possession of an independent state. But in many contexts (Ireland, Czech and Slovak territories, Ukraine) such modernising states have provoked a *cultural nationalism* marshalling a communitarian revolt against the assimilation of populations to an alien dominant culture (Hutchinson 1987). Such nationalists have sought to 'regenerate' premodern ethnic identities operating below the state level that, when embedded by religious institutions, written vernacular cultures, and legal systems and professions, have persisted into the modern era and provided inspiration and resources for their campaigns to capture the modern state.

Moreover, states, themselves, have been shaped in their modernising policies by older ethnic identities, and, throughout the modern period, states and popula- tions have fallen back on ethnocommunal moral and political resources in the face  of unforeseen contingencies such as warfare, economic dislocations and large- scale international migrations, ideological challenges, and 'natural' disasters.

Warfare and imperial collapse has resulted in the overthrow and rise of states, the shifting of states into new geopolitical spaces, the turning of dominant groups into national minorities and vice versa, and large-scale movements of population. This geographical, demographic, and status mobility has required a redefinition of political communities with respect to each other, as we saw after the Versailles settlement and the collapse of the USSR. Economic changes have regularly also transformed the status of regions and classes within 'nation-states' and the power of national populations vis-à-vis each other. During the 1870s, agrarian depressions, rapid urbanisation and large-scale migrations of Jews generated a populist nationalism extending from the USA to Tsarist Russia. Recurring 'waves' of secular and religious salvation movements have swept across state boundaries, creating a sense of threat to national identities. The current Islamic revival has fanned European ethnocentric reaction against resident Muslims, including France where fears have been expressed about the erosion of secular republican traditions by militant Islam. Unexpected natural events – diseases, famines, ecological disturb- ances, shifts in fertility patterns – outside the control of states have engendered defensive ethnic mobilisations. The inability of the British government to avoid the great famine in mid-nineteenth century Ireland permanently alienated the Catholic Irish from the union with Britain, and changes in birth rates relative to 'significant others' have heightened tensions between ethnic populations within states (as between Russians and the Central Asian peoples in the former USSR).

We find these recurring patterns of ethnic mobilisation at work in republican France, widely conceived to be the first civic nation and modern society. The very universalism of the French revolution, however, drew on older ethnic conceptions of France as having a special mission to Europe, as heir of Roman and Carolingian civilisations and as the chosen defender of European Catholic Christendom (Armstrong 1982: ch. 5). Moreover, although France was a powerful centralised and secular state, it was never able to uproot a living Catholic culture, which sustained a significant counter-republican crusade up to the present. The state was destabilised throughout the modern period by invasions, changes of regime, boundary changes, social revolutions, and mass migrations, and in the face of such uncertainties, rival political projects have invoked ethnic legitimations. War and invasion almost immediately nationalised the Revolution, and after the restoration of monarchy, republicans qualified their rationalism by rooting the revolution in a historic French nation and appropriating traditional ethno-religious symbols and heroes. By the 1830s Michelet presented the Revolution as the culmination of a democratic nation, epitomised by the medieval Saint Joan of Arc. Victor Hugo gave momentum to the romantic cult of Gothic France, as embodied in its great cathedrals that now exemplified not the glories of Catholicism but rather the democratic and national genius of its medieval craftsmen and guilds. Counter-revolutionaries sought to reground the legitimist cause in a period of increasing democratisation by reclaiming St Joan as a symbol of popular Catholicism and monarchism. Defeat in the 1870s and the loss of territories at the hands of Germany, and German invasions in two world wars have all resulted in mass revivals of St Joan as national liberator (Gildea 1994: 154–65). To republicans and their opponents, the great cathedrals have been enduring symbols of an indomitable French nation – the cathedrals of Metz and Strasbourg, poignant reminders of provinces in captivity after 1870, and the shelled cathedral of Reims, a representation in 1916 of a suffering people (Vauchez 1992: 64).

Even the exemplary civic nation then rests on an ethnic substratum. As Anthony Smith (1999) has argued, the core of nationhood is located in its myths, memories and culture rather than in allegiance to a state. Extreme crises – periods of conquest – demonstrate that this nationalist ideology has a real resonance. For while it is possible to overthrow a state and control a territory, it is difficult to expunge and penetrate (from above), a way of life, particularly when it is embedded by a dense web of religious institutions, linguistic practices, literatures, legal customs, and rituals, which then can become sites of collective resistance. The long historical perspective of nationalists, which includes eras of defeat, enslavement and recovery, evokes the capacity of communities to overcome disaster by mobilising an inner world of spiritual energies. Poles under the Soviet yoke rallied under the umbrella of the Catholic Church, remembering the survival and resurrection of their nation despite two centuries of division and occupation by empires.

In short, national identities endure even when stripped of their protecting state, and the legitimacy of nation-states rests ultimately not on just the provision of economic and social progress but on more deep-seated attachments, sustained by historical memories, to the defence of a homeland, a unique culture, and independence of a community.

## Nations as fluctuating entities

If the core of the nation lies in the cultural community, is it not the case that its political carapace, the nation-*state*, is no longer able in a global world to fulfil its essential functions, including the defence of the nation from external threat, the management of the economy, and the provision of basic welfare? Hence the rise of regional transnational institutions such as the EU.

This perspective is vitiated by the assumption that once upon a time there were sovereign nation-states. In much nationalist scholarship (Hroch 1985; Hobsbawm 1990) we see a teleology operating in which nations rise from being elite organisations to mobilise the masses and incorporate them into a unitary society that controls economic, military, cultural and political frontiers. However, as we noted above, nation-states and states in general have been shaken periodically by unexpected military, economic and ideological challenges during the nineteenth and twentieth centuries.

Nineteenth-century Britain remained a world power, in part because of its skill in mustering coalitions of states against the dominant great power on the European sub-continent. Periods of 'splendid isolation' when Britain would enjoy a relative autonomy as a global power have alternated with a pooling of sovereignty in the two World Wars. In the economic sphere states have employed different strategies to compete in a transnational economic market, depending on their relative strengths and the degree of 'openness' of the world market itself. As the pioneering industrial society, Britain saw it in its national interest to promote free trade, though it had to shift to protectionism after the First World War destroyed the a 'golden age' of liberal internationalism. By contrast 'late-comer' Germany pursued more protectionist policies.

Not only strategies have evolved in response to contingent challenges. There have been oscillations between national and imperial, class, regional, and religious identities throughout the modern period (Connor 1990). The threat of working-class insurrection has haunted middle-class nations in Western Europe at various intervals from the early nineteenth century until 1968. Regional identities too have fluctuated. Eugene Weber's analysis (1976) of the strength of regionalism in the 1870s implies a decline in the pervasiveness of French nationalism since the period of the revolutionary wars.

The notion of a golden age of sovereign nation-states is a myth. If the autonomy of even Britain and France was limited, this was even more true for small countries. European nation-states, as William Wallace (1997) has noted, have varied enormously in how they have articulated state–society, state–economy, and state–interstate relations. Nations and nation-states vary considerably in the social niches they wish to regulate by explicit reference to national norms. This says nothing about the potency of national identities *per se*. Following Banton (1994), one might argue that a switch from avowedly national to international class loyalties (for example industrial action against a co-national employer in support of foreign workers) may not indicate changes in the values attributed to national affiliations, but rather a changing conception of what relationships should be governed by national norms. An adherence to the nation may not fluctuate much despite apparent changes in behaviour.

Nonetheless, it is obvious that oscillations in nationalist vis-à-vis class, religious and regional loyalties have occurred in two centuries, marked by periods of liberal and communist revolution, Islamic resurgences, and huge mass emigrations. Clearly there are two issues that must not be conflated: why national groups make strategic choices over the range of roles they wish to regulate, and why there are fluctuations in the salience of national loyalties. The former are in effect rational decisions about how to achieve national goals, through, for example, pooling of sovereignty; decisions that are in effect conditional, and in principle reversible. The latter represents major shifts of loyalty away from national to other allegiances, perhaps to a European identity. Differentiating between the two may be complex, but such major shifts are usually accompanied by explicit justifications and controversy. We should look to structural factors to account for such shifts. Whether there have been major shifts will be addressed in later section.

## Nation-states and Europe

Is the increasing integration of Europe bringing about the enmeshing of national with European identities, so that the nation as a self-contained individuality is giving way? Most commentators admit that such Pan-European consciousness as exists is confined to elite political, business, bureaucratic, trade union and media networks, but claim that as European integration deepens, so a participation in this project will broaden. These perspectives imply a new cultural basis is being created of a European pluricentred system of decision-making.

This is doubtful for two reasons. First, there has always been a consciousness, at the elite level, of belonging to a European as well as to a local culture. Second, from their very beginning, nations, aware of their part in a multi-actor civilisation, defined themselves as contributors to a European civilisation, and the modern history of Europe is the story of a struggle between the great powers over which nationalist vision of Europe would prevail.

From the early Middle Ages a Europe existed (at least at the elite level) as a family of cultures (cf. Anthony Smith (1992)), knit by Latin Christianity built on the heritage of the Roman Empire, dynastic intermarriage, the rise of a system of diplomacy and later international treaties. In the early modern period a French royal-court culture defined the codes of the European aristocracy, and later the movements of the Enlightenment and Romanticism provided a common conceptual language of European politics and culture, including the emerging nationalisms of the subcontinent.

Even before this, when ethnic identities crystallised they often defined themselves by reference to a European mission, as participants against an extra-European 'other' or in an intra-European battle of values. The thousand year war against Islam saw the Spanish, Poles, Hungarians, Serbs, and Russians legitimising themselves as *antemurale* defenders of Christian Europe, identities that continue to exert a hold. The wars of the Reformation and Counter-Reformations resulted in English, Dutch, French and Spanish states defining themselves as elect defenders of Protestantism or Catholicism, but only after civil wars within emerging national states in which proponents of the rival religious causes looked for support to European allies. In short the (religious) battles to define the nation and European civilisation were interlinked. Foreign intervention could effect the triumph of one side: William of Orange secured the English Glorious (Protestant) Revolution of 1688.

Modern national identities crystallised round the assault of the French-led Enlightenment on the European ancien régime. First Republicans, then Napoleon, evoked France as the modern Rome that would ensure a civilisational zone of peace and justice. In reaction to this, an English constitutional-monarchical and German romantic nationalism formed, with the Germans rejecting a rationalist unification of Europe in favour of a Christian confederation of nations on the model of the Holy Roman Empire (Kohn 1967). As before, these competing national ideals furnished a European repertoire for many emerging nationalisms, and the choice of national conceptions was shaped by location within the different politico-cultural zones of Europe. German organic conceptions influenced many Central and Eastern European nationalities. There were also rival visions *within* nations which looked for inspiration and sometimes support from 'dominant models'. In Russia Slavophiles admired an English constitutionalism led by an enlightened aristocracy, whereas Westerners tended to look to French republicanism.

Indeed, the struggle between models was perceived to be a battle for the identity of Europe. The nationalism of stateless nations or small nation-states was often expressed in moral terms, with Poles and the Irish viewing themselves as exemplary Christian nations destined to redeem a fallen Europe. The nationalism of 'great states' tended to express the traditional ambitions of such states to command the subcontinent. Napoleon sought to unite Europe within a French imperium that in his continental system was economic as well as political. After national unification was achieved by the defeat of France, Germany in the two World Wars made attempts to achieve a European Empire, again using economic as well as military instruments to secure its ends.

Intrinsic to many national identities, then, is an idea of mission to European civilisation, that derives from the sense of belonging to a common heritage, characterised by status competition, mutual borrowing, and concepts of the balance of power. This Europe is not unitary but multiple, and is perceived from within different national prisms. For great powers, 'Europe' implies a leadership role, whereas smaller nations have seen relationships with European neighbours as a means to escape the threat of absorption by adjacent great powers, hence Irish nationalists looked to Republican France and Germany at different times as a counter to Britain.

Europe also divides into culture zones, often dominated by competing powers, such as France in the 'West', Germany in the centre, and Imperial Russia in the East, and such states have provided the models through which other communities defined themselves. Those perceiving themselves to be on the margins, especially those on geo-cultural fault lines, may compensate by demanding recognition for a historic role as frontier guards.

Because of the interpenetration of European cultures, this multiplicity has been reflected within nations, and rival projects in their battle to secure their vision of the nation have looked to 'Europe' both as a source of allies and of threats. 'Europe' can be simultaneously 'other' and as the means of returning to one's authentic traditions. Hence in nineteenth and twentieth century Spain we find a struggle between a conservative conception of the nation, based on the *Reconquista*, as defender of Catholic Europe and a modernising ideal originating with the Enlightenment, for which 'a return to Europe' entailed a moral regeneration of the nation (Jauregui 1999).

## Nation-states and the European Union

In the light of this do we see the rise of the EU as a fundamental revision of the traditional Europe of nation-states? Nations, I have argued, cannot be conflated with states and their elites, but are communities of histories and cultures. The pooling of sovereignty and the limited regulatory reach of contemporary nation-states over many spheres is nothing new. The hybridisation of national and European ideals has been of long standing, and it is achieved on national foundations.

Can the rise of the European Community then be explained as a new strategy of national elites to maximise their sovereignty in an increasingly globalised world? Or does the federal vision of its founders represent a fundamental revulsion against the national principle in the name of wider (European) civilisational loyalties? Is the hybridisation taking on a new character, in which we see a process of replacement of national by European identities as the integration process takes off?

Alan Milward (1992) has argued powerfully that the EU has served to rescue the nation-state, but there is also a strong elite-led federalist agenda that arose from the revulsion against nationalism in the ruined Europe of 1945. The evidence for continuity rather than revolution is debatable. The European Union can be seen as the latest in a series of attempts to unite Europe politically as an instrument of national ambitions. As we saw, France and Germany in the modern period each attempted in time of war to establish a European power bloc as a global actor against imperial competitors. In the post-war period the goal was to forge, in alliance with the USA, a stable political and economic bloc to combat the overwhelming threat from the USSR, and the initial instrument, the European Coal and Steel Community, had its precursor in the German war economy in occupied Europe. What is distinctive about the current project is the *alliance* of the former enemies, France and Germany, and the *voluntary* agreement of other European nation-states under their leadership to pool their sovereignty in a supranational institution, moved by the general revulsion against the national rivalries that had brought Europe to the point of destruction.

The formation and accession of states to the European Community and the politics of the European Community can be explained by national motives. In most cases the desire to form or join arose from a conception of national interest. The motivations of France (to constrain a temporarily weakened Germany within a French-dominated Europe) and Germany (to relegitimise itself as nation-state committed to European democracy) are well known. Joining 'Europe' can also be a strategy of freedom from economic dependence on a powerful neighbour (e.g. Ireland in relation to Britain). In some cases, joining 'Europe' was seen as ensuring the victory of one's conception of the nation against internal rivals. Spanish democrats, like their counterparts in Greece, regarded accession as a validation and protection of the authentic 'enlightened' nation against opponents longing for a return to military authoritarianism and religious reaction. The story is similar for Eastern European aspirants. For all member states participation in the European Community gives them the status as joint decision-makers on the world stage, particularly compelling for small nation-states, to whom the EU Presidency rotates periodically, giving them their Warholian 'fifteen minutes of fame'.

In reality, European Community politics is driven by the national interest of the larger states, notably France and Germany, and this was reflected in the structure of power: the centre was the Council of Ministers, the Commission was weakened by having a tiny bureaucratic staff, and the Parliament was little more than a talking shop. Even the dramatic 'deepening' represented by Maastricht, it can be argued, was dictated by the interests of the European nation-states, recognising that the sudden collapse of Communism could result in a return to the politics of the 1930s with a re-unified Germany, an unstable Eastern Europe of economically distressed states trying to establish democratic traditions, but with problematic national minorities, and further east an insecure and bellicose Russia. Strengthening the European Union arose from the French desire to constrain a re-united Germany within a 'European' set of economic institutions and the German willingness to offer up its economic autonomy in return for movement towards Political Union (and perhaps admission of the former communist states, and thereby stabilising its eastern borders and extending its influence) (Anderson 1997).

Nonetheless, the EU has a supranational as well as an intergovernmental character, and its range of regulatory functions, now including monetary policy, is steadily increasing. This suggests a European-wide federation might arise as an *indirect effect* of the competitive goals and fears of the European nation-states, just as before the nations of Europe formed as an unintended consequence of the competition of dynastic states. The question is then: can the European dimension co-exist with the national dimension, and on what basis?

Can a European identity be found that will eventually transcend national loyalties and underpin a European state? Or is the emerging EU *sui generis*, a novel entity recognising the multiple sovereignties of post modernity? Or again, is the future to be a European order acknowledging the primacy of nation-states in a constitution that regulates the respective powers of supranational and national institutions? I will explore each of these possibilities in the context of the problems facing the Union, including eastern enlargement.

The introduction of symbols such as an EC flag and anthem and the pre-occupation with a European *demos* suggests the desire to create a European *national* community. But symbols in themselves have no efficacy unless they evoke a sense of a concrete collectivity, and even the outstanding civic nation, France, I have argued, is founded on an ethnic substratum – a historic political capital, Paris, the prestige of French language and culture, a history of '*gloire*', and clear boundaries 'naturalised' by war and physical barriers. Whereas nations evoke heroic images of collective will, a concrete cultural community and a sacred home-land, the 'European' identity the EU wishes to create is vague and contested. As political centres, Brussels and Strasbourg, evoke no sacral aura, and the EU lacks unifying cultural sites, and clear geographic boundaries. It offers no equiva-lence to national commemorations (e.g. Remembrance of the Fallen) that have a such a powerful popular resonance. The European project is articulated by reference to a indefinite future-oriented *telos* (the image of a moving train towards ever closer union that one must get on) that represents a rejection of the past of national rivalries.

Cannot a European constitutional patriotism guaranteeing civil rights and progress be realised subjectively as an act of faith in the future? The model of the USA is often invoked as a successful ideological project to found a new society based on universal enlightenment principles and on a deliberate rejection of the (European) past. Like the architects of the USA, European federalists veer between conceiving of the project as a heroic act of will and as following a *telos*. The USA, however, can plausibly differentiate itself from the past because it is a 'New World' nation of emigrants who have consciously left their place of origins and gained self-definition through the myth of a popular war of liberation against European imperialism, revolutionary heroes and sacred texts (the Declaration of Independence and its Constitution) that inspire allegiance. Moreover, the USA was built on English cultural values and the only pre-existing ethno-territorial identities it faced were pulverised by war and expropriation. In contrast, the EU was founded by the elites of defeated nation-states and has at best a pragmatic rationale, administered by bureaucrats.

John Pocock (1997) maintains that this trauma of defeat both created the European Community and crippled it. The ideology of Europeanism on which it rests is postmodernist, directed against moral absolutism and the grand narratives of European nation-states. It is largely deconstructionist in character, retaining for itself an essential lack of identity. It offers no synthetic or universal history to replace that of the nation-states. The very indeterminacy of 'Europe' presents tactical advantages, since like a text it can be 'read' in very different ways by the different constituent nationalities, and its borders can be extended elastically to fit the needs of a developing project. But this lack of clear criteria of membership enhances the manipulative capacity of powerful states in what is essentially a pragmatic imperial project, seeking to override the resistance of routinised national identities.

Postmodernists might reply that the European Union neither can nor should attempt to be a supernation, because in a global age the idea of a territorially-bounded sovereign actor is obsolete and dangerous. The EU is based on a consciousness of the catastrophic consequences of national rivalries in Europe and the vital need to discipline them within a political framework that would also recognise transnational (or subcontinental) and regional identities and interests. What holds it together is not just the *rational* advantages perceived by *elites* in pooling sovereignty, but a deeper *moral* revulsion of *peoples* against nationalism, combined with a sense that national identities are more securely preserved by detaching them from nation-states. The European Union thus does not need to be conceived as a surrogate nation-state with all the absolutisms that implies, including a moral messianism (*pace* USA). Its justification is as a pioneer of a new form of democratic political community, acknowledging that there are now multiple and overlapping centres of power and that authority is to be located appropriately to the problem at hand. The European Union liberates both dominant and minority nations from their fetish of the nation-state, and this is reflected in the trend to regional devolution. Moreover, a citizenship conceived in European terms because of its thinness would be less exclusive of immigrant minorities and compatible with the multicultural realities of contemporary industrial societies.

There is something in these arguments. A loyalty to the 'European' ideal is visible particularly in the case of discredited aggressor states (Germany, Italy) and the (Benelux) smaller states directly threatened by the quarrels of the great powers. But the postmodernists are open to two objections. First, they underestimate the degree to which national identities remain engrained, and are capable of being revitalised. The commitment of post-war Germans to a European democratic idealism to overcome the otherwise 'unmasterable past' did not interfere with the impetus to national re-unification unity in 1990, in spite of statements of alarm from European Community leaders. Second, they do not explain how an indefinite ideology can mobilise European populations to collective action in crisis. A postmodernist celebration of the multiplicity of identities is possible in a stable and prosperous world without obvious external or internal threats. But only a potent and definite identity is capable of orienting and mobilising collective action in order to overcome threats such as eruption of wars (in the Balkans), Islamist terrorist threats, economic recessions, and the prospect of large-scale immigration. A negative anti-Americanism is not a sufficient binding force, and indeed could be dangerously destabilising in the current world crises.

The very expansion of powers by the European Union intensifies a need to find some form of legitimation for their use. For monetary union to be successful will require fiscal coordination and significant powers of taxation to distribute resources from richer to poorer regions of Europe to compensate for the loss of exchange rate adjustments. The stronger the EU centre grows, the more it requires such cultural power to mobilise consent. But it possesses not even a common language, let alone a bank of myths, memories, and symbols to convey a sense of belonging to a community of sentiment. At the moment, the EU judged by a range of measures including electoral turn-outs, lacks popular legitimacy compared with the nation-states. The question remains, then, how is the EU to co-exist with this national dimension?

If it is implausible to construct a strong sense of Europeanness in its own terms, can one conceive of a Europe as a family of nations, gradually developing common values on a continental scale through a sense of quasi-kinship? The analogy is with conglomerate states such as Britain that may be conceived as a supernation built upon a family network of English, Welsh and Scottish ethno-national ties. There does seem to be a tendency for conglomerate states to use a language of kinship. Even the USSR, organised on avowedly supranational principles, depicted the Russians as the elder brother of the Soviet nationalities.

The very notion of an 'elder brother' acknowledges that such states were built upon a dominant national community which supplied the linguistic and cultural cement of the state, though the conflation of Britishness with Englishness and Soviet identities with Russian values was hidden. It is inconceivable for the EU to be based on a single hegemon, given the memories that this would evoke, though France continues to claim leadership by virtue of its historical pre-eminence in Europe. Is there a core quasi-ethnic grouping available to the EU? Possibly, in the loose sense of the original member states who share the EU founding myth and the sense of status that this implies. Within this group there is the coupling of the two nation-states that fought for European hegemony during the nineteenth and twentieth centuries, France and Germany, who have dominated EU decision-making since its origins. At points of crisis, German and French opinion makers and politicians have called for a renewal of this alliance and the formation with the Benelux countries of an inner core to further advance integration (see Lamers 1997).

The problem is that a kinship system implies hierarchy rather than equality and can build up centrifugal resentments as the case of the USSR, and lately, the UK demonstrates. Although this is reduced by the dual axis, the questions remain: Who is to be the elder brother, and who is perceived as belonging to the inner core of the family, as opposed to being a distant cousin, or even an adopted orphan (e.g. Turkey)? The EU's project of 'widening' and 'deepening' as it expands to take in Eastern European countries revives these questions as the existing status order is shaken both by territorial expansion and by the struggle for dominance over the strengthened institutions. The Franco-German accommodation (like the former Austrian–Hungarian Habsburg alliance) has always been pragmatic rather than fraternal: there are tensions at the elite level between the French centralist and the German federalist visions of the EU and popular suspicions below the surface. These anxieties have been exacerbated by the combination of German re-unification with EU expansion to the East that has awakened French fears of a revived German hegemony shifting the centre of gravity of the Union from the West. The very multiplication of actors within the EU following the entry of smaller and poorer Eastern states would seem to presage not only the loss of national vetoes through proposed majority voting but also the threats to the power of the richer and larger states.

Increasing centralisation raises the stakes in the battle over whose conception of Europe is to prevail which, when combined with the increase of members, intensifies the need to find a cement for this arrangement. Will the countries from what has been regarded as the periphery or even the outside of Europe perceive the 'integration process' as a form of imperialism, in which they have to submit to an onerous framework designed for advanced industrial states? Can Europe rely on institutional brokering and conjured rhetoric of common interest, or will the very expansion of the EU increasingly expose its empty heart?

The danger that the EU, as presently constituted, may collapse from its own contradictions is all the more likely as an unaccountable elite-driven integration process gathers momentum in spite of the absence of a substantiated European democracy (with a *demos*) that might legitimise the surrender of nation-state powers. Major gaps with popular opinion have been exposed already by referenda in France, Ireland and Denmark. The incapacity of national representative institutions to regulate such central areas as monetary policy and frontier controls makes it all too possible that grievances over unemployment, immigration and race and ethnicity will express themselves in large-scale populist direct action.

One possible answer to this widening gap between the peoples of Europe and the expanding EU political sphere is a written constitution that would authoritatively define the respective national and Union jurisdictions, and return substantial authority to the only credible repositories of democratic practice, the nation-states. Different versions of such an arrangement, enshrining the ideal of 'ever closer union of peoples', have been mooted: including a federal state sustained by a Constitutional Court on USA or German models. But constitutions have to have within them the potential for adaptation so that they can address circumstances unimaginable to their formulators. The experience of the USA, Canada and Australia suggests that a written constitution becomes a battleground between ideological groups seeking to expand or limit the central state and alter its rulings on fundamental rights, and that the supposedly neutral Constitutional Courts become politicised in the process. In the USA such conflicts over states' rights tied to the issue of slavery led to civil war.

A major difficulty of codifying decisively the respective spheres of the EU and nation-states is that nations change in what they perceive to be their core regulatory concerns, as they encounter the challenges of an ever-changing world. If that is so even within a single state, a constitution formulated for a union of many nation-states will almost certainly be the site of perpetual political conflict.

## Conclusion

The movement for European integration is justified by several rhetorics – the extension of democracy and human rights, enhancing economic progress, becoming a world actor, taking responsibility for European security. All of these have their point, but this is above all an elite-driven, even an Imperial (Franco-German) project, infused with a strong subterranean desire to contain the resurgence of historical national differences at the very centre, as well as on the eastern fringes, of Europe. The drive to integrate, however, exacerbates the problem. Centralising powers in European institutions raises expectations of what the EU can deliver while multiplying the problems it must resolve, and it intensifies the gap between elites and peoples by transferring powers from national parliaments to arcane and all but unaccountable institutions. A resentment of an invasive Imperial centre is the classic breeding ground of European nationalism, especially when the Imperial elites are divided by their national visions of Europe.

Myths and symbols provide key components of understanding and directing change. Even in normal times, as Michael Billig (1995) has demonstrated, the discourse of politicians is laden with national myths, images and a national rhetoric, often derived from warfare, which insiders take for granted. The legend of the nation is of a community knit by love and common sacrifice. Its myths and symbols orient its members to fundamental values – to homeland, the defence of 'irreplaceable cultural values', and to the freedom of its people. Images establish a common bond between leaders and led and legitimise even in 'normal times' difficult decisions – the imposition of heavier taxes in economic difficulties, the redistribution of resources between richer and poorer regions or classes. At times of extraordinary crises – the outbreak of war or economic depression – mythic images of kinship can inspire great sacrifice on behalf of the nation-state. One of the characteristics of such myth–symbol complexes is that they remain empty or alien to the outsider.

What images will the politicians of an increasingly differentiated European Union invoke to secure collective sacrifice for the common good? And how will they deal with extraordinary crises? Large-scale surveys indicate there is indeed a *consciousness* of being European, but an identity is more than a sense (it supplies fundamental prescriptions about conduct), and this consciousness is mediated through the different and often competing national identities of Europeans. The recent terrorist attacks offer a significant challenge to the Union. There are likely to be many more. Are there Indonesias about to erupt within Europe or on its borders? The political earthquake ten years ago engendered the proliferation of ethnic nationalisms in the East. The Middle East threatens to explode with potentially disastrous consequences for Europeans. We see evidence of ecological and climatic change, together with the rise of religious fundamentalism which brings with it the possible breakdown of North African societies and mass population movements.

One of the things one learns by taking a long-term historical approach is that the unexpected is the norm. We also know that nations and nation-states have a track record of surviving the most momentous crises. Has the EU similar moral and political stamina? We shall have to wait and see.

# References

Albrow, M. (1996) *The Global Age*, Cambridge: Cambridge University Press.

Anderson, B. (1991) *Imagined Communities*, London: Verso.

Anderson P. (1997) 'The Europe to Come', in P. Gowers and P. Anderson (eds) *The Question of Europe*, London: Verso.

Armstrong, J. (1982) *Nations Before Nationalism*, Chapel Hill: University of North Carolina Press.

Banton, M. (1994) 'Modeling ethnic and national relations', *Ethnic and Racial Studies* 17, 1: 1–29.

Billig, M. (1995) *Banal Nationalism*, London: Sage.

Castells, M. (1996) *The Rise of the Network Society*, Oxford: Blackwell.

Connor, W. (1990) 'When is a nation?', *Ethnic and Racial Studies* 13, 1: 92–103.

Gellner, E. (1983) *Nations and Nationalism*, Oxford: Blackwell.

Giddens, A. (1990) *The Consequences of Modernity*, Cambridge: Polity.

Gildea, R. (1994) *The Past in French History*, Yale: Yale University Press.

Guibernau, M. (2001) 'Globalisation and the nation-state', in M. Guibernau and J. Hutchinson (eds) *Understanding Nationalism*, Oxford: Polity.

Hobsbawm, E.J. (1990) *Nations and Nationalism Since 1780*, Cambridge: Cambridge University Press.

Hroch, M. (1985) *The Social Preconditions of National Revivals in Europe*, Cambridge: Cambridge University Press.

Hutchinson, J. (1987) *The Dynamics of Cultural Nationalism: The Gaelic Revival and the Creation of the Irish Nation State*, London: Allen & Unwin.

Jauregui, P. (1999) 'National pride and the meaning of "Europe": a comparative study of Britain and Spain', in D. Smith and S. Wright (eds) *Whose Europe? The Turn Towards Democracy*, Oxford: Blackwell/The Sociological Review.

Kohn, H. (1967) *Prelude to Nation-states: The French and German Experience 1789–1815*, New York: Van Nostrand.

......s, K. (1997) 'Strengthening the hard core', in P. Gowers and P. Anderson (eds) *The ..tion of Europe*, London: Verso.

Milward, A. (1992) *The European Rescue of the Nation State*, London: Routledge.

Pocock, J.G.A. (1997) 'Deconstructing Europe', in P. Gowers and P. Anderson (eds) *The Question of Europe*, London: Verso.

Smith, A.D. (1986) *The Ethnic Origins of Nations*, Oxford, Blackwell.

—— (1992) 'National identity and the idea of European unity', *International Affairs* 68, 1: 55–76.

—— (1999) *Myths and Memories of the Nation*, Oxford: Oxford University Press.

Vauchez, A. (1992) 'The Cathedral' in P. Nora (ed.) *Realms of Memory, Volume 2*, New York: Columbia University Press.

Wallace, W. (1997) 'The nation-state – rescue or retreat?' in P. Gowers and P. Anderson (eds), *The Question of Europe*, London: Verso.

Weber, E. (1976) *Peasants into Frenchmen: The Modernization of Rural France (1870–1914)*, Stanford: Stanford University Press.

# 4 Democracy without demos

## European integration as a process of the change of institutions and cultures

*Richard Münch*

### Introduction

The discussion about the cultural aspect of European integration is characterised by two elements: on the one hand, there is the demand to have the economic project of the single market's integration finally followed by a cultural project of the production of meaning. On the other hand, there is the fear of Europe's cultural variety falling completely victim to the integration machinery in Brussels. Obviously, the attempt is made to square the circle using harmonising formulae such as 'unity within variety', and reassuring principles like 'subsidiarity' (Zetterholm 1994; Kaelble 1997). But what precisely can we understand by these? How can cultural unity be compatible with cultural variety at all? Isn't that a contradiction in itself? Let us, therefore, take a closer look at the process of European integration from this point of view. We will see that the question as to European unity within the cultural variety of national traditions is basically not quite correct. A clearly out-lined European cultural unity will not arise, nor will the nations and their cultural traditions form its elementary parts. The process of European integration gives rise to a considerably more varied structure consisting of a myriad of levels and arenas. Here, the nations and their cultural traditions are losing in identity-forming strength and, instead, give way to integration through a growing division of labour, whose elementary units are not the nations but rather the individuals. The economic integration and its market logic goes hand in hand with a homo-logous transformation of the logic of solidarity, law and politics. The corresponding changes are stabilising each other. In this way, European integration occurs as a comprehensive and thoroughgoing process of institutional and cultural change (Münch 1993).

### A single European market without a European social union?

The shift in the EU Council of Ministers' decision-making process from unanimity to a qualified majority in all questions of single-market integration, as stipulated in the Single European Act of 1986/87 (SEA), along with the turning away from the goal of a complete harmonisation of legal prescriptions, technical rules and standards in favour of their mutual recognition by the member states, as stipulated in the White Paper on the completion of the Single Market, put an end to a long-lasting period of stagnation in the integration process and led to the successful establishment of the Single Market at the end of 1992. The Maastricht Treaty of 1991 paved the way for the European Economic and Monetary Union (EMU) in 1999. A focus on the realisation of the single market by means of removing barriers and in favour of free economic circulation, and the EMU's safeguarding by a policy of stability, formed the guarantees of success for this economic integration project. The accompanying social–political support, however, was deliberately kept within very close limits. Art. 138 (formerly Art. 118a, before the renumbering of the Treaty of Amsterdam) enables the enactment of legislative measures with a qualified majority, which set minimum standards for an improvement in the working conditions and the protection of health and safety at work. Art. 139 (ex Art. 118b) empowers the Commission to 'develop a dialogue between the social partners on a European level which may involve contractual relationships, if required'. Arts 158 and 162 (ex Arts 130a and 130e) require a closer cooperation between the member states in order to reduce the welfare divide existing between them. Out of the 200 legislative measures which were passed for the creation of the single market in 1992, no more than 12 referred to its social–political support. The passing of the directive on protection at work (89/391)[1] is considered a special success, as it goes beyond the level of protection prevailing even in the highly developed member states.

A good deal of hope was also invested in the new social dialogue at both a sectoral and an intersectoral level, which was inaugurated in the social records of 1993. It is true that previous social dialogue had generated a series of common statements at both a central and a sectoral level, yet there were no binding general agreements. This should change as a result of the new social dialogue. So far, however, this has brought about only two agreements on a central level: on maternity leave and part-time work. On a sectoral level, in contrast, no agreement has been reached yet (Keller and Sörries 1997, 1998, 1999).

Altogether, it is shown that the social element of the single market's integration lags far behind the economic one (Leibfried and Pierson 1998). The project of having the single market complemented with a social union, which was supported by Jacques Delors, above all, has been declared a failure by many people; this is considered a victory of the employers over the trade unions, of the neo-conservative governments over their socialist challengers, and of neo-liberalism over the programme of social balance. Nevertheless, voices can be heard that still do not give up the struggle for a social Europe and that consider the success achieved so far in European social politics a start. If one pursues the matter with enough patience, so they claim, this initial success may be exploited further, even without the birth of a European state, which sceptics consider essential for this purpose, but which is not realisable in the long run and possibly not even desired, at least not by everyone (Kowalsky 1999: 322–6).

## A European single market and national welfare systems?

According to the prevailing interpretation, the political balance of power has prevented the building of a European social union so far, alongside structural reasons such as the far-too-big differences in the member states' economic power, social systems and mentalities. Therefore, many experts have argued for a strengthening of national social politics in order to balance the insecurities produced both within the European Single Market and within the world market by the ever tougher competition (Leibfried and Pierson 1997; Scharpf 1998; Streeck 1998). This plea is confirmed by estimations saying that, as before, 95 per cent of all cases in industrial and social legislation are judged according to national law (Schuster 1996). It would be wrong, however, to conclude that the absence of the European social state leaves an even wider scope for the maintenance of the national welfare state. In fact, the European single market initiates a comprehensive process of transformation, which also affects to a certain degree the member states' welfare state institutions and the related welfare cultures and their ideas of justice. Both national cultures and people's identities undergo substantial changes.

The integration of the single market triggers a process of change in structures, institutions and cultures on all levels, from the European via the national and regional down to the local level. The liberalisation of the world market has an additional effect on this process of change. The European transformation process is part of a worldwide project of networking with a simultaneous differentiation of levels. This transformation process, which is set in motion by the integration of the single market in the context of a more open world economy must, however, not be interpreted in the sense of the 'functionalist' integration theory which claims that an economic integration will, in the long run, involve, at least, Europe's political, social and cultural integration as a result of 'spill-over effects'. In line with this integration model, the process which earlier resulted in the formation of the national welfare states, should be repeated on a European level. Accordingly, the political and social-integrative institutions and their related culture on a European level would be very similar to those pertaining to the nation-state: representative democracy, rule of law, neo-corporatism and an egalitarian welfare culture. The highly developed welfare states serve as models for the development of the European Union, whilst the less developed Southern European states are considered the latecomers in a development leading toward a very particular goal for everybody: a federal European representative democracy formed in line with the principles of the welfare state under the rule of law. The variety of nation-state institutions and cultures would be absorbed by an institutional and cultural unity on a higher level. This model of functionalist integration takes far too little account of the structural changes initiated by the single market integration: democracy, the rule of law and social integration will change their character under the new structural conditions.

## De-limitation of markets and solidarities: dissolution of national solidarity

The abolition of national frontiers for economic circulation changes the solidarity structures which formed the basis of the national welfare state. New sales potentials will arise for domestic products and services beyond the national borders. Vice-versa, foreign products and services will, however, also have free access to the domestic market. The same applies to capital investments and the workforce. Out of these four elements of economic circulation, the mobility of goods and capital grew fastest by far within the European single market. Both goods and capital flows tend to respect national borders less and less. As far as services and workers are concerned, in contrast, mobility is clearly lower and it is least so for workers. As regards the service sector, easily transferable forms such as insurance act as the pioneers. In the case of workers, the prevailing South–North mobility of those with lower qualifications even declined as a result of the halt in recruitment and high unemployment in the highly developed countries. In contrast, the immigration of asylum seekers from outside the EU has increased substantially. However, it should be discounted here, as we are dealing with the intra-European migration. A new mobility has arisen only in the construction sector, which led to related control measures, due to the precarious situation in the job market. According to the EU directive 96/72 EC,2 the wage conditions agreed at the place of work are applicable. Neo-liberal critics describe this as a restriction on competition, whilst those who are on the left, consider it insufficient (Kowalsky 1999, 122–7). Otherwise, the new mobility is more or less a matter of highly qualified experts in research and development.

This means that the opening of the borders offers new economic chances whilst, at the same time, making competition even tougher. As far as the workforce is concerned, competition is fuelled more by the mobility of capital than by the mobility of work. Capital is increasingly – though still hesitantly – looking for locations where the right staff is available for a particular purpose. It is therefore logical to open up new production locations in Eastern Europe and to inaugurate a new research plant for bio-technology close to MIT in Cambridge, Massachusetts.

The divergence between mobility of capital and mobility of labour exercises an increasingly competitive pressure on employees. It is felt, in particular, among the least qualified workers, who have to acknowledge that they can be easily replaced by machinery and/or cheaper workers in different locations. The situation is completely different for highly qualified staff. They are faced with new opportunities, which they may exploit to increase their incomes (Nelson 1995; Haller 1997; Reich 1991). People who are working successfully with a high productivity no longer depend on the support of simple production workers and service providers on the spot, since the division of labour can be differentiated on a European and even worldwide level, in a world of open borders. The extension of transport and communication networks, along with the acceleration of transport and communication through new technologies allow for the ever more extensive exploitation of open borders, for a division of labour throughout Europe and the world as a whole.

Consequently, nationally limited production and value creation chains are increasingly superseded by those which branch out across Europe and the world (Narr and Schubert 1994; Thurow 1996).

Sectors and groups of workers which are strong in competition are oriented toward the European and global markets and seize the chances offered to them outside the national borders. Correspondingly, they cannot and no longer want to join forces to the same extent as before with weaker sectors and groups. The national welfare consensus breaks apart and necessarily has to give way to a network of economic cooperation and the inevitably resulting solidarity, which is far more geared toward the outside and far more differentiated inside. One group of people is presented with better economic opportunities, in which the other group can no longer participate as before. High incomes for strongly competitive sectors and groups of employees no longer imply necessarily high incomes for the others, too, since the ties of the value creation chain and the related solidarity between them have been cut. As a result of the competitive pressure from outside, suppliers are kept on a short lead, services (cleaning of buildings, drivers' services, messenger services, canteens) are outsourced and subjected to stronger competition. The differing wage levels in various sectors are exploited to the full, the inefficient operation of public enterprises is reduced or removed completely with their privatisation. In addition to this, the greater opportunity for mobility of both capital and top executives limits the scope for re-distribution through the state. This is accounted for to a great extent now, as the earlier extension of the welfare state and all its blessings for everyone has reached the limits of its financiability. The new policy of austerity is the first step toward recognising the new realities on a still very high level of redistribution through the state. The efficiency revolution, under the leadership of globally-active consultancy firms, which penetrates even the last niches of society, implies that no one will pay more money for a performance than its actual worth. The principle of achievement celebrates new triumphs.

## Extension, branching and differentiation of the division of labour: from mechanical to organic solidarity

The opening of national borders does away with barriers that previously kept people at a distance. This increases the opportunities to establish relationships of trade, capital investment and cooperation. Nevertheless, these new opportunities are not seized to an equal extent by all. They are a concern of elites who limit and qualify their relationships inside national borders, at the same time as they take up new relationships outside. Along with the new opportunities for relationships, the number of more or less long-term associations is growing, as is the number of memberships for mobile people. This covers an ever increasing number of associations bringing people together for specific purposes, beyond formerly existing borders. Cross-border traffic brings products to any place around the world, from the most simple food products to the most demanding technical or artistic creation.

Correspondingly, options and *possibilities* for differentiation are growing for people (Gross 1994). Yet at the same time, the *necessities* for differentiation are increasing. The openness of borders leads to a decline in spaces protected against competition. Tougher competition is the drawback of extended economic opportunities. Those willing to earn money compete more strongly for jobs, suppliers of products and services for clients, locations for investors. They can meet this competition by offering better quality at the same price or asking a lower price for the same products based on higher productivity. This strategy has worked perfectly in Germany for a long time and has led to a permanent rise in productivity. As soon as the limit of this strategy has, however, been achieved, people have to undergo more substantial changes. In his study on the division of labour, Durkheim revealed three ways out: emigration, suicide and specialisation. Since, as a rule, people cling strongly to their home and their life, it is only the third way that remains open to them, namely specialisation (Durkheim 1964: 256–82; 1982: ch. 5, 1).

In a world of unprotected spaces, emigration is an option only for those living in the world's poorest regions. The unequal level of development of the world's regions and the shortening of distances through transport and communication have, in fact, an influence in increasing the migration rate. Nevertheless, the majority of people remain within the poorer regions, whilst only a small number succeed in reaching the richer ones. Basically, war and destruction along with more limited opportunities to earn an income and an improved awareness of better opportunities in other locations, are the main reasons behind the swelling of the migration streams.

In the highly developed regions, specialisation offers the only realistically feasible way out of a situation of overflowing competition, which otherwise results in an increasing narrowing of the scope of distribution. This means that more and more products and services have to be launched on to the market in ever shorter product cycles (Durkheim 1964: 270–5). Specialisation implies the offering of products and services which did not exist in this particular form before. Correspondingly, an ever greater number and sequence of inventions is required, which have to be made into products ever faster. The basis for this is the more comprehensive and thoroughgoing exploitation of the potential offered by science. All those disciplines which cannot be used to this end, will find it more difficult to survive. The humanities, which are strongly affected by this development, therefore have to find a completely new definition and replace the devotion to high culture by the training of marketable qualifications. This shows that the strategy of reducing competition through specialisation is inseparably linked with the permanent rise in economic growth. Without this growth, distribution struggles tend to become harder and ultimately have to lead to violent clashes. It is only the establishment of a global compulsory regime, rationing the limited resources that could avoid such consequences.

Therefore, there are three alternatives to the reduction in distances and the related growth in competition in the European single market and the world market: specialisation accompanied by permanent economic growth; violent distribution struggles; or a compulsory global regime. Since economic growth and the acceleration of product cycles and of structural change involve an ever growing number of ecological and social strains and anomic phenomena, in the face of the other two available alternatives, the channelling of economic growth onto paths which are both ecologically and socially friendly, turns out to be the most urgent problem for the future.

The increasing specialisation is the individual side of a process which is reflected on the societal side by the ever more graduated division of labour and the related exchange of products, semi-products and services. However, the division of labour, which reaches farther on the outside and is more differentiated inside, not only has an economic aspect, but also a solidarity-related one. Division of labour necessarily implies cooperation. It brings people together who were separated before, above all beyond the previously existing national borders. Yet it also separates people who formed a homogeneous group before. Cooperation is an elementary form of solidarity uniting people of different origins and identities. For this, Durkheim coined the term 'organic solidarity'. This solidarity resulting from variety must be differentiated from the older form of mechanical solidarity of people sharing a common identity within a homogeneous group. In the process of the increasing division of labour, mechanical solidarity, which is rooted in simple tribal societies, begins to lose its contours, whereas organic solidarity assumes growing significance. In the process of European integration and, beyond, in the process of global sociation, we can observe a new boost in this direction (Durkheim 1964: 147–99).

The national welfare state is the highest embodiment of mechanical solidarity so far. It is expressed in the latter's high level of guaranteeing relatively equal conditions of life, at a high standard of welfare. The state quota, i.e. the share of public spending within the GNP, or the degree of decommodification, as established by Esping-Andersen, i.e. the independence of the individual standard of life from individual market performance, could be regarded as a yardstick of mechanical solidarity. According to this yardstick, the social-democratically oriented Scandinavian welfare states and that of the Netherlands have attained the highest level of mechanical solidarity; the level of the conservatively formed welfare states on the European continent (Germany/France) is slightly lower; the level of the conservative-liberally marked welfare state of the UK – which has also been shaped by the Labour party – is substantially lower; and the level of the liberal welfare state of the USA clearly lags behind. Another feature of mechanical solidarity is the relative homogeneity of working people, which is mirrored by their representation in large associations (large trade unions). This aspect also differs in the welfare states mentioned above (Esping-Anderson 1990; Cattero 1998; Lessenich and Ostner 1998).

The extension and branching of the division of labour to the outside and its differentiation inside push back the mechanical solidarity of the welfare states which has evolved historically. It is increasingly replaced by the farther reaching and more strongly branched yet also internally differentiated organic solidarity of cooperation. This development is reflected, on the one hand, by the ever stronger interlacing of economic circulation within the single market and, on the other hand, by the ever stronger internal differentiation of the workforce. Trade, direct investment and value creation chains beyond national borders, differentiation of professions and interest representation accompanied by a simultaneous loss in significance of large associations, are the characteristic features of the growing organic solidarity both inside and out.

## European law: from material to procedural justice

The development from mechanical to organic solidarity corresponds to the formation of European law and the withdrawal of national legal traditions. At the same time, a common European culture is taking firm contours, whilst national cultures tend to fade. Likewise, a European collective consciousness is arising with a simultaneous weakening of national identities.

According to Jacques Delors, more than 80 per cent of the entire economic activity is regulated by European law. If we disregard the regulation of the agricultural market – which has its very specific reasons – this economic law is more distinctly geared toward safeguarding the free flow of goods, economic liberties and competition than that of the individual member states. It concerns the granting of free movement of the factors of production, equal opportunities and fair competition. Since all other areas of law are much less developed, this character, which is committed to market logic, leaves its mark on European law as a whole. It therefore appears obvious that its logic affects the other legal areas, too, especially as there is no EU state with enough political power to introduce a different legal logic. In the field of consumer protection, for instance, it is shown that the principle of the mutual recognition of product standards leaves greater self-responsibility to the consumers than was the case with the preventive protective policy of the highly developed welfare states (Reich 1996; Micklitz 1997).

A change in paradigms from material to procedural protection of fundamental rights can be observed here. Less so than the national welfare states, the European Union is taking consumers under its wing by way of material legal prescriptions and detailed uniform standards. Therefore, the role of the national courts and of the European Court of Justice will be even more important when it comes to ensuring a fair balance of interests between consumers and manufacturers when implementing EU law in cases of dispute. The coordination of freedom of action and balance of interests will shift to some extent away from material legislation toward jurisdiction. The logic of this jurisdiction is characterised by the principle of free movement and is, accordingly, mainly geared toward the correction of practices that distort competition, or that lead to unfair competition, fraud and misinformation at the expense of consumers. Consumers are not protected materially, but are, instead, empowered to make autonomous decisions.

## European social law: from social balance to fairness

Market logic corresponds to a legal logic guaranteeing individual legal subjects the sovereign execution of their rights to freedom with equal opportunities. Market logic and the related legal logic complement each other. The matching political logic embodies a regulative policy securing the functioning of both the market and competition, and the equal participation of everybody in this competition. This framework does not provide much space for a redistributive policy. Accordingly, the small amount of social policy developed at the EU level is geared toward the improvement of competitive chances in weakly structured regions, the reduction of discriminatory restrictions on access to the market, the portability of social payments and the maintenance of the employees' competitiveness (Leibfried and Pierson 1998; Kowalsky 1999). Regional, social and cohesion funds are intended to strengthen competitiveness. The legislative measures on protection at work serve to maintain labour, equal rights for women remove discriminatory restrictions on competition. The European employee representatives are not organs for co-decision, but rather institutions for information and consultation. They provide both employers and employees with a better basis for information for their relative decisions, ensure more transparency and mutual openness. The decisions of the European Court of Justice which refer to social policy comply with this market-creating logic. They abolish discriminatory practices which exclude individual workers from market opportunities, yet they do not protect employees against the strength of the market or related competition. The Title on employment in the Amsterdam Treaty sets the Union the goal of achieving a high level of employment. The core of this programme is the promotion of the *employability* of the workforce, yet another category which does not protect against the market power but is intended to provide market abilities. The Employment Title is not intended to make any prescriptions to the individual states but, instead, to facilitate mutual learning through a variety of measures via a committee. Moreover, transparency and competition for the best solutions are sought.

We can recognise so far the direction of the change in paradigms of law in the transfer of legislation and jurisdiction from the nation-state to the European level. A political logic and a legal logic corresponding to the market logic are emerging. Apart from agricultural policy, political logic foregoes redistribution and, instead, prefers regulation, which keeps the access to the market open to everybody, removes discrimination and maintains and/or produces competitiveness. The legal logic is committed to guaranteeing that legal subjects may exercise their rights without restriction. It does not aim at material justice, but at formal procedural justice. All three types of logic are based on an understanding of justice which does not look for equality of results but rather equality of opportunities, not provision but fairness. Legislation is largely confined to economic law whose core can be found in competitive law influencing all other legal fields.

Compared to national law, European law is more abstract, open and flexible. Its guidelines assume greater significance than rulings and decrees. They establish a frame which the member states have to concretise in accordance with their specific situation. European norms determine minimum standards allowing for the approval of less competitive member states and leaving enough scope toward the top for the more competitive states. As politics sets material law to a lesser extent, the courts – headed by the European Court of Justice – assume greater importance than in the nation-states. According to the corresponding logic of market and procedural justice, they play this role with the goal of ensuring a fair balance of interests and safeguarding competition and access to the market, yet not with the goal of realising equal living conditions for everyone materially (Lenaerts 1992; Zuleeg 1995; Joerges 1996).

## Between abstraction and individual self-responsibility: the change in national legal traditions

The logic of solidarity forms a link between market logic on the one hand and legal logic and political logic on the other. All four types of logic are linked with each other in a relationship of structural homology. The corresponding logic of solidarity is based on cooperation, which is extended and branched toward the outside and differentiated inside in the framework of the division of labour. The cooperation of organic solidarity, which is caused by complementary interests, replaces mechanical solidarity based on a communal spirit. Whilst mechanical solidarity merely entails a direct connection of the individual members of society to the collectivity, a wealth of loyalty duties have to be coordinated in the case of organic solidarity. The collective consciousness is weakening and determines behaviour less concretely. It is more abstract and forms but a frame which is filled by the individuals and their decisions in accordance with the relative situation. The scope for the unfolding of individual consciousness and individual identity is growing to the same extent as the collective consciousness is becoming weaker and more abstract. The abstraction of collective consciousness and the unfolding of individual consciousness intensify each other. The ever growing number of associations form the intermediary instances between these two poles. With Georg Simmel we may add here that loyalty is not only constructed concentrically from the family to the community to the nation and to Europe, but also exists side by side horizontally in the form of business relationships, partnerships and membership of associations so that the individual will gain and have to determine his/her personal identity at the point of intersection of a myriad of social circles. He/she has to take up the chance for autonomy with self-responsibility and mediate between the different claims to loyalty. In this way, the process of European integration implies a tremendous boost to individualisation (Simmel 1908/1992: 456–511).

Europe is not so much formed from individual nations, their collective solidarities and their national cultures, but more from the strongly differentiated cooperation of individuals which, in turn, is formed by an ever growing number of associations. The individualisation of responsibilities pushes the uniform collective organisation of social life through the nation-state into the background thus giving way to the more varied and differentiated coordination of action within Europe. European society evolves as a multi-level network society. In a society of this kind, individual, self-responsible action can no longer be coordinated by direct political control and substantive law, but merely by framework legislation and procedural law, which must be formed variably in accordance with the situation. Correspondingly, the focus of the coordination of action is transferred away from the state toward the individual negotiation of contracts. In-between, the coordination of action through the settlement of conflicts by the courts is gaining in significance. National legal cultures do not fade just because they are covered by European law, but, above all, because their substantive law based on a strong collective solidarity is not suited to a situatively variable coordination of action between self-responsible individuals. Therefore, it is not the legal subjects who are the bearers of national legal traditions. They are detached more and more from the national legal community and open toward the more varied, situatively variable coordination of action through European law. It is rather the jurists trained in national law who appear to be the keepers of the Holy Grail. This last bastion of national legal cultures is disappearing along with the appearance of a growing number of young jurists trained in European law.

National legal cultures are destroyed from two sides: from the top by European law and from the bottom by the individualisation of the ways of life. Nevertheless, national legal traditions will not disappear overnight. Since the framework measures of European law leave some scope for specific national interpretations, and since the implementation is in the hands of the national administrations, European law will be adjusted to national patterns of thought and ways of argumentation, and it will frequently be implemented very slowly, with a great delay and a good deal of dilution. On the one hand, the ever growing number of procedures instigated by the Commission against the member states for violating the contracts, i.e. for failing to adopt European law, shows the growing European legal formation but, on the other hand, it is also proof of the continued resistance displayed by the bearers of national law. Nevertheless, the position of national law has changed. It has lost its position of sovereign validity and has been pushed into a mediator role between European law and the individualised conditions of life. Its character is being changed by both these aspects. It is a traditionally anchored interpretation forum for abstract law and procedural justice as fairness under the terms of individualised conditions of life. And it forms a link with the national past on the way toward a more open European future.

Industrial and social legislation is not spared by this process of change, although it is still oriented to the different national traditions in 95 per cent of cases. The pressure to abstraction, formalisation and proceduralisation, which is exercised by European law, and the pressure to individualisation, which results from the changing conditions of life, involve a long-term refurbishment of national industrial and social laws, too (Kowalsky 1999: 352–68). These will move away from the production of collective solidarity toward the support of individual provision on the basis of elementary security. Industrial relationships will also continue to change: they will move away from collective contracts toward individual contracts, away from comprehensive wage contracts toward variable company-related agreements, away from the total safeguarding of the 'normal job situation' toward the support for part-time and temporary jobs, away from the avoidance of precarious jobs toward their support by way of negative income tax, away from the administration of unemployment through authorities toward the activation of those able to work through private agencies and employment organisations (Keller and Seifert 1995).

The representation of vast masses of employees through large trade unions will have to give way to a pluralism of individual representation of interests. The decline of trade unions has not merely been caused by the new power of capital in the global economy, but also by the working population's growing out of a state of tutelage. The ever more educated workforce in ever more differentiated areas of work can no longer be contained within the narrow scheme of collective representation through one trade union (van Ruysseveldt and Visser 1996; Ebbinghaus and Visser 1997; Müller *et al.* 1997). The steadily growing qualification and differentiation of jobs is, at least, as much responsible for the decline of the trade unions as is the fact that it is possible to invest capital globally.

The welfare cartel of state, large welfare associations and local institutions will have to open and create more space for new and more specialised social associations. The welfare cartel will be replaced by a new welfare pluralism. This comprehensive, thoroughgoing institutional change will go hand in hand with a change in the national work and welfare cultures. The social-democratic model of Scandinavia, the conservative pattern of Continental Europe and the conservative-liberal regime of the UK will converge into a new regime that will be shaped by the setting of frameworks, abstraction, formalism and proceduralism of European law on the one hand, and by the individualism of the new conditions of life on the other. Justice as social balance will be superseded by justice as fairness in the sense of equal opportunities and the principle of achievement.

## Negative and positive solidarity in the process of the increasing division of labour

In his study on the division of labour, Emile Durkheim introduced a differentiation between negative and positive solidarity in addition to the differentiation between mechanical and organic solidarity (Durkheim 1964). In legal philosophy, the corresponding differentiation of positive and negative freedom has established itself (Kant 1797/1956: 307–634; Höffe 1999: 40–57). Negative solidarity co-ordinates the individual scope of action so that the exercise of the freedom of action for one will not be to the detriment of the freedom of action for the other. It finds an expression in property rights. The latter regulate the access to material objects. Conflicts are avoided by a clear determination of this access. The negative solidarity embodied in property rights ensures a distance between individuals thus avoiding conflicts in the exercise of their freedoms. Nevertheless, it does not establish a relationship of cooperation between individuals. Such a relationship is the characteristic feature of positive solidarity. The latter is expressed legally in contract law, family law, commercial law, procedural law, administrative and constitutional law. These fields of law determine the position and relationship among individuals, their mutual rights and duties and their cooperation.

In Durkheim's view, only positive solidarity will produce social integration. This can be assumed, since the determination of property rights implies relationships of mutual respect of property. In the relationship to material objects, there is always a relationship included between people; without their consensus regarding the distribution of rights to material objects, such laws would not have a secure validity. This is the side of positive solidarity. It is conceivable in two forms: One of them is mechanical solidarity, where the collective consciousness takes such an extensive space that little or no room at all is left for the individual consciousness. The individual is tied directly to the omnipresent society. The other form is organic solidarity, where the collective consciousness is restricted to a smaller part of human awareness, makes itself seen less clearly, is becoming more abstract and gives way to a considerably wider unfolding of the individual consciousness. The more specialisation and the related division of labour progress, the more can individuality spread. Individuals are less directly tied to society as a whole, but more indirectly through the inclusion into a differentiated, finely woven network of cooperation relationships.

The scope of this organic solidarity covers a far wider field and considerably more people than that of mechanical solidarity. The corresponding law regulates the cooperation between natural and legal persons. The related means of formation is the contract, which is worked out by the contract partners in accordance with their situation and needs. The contract *law*, in turn, determines in a generally binding way the criteria to which contracts have to adhere in order to have a claim to societal validity and be able to hope for corresponding legal support. This covers the non-contractual foundations of individually negotiated contracts which express a consensus and a related collective solidarity that go beyond the contract partners. Here we find that small remainder of mechanical solidarity without which societies cannot exist without descending into anomie and a complete insecurity of the individual existence – not even those societies which display a widely differentiated division of labour and which are strongly individualised.

The remaining share of mechanical solidarity can, in turn, be more or less great. It can be assumed, however, that it will become smaller, less present and more abstract, the more comprehensive the division of labour becomes, the more it differentiates and the more scope for individualism it creates in this way. This means, it must be necessarily smaller in a European society than in the different European nation-states. In turn, European collective consciousness is becoming more abstract and comes to the fore less clearly. The related development of the collective view of justice turns away from a guarantee of equal conditions of life for all and goes toward the granting of equal chances for the realisation of individually chosen ways of life. Justice as social balance in the comprehensive sense of a welfare state re-distribution increasingly forms a contradiction to the individualised conditions of life of the widely diverging and differentiated division of labour. Sociation is resulting less and less from collectively coordinated action and more from individual contributions to a finely woven network. There is no room for homogeneous collectives. Social security is not a result of the individual's firm inclusion into a collective, but rather of the openness and of a wealth of various points of intersection of the network so that there are many points of entrance for the individual. This also means, however, that this openness has to be shared with many other people and has to be made a personal benefit through personal contributions. The open network society offers a variety of chances for individual self-realisation, which are, however, not exploited equally by all and cannot be exploited by all. Its social dimension is, in particular, its openness, which is inseparably linked to individually differing successful exploitation.

Individuals, who are far apart from each other, but nevertheless influence each other in many ways, are in the best position to agree on the maintenance of open chances and equal opportunities. Their solidarity support will focus on the granting of these equal and open opportunities for individual self-realisation as well as on the maintenance of a social security network, which will lead everybody who has stumbled back on to the open field of the realisation of chances in competition (Rawls 1971). This justice understood in the sense of fairness stands out against the understanding of justice as social balance by comprehensive welfare state re-distribution and its wider power of inclusion. It can include more people of different origins under one common roof. Justice as social balance, in contrast, is tied to more cohesion and depends on more unity. Its high degree of equality of results is only possible due to strong isolation toward the outside and the correspondingly low chances for strangers to enter the group in question. The internal morality of fraternity among companions is coupled with an external morality of non-fraternity toward strangers. Justice in the sense of fairness levels off this difference. It makes equal rights accepted for all without frontiers. Yet, this can only be understood as equal opportunities in this particular case. It is exactly at this point that the form of inclusion of the American liberal society differs from that of the European welfare states. The American society could be more open to immigration not least of all as its internal solidarity was widely limited to the granting of equal opportunities. The European welfare states, however, had to be more isolated toward the outside, as they fostered a greater equality of results inside. The fortress Europe is the other, less fair, side of the European welfare state's social justice. The left-wing concentration on the welfare state and the right-wing rejection of strangers are two sides of one and the same coin. Inasmuch as the trade unions in Germany oppose the government's plan to offer 'green cards' to foreign computer specialists in order to overcome the shortage of qualified experts in this branch of business, they team up with right-wing opposition to immigration.

The European integration process is a step toward open sociation and justice as fairness which, however, stops exactly at the point where the 'fortress Europe' is delimited to the outside. Compared to the nation-state justice as social balance, however, European justice assumes far more the character of fairness. This development is not only limited to the European level, but also penetrates all levels of European society, i.e. also the EU's individual member states. The idea that the inadequate extension of the European social union can be compensated for by an even stronger clinging to nation-state social security must necessarily fail due to the fact that the structural change in solidarity affects all levels. Yet, national social policy is faced with narrower limits than before, since it loses its sovereignty completely in the competition for investors within the European single market, as far as the imposition of tax, redistribution and social regulation are concerned. Since a member state's industry can attain more growth in the home market, it ultimately has a growing GDP at its disposal, which can also be used for welfare purposes.

In this sense, the welfare potential is even rising. The fact that this potential can be used less than before for redistribution and a comprehensive social security, is not simply a matter of capital taking on an international character, whilst work remains tied within the national boundaries. This is but one aspect of a much more comprehensive structural change which withdraws the foundations of a nationally closed mechanical solidarity from the welfare state and involves an internally much more differentiated organic solidarity which goes far beyond national boundaries. A structural contradiction arises between this emerging solidarity of networks and the traditional welfare culture. The welfare culture is becoming a fetter on the new solidarity structure which is in the process of development. A phase of social struggles, institutional and legitimacy crises will set in, from which, in the long run, a new institutional structure and a new legal culture will result that are in harmony with the new solidarity structures. The dynamics of this structural change start from the unfolding of new opportunities and competition through the opening of national markets, with the ever closer networking of these markets by communication and transport playing an essential role. The structural change occurs in line with Marx's model. The unfolding of productive forces through open markets is in contradiction with the established production rela-tionships, that tie up the further development of productive forces, but which will tear in the long run and give way to new production relationships and their more satisfactory superstructure of law and justice. Nevertheless, this process does not lead straight into the paradise of communism, but rather into the realm of the open multi-level network society (van Ruysseveldt and Visser 1996; Müller *et al.* 1997).

This far-reaching structural change has so far not been sufficiently grasped. This is not least of all underlined by the fact that the search for solutions is focused on the maintenance of the 'achievements' of the national welfare state, whether it is by transfer to the European level and/or safeguarding of the national level. It is generally neglected, however, that the social justice of the national welfare state was coupled with both European and global injustice. The emphasis is on comple-menting the 'negative integration' of the single market through the removal of all tariff and non-tariff barriers to free economic circulation by a 'positive integration' through social policy. This pattern of thought was introduced into the theory of international relationships by Jan Tinbergen (Tinbergen 1965; Scharpf 1996; Jachtenfuchs 1998). Fritz Scharpf has taken up and applied the idea to the question of European integration. He starts from the assumption that the national welfare states succeeded in producing a 'balance' between negative, market liberating and positive, market regulating integration, since their constitutions not only grant the right to freedom, but also the right to equality, not only in property rights, but also social rights so that the inequalities created by the market are kept within close limits by social policies. In the European Union, however, negative integration outweighs positive integration, since the latter depends to a far greater extent on a working government that intervenes in society. The big differences in the economic performance alone that prevail between the poor and the rich member states, do not allow for an agreement on uniform social standards. For the poorer countries, the high standards of the rich countries would mean a loss in competitiveness. The differences in institutional regulations do not even allow for a harmonisation between the countries on one and the same level of development. It is only possible to ensure progress in positive integration where the costs and differences in national institutions appear low, where unified regulations make cross-border economic traffic easier and where the rich countries practice a sort of definitional power due to their know-how. This can be observed, for instance, in the protection against health risks at work, in the utilisation of consumer goods as well as in individual cases of environmental protection. As far as social policy is concerned, however, these prerequisites do not exist. It is true that the European Social Fund has grown continually as regards its share of the Union's overall budget – both in absolute and relative terms – namely from ECU 24.5 m, i.e. 1.5 per cent of the overall budget in 1968 to ECU 6.8 bn, i.e. 7.8 per cent in 1998 (Kowalsky 1999: 249). Nevertheless, these are but modest sums taking into account the fact that in Germany, for instance, the social budget amounted to 34.4 per cent of the GNP in 1997 (Institut der deutschen Wirtschaft 1998). The question therefore is as to whether an extension of qualified majority voting in the Council of Ministers to social policy, or even the introduction of simple majority voting will bring about a greater ability to act. An argument against such a measure is that the Union's integration has not advanced far enough. What is lacking in particular is a system of parties and associations that can overcome national differences as well as a cross-border public, i.e. that a European demos has not yet taken shape. If we arrive at this conclusion and if we see the positive integration of the national welfare states as a quality that has to be maintained in any case, we have to look for bases for national social policy. Scharpf points to Arts. 36, 48(3), 56(1) and 100A(4) of the old numbering of the Community Treaty, which allow the member states a higher protective level – beyond European regulations – and restrict the import of goods and, as a result, protect the domestic industry from foreign competition, if this is deemed necessary for the protection of the lives of humans, animals or plants as outlined in Art 36 of the old numbering (new: Art. 30). However, it will not be possible to refer to these articles in the field of social policy so that, in the end, the question arises as to whether the rich member states will be able to maintain their high level of social security even under the condition of open borders.

A fact speaking against such a development is that companies will no longer be able to pass on the rising taxation resulting from the competitive pressure of cheap foreign suppliers to the consumers as easily as before, and that they themselves can switch to less expensive locations. Therefore, Scharpf supports the discharge of companies by taxes and social payments and the corresponding conversion to the financing of social security through taxes. A model for this is Denmark, where 85 per cent of social spending is raised through taxes. Since, however, certain limits are set to this strategy, the only thing that will remain, in the end, is the claim that the European Union abandons the preference for negative integration through the removal of obstacles to competition and, instead, gives equal ranking to positive integration through regulation of the market, as this was the case in the national welfare states in the past. Nevertheless, this is merely a demand that can hardly be realised since the limits to majority decisions at a European level have been set far too restrictively for a long time. If we see the national welfare state as the model for a mutual balancing of both negative and positive integration at a European level, our argumentation will obviously finish up a blind alley. We can see that the national welfare state comes under competitive pressures and has to eliminate some social security without, however, the European Union being in a position to bring about an equivalent compensation. To draw up an unbiased analysis which is not tied to certain values right from the start, the national welfare state can, however, only represent a limited historical epoch that cannot be extended infinitely. The forms of linkage of both negative and positive integration discovered in this epoch cannot be transferred to another epoch without alterations, where the nation-state is attributed but a restricted role in a multi-level system of local community, region, nation, Europe and the world. This model of the national welfare state, which is frequently contrasted to the American model of economic liberalism as the 'European social model' is too much bound to the past. Durkheim's classic contribution, featuring an almost identical conceptual framework of negative and positive solidarity, which is included in his modernisation theory, should be accounted for in this debate (Durkheim 1964: 111–32). The new solidarity network should be particularly recognised. It is unfolding through 'negative integration' alone in a cross-border way as a result of free movement of economic factors and as a result of the further-reaching, more differentiated division of labour.

What Scharpf calls 'negative integration' is part of the 'positive solidarity' for Durkheim. At the same time, Scharpf understands 'positive integration' very much as mechanical solidarity which, however, has no more room within the European and – beyond this – the global multi-level network society. That 'positive integration' assumes a different character in such a network than in a nationally closed welfare association has to be accounted for sufficiently. Also, the accompanying change in the understanding of justice has to be interpreted appropriately. The need for structural adequacy of solidarity, legal and domination logic and the homology pressure exercised by the single market's integration on solidarity, law and politics should be adequately recognised. If 'positive integration' is normatively synchronised with the national welfare state's integration achievements, it is becoming utopian in the face of the new structural realities.

The same questions can be raised with regard to other common interpretation patterns such as 'disorganised capitalism' or 'neo-voluntarism' (Lash and Urry 1987; Streeck 1996). They are concepts that establish the dissolution of the social integration of the welfare state. They should, however, also offer a perspective for the new forms of sociation whose first contours begin to loom on the horizon. The theory of the welfare state seems so closely linked with the latter's ideology and politics that its supporters have not found a workable model so far that would be appropriate for the formation of the structural change and represent a realistic alternative to neo-liberalism. This is why its protagonists are in a difficult position in competition with neo-liberalism. The newly invented 'Third Way' indeed presents such an alternative (Giddens 1998).

The term 'disorganised capitalism' was used by Lash and Urry to describe the decreasing organisation of capitalist production through legislation and agreements between employers associations and trade unions as well as through the cooperation of company management and employees' representatives. As the term suggests, attention is geared toward the removal of existing institutions without the new matter being recognisable for its own quality and as an element of an emerging new form of sociation in further reaching, more strongly branched and more differentiated networks. The term of 'neo-voluntarism' was introduced by Wolfgang Streeck in order to direct attention to the more open creation of the relationship between employers and employees and the related new formative power of capital in its relation to work. Streeck claims that the programmes of the Social Action groups in the 1970s and of the Social Dimension groups in the 1980s had the goal of adding a social union to the economic union, which has approximately the same quality as the national welfare states, but that they failed as a result of the strong resistance on the part of the member states who were unwilling to give up their national sovereignty. The consequence of this, he says, is a discrepancy between the fully unfolded international economy and a limited international, but mostly only nationally oriented social policy.

In Streeck's view, this situation is certainly in the interest of the national governments, since they will maintain their sovereignty as a matter of form in this way, yet can always blame their failures on the cross-border powers of the market which are outside their reach (Streeck 1996). This arrangement is additionally supported by the fact that the class interest of capital has an advantage as compared to labour's class interest and can, therefore, impose its position much more easily. Capital's interest is best assisted by the liberalisation and deregulation of markets. According to Streeck, this is achieved on a European level by the fact alone that nothing is added to the concept of completion of the Single Market, i.e. that there are no measures in the direction of a positive integration through a European market regulation. Since this requires the approval of all member states, such attempts fail if there is the veto of only a single member state. Capital, in contrast, does not require a European organisation, since its interests come to fruition practically on their own. Labour's class interest takes a completely different character. It has to aim at a European re-regulation, at a European social union, that means it has to organise itself on a European level. Nevertheless, this attempt fails due to the too powerful national differences. The same applies to the negotiations between employers and trade unions. The employers can do without these negotiations, since their interests will be achieved on their own, whilst the trade unions depend on them and are, therefore, in a more difficult position.

There are only two, narrowly defined, areas where sophisticated European social regulations have been attained: equality for women and the field of health and safety at work. Three out of the ten existing directives on social policy refer to the first area, with four covering the second. Equality for women was supported by provisions in the Treaty of Rome, by the fact that there previously existed only a loose anchoring in national social systems and by the civil law character of equal opportunities. Safety at work was based on the interest in uniform safety standards for machinery in order to allow their sale across the borders. However, outside these restricted areas, a type of social policy is establishing itself at the Union level that abandons legislation and regulatory interventions and, instead, prefers cohesion by allowing for deviations depending on the interest situation of a member state. It prefers unity by subsidiarity in the sense of allowing for private law, individually negotiated agreements instead of public law regulations. It also favours governing through conviction, recommendation, expertise and explication, governing through consultation, governing through the supply of a range of regulations from which member states are free to choose (for example, in the case of European company committees), as well as governing through the diffusion of regulations on a multi-national political market. Moreover, national social policy is restricted increasingly: it has to adjust to the requirements of the cross-border mobility of the workforce, adapt to the interdependence of the action of relevant actors (e.g. entrepreneurs) outside their territory and accept competition with other nations for mobile factors of production.

What, according to Streeck, is the only thing that remains as a strategy for the safeguarding of positive integration as a counterpart to negative market integration, are the national modernisation coalitions between the state, the employers and the trade unions (alliances for work), which aim at a re-regulation under the new conditions and a simultaneous modernisation of the location through technical rationalisation and qualification for work. There is no doubt that capital dominates in such coalitions. The successful realisation of this recommendation, in contrast, will face a problem, namely the fact that it has to unite three main actors under one roof who exist less and less as closed corporate actors. Instead, all three sides of this national alliance for renewal fragment into parts each having their particular interests. The model is based on a pattern of the welfare state striving for equal security for a vast majority of uniformly marked employees. However, this world of the social-democratic 'standard' employee has ceased to exist. It has been replaced by a considerably more varied structure of most different milieus. In this way, even Streeck's analysis which was made explicitly with the intention of leading to a rejection of the model of the national welfare states, ends up in a dilemma. It still intends to take something of the former welfare state over into the new world, although the structural preconditions for such a renewal of the national welfare state gradually vanish.

## Creative destruction: constructing new forms of social integration

The change in national social policy initiated by European integration is by no means merely a process of lowering social standards. It is also a process which overcomes long-established practices with exclusionary effects. Let us take employment policies as an example. We certainly cannot say that the European welfare states were successful here over the past 20 years. Most of them have rather been unable to reduce the high unemployment rates thus far. It is only the Netherlands, Denmark and the UK that have been able to record first successes in the late 1990s. The high level of job security costs in the European welfare states resulted in a general reluctance of employers to offer new jobs. Instead of creating new jobs, overtime work has been extended in favour of those with a job and at the cost of those without a job. Collective job security has become a privilege of those included, but has established high barriers for those who do not form part of that collective. In the individual welfare states, the binding power and inertia of well-established institutions, as well as interest coalitions of employers, employees, employer associations and trade unions to continue with historical practice – because of the calculability of risks, privileges, the saving of transaction costs and avoidance of unforeseeable risks pertaining to institutional reforms, and company blindness towards the exclusionary effects of institutionalised forms of inclusion – have all contributed to the maintenance of welfare institutions. This has resulted in the petrification of the society and the inability of governments to approach the unemployment problem with fresh new strategies. The welfare state has become a total security system for everybody with the effect of constricting the activities of entrepreneurs in the widest sense (economical, political and moral) who are needed for the mobilisation of society. This leads to a high rate of unemployed people who are excluded from those networks which provide support, social status and the feeling of self-esteem. Good economic compensation does not help to secure social status and self-esteem.

It is in this situation of paralysis that international competition and the co-ordination of employment policies in the European Union by means of 'soft instruments of steering' such as monitoring and benchmarking, do not simply restrict the range of available measures aimed at reducing unemployment rates, but rather open up new ways of mastering that problem. In the Employment Title of the EC Treaty, as amended by the Amsterdam Treaty of 1997, and in the results of the Extraordinary European Council on Employment in Luxembourg in November 1997, the member states consented to give the growth of employment high priority (European Commission 1998). Employment policies of the member states should be based around four pillars: (1) improving employability by training programmes; (2) furthering job-creating entrepreneurship; (3) enhancing the adaptability of work organisation in order to meet demands for flexibility and change; (4) increasing equal opportunities for those who are disadvantaged. In order to promote employment growth, a coordinated system of information on employment statistics and different national employment strategies for reasons of monitoring and benchmarking has been introduced. It is expected that this system should help to identify the effects on employment of a whole set of rules and measures applied in the different employment policies of the individual member states. From the point of view that is committed to the 'positive integration' of the welfare state, this type of 'soft steering' appears just like a further example of the European Union's limitation to 'negative integration' in the sense of enhancing competition by abandoning all barriers to the free border transgressing circulation of capital, commodities, services and labour and its refraining from positive integration in the sense of compensating for market failure, market intervention and redistribution with the aim of producing welfare for all and not only for those who are the winners of market competition (Scharpf 1996). Such a position takes as an unquestioned fact that the established welfare systems on the national level are indeed the best of all imaginable worlds and thus in need of being safeguarded in the nation-state and transferred as much as possible to the European Union. In this perspective, we see but one side of the coin, whilst the other, far too much neglected side, is the fact of erecting an authoritarian regime in a democratic guise exercising paralysing effects on individual activity, innovation and mobilisation of the society, by taking half of the earned income from the active people for the political formation and administration of society and the production of a class of unemployed people lacking access to networks, social status and the feeling of self-esteem. It is, therefore, one-sided and means a restriction to the analytical perspective if we take the 'positive integration' of the national welfare state as the only valid model of a 'good' society and as the binding goal of mastering the social effects of European market integration and economic globalisation. Monitoring and benchmarking are surely 'soft means of steering', they do not determine a European employment policy with binding power, they do not establish any binding intervention in the market and are thus far removed from the institutionalised national forms of 'positive integration'. They are possibly the weakest forms of complementing the liberalisation of the labour market by 'negative' European market integration with 'positive integration'.

The effects of monitoring and benchmarking on the learning capabilities of national policy makers should, however, not be underestimated. Together with enhanced market competition, they initiate institutional competition and restrict the range of justifiable strategies to such measures which are confirmed by success under the condition of open markets. In this sense, there is a trend of convergence of the member states in the measures of 'best practice'. Nevertheless, this trend is limited by the consistent pressure of policies. There is no guarantee that an element of policy, which is successful in one national institutional setting, will also be the right solution to the problem in another setting. Lack of support from complementary institutional elements and lack of legitimacy can always result in failure. The policy element might be adapted to the established institutions and lose its effectiveness, because it is robbed of its original meaning or it might be rejected because it does not fit in the new setting. Only under favourable circumstances will it contribute to a lasting transformation of the institutional setting and legitimating culture: if there is enough suffering from failures of the established institutions and if there are political entrepreneurs which are able to mobilise a broad movement of institutional reform. Margaret Thatcher's reform policies in the paralysed Britain of the late 1970s and early 1980s are the most interesting example for studying the preconditions of such thoroughgoing societal change. Preoccupation with Thatcher's deconstruction of the welfare state has hindered many analyses of her policies for the construction of a new liberated and more dynamic society. The cautious consolidation of Thatcher's achievements by Tony Blair's New Labour government is sound proof of the wide acknowledgment of Thatcher's work of 'creative deconstruction' in the sense of Schumpeter's description of the entrepreneur's role (Schumpeter 1950/1993: 134–42). Here it is the role of the political entrepreneur.

In the perspective outlined, we point to the innovative and constructive side of institutional reforms which eradicate established patterns of welfare regulations.

This is also true for the effects of European monitoring and benchmarking. The other side of restricting the nation-state's range of policies to those which prove to be successful under international market and institutional competition is the overcoming of 'company blindness', the breaking up of coalitions in vested interests, the uncovering of undeserved privileges and the discovering of the negative effects of prevailing patterns of behaviour. In this way, a whole range of possible measures become visible and available, which were unknown and impossible before. This is the side of extending the range of policies compared to the earlier state of encapsulated national employment policies of the welfare state resulting from the establishment of the European multi-level regime in the field of social policy. Here, political regulation is not more difficult in the European multi-level system than in national politics, as is generally thematised, but, in fact, is actually easier, namely better informed and more open. The example clearly demonstrates that it is a one-sided ideological restriction of our perspective of what goes on in the processes of European (and global) market integration, if we see them only as a destruction of positive integration by the national welfare state in favour of negative supranational integration without a corresponding and equally 'strong' positive integration on that level. This perspective blinds us to the disintegrative side of the national welfare state, both with regard to exclusionary effects beyond and within the nation-state. It also lacks sensitivity to the negative effects of too much integration: paralysis, avoidance and even suppression of open conflict, constriction of freedom, standardisation of life and lack of innovation. An open-minded analysis of European integration and global sociation has to look at both sides of the coin: the destruction of established yet limited and out-dated forms of particularistic nation-state integration *and* the construction of new, more flexible, individualised and encompassing forms of multi-level integration.

This process of social transformation can no longer be analysed in terms of class interest; it is too much part of the ideological superstructure of a historical epoch, which we have left behind us in the meantime (Streeck 1996). The interests of 'capital' and of 'labour' are so strongly differentiated with new and growing forms of fusion, such as the capital-owning employee and the labour force entrepreneur that it is no longer possible to carry out an analysis of what is going on in terms of 'capital interests' and 'labour interests'. The positions of branches and of companies within branches is so different that it is impossible to derive from them a common interest in national, European or global regulation in general or in specific forms and substances. The same goes for the employees, who range from the simple, unskilled workers and service people through different levels of qualification to highly qualified specialists. The fact that we have an increasing number of types of labour contract which do not conform to the traditionally established 'normal' and standardised type of labour in terms of life-long, full-time employment with regular working time, with one employer, is by no means merely a sign of the 'weakened' position of labour in conflict with capital. In this area, we not only find people in a depressing situation of precarious employment, but also women who work part-time by choice so that they reach a better reconciliation between family and work, as well as a growing number of specialists who are independent and sufficiently powerful that they prefer to work for changing employers for a limited time only. And there is also the increasing number of young, mobile people who take up the entrepreneurial role in very small new businesses within the rapidly growing IT and media industries. We are witnessing a new gold rush, with a tremendous dynamic and in depth transformation of the whole economy. For the young, mobile labour force entrepreneurs, the employee capitalists and the new, small business entrepreneurs, the regulations of the welfare state are out-dated remainders of a class society far back in the past. They see such regulations much more as restrictions on their activism than as means for social integration. What is emerging is a society of individual activists which needs new forms of integration. Consultancy agencies, employment agencies, job exhibits, job fairs, Internet mailing lists and networks of the most different kinds are much more important in this new world than employment administrations of the state, labour law and old-fashioned trade unions. An analysis of European integration and globalisation in terms of the assumed class interest of capital and labour is too much oriented to the past and prevents us from looking at the constructive side of what is going on in this exciting epoch of massive 'creative destruction' by entrepreneurial activity.

## Not a Europe of nations, but a Europe of individuals: a transformation process full of conflicts

Whilst common features are increasing at the European level, those within the member countries and their cultures are declining; vice-versa, the differences between the nations are declining whilst they are increasing within the nations. The common features within Europe are, however, of an abstract type and mould a formal framework for a varied, widely branched and finely differentiated network of more or less permanent loyalty relationships. In the framework of this network structure, there is increasingly less room for strong collective solidarities, collective identities and cultures. They are replaced by a pluralism of varied and widely branched associations and cultural patterns. Therefore, the nation-states and their national solidarities and cultures will not be an obstacle to further integration in the long run, since they will lose in power and importance anyway. The Europe of the future will not be a Europe of native countries and national cultures, but rather a Europe of self-responsibly acting individuals and of a plurality of life concepts that can no longer be homogenised nationally (Durkheim 1964: 133–8).

The single market alone brings about a comprehensive European and, at the same time, globally oriented, consumer culture. National, regional and local consumer traditions are inevitably flooded more and more by products arriving from all across Europe and the world and lose their identity-forming strength. To be able to survive at all, local producers have to maintain their position with new products and practices by increasing their marketing, and conquering consumers from outside their own region. The open market no longer allows for the maintenance of traditions merely for tradition's sake, but only their formation in line with market requirements. In this case, it is not only material consumption that matters, but cultural practices, ranging from eating habits right through to music, theatre, literature and fine arts. Of course, in this process, everything that is European or global is interpreted according to local traditions (Robertson 1992). It would, however, be too short-sighted to deduce the continued existence of local traditions from this fact. Local traditions as such will not survive, but will necessarily change their character by being filled with things from outside the local range, unite with these things and try to recruit customers outside the local market. In this way, a colourful mixture of local and extra-local traditions is created so that places no longer differ through their own particular traditions, but, at best, by the more or less motley shades of their colourful range of goods on offer. Consumers will find more or less the same everywhere. We can therefore see that cultural traditions lose their local foundation and identity-forming strength within a common market. The differences between local, regional and national cultures shrink; instead, the local, regional and national scope of cultural practices is growing, i.e. their internal differences are increasing.

Along with the outside adjustment and the simultaneous internal differentiation of cultural practices, social milieus, ways of life and styles of consumption differ less and less between nations, whilst they differentiate into ever smaller fragments internally. Lifestyles and types of consumption develop across national traditions. They create milieu-specific common features between nations, whereas new differences arise within nations. Here, too, it is shown that Europeans are becoming more similar beyond national borders whilst at the same time differentiating more strongly internally according to milieus. There are smaller differences between culture-consuming city tourists from Germany, the UK or the Netherlands than between German cultural tourists and German mass tourists lazing around on the beaches of the Adriatic Sea. Likewise, there are many similarities between mass tourists from different countries, whilst they are worlds apart from the culture-oriented tourists from their own country.

The finding that common features are growing throughout Europe, whilst the common features within the nations are declining, that Europe is integrating, whilst the nation-states differentiate internally, shows that this structural change involves substantial conflicts in the nation-states. European integration implies, to some degree, the disintegration of nation-states. The turning toward Europe is first and foremost a matter of modernising elites, of the strong as a whole, whilst the weak cling to their old national solidarities or withdraw to smaller regional and local solidarities. The modernising elites carry out the entrepreneurial role of 'creative destruction' in Schumpeter's sense. It is not surprising, therefore, that the processes of European and global integration and the weakening of nation-states are accompanied by nationalistic and regionalist counter-movements. The big parties lose in integrative strength and are therefore losing ground in almost all European countries, above all to the benefit of right-wing populist and right-wing extremist parties (Betz 1994). It is not only the conservative parties alone that have to cede votes to the new extreme Right, but also the social democrats and the socialists. They are torn apart by the diverging movements of modernists and traditionalists. They no longer succeed in uniting the wide range of workers. Some of them abandon parties since they feel strong enough to maintain themselves in the competition of an ever more open society, whilst the others do so as they no longer believe these parties can offer them the desired protection against the growing competition from outside. The typical social democratic electorate is dissolving in the context of society's differentiation process. This phenomenon is another result of the interplay of Europeanisation and globalisation, on the one hand, and of internal differentiation, on the other.

Regionalist movements come to life since, on the one hand, the nation-state no longer offers the support required and, on the other, as both the European single market and the world market submit the regions and local communities below the level of the nation-state to a stronger competition between locations. Therefore, the stronger regions want to discharge part of their commitment toward the weaker ones, whilst the weaker regions count on that support in the wider European framework, support which they believe is withheld from them by their own nation-state centre.

The above-mentioned process of abstraction and differentiation of the collective consciousness in the context of European integration can be excellently under-lined with data from Eurobarometer surveys. An avant-garde of 4 per cent of the national populations are developing a European identity, thus standing out against national ties; a small group of 6 per cent combines both identities whilst giving preference to Europe; a larger group of 42 per cent still see themselves first and foremost as members of their own nation, but secondarily also as Europeans; no less than 45 per cent, however, still consider themselves exclusively members of their own nations (European Commission 1999: B13). Accordingly, they still expect the nation-state to offer a collective solution to current problems. Therefore, they react with uncertainty to the nation-state's dwindling integrative and problem-solving power. They are ill-prepared for a self-responsible lifestyle. As a result, they provide potential supporters for right-wing populist and right-wing extremist counter-movements to the process of Europeanisation and globalisation. In this process, the nation-states have to pass the crucial test between the diverging movements of modernisers and traditionalists, Europeans and nationalists (Münch 1998: 306–19). The conflict is enhanced by the fact that it is linked with the differen-tiation of national societies according to education, income and professional status. The turning toward Europe and the related modification of national solidarity is, above all, a matter for the higher status groups, whilst clinging to the nation primarily involves the lower groups (European Commission 1999: B31).

## The new Europe: democracy without demos

It is striking to note that the dissatisfaction with democracy at the European level goes hand in hand with the lack of a turn toward Europe and a lower status with regard to education, income and profession (European Commission 1999: B19). The generally low degree of satisfaction with democracy at a European level triggered a feverish search for an adequate remedy to this so-called European democracy deficit (Reif 1992, 1993a, 1993b). Most proposals in this direction, however, start from a far too simple transfer of the model of a nation-state representative democracy to the level of the European Union. They account only insufficiently for the above-mentioned structural change and the homology requirements in the harmonisation of European market logic, solidarity logic, political logic and legal logic. The search involves European neo-corporatist cooperation between state and associations, the European party system, the mighty European parliament, the European government and, not least of all, the European public. None of these structures of the European nation-states will, however, do justice to the branching and differentiation of markets, solidarities, legal regulation and political frame setting as they tend to form the European Union. The form of democracy that is possible under these conditions conforms much more to the American multi-level system of checks and balances, pluralism of interests, a wealth of partial publics and a situation-related harmonisation of interests and rights, starting with the formulation of laws right through to their implementation and to litigation, with special importance being attributed to courts as sites for the coordination of freedom of action.

Such a pluralistic multi-level democracy does not take place in the central political formation of opinion and will of a demos and/or its representatives, but rather in a myriad of arenas on many different levels. It includes a larger number of actors. All stages of the political process are contested: programme formulation, legislation, implementation and the settling of conflicts by the courts. Legislation aims at providing a framework which is concretised in the wider arenas; it occurs in processes of trial and error, starts as a faulty piece of unfinished work and remains so with the only hope that ever new chances arise to correct mistakes. Instead of a neo-corporatist cooperation of state and privileged large associations, a wider pluralism of interests and a permanent competition for influence and smallest advantages dominate the scene. Politics does not have a centre and does not aim at the whole thing, but rather at small partial solutions to small partial problems. It is represented everywhere, in the family, at schools, in clubs, in companies, in administration, in court action, wherever laws and interests have to be coordinated. These are not guided into pre-set tracks once and for all by a general law, but have to be concretely coordinated according to the particular situation and, if necessary, with the help of court action. Accordingly, the courts assume a much more important role in conflict settlement than in the nation-states' representative democracy.

A pluralistic multi-level democracy is a democracy without a uniform demos. Its quality is shown neither in the representative formation of opinion and will (by leading elites, as a rule) nor in a Pareto-optimum output, which brings everyone into a better position than before, but rather in the wealth of arenas and of active groups, in the openness of procedures, in the fairness of competition for influence, in the equality of chances for participation, in the revisability of decisions, in the permanent correction of mistakes. By leading us toward such an open and pluralistic multi-level democracy, European integration involves a thoroughgoing change in the political and legal cultures of its member states.

How can the legitimation of EU politics and EU law be interpreted and, if necessary, formed anew under the above-mentioned structural conditions so as to remedy the 'legitimation deficit' that is linked to the so-called democracy deficit? To say it right from the start: none of the models developed for this purpose does justice to the structural conditions that deviate so strongly from nation-state politics. All of them suffer from a far too strong orientation to the usual nation-state representative democracy (Wildenmann 1991; Joerges 1994; Jachtenfuchs and Kohler-Koch 1996). Let us list the models briefly: first of all, there is the model of a Europe of market interests which limits the European Union to the role of an economic association designed to ensure free economic circulation within Europe, whilst everything else remains a matter of nation-state politics (Behrens 1994). This model is no longer applicable, especially since the organisation of the single market and the economic and monetary union strongly affect other political areas so that there is a basic restructuring of social conditions in such a way that the nation-states can no longer play their traditional role of political control and formation of society on the basis of a representative democratic formation of will. Meanwhile, politics takes place on a variety of levels and in many arenas above, within and below the nation-state formation of will, so that it can no longer be legitimated with a reference to such a centre of will formation.

There is no improvement with the model of legitimation through the competence of experts (Ipsen 1972; Majone 1989, 1994a, 1994b). According to this model, European politics is a matter of experts acting on behalf of the national governments and deciding on purely factual aspects. Once again, the procurement of legitimation is first and foremost a matter of representing the national electors' will in the Council of Ministers. On the one hand, EU politics draws its legitimation from the factual knowledge of experts and, on the other hand, from the inter-governmental cooperation of sovereign governments legitimated by representative democracy. This model also fails due to the variety and differentiation of political arenas above, within and below the nation-state democratic formation of will.

The model of a dual structure of a supranational and inter-state decision-making procedure is as unworkable as the models outlined before (Weiler 1981). It is based on the combination of two representative democratic procedures of the political formation of will, even so, reality keeps moving away from it more and more. Politics takes place on too many levels and in too many arenas to be able to be forced into such a straitjacket.

Just like the models of legitimation of EU politics and EU law, the proposals on the EU's democratic new formation – possibly through the creation of a European constitution – also fail as a result of their too close connection with the traditional nation-state representative democracy. This goes both for the model of a federal state and for the model of a confederation of states or the model of a nationality state. The federal state model sees its hopes for democratisation backed by the European Parliament and by the wish that the European Commission be transformed into a government responsible to the Parliament, whilst the Council of Ministers works as a second chamber (Reif 1992, 1993a; von Bogdandy 1999). This is a parliamentary-democratic version of the federal state. Another, presidential-democratic, variety puts a president at the head and attaches greater significance to the second chamber. The model of a confederation of states is more obliged to the status quo, considering the European democratic formation of will a matter of the transfer of the nation-state formation of will to European politics through the governments of the member states (Kirchhof 1994). The decisive place for this operation is the Council of Ministers. A nation-state related variation of this model hopes to obtain more European democracy from the stronger tying of national governments to their national parliaments as far as European politics is concerned (Lepsius 1991).

All these models start from the illusion that politics can be focused on decisive places and gains its legitimation from a representative-democratic formation of will, whether it is at a European or a national level. In future, however, this will be less and less possible, at either level. The search for a European public, a European party system, a European system of associations and a European neo-corporatist cooperation of a European state and representative large associations will fail due to the overly simple transfer of an obsolete model of nation-state representative democracy to European politics. Also, the search for an adequate integration of the nation-state formation of will into European politics in models of a confederation of states or nationality states adheres too much to the declining era of the nation-state representative democracy. Neither model – the federal state or the confederation of states and/or nationality state – sufficiently takes into account the fact that Europe will not take the form of a nation and will be increasingly less composed of nations. Europe will, instead, become a considerably more varied structure of local communities, of more or less strong regions, ever more fading remainders of nations and a wealth of horizontally arranged groups of interests, but, above all, of self-responsibly acting individuals. There will not be one central place for politics and no central public, but many places and partial publics. Under such structural terms, European politics can no longer find its legitimation in obsolete forms of a democratic formation of will. The resource of its legitimation will, instead, be its division into levels and arenas, its openness to participation, its unfinished character, its revisability, and its capability to correct mistakes permanently (Münch *et al.* 2001).

## Notes

1 Council Directive 89/391/EEC of 12 June 1989 on the introduction of measures to encourage improvements in the safety and health of workers at work, Official Journal L 183, 29/06/1989, p. 1–8.
2 Directive 96/71/EC of the European Parliament and of the Council of 16 December 1996 concerning the posting of workers in the framework of the provision of services, Official Journal L 018, 21/01/1997, p 1–6.

## References

Behrens, P. (1994) 'Die Wirtschaftsverfassung der Europäischen Gemeinschaft', in G. Brüggemeier (ed.) *Verfassungen für ein ziviles Europa*, Baden-Baden: Nomos.

Betz, H.-G. (1994) *Radical Right-Wing Populism in Western Europe*, New York: St Martin's Press.

Bogdandy, A. von, (1999) 'Die Europäische Union als supranationale Föderation', *Integration* 2: 95–112.

Cattero, B. (ed.) (1998) *Modell Deutschland – Modell Europa*, Opladen: Leske & Budrich.

Durkheim, E. (1964) *The Division of Labor in Society*, trans. G. Simpson, New York: The Free Press (*De la division du travail social*, Paris: Presses Universitaires de France, 1893/1973a).

—— (1982) *The Rules of Sociological Method*, ed. by S. Lukes, trans. by W.D. Halls, London: Macmillan (*Les règles de la methode sociologique*, Paris: Presses Universitaires de France, 1895/1973b).

Ebbinghaus, B. and Visser, J. (1997) 'Der Wandel der Arbeitsbeziehungen im westeuropäischen Vergleich', in S. Hradil and S. Immerfall (eds) *Die westeuropäischen Gesellschaften im Vergleich*, Opladen: Leske & Budrich.

Esping-Anderson, G. (1990) *The Three Worlds of Welfare Capitalism*, Cambridge: Cambridge University Press.

European Commission (1998) *Joint Employment Report 1998*, Luxembourg: Office for the Official Publications of the European Communities.

—— (1999) *Eurobarometer 52*, Luxembourg: Office for the Official Publications of the European Communities.

Giddens, A. (1998) *The Third Way*, Cambridge: Policy Press.

Gross, P. (1994) *Die Multioptionsgesellschaft*, Frankfurt am Main: Suhrkamp.

Haller, M. (1997) 'Klassenstruktur und Arbeitslosigkeit – Die Entwicklung zwischen 1960 und 1990', in S. Hradil and S. Immerfall (eds) *Die westeuropäischen Gesellschaften im Vergleich*, Opladen: Leske & Budrich.

Höffe, O. (1999) *Demokratie im Zeitalter der Globalisierung*, Munich: CH Beck.

Institut der deutschen Wirtschaft (1998) *Zahlen zur wirtschaftlichen Entwicklung der Bundesrepublik Deutschland*, Cologne: Institut der deutschen Wirtschaft.

Ipsen, H.P. (1972) *Europäisches Gemeinschaftsrecht*, Tübingen: Mohr.

Jachtenfuchs, M. (1998) 'Entgrenzung und politische Steuerung', in B. Kohler-Koch (ed.) *Regieren in entgrenzten Räumen*, Opladen: Westdeutscher Verlag.

Jachtenfuchs, M. and Kohler-Koch, B. (eds) (1996) *Europäische Integration*, Opladen: Leske & Budrich.

Joerges, C. (1994) 'Legitimationsprobleme des europäischen Wirtschaftsrechts und der Vertrag von Maastricht', in G. Brüggemeier (ed.) *Verfassungen für ein ziviles Europa*, Baden-Baden: Nomos.

—— (1996) 'Das Recht im Prozeß der europäischen Integration', in M. Jachtenfuchs and B. Kohler-Koch (eds) *Europäische Integration*, Opladen: Leske & Budrich.

Kaelble, H. (1997) 'Europäische Vielfalt und der Weg zu einer europäischen Gesellschaft', in S. Hradil and S. Immerfall (eds) *Die westeuropäischen Gesellschaften im Vergleich*, Opladen: Leske & Budrich.

Kant, I. (1797) 'Die Metaphysik der Sitten', in I. Kant, *Werke in sechs Bänden*, vol. 4, edited by W. Weischedel, Frankfurt am Main: Suhrkamp, 1956.

Keller, B. and Seifert, H. (eds.) (1995) *Atypische Beschäftigung – verbieten oder gestalten?*, Cologne: Bund-Verlag.

Keller, B. and Sörries, B. (1997) 'The new dialogue: procedural structuring, first results and perspectives', *Industrial Relations Journal, European Annual Review*, 77–98.

—— (1998) 'The sectoral dialogue and European social policy: more phantasy, fewer facts', *European Journal of Industrial Relations*, 4: 331–48.

—— (1999) 'The new European social dialogue: old wine in new bottles?' *Journal of European Social Policy* 9: 111–25.

Kirchhof, P. (1994) 'Das Maastricht-Urteil des Bundesverfassungsgerichts', in P. Hommelhoff and P. Kirchhof (eds) *Der Staatenverbund der Europäischen Union*, Heidelberg: C.F. Mueller.

Kowalsky, W. (1999) *Europäische Sozialpolitik: Ausgangsbedingungen, Antriebskräfte und Entwicklungspotentiale*, Opladen: Leske & Budrich.

Lash, S. and Urry, J. (1987) *The End of Organized Capitalism*, Madison, Wis. University of Wisconsin Press.

Leibfried, S. and Pierson, P. (1997) 'Halbsouveräne Wohlfahrtsstaaten: Soziale Sicherung in der europäischen Mehrebenen-Politik,' *Blätter für deutsche und internationale Politik* 12: 1457–67.

—— (eds) (1998) *Standort Europa. Europäische Sozialpolitik: Sozialpolitik zwischen Nationalstaaten und Europäischer Integration*, Frankfurt: Suhrkamp.

Lenaerts, K. (1992) 'Thoughts about the interaction between judges and politicians in the European Community,' *Yearbook of European Law* 12: 1–34.

Lessenich, S. and Ostner, I. (eds) (1998) *Welten des Wohlfahrtskapitalismus. Der Sozialstaat in vergleichender Perspektive*, Frankfurt am Main/New York: Campus.

Lepsius, R.M. (1991) 'Nationalstaat oder Nationalitätenstaat als Modell für die Weiterentwicklung der Europäischen Gemeinschaft?', in R. Wildenmann (ed.) *Staatswerdung Europas? Optionen für eine Europäische Union*, Baden-Baden: Nomos.

Majone, G. (1989) *Evidence, Argument and Persuasion in the Policy Process*, New Haven: Yale University Press.

—— (1994a) 'The European Community: an "independent fourth branch of government?"', in Gert Brüggemeier (ed.) *Verfassungen für ein ziviles Europa*, Baden-Baden: Nomos.

—— (1994b) 'The Rise of the Regulatory State in Europe', *West European Politics* 17, 3: 77–101.

Micklitz H.-W. (1997) 'Legitime Erwartungen als Gerechtigkeitsprinzip des europäischen Privatrechts', in L. Krämer, H.-W. Micklitz and K. Tonner (eds) *Recht und diffuse Interessen in der Europäischen Rechtsordnung*, Baden-Baden: Nomos.

Müller, W., Steinmann, S. and Schneider, R. (1997) 'Bildung in Europa', in S. Hradil and S. Immerfall (eds) *Die westeuropäischen Gesellschaften im Vergleich*, Opladen: Leske & Budrich.

Münch, R. (1993) *Das Projekt Europa: Zwischen Nationalstaat, regionaler Autonomie und Weltgesellschaft*, Frankfurt: Suhrkamp.

—— (1998) *Globale Dynamik, lokale Lebenswelten*, Frankfurt am Main: Suhrkamp.

Münch, R., Lahussen, C., Kurth, M., Borgards, C., Stark, C. and Jauß, C. (2001) *Democracy at Work: The Politics of Clean Air in Britain, France, Germany and the United States*, Westport, Conn.: Greenwood Press.

Narr, W.-D. and Schubert, A. (1994) *Weltökonomie: Die Misere der Politik*, Frankfurt am Main: Suhrkamp Verlag.

Nelson Joel, I. (1995) *Post-Industrial-Capitalism: Exploring Economic Inequality in America*, Thousand Oaks, CA: Sage Publications.

Rawls, J. (1971) *A Theory of Justice*, Cambridge, MA: Harvard University Press.

Reich, N. (1996) *Europäisches Verbraucherrecht*, 3rd edition, Baden-Baden: Nomos.

Reich, R. (1991) *The Work of Nations: Preparing Ourselves for 21st-Century Capitalism*, New York: Vintage Books/Random House.

Reif, K.-H. (1992) 'Wahlen, Wähler und Demokratie in der EG: Die drei Dimensionen des demokratischen Defizits', *Aus Politik und Zeitgeschichte*, B 19: 43–52.

—— (1993a) 'Das Demokratiedefizit der EG und die Chancen seiner Verringerung', *Politische Bildung* 3: 37–621.

—— (1993b) 'Ein Ende des "Permissive Consensus": Zum Wandel europapolitischer Einstellungen in der öffentlichen Meinung der EG-Mitgliedsstaaten', in R. Hrbek (ed.) *Der Vertrag von Maastricht in der wissenschaftlichen Kontroverse*, Baden-Baden: Nomos.

Robertson, R. (1992) *Globalization: Social Theory and Global Culture*, London: Sage.

van Ruysseveldt, J. and Visser, J. (1996) *European Industrial Relations in Transition*, London: Sage

Scharpf, F.W. (1996) 'Negative and Positive Integration in the Political Economy of European Welfare States', in G. Marks, F.W. Scharpf, P.C. Schmitter and W. Streeck, *Governance in the European Union*, London: Sage.

—— (1998) 'Jenseits der Regime-Debatte: Ökonomische Integration, Demokratie und Wohlfahrtsstaat in Europa', in S. Lessenich and I. Ostner (eds) *Welten des Wohlfahrtskapitalismus: Der Sozialstaat in vergleichender Perspektive*, Frankfurt am Main: Campus Verlag.

Schumpeter J.A. (1950/1993) *Kapitalismus, Sozialismus und Demokratie*, Tübingen and Basel: UTB für Wissenschaft, Francke Verlag.

Schuster, T. (1996) 'Die soziale Dimension der Europäischen Union', *Integration* 19: 245–51.

Simmel G. (1908/1992) *Soziologie: Untersuchungen über die Formen der Vergesellschaftung*, Frankfurt am Main: Suhrkamp.

Streeck, W. (1996) 'Neo-voluntarism: a new European social policy regime?', in Gary Marks, Fritz W. Scharpf, Philippe C. Schmitter and Wolfgang Streeck, *Governance in the European Union*, London: Sage.

—— (1998) 'Globale Wirtschaft, nationale Regulierung', in B. Cattero (ed.) *Modell Deutschland – Modell Europa*, Opladen: Leske & Budrich.

Thurow, L. (1996) *Die Zukunft des Kapitalismus*, Düsseldorf: Metropolitan.

Tinbergen, J. (1965) *International Economic Integration*, 2nd edition, Amsterdam–London–New York: Elsevier.

Weiler J.H.H. (1981) 'The community system: the dual character of supranationalism', *Yearbook of European Law* 1: 257–306.

Wildenmann, R. (1991) *Staatswerdung Europas? Optionen für eine Europäische Union*, Baden-Baden: Nomos.

Zetterholm, S. (1994) *National Cultures and European Integration*, Oxford/Providence: Berg.

Zuleeg, M. (1995) 'Der rechtliche Zusammenhalt der Europäischen Gemeinschaft', in W. Blomeyer and K.A. Schachtschneider (eds) *Die Europäische Union als Rechtsgemeinschaft*, Berlin: Duncker & Humblot.

# 5 Integrating immigrants and minorities in a wider and deeper Europe

*Andrew Geddes*

## Introduction

Debates about the 'integration' of immigrants – for this term with its functionalist imagery and allusions to mathematical processes of building a whole number is still the preferred term in many European countries – are strongly, perhaps even indelibly, imprinted with the hallmark of nation-states that have had difficulty thinking of themselves as immigration countries. One result has been that European countries – particularly older, north-west European immigration countries – have tended to seek to 'nationalise' their immigrant and ethnic minority populations, or at least seek to do so, in relation to host society institutions and norms (Banton 2001; Favell 2001). Indeed, there seem since the mid-1990s to have been renewed attempts to assert policy approaches that downplay the rights of groups defined in cultural or ethnic terms and emphasise the responsibilities of individuals. In such terms immigration can be construed as a challenge to the nation-state and to the organisational practices and ideas that animate these practices within these states.

Yet, there is another element to this discussion that involves turning this relationship around and analysing the ways in which changes in nation-states and changed relations between them affect understandings of migrants and minorities. This chapter focuses on two elements of these: welfare state pressures as an instance of changed relations within states and political and economic integration within the European Union (EU) as an instance of changed relations between them. This is linked to a policy discourse that places far more emphasis on the responsibilities of individuals and far less on the rights of groups. This focus and policy discourse applies more generally to the population as a whole, but has particular effects on immigrants who – often for reasons linked to understandings of culture and difference – are viewed as a particular 'integration problem'. Yet, this perception of these groups as an 'integration problem' has less to do with the culture or identity of these groups than it has to do with the changes in background institutional conditions such as welfare state pressures that change the perceptions of migrants and minorities. Welfare state pressures and changed welfare state ideologies have prompted a tighter demarcation of the boundaries of the community of legitimate receivers of welfare state benefits and more efforts to exclude those seen as undeserving, such as so-called 'bogus asylum seekers' (Bommes and Geddes 2000).

This is less to do with a change in the character of migrants than the pressure on European states and the effects that this then has on perceptions of those forms of migration deemed unwanted or in some way abusive.

The EU signifies changed relations between states and a unique form of supra-national integration with implications for politics and society within the 15 member states, as well as in surrounding states and regions. The EU has both boundary-removing and boundary-constructing features tied very closely to the forms of material and symbolic power associated with market integration. The chapter focuses on the EU migrant inclusion agenda and the ways in which it is shaped by the sources of material and symbolic power associated with European integration. These derive from the EU's core market-making purposes. This creates possibili-ties for Europeanised forms of inclusion that reflect the bounded nature of the European project. As the EU removes some barriers so it establishes others with the effect that rights and freedoms in a European context need to be understood in relation to the internal and external boundaries associated with this project. This has meant the exclusion of legally resident third country nationals from rights of EU citizenship and the establishment of tighter controls at the external frontiers of the EU on those forms of migration defined as unwanted (coupled with the co-option of surrounding states and regions into this control frame). The focus of the chapter is EU measures relating to the protection of the rights of migrants and minorities. The chapter analyses the inclusion by the Amsterdam Treaty of anti-discrimination provisions (Article 13),[1] the subsequent anti-discrimination legislation (two directives and an action programme in June 2000).

## Migrants and minorities in an integrating Europe

The EU presents us with a bounded form of supranational membership tied to the EU's core economic purposes and a form of economic entitlement for EU citizens linked to the exercise of rights in the single market. EU citizenship is a right derived from prior possession of the nationality of a member state. There are around 11 million legally resident third country nationals in the EU, plus a less difficult to identify number of people who fall into the category of illegal immigrant. The origins of these migrants and their descendants are diverse: labour migrants, family members, ethnic returnees (German *Aussiedler*, for example), asylum seekers and refugees, and clandestine migrants to name four of the main categories. If some temporal ordering is introduced then we can say that earlier migration to Europe after the Second World War was politically-historically structured by guestworker agreements and by post-colonial ties.

The 'new migration' into Europe since the end of the Cold War has not been subject to the same kinds of structuring effects. One example of this was provided by the Portuguese regularisation of irregular migrants conducted in the summer of 2001 – around one third were found to have come from the Ukraine: hardly a country with which Portugal can be said to have had close ties. From this we can extract a more general point about the diversity of Europe's immigrant and ethnic minority population as well as the effects of what can be characterised as the conceptual and geo-political widening of the migration issue. By this is meant the ways in which new forms of migration and new forms of state response have developed in post-Cold War Europe to international migration in its various forms, with effects on central, eastern and southern European countries. There have been consistent attempts to restrict access at the EU's external frontiers to those forms of migration defined as unwanted. People who fall into the category of 'unwanted migrant' face an increasingly frosty reception in EU member states. They are more likely to be viewed as a threatening presence and as potential abusers of the welfare state. This relationship between migrants and the welfare state plays a key role in the definition of some forms of migration as a threat and others as an opportunity (usually in economic terms). While there is no alternative in view to the national welfare state, the development of EU cooperation on migration (free movement as well as aspects of immigration and asylum) is linked to the national welfare states of the member countries: the defence of these welfare states and their re-orientation. This tension appears to have been heightened by the opening to new economic migration in some European countries coupled with renewed attempts to keep out those migrants who fall into the 'unwanted' categories as defined by state policies.

Although there are of course differences in the organisation of these welfare states, it's possible to argue that the relation between migration and welfare is of critical importance. Changes in these welfare states have important effects on our under-standing of migration and migrants. Throughout the 1990s a sharper distinction was between those deemed deserving and those deemed as undeserving of welfare state benefits. As Michael Bommes has shown (2000) there has been in Germany a downplaying of national semantics since the 1990s with an associated change in emphasis from the German national community as based on ethnic belonging towards a national community of GNP contributors. Guestworker immigrants have been included within this national community of GNP contributors, albeit often at a lower level, while newer migrants have been excluded. These new forms of welfare state exclusion have also applied to *Aussiedler*, ethnic co-belongers, but placed outside of the community of legitimate receivers of welfare state benefits since the mid-1990s and treated more like other immigrants.

It could be seen as ironic that just as there seems reason to cast some doubt on the continued ability of European states to affect the kinds of integration associated with nation-state building there seems also to have been a reassertion of 'national models'. The UK, the Netherlands and Sweden were all once seen as examples of multicultural responses to immigration (Geddes 2003). In these countries there is now far less enthusiasm for identity-affirming multicultural policies and far more enthusiasm for an approach that emphasises the responsibilities of individuals. This does not just apply to migrants and their descendants. The social expectation of integration applies far more generally; but the integration – or lack of it – of migrants and their descendants is seen as a particular problem. Moreover, this problem is one that is often defined in terms of race, culture or ethnicity.

In this type of context, if we understand a central political activity to be the pursuit of shared meaning then debates about immigrant integration are a good example of conflict over the concepts used in framing political judgements on social problems and public policies (Edelman 1988). The result has tended to be the adoption of policy frames that organise or reorganise the conceptual and organisational boundaries of a given community (usually national) so as to include or exclude newcomers. This national point of reference has been particularly evident in 'older' immigration countries in north-west Europe.

The geopolitical and conceptual widening of international migration to include new countries and new types of migration causes some pause for thought and raises questions about these national frames of reference and their continued relevance. For instance, state contexts in southern, central and eastern Europe differ from those in older immigration countries. If state penetration of society is at a lower level then this could affect the capacity of states to affect 'integrative' outcomes. So too could the development of economic and political integration that creates rights that cross frontiers within the European Union. This then links to the ideas about the 'neo-medieval' EU developed by Zielonka (2001). For Zielonka, the term captures both the heterogeneity and boundary-changing nature/potential of the EU. It also indicates a development that both reflects this diversity and is normatively desirable.

The argument of this chapter is that in a multiple and heterogeneous EU where there are some doubts about traditional understandings of integration centred on the welfare state then we also need to account for the role that legal certainty can play for immigrant, ethnic and national minorities. Such groups can be in a structurally weak position and thus vulnerable if a multiple and heterogeneous EU brings with it uncertainty and insecurity without the kinds of certainty imparted by anti-discrimination laws. It is argued that such laws are compatible with a vision of a multiple and diverse EU and indeed, that they are essential if all the peoples of Europe are to be given a sounder footing on which to advance claims for inclusion at local, national and EU level.

## Legal certainties in a neo-medieval Europe

It is well known that there has been a rapid development of EU immigration and asylum responsibilities in the 1990s (Geddes 2000a). The EU has paid less attention to anti-discrimination laws, minority rights and action against racism and xenophobia. This began to change in the 1990s, but often the only action taken was a ritual declaration appended to the conclusions of various summit meetings of the heads of government (European Parliament 1998). The result was that EU policy developments were lopsided in the sense that they focused on the control of those forms of international migration defined by state policies as unwanted, such as 'illegal' immigration and asylum seeking. Little attention was paid to issues relating to immigrant integration or the protection of minorities. The Treaty basis for such action was limited and these were seen as largely national concerns. If we employ the distinction made by Hammar (1990) then we can say that the EU has focused on immigration policies (concerned with the regulation of international migration in its many forms) rather than immigrant policies (addressed towards the social and legal position of migrants and minorities).

If we try to pinpoint the motive forces underpinning the development of EU immigration cooperation and integration then a strong intergovernmental impetus can be identified. The EU has actually been quite useful to member states because it has allowed them to establish new institutional venues at European level where the domestic legal and political constraints on immigration policy-makers have been relaxed. National governments have thus been able to 'escape to Europe' in a bid to solve problems of international regulatory failure and seek new forums for the pursuit of restrictions on 'unwanted' immigration (Hollifield 2000; Stetter 2000). A key element of this response has been the co-option of surrounding states and regions into these processes. For instance, policy developments in southern Europe – particularly the repressive elements – have been strongly influenced by the EU *acquis* (Pastore 2001). For candidate states in central and eastern Europe there have been onerous requirements associated with the incorporation of the EU *acquis* into national law as a condition for membership (Lavenex 1999). The result has been that the uncertainties of political, social and economic transformation in central and eastern Europe have also coincided with the development of immigrant and ethnic minorities communities in these countries, as well as longer-standing minority populations. The uncertainty elicited by transition and the sometimes onerous economic requirements of EU membership have led to instances of migrants and minorities being scapegoated (see, for instance, Fonseca 1995).

While policy developments could be characterised as lop-sided there is also the issue of the underlying conceptualisation of the relationship between international migration and its sequels and European integration. It is at this point that Jan Zielonka (2001) entered the fray. He detected a flaw in the exercise of exporting the EU immigration and asylum *acquis* to the CEECs. He argued that the venture was predicated on attempts to reconstruct the kinds of 'hard' borders that had been a familiar aspect of the response in 'older' immigration countries. The allusion is to national policies that seek to regulate the flow of international migrants through centrally directed command and control policies. He argues that this is not appropriate in central and eastern Europe and that this defect will become more apparent as the EU moves eastwards and the divergences within the EU, in socio-economic terms, for instance, grow larger. He argues that 'The very notion of a hard, external border as envisaged by the single market project and the regime of Schengen is basically flawed and unlikely to survive the following enlargement' (p. 508).

In such terms the EU is less of a 'post-Westphalian state' with hard and fixed external borders, socio-economic homogeneity, a European cultural identity, one type of citizenship and 'absolute sovereignty' regained at European level (if it ever aspires to be). Instead, he argues that the EU is more of a 'neo-medieval empire' with overlapping authorities, divided sovereignty, varied institutional arrangements, multiple identities and diversified types of citizenship with different sets of rights and duties. The word that might spring to mind when medievalism is mentioned is feudalism, but for Zielonka it conjures up a vision of a diverse, heterogeneous and normatively desirable future for a wider EU. Zielonka's point is that the future enlargement can only magnify, accelerate and confirm these trends towards diversity, multiplicity and differentiation. In turn, this implies that the EU must embrace alternatives to absolute sovereignty that involve overlapping authority, multiple cultural identities and flexible institutional arrangements in order to promote free movement within and across its borders. As such, the post-Westphalian state is redundant and new forms of neo-medievalism become the appropriate response (see also Caporaso 1996).

Leaving aside the point that this vision of multiplicity and overlapping spheres is likely to strike fear into the hearts of EU lawyers, the question that this chapter discusses is the relationship between this vision of a progressive 'neo-medievalism' and the protection of the rights of migrants and ethnic minorities. It is argued that these people are typically in a structurally weak position and that they are likely to be in the frontline if scapegoats are needed to be blamed for the uncertainty and insecurity that some people may feel in the face of some aspects of the multiplicity and heterogeneity associated with European integration. In this context it is argued that some good old-fashioned legal certainty in the form of EU anti-discrimination legislation that directly binds member states is a necessary accompaniment to a wider and deeper EU. The chapter now moves on to discuss the development of EU legislation that protects migrant and minority rights and the forms of mobilisation that have developed around these issues at European level.

## Pro-migrant mobilisation in the EU

Since the 1990s it has been possible to identify new forms of political mobilisation around migrant and minority rights issues at EU level. This is not ethnic mobilisation as such in the sense that it represents direct mobilisation by Europe's immigrant and ethnic minority populations. Rather, this form of action can best be understood as a form of interest co-option by EU institutions coupled with entrepreneurialism by pro-migrant groups which thus conforms with the more general pattern of interest group activity at EU level (Geddes 2000b). In the area of international migration many of the groups that have been particularly active (the Churches Commission for Migrants in Europe, Amnesty International, Caritas, etc.) have brought with them the moral and symbolic capital associated with church-based or human rights organisations to support their arguments that the EU needs to consider migrant and minority concerns as part of its developing agenda.

When referring to the co-option of these groups, I don't mean that they are entirely creatures of the EU institutions. Rather, I refer to the ways in which supranational institutions, the European Commission in particular, will support (in some cases even establish) groups with which they can consult. This fulfils a Commission need to discuss with representatives of civil society and thus add some legitimisation to what can be rather detached policy development. There's another point here too. The close links between the Commission and lobby groups can lead to the formation of pro-European integration alliances where the identification of 'problems of Europe' can prompt the solution of 'more Europe' to counter these supposed weaknesses. In these terms, ideas such as 'social inclusion' have been useful opportunities for the Commission because the terms present an ideal combination of vagueness and normative desirability which can be the source of arguments for EU task expansiveness in the longer-term (Geddes 2000c).

The academic literature on these new forms of EU level political action has made connections with what has been called the political sociology of the international. This concerns analyses of the ways in which Europeanised sources of power and authority have led to the development of a European political field with its own forms of culture, capital and habitus. Favell (2001), for instance, takes the emergence of pro-migrant NGOs at EU level as evidence for the emergence of a new political field and a nascent 'sociology of the international [that] aims to understand the internal relations, conflicts and power brokering of political actors and organisations within a particular policy arena that is in the process of thereby constituting itself'. Europeanisation thus has implications for the organisation of political action and for the link between active citizenship and the nation-state as its primary locus.

If we take the point about the organisation of political action then we need to be specific about the forms of political action enabled at EU level. The EU is a creature of Treaty, but more than this, it is a creature of a Treaty informed by a strong commercial imperative. At the heart of the European project are market-making, the completion of the European single market, and more recently, the establishment of the European single currency. We should not expect the EU to be a progressive exponent of new forms of multiculturalism or identity politics because it is not that type of organisation. If claims for inclusion by pro-migrant groups are to be made then they need to draw from the specific legal resources associated with European integration. In the area of anti-discrimination, the EU has commitments dating back to the Treaty of Rome (1957) that prohibit discrimination on grounds of nationality, while also seeking equality between men and women in the workplace. There were no provisions on other forms of discrimination such as those based on race, ethnicity or religion. Partly because these were not salient concerns at the time that the Treaty was drafted back in the 1950s and partly because these have also been viewed as national responsibilities. The arguments of pro-migrant groups centred on connecting migrant and minority rights to the existing legal resources associated with European integration and thus arguing that extended anti-discrimination provisions were a necessary accompaniment to single market integration and the kinds of principles that informed it.

Pro-migrant groups have thus drawn from Europeanised sources of material and symbolic power that generate ideas about inclusion with a strong economic focus. Moreover, these ideas were linked to the bounded nature of the European project in the sense that the EU has both barrier-removing and barrier-building features that lead to a relatively hard shell being built between itself and neighbouring states and forms of movement that privilege those empowered to move by the EU treaties and associated legislation while restricting those forms of movement not supported by treaty or legislation. In a sense, therefore, the EU faces the boundary issues raised by the articulation between closed states and open economies. In these terms, the Europeanisation of debates about migrant inclusion confounds both a narrow state-centrism and post-national universalism.

This still leaves the question of how we are to explain the resources available to pro-migrant groups. In his analysis of the politics of migration in liberal states, Freeman (1995) argued that there were tendencies towards both expansive and inclusive policies because of the ways in which the concentrated beneficiaries of policy have a clearer incentive to organise compared to the diffuse bearers of costs. He argued that business interests would be likely to push for expansive migration policies while pro-migrant groups would be advocates of more inclusive policies that extend rights to migrants. This work has been developed by those who argue that the venues in which decisions about migration are taken are particularly important. Guiraudon, for instance, has argued that relatively shielded judicial and bureaucratic venues offer more scope for the protection of migrants' rights because these are less exposed to broader public debates.

What does this mean for pro-migrant groups at EU level? If we think about the resources that pro-migrant groups at EU level are likely to possess then it's fair to say that they tend to be relatively weak. Public opinion across the EU tends to be anti-immigration and anti-immigrant while non-national migrants have limited access to local and national political systems, never mind to the EU political system (EUMC 2000). Yet, this need not stultify the scope for pro-migrant advocacy. Venue-switching, Guiraudon (2000) argues, is an important device because it can lead to decisions being made in relatively shielded bureaucratic or judicial venues. As a result, some political opportunities can arise where decision-makers are relatively shielded from anti-immigration/immigrant pressures, such as behind the relatively closed doors of the European Commission and the European Court of Justice (ECJ). The European Commission's technocratic origins mean that it tends to search for technical solutions to political problems. It can also be responsive to the ideas that pro-migrant NGOs bring forward. In this sense, the EU's 'democratic deficit' arising from the lack of direct political participation, may offer new political opportunities. Problems can arise if decisions made behind closed doors are subject to wider public scrutiny later down the line.

It is in these terms that pro-migrant mobilisation at EU level has been identified that seeks to capitalise on shielded EU venues and EU sources of legal and symbolic power (Geddes, 2000b). It's also worth bearing in mind that EU laws can feed back into domestic contexts and challenge national ways of doing things. Keck and Sikkink (1998), for instance, argue that transnational advocacy can create a 'boomerang effect' where resource-poor national organisations can be strengthened by resource-rich international organisations.

At this stage, we need to become a bit more specific. We have identified the kinds of spaces created for pro-migrant mobilisation and the kinds of action favoured in a European context. But what are the components of this EU-level migrant-inclusion agenda? Their main elements can be identified: extended anti-discrimination provisions, the extension of the rights of EU citizenship to legally resident third country nationals (TCNs); and asylum procedures judged fair and humane to the extent that they accord with international standards.

The most problematic issue has been the rights of asylum seekers. Across the EU there have been attempts to (i) reduce the ability of asylum seekers to access the territory of EU member states (ii) use internal measures such as dispersal systems, accommodation centres, the denial of labour-market access, and the use of vouchers rather than cash-paid welfare state benefits and (iii) construct a central and east European 'buffer zone' to absorb some of the migration pressure. Prominent EU-level NGOs such as the European Council on Refugees and Exiles (ECRE) who contest the asylum sphere have been strong critics of what they see as a race to the bottom by EU member states that bears only tenuous relation to the international commitments of the member states. This may also reinforce the point made earlier. EU cooperation and integration may actually have enabled the member states to develop new ways of regulating those forms of migration that their policies define as 'unwanted'. EU member states can thus retain a symbolic commitment to the right to asylum while eroding the ability of people who want to enter the territory of EU member states and exercise this right. The aim of policies is to reduce the ability of asylum seekers to make a claim on the societies in which they find themselves. This is designed to ensure that this form of migration, unlike others in the past, is reversible and does not lead to permanent settlement. Another consequence is the development of a diversion effect – similar to that which affects southern Europe – as migrants unable to enter EU member states settle in central and eastern Europe.

The two other elements of the EU-level migrant inclusion agenda mentioned above can now be discussed. The extension of anti-discrimination legislation and the extension of citizenship rights for TCNs can be analysed alongside each other because the relative progress of each tells us interesting things about the claims for inclusion enabled at EU level. EU citizenship rights for third country nationals would shatter the derivative character of EU citizenship by creating forms of membership that were not dependent on prior possession of the nationality of a member state. This debate was located on unpromising political terrain given that the member states had made it very clear that (i) nationality laws were their prerogative and (ii) the EU citizenship established by the Maastricht Treaty was derived from prior possession of the nationality of a member state.

In contrast, anti-discrimination legislation had the advantage of drawing from some existing anti-discrimination provisions (nationality and gender), as well as the Community legal principle of equal treatment. Although there were not specific 'race' or ethnicity measures, these resources could be used to argue that racial and ethnic-based discrimination should also be tackled. Moreover, these concerns could be linked to market-making functionality because such discrimination would hinder the effective operation of the single market.

The two main organisations that contested the area of migrants' rights have been the European Union Migrants' Forum (EUMF) and the Starting Line Group (SLG). The EUMF was established by the Commission as a representative forum, but has had a troubled recent history and during 2001 its future was in doubt because of various questions about its internal organisation. The SLG was discontinued in rather happier circumstances following the successful incorporation of anti-discrimination legislation into the Treaty. New projects have been established within the ambit of the Brussels-based Migration Policy Group with which the SLG was closely associated.

Both the EUMF and SLG organisations made claims about their representativeness based on the large numbers of affiliated organisations. The Francophone orientation of the EUMF underpinned a focus on *citoyenetté* and the extension of EU citizenship to legally resident third country nationals. The EUMF was established by the Commission as a representative forum for Europe's migrant and migrant-origin populations. There was a terminological problem because many of those whose concerns were supposed to be addressed by the EUMF were *citizens* not migrants. This was because post-colonial migration into the Netherlands, UK and France, for instance, occurred by people from former colonies who were nationals of the countries to which they moved. Beyond this, the EUMF also had difficulty establishing the role intended for it by the Commission. It was difficult to establish a coherent platform in relation to specifically EU developments from the diverse interests of a large number of migrant organisations from across the EU. The claims of the EUMF were also contested by the British-influenced Standing Committee on Racial Equality in Europe that argued that racism was the key issue that needed to be addressed.

In terms of its specific advocacy, the EUMF's proposals to the pre-Amsterdam intergovernmental conference in 1996 supported legislation to combat racial and ethnic-based discrimination, but largely centred on a proposal to amend Article 8a of the EU Treaty with the effect that it would read: 'Citizenship of the Union is hereby established. Every person holding a nationality of a member state or who has been lawfully residing in the territory of a member state for five years shall be a citizen of the Union'. It was then proposed to amend Articles 48–66 covering free movement so that these rights would also be extended to third country nationals on the basis of legal residence rather than prior possession of the nationality of a member state (EUMF 1996).

The EUMF's strategy also requires some attention. It's well known that the Commission relies on the kinds of expert input into the policy development process that interest groups can provide (Mazey and Richardson 1993). Thus, inputs that fit with the EU's prevailing technocratic ethos are particularly highly valued. The EUMF was viewed as failing to bring forward specific proposals and for serving as a forum for complaint rather than input into policy development. At the December 2000 meeting of the EUMF, for instance, a senior Commission official noted that the Commission funded the EUMF and that as a result it wanted to know what the EUMF members thought about the two Commission communications on immigration policy and on asylum issued in November 2000. He argued that as the Commission was paying for the meeting then it could legitimately expect some input from the EUMF.

Ultimately, however, the claims about nationality and citizenship made by the EUMF faced the major problem of not drawing from existing EU resources. Nationality law was specifically identified by the Maastricht and Amsterdam Treaties as a matter for the member states with EU citizenship a derivative of prior possession of the nationality of a member state. The conclusions to the Tampere summit meeting of the European Council held in October 1999 referred to the need to approximate the rights of TCNs with nationals of member states, but also stated that the route to repairing the incomplete membership status of 'denizenship' (legal and social rights short of full citizenship) was the acquisition of national citizenship.

We can now move on to explore the strategy of the Starting Line Group. The UK and Dutch influence on the SLG underpinned a strong focus on anti-discrimination. The Starting Line Group was organised along lines that were more in accordance with usual Commission-lobbying strategies. The SLG relied in particular on expertise and academic networks, particularly legal expertise. These would be used to formulate concrete proposals for action. The SLG was particularly influenced by Anglo-Dutch perspectives on anti-discrimination with reference to legislation that tackled both direct and indirect discrimination, with a particular focus on the workplace and scope for positive action. This reflects the involvement in the group's origins of the British Commission for Racial Equality and the Dutch National Office Against Racism. The SLG was also able to draw from established legal resources. The EU was already committed to anti-discrimination (gender and nationality in the Treaty of Rome). It is also committed to the principle of equal treatment (Directive 76/207 of 1976). An interesting point here is that these kinds of proposals did not imply a race to the bottom or lowest common denominator policies. These terms are often used to characterise decision-making in intergovernmental forums where unanimity is the basis for decision-making.

## Arguing for inclusion

Having compared the strategies of the main groups lobbying for migrant inclusion – the claims they made and the material and symbolic resources from which they drew – we can now move on to explore the content of EU anti-discrimination legislation more carefully. This involves, first, analysing the inclusion of a new Article 13 in the Treaty of Rome by the Treaty of Amsterdam that established a legal basis for action to combat discrimination based on race, ethnicity, religion, gender, age, disability and sexual orientation. We can then outline the progress of the 'world record' directives on 'race equality' and equal treatment in the workplace that took just six months to go from proposal to law. It is argued that while intergovernmental impetus underpinned the inclusion of Article 13 as a specific anti-discrimination provision, that the frame provided by pro-migrant groups and the cultivation of alliances with Commission officials was a vital backdrop when solutions were sought to the problems of racism and xenophobia that were brought into sharper focus by the entry of the extreme right-wing Freedom Party into the Austrian coalition government in February 2000.

The inclusion of specific Treaty anti-discrimination provisions can be linked to member-state concerns about racism and xenophobia. The French and German governments were instrumental in the creation of the Kahn Committee, which called for expanded anti-discrimination legislation (ECCCRX 1995; European

Parliament 1998; Chopin and Niessen 2001). The change of government in the UK in 1997 also removed the opposition to the inclusion of specific anti-discrimination provisions held by the Conservative government. Ideas about anti-discrimination had been actively circulating at EU level throughout the 1990s. The new Article 13 reflected these ideas and brought together a number of equality concerns (race, ethnicity, religion, age, disability, gender and sexual orientation) under one Treaty heading. The key factor was, however, the intergovernmental impetus given by the widely held view that 'something needed to be done' about racism and xenophobia and the unblocking of the process after the change of government in the UK. This does leave another issue: the rapid progress from proposal to legislation (December 1999–June 2000) of the anti-discrimination directives.

In seven months between December 1999 and June 2000 the Commission proposals on anti-discrimination legislation were turned into two directives on race equality, equal treatment in the workplace and an accompanying action programme to support implementation of the legislation. This 'world record' progress is particularly interesting because these areas were new policy issues for the EU (Tyson 2001). Ideas had been circulating, but there had not previously been a Treaty basis for legislative action. Indeed, the Commission itself had been sceptical about progress. It hoped that its package of measures – the two directives and action programme – would be adopted by the end of the French Presidency in December 2000. The Portuguese government which held the Council Presidency were keen to secure some prestige associated with adoption of at least one directive, but found it difficult to judge the issue on which progress towards legislation was most likely.

February 2000 was the key month. By this time, the Council working group composed of national officials had only had time for a first reading of the proposals. Parallel to this were developments linked to the entry into the Austrian coalition of Haider's Freedom Party (FPÖ). On 31 January 2000 14 member states announced that they would suspend bilateral official contacts at political level with an Austrian Government integrating the FPÖ, but on 3 February, a coalition government was formed in Austria with the FPÖ. A week later (11–12 February), an informal meeting of the Ministers for Employment and Social Affairs in Lisbon had been scheduled. The French minister Martine Aubry and her Belgian colleague were the most vocal in calling for action against the new Austrian government. This had a symbolic dimension when the French and Belgian ministers refused to participate in the usual end of meeting group photo.

What effect did this have on the negotiations? The British, Dutch and Swedish governments were happy with the content of the directives because they accorded fairly closely with measures already adopted in national law. They had one or two particular concerns, but the adoption of the directives would be fairly costless because there was a good fit with national legislation and thus little adaptive pressure. The Portuguese presidency was keen to push for a resolution. The issues were potentially trickier for the French because their policy approach had consciously eschewed British- and Dutch-style ethnic minorities policy and preferred the assimilationist approach central to 'national integration'. But, as

Geddes and Guiraudon argue (2002): 'the bottom line of the Lisbon summit was that deeds should match words and that verbal condemnation of xenophobic parties had to be followed by legislative acts'. The point here is that French support was linked to a more traditional anti-racism – opposition to a far right politician who had praised the Waffen SS – and this fitted with a French conception of what anti-racist measures should be about. In fact, the proposals offered a civil rights approach to the integration of migrants and minorities with a particularly strong workplace emphasis. This was also a directive on which no member state wanted to be seen as the back-stop. The Austrians supported the new legislation, as too did the Germans who were keen to avoid being portrayed as the 'bad guys' on this issue.

The 'levelling-up' that occurred with the adoption of the directives and action programme arose because proposals for extensive and radical anti-discrimination laws were enabled at EU level by the conjunctural factors associated with the entry into the Austrian coalition of the Haider government and the impact this had on both political will and the speed of negotiations. Having affirmed their political will in the summit conclusions, the ministers left the Council working group to negotiate behind closed doors. The European Parliament (EP) informed the Portuguese Presidency on 8 May 2000 that it would give its opinion on the race directive first. Until this point the race and employment directives had been discussed in parallel. Afterwards and until political agreement was reached a month later on 6 June, the working group focused on the race directive during long meetings. Interviews with participants in this process have suggested that Community legislation and jurisprudence on gender equality provided a frame of reference for the directive on racial discrimination. Given that these were new areas, it was important for the proposals to draw from an existing equal opportunity frame. The fact that the references were to equal treatment also tallied with traditional French concerns about *égalité*. The Portuguese presidency was also keen to see rapid progress on the directives, which disadvantaged some interested parties. The federation of employers' organisations (UNICE) closely monitors EU developments. UNICE assumed that the issue of proposals in November 1999 gave them three or four months to reflect before issuing their viewpoint. By this time, the deal had been done and the political will for legislation based on the Commission proposals was present in the Council. The legislation does have major implications for employers because its provisions on the burden of proof could generate substantial litigation against employers, but the employers were too late to affect the content of the legislation. The European Parliament's influence was more significant because it 'played the clock'. The SLG was also close to some European Parliamentarians and used them to re-introduce proposals that the Commission had dropped.

If we try to bring the discussion together, the strategy adopted by the SLG was successful because it drew from existing EU legal and symbolic resources related to Treaty and legal provisions and the kinds of arguments about 'inclusion' that could be made on this basis. The progress of the legislation was speeded by specific political factors which played an important part in the generation of political will and the 'world record' directive. It should be remembered that this was ostensibly an unpromising issue because of the absence of previous experience and the diverse and deeply rooted policy responses in the member states. The EU can thus affect deeply rooted national responses to immigration and its sequels, and establish legislation with direct effect that extends rights to EU citizens and third country nationals in relation to racist discrimination and discrimination in the workplace.

## Conclusion

Immigration challenges the nation-state – the organisational practices within these states and the ideas that animate these practices. This chapter has attempted to show the ways in which changes within states and changed relations between states affect understandings of migrants and minorities. Welfare state pressures and European integration have led to a tighter demarcation of the community of legitimate receivers of welfare state benefits with attempts to exclude new immigrants. At the same time, there is a policy discourse that places far more emphasis on the responsibilities of individuals and far less on the rights of groups. This applies more generally, but has particular effects on immigrants who – often for reasons linked to understandings of culture and difference – are viewed as a particular integration problem. Yet, this perception of these groups as an 'integration problem' has less to do with the culture or identity of these groups than it has to do with the changes in background institutional conditions such as welfare state pressures that change the perceptions of migrants and minorities.

The chapter developed these points through analysis of the evolving EU migrant inclusion agenda, and addressed two main questions: what role does the EU play in offering new sources of inclusion for immigrant and ethnic minorities? What does this mean for the usual national frame of reference for these integration policies? To answer these questions the chapter examined the development of pro-migrant mobilisation at EU level and the legal and symbolic resources that groups could draw from when making claims for inclusion. It was shown that proposals dealing with anti-discrimination drew from existing Community legal resources and had a greater chance of success than those that focused on nationality and citizenship. The progress of the legislation – in particular the speedily agreed directives of June 2000 on race equality and equal treatment in the workplace – were also impelled by the political will that emerged within the Council working group in the aftermath of the FPÖ's entry into the Austrian coalition. The result is that the EU offers new sources of inclusion for migrants and minorities based on a form of inclusion that draws from existing EU legal resources, which have a strong link to market-related functionality. These create new supranational resources for pro-migrant mobilisation with the capacity to feed into domestic contexts. These derive from the forms of material and symbolic power associated with European integration and a limited vision of economic citizenship that confounds more ambitious views about post-national membership and the EU's progressive potential.

We can also ask what these anti-discrimination measures mean for the future development of the EU. If the EU is indeed to develop as some kind of 'neo-medieval empire' that embraces diversity and multiplicity and understands these as integral components of its identity then it could be argued that some legal certainty is necessary to protect those who may be vulnerable if uncertainty and insecurity accompany multiplicity and heterogeneity. The boundary issues created by European integration and the insecurity and uncertainty that can be linked with them can also lead to the targeting of migrants and minorities. In this context, the legal certainty associated with EU level anti-discrimination legislation that binds member states is a necessary component of a wider and deeper EU and the realisation of the principle of equal treatment for all those who live within its territory.

## Note

1  The Treaty of Amsterdam (1997) amended the Treaty of Rome (1957), inserting a new Article 13 which empowered the EU to take action to combat discimination on a number of grounds.

## References

Banton, M. (2001) 'National integration in France and Britain', *Journal of Ethnic and Migration Studies* 27, 1.

Bommes, M. (2000) 'National welfare state, biography and migration: labour migrants, ethnic Germans and the re-ascription of welfare state membership', in M. Bommes and A. Geddes (eds) *Immigration and Welfare: Challenging the Borders of the Welfare State*, London: Routledge.

Bommes, M. and Geddes, A. (2000) *Immigration and Welfare: Challenging the Borders of the Welfare State*, London: Routledge.

Caporaso, J. (1996) 'The European Union and forms of state: Westphalia, regulatory, or post-modern?', *Journal of Common Market Studies* 34, 1: 29–52.

Chopin, I. and Niessen, J. (2001) *The Starting Line and the Incorporation of the Racial Equality Directive into the National laws of the EU Member States and Accession States*, Brussels/London: Migration Policy Group/Commission for Racial Equality.

ECCCRX (European Council Consultative Committee on Racism and Xenophobia) (1995) *Final Report*, Ref. 6906/1/95 Rev 1 Limite RAXEN, Brussels: General Secretariat of the Council of the European Union.

Edelman, M. (1988) *Constructing the Political Spectacle*, Chicago: University of Chicago Press.

EUMC (European Union Monitoring Centre on Racism and Xenophobia) (2000) *Attitudes Towards Minority Groups in the European Union*, Vienna: European Union Monitoring Centre on Racism and Xenophobia.

EUMF (European Union Migrants' Forum) (1996) *Proposals for a Revision of the Treaty on European Union at the Intergovernmental Conference of 1996*, Brussels: European Migrants' Forum.

European Parliament (1998) *EU Anti-Discrimination Policy: From Equal Opportunities Between Men and Women to Combating Racism*, Brussels: European Parliament Directorate General for Research Working Document, Public Liberties Series LIBE 102.

Favell, A. (2001) 'Integration policy and integration research in Europe: a review and critique', in T.A. Aleinikoff and D. Kluesmeyer (eds) *Citizenship Today: Global Perspectives and Practices*, Washington: Carnegie Endowment for International Peace.

Fonseca, I. (1995) *Bury Me Standing: The Gypsies and their Journey*, London: Chatto and Windus.

Freeman, G. (1995) 'Modes of Immigration Politics in Liberal States', *International Migration Review* 29, 3.

Geddes, A. (2000a) *Immigration and European Integration: Towards Fortress Europe*, Manchester: Manchester University Press.

—— (2000b) 'Lobbying for migrant inclusion in the European Union: new opportunities for transnational advocacy', *Journal of European Public Policy* 7, 4: 632–49.

—— (2000c) 'Thin Europeanisation: the social rights of migrants in an integrating Europe', in Michael Bommes and Andrew Geddes (eds) *Immigration and Welfare: Challenging the Borders of the Welfare State*, London: Routledge.

—— (2003 forthcoming) *The European Politics of Migration*, London: Sage.

Geddes, A. and Guiraudon, V. (2002) *The Anti-Discrimination Policy Paradigm in France and the UK: Europeanization and Alternative Explanations to Policy Change*, paper presented at the joint sessions of workshops of the European Consortium for Political Research, Turin, March 2002.

Guiraudon, V. (2000) *Les politiques d'immigration en Europe*, Paris: L'Harmattan.

Hammar, T. (1990) *Democracy and the Nation State: Aliens, Denizens and Citizens in a World of International Migration*, Aldershot: Avebury.

Hollifield, J.F. (2000) 'Immigration and the politics of rights: the French case in comparative perspective', in M. Bommes, and A. Geddes (eds) *Immigration and Welfare: Challenging the Borders of the Welfare State*, London: Routledge.

Keck, M. and Sikkink, K. (1998) *Activists Beyond Borders: Advocacy Networks in International Politics*, Ithaca NY: Cornell University Press.

Lavenex, S. (1999) *Safe Third Countries: Extending the EU Immigration and Asylum Policies to Central and Eastern Europe*, Budapest: Central European University Press.

Mazey, S. and Richardson, J. (1993) *Lobbying in the European Community*, Oxford: Oxford University Press.

Pastore, F. (2001) 'La politica migratoria', in M. Caciagli and A. Zuckerman (eds) *Politica in Italia: I Fatti dell'anno e le interpretazione*, Bologna: Il Mulino.

Stetter, S. (2000) 'Regulating Migration: Authority Delegation in Justice and Home Affairs', *Journal of European Public Policy* 7, 1: 80–103.

Tyson, A. (2001) 'The negotiation of the European Community Directive on Racial Discrimination', *European Journal of Migration and Law* 3, 2: 199–229.

Zielonka, J. (2001) 'How new enlarged borders will reshape the European Union', *Journal of Common Market Studies* 39, 3.

# 6 Migration, cultural diversification and Europeanisation

*Krystyna Romaniszyn*

## Introduction

This chapter expounds a thesis coined by the author (Romaniszyn 1999a, 2000a) holding that international migrations amplify the cultural diversity of an 'affected' society, be it a recipient or a sending one. The following analysis aims to supply yet another dimension for the discussion of the process of Europeanisation highlighted in this book. The analytical scope of the text embraces cultural changes brought about by the international inflows in the in-migration and out-migration countries in the areas of: work, organisation, and consumption patterns; social norms and social status; local communities; collective and individual identities, ethnic stereotypes, interethnic relations, and ethnic structure.

The chapter is in three main parts. It begins by outlining basic developments regarding international inflows into Europe. Next follows the presentation and discussion of the impact of migration on the above-specified aspects of culture[1] of the host and sending countries. It concludes by considering dilemmas regarding the management of cultural pluralism resulting from international inflows, and how this relates to and influences the process of Europeanisation.

## The besieged fortress of Europe

Mass international migrations have accompanied the history of Europe for the past century. During that time the map of the receiving regions and those where the migration pressure had been built up has changed dramatically. In the last few decades the formative factors which have strongly influenced the migratory movements on the European continent included a cessation of the foreign labour recruitment programmes, the collapse of the Soviet bloc, European integration, and the globalisation processes. The factors at work have resulted either in generating migratory pressure – a tendency that prevails – or in counteracting it. Generally, the response of the European Union member states to the increased migration potential is characterised by the implementation of restrictive and exclusionary immigration policies and the adjustment of the monitoring system in order to protect these countries against uncontrolled immigration, and to curb controlled immigration. These new immigration politics have very quickly been accused of creating a 'Fortress Europe'. The metaphor generated another one, relating to central European states, Poland, the Slovak and Czech Republics and Hungary, which were labelled a 'buffer zone' or a 'cordon sanitaire' (Joly 1996) which shields Western Europe against the inflows from the East.

Basic, observed and assembled facts and trends pertaining to contemporary, international inflows in Europe may be summed up as follows. The first, large dimension of the phenomenon relates to the volume, the scale, and the targets of international inflows. The last two decades, the 1980s and 1990s, witnessed mass and diversified international population movements all over the globe which won them the name and reputation of '*the migration era*' (Castles and Miller 1993). The level of inflows into sixteen western European recipient states in the year 1990 totalled approximately 1.2 million people, while in 1997 it reached circa 1.6 million (Okólski 1999: 150). Such an intensification of international flows was brought about by the activation of traditional sending regions and countries and 'the awakening' of new ones which have marked new migratory routes. Increased by the globalisation process, these movements themselves add to its acceleration. Additionally, a powerful migratory mechanism to be found all over the world, that is a pulling-in by the links established between countries and regions, significantly builds up the volume of migration. A relevant example is the recent labour migration from Tunisia to Italy.

> The tendency of Tunisians to migrate to Italy was further boosted when the 'Habib' boat started operating between the ports of Tunis and Genoa. The cost and speed of transport was reduced and the links between the two countries increased . . . [Additionally,] the transmission of television programmes promoting Italy's wealth induced many people to think that the neighbouring country was 'the promised paradise'.
>
> (Daly and Barot 1999: 40)

Research carried out in selected Central and Eastern European states also shows a correlation between developed transportation systems connecting this region and Western Europe, easy access to detailed information about opportunities in the target countries, and the migratory inflows to and from the region (Romaniszyn 1997: 30). Undoubtedly the current level of communication and transportation, increased by globalisation, which after all involves the intensification and diver- sification of linkages, and accompanied by an imbalance in living standards, altogether augments the amount of international migration. Besides, in Europe, the political changes of 1989 facilitated East–West migration, which has formed a vital part of inflows since the beginning of the 1990s. 'Western Europe has reacted to the new wave of immigration with a mixture of fear, rejection and massive administrative measures' (Fassmann and Munz 1994: 534). This widespread anxiety compelled some Western European scholars to speculate whether the East–West migration would more likely follow the rational or the Doomsday model (Cohen 1991: 19–29). Ten years after, there is no doubt that the former model has established itself, as the newcomers from Central and Eastern Europe have sought jobs and wages attractive to them in affluent western states, while responding to the demand for cheap labour there. In effect, 'as early as around 1992 or 1993 westbound migration from the East started to slow down' (Okólski 1999: 161). Thus the opinion that 'all scenarios predicting the imminent exodus of 5 to 25 million people from Eastern Europe and the former Soviet Union/CIS to the West are exaggerating the dimension of the expected flows' (Fassmann and Munz 1994: 534) has turned out to be an accurate prediction. Nevertheless, existing imbalances in economic development, matched with rising consumption aspirations and expectations (Romaniszyn 2000b: 140), will continue to push subsequent 'generations' of the labour migrants from the East to the West.

For their part, Central and Eastern European countries of the former Soviet-block witnessed an enormous intensification of international inflows in the last decade, mainly from the East and the South.[2] The recorded level of annual inflow ranged from approximately 1000 in Bulgaria and Romania to some 10,000–15,000 in the Czech Republic and Hungary; in Poland inflows seem to be increasing from 2600 in 1990 to 8400 in 1997 (Okólski 1999: 150). However, the stated figures *exclude* asylum seekers, transit migrants (mostly illegal), and clandestine labour migrants. Newly developed migratory routes *within* this region are 'populated' by labour or petty-trade migrants generally moving from the Ukraine, Bulgaria, Byelorussia to Poland, the Czech Republic, and Hungary; and by labour migrants from the Ukraine to Russia (Romaniszyn 1997: 28). The whole region has also been crossed, often illegally by the transit migrants from the East and the South heading for Western Europe, and above all Germany. There are no reliable figures regarding illegal migration from outside Europe crossing the 'buffer zone' on the way to the West. However, the volume of these inflows must be substantial since, according to the available estimates some 150,000 to 250,000 migrants from Asia and Africa are in the Commonwealth of Independent States (CIS) territories at any given time awaiting departure to the West (Okólski 2000: 333). For instance, in one case 'in 1997 alone, some 1,600 convoys with illegal migrants in transit were detained in Poland, including 215 in excess of ten people' (Okólski 1999: 166), and it may well be assumed that not all the convoys crossing the country were detained. Finally, the 'buffer zone' itself has become a destination region for immigrants from outside Europe or the former Soviet Union. In Poland, the Czech Republic, and Hungary communities of these newcomers have already developed. These are respectively Vietnamese and Armenian, Vietnamese and Chinese, and Chinese communities.

Yet another considerable change has taken place in southern Europe. Since the 1980s, along with joining the European Union, the former sending countries of Greece, Italy, and Spain, have begun to take in large numbers of foreign workers, mostly undocumented ones, transforming themselves into recipient states. All in all, in the mid-1990s Europe hosted almost 22.5 million documented foreign residents (Okólski 1999: 151). There is, however, no doubt that an unknown number of the undocumented, and thus unrecorded immigrants, have also found their way into the European Union 'Fortress' and its 'buffer zone'.

Secondly, the majority of contemporary migratory flows have not resulted from formal recruitment, but are self-initiated by entrepreneurial migrants. This

corresponds with, and perhaps stems from, the growing importance and development of the service sector in national economies employing the newcomers, legally
and illegally. These movements are further augmented by the operation of a
powerful migration-networks mechanism (Romaniszyn 2000b). These efficient
microstructures, which have developed across the world and have been recorded
in a number of fieldwork studies, link sending and receiving countries and provide
subsequent inflows of migrants, legal and illegal. Migrant networks also play a vital
role in adjustment to the receiving country and in development of ethnic enclaves
in a host country's economy. Kin and friends of the same ethnic origin 'provide
essential information on the setting up of businesses, the economic inputs required,
the problems encountered and the labour requirements' (Boyd 1989: 653).
Trafficking networks function in a similar way, well organised and proving to be
a lucrative and efficient industry. Indisputably the development, expansion,
and operation of these networks, speeds up the inflow of illegal migrants into
the 'Fortress' and its 'buffer zone' (Romaniszyn 1997: 23ff.). All in all, due to the
operation of numerous factors, the 'Fortress' remains besieged; what changes are
the locations where migratory pressure amounts, and the categories of inflows.

Thirdly, and metaphorically speaking, migratory inflows bring about the
'migration of cultures', as migrants are the bearers of their own ethnic or national
culture, and are perceived as such, at least at the beginning of their stay. Moreover,
their mass settlement or permanent residence in the recipient society results both
in a change of the country's ethnic structure, and in diversification of its culture.
Cultural change that follows is to be seen as the most fundamental consequence
of contemporary migration inflows into the European receiving countries.

Within a few decades after the Second World War, mass migration had led
to the creation of multi-ethnic, and hence multi-cultural, societies with large,
distinctive, and basically non-European minorities. It is true that the European
receiving societies had been unprepared for the acceptance of a vast number of
permanent immigrants. This seems to be changing. Nevertheless, policies towards
immigrants still seem incoherent. On the one hand, governments try to defend a
dominant culture of the nation-state and to integrate minorities. While, on the other
hand, they attempt to safeguard the rights of immigrants wishing to preserve their
cultural distinctiveness. As stated previously, newly adopted policies and joint
agreements on migration, on the whole, enforce restriction. But there is also a wealth
of discussion about the measures necessary to tackle the inequalities and exclusion
confronting minority groups and immigrants. Needless to say, the permanent
presence of immigrants calls for skilled governance of the emerging ethnic and
cultural pluralism within a nation-state, that welcomes its cultural identity,
coherence and stability, in their numerous aspects.

## Cultural diversification resulting from migratory flows

The following discussion on cultural diversification brought about by migratory
inflows rests upon the assumption that the culture of the host and sending societies

succumbs to the influence of migrants as bearers of different cultures, and their communities. The assumed influence will be presented and analysed on the evident instances regarding particular aspects of culture, previously enumerated. Firstly, the constant presence and operation of migrants in the recipient countries' markets affect the economic culture of these societies.[3] Organisation and work patterns displayed by the migrant entrepreneurs are not only perceived, but often adopted by local businessmen and competitors mobilised by the economic activity of newcomers. This mobilisation is a response to a strong competition stimulated by immigrants, in case they are better organised or just offer cheaper services and goods. On the other hand, the ample supply of cheaper foreign labour and the opportunity provided by the purchasing power of foreign businessmen may augment the revival of old, or the development of the new, forms of work organisation.

A good illustration is provided by contemporary labour migration of women. Throughout the world cheap female migrant labour is the cornerstone of the revival of the nineteenth-century style sweatshops in the metropolises of advanced industrial states such as in New York, Paris and London (Morokvasic 1984: 890). After 1991, such sweatshops have also reappeared in Poland due to cheap labour provided, basically, by women from the former USSR. The latter case may be exemplified with reference to the so-called 'Russian bazaars' in Poland that appeared after 1989. These are the market areas originally frequented by travellers from the former USSR, which soon became the hubs of trade with the newcomers from the East.[4] The bazaar turnover has resulted essentially from trade with the foreign entrepreneurs, be they buyers or sellers. In turn, the international bazaar trade has engaged local Polish businesses and has encouraged their development. The mushrooming of small, private, sometimes family firms producing strictly for Eastern customers frequenting the bazaars exemplifies the re-emergence of a long absent work organisation pattern. This entrepreneurial form had been muted under socialism installed in the country since the Second World War, and it has been the trade with migrants from the East that has prompted its revival. Thus, trade with foreign migrant entrepreneurs has added to a change in the country's economic culture. Further development of this area due to inflows of foreign businessmen brings us to the issue of the reception of American organisational culture, of 'McDonaldisation'.

The phenomenon epitomises a 'migration' of economic ideas brought in by the newcomers who establish new branches of the model firm in the receiving country. These ideas, in their own way, diversify, and thus change the economic culture of the 'affected' societies. This process can also be traced within the Polish example discussed above, as there are reasonable grounds to assume that McDonaldisation has already been brought into this, as well as into other central European states. The McDonaldisation culture, depicted in Ritzer's (1996) theory, succeeds because it offers consumers, workers, and managers efficiency, calculability, predictability, and control. These four basic principles of fast food management have spread also to other services such as education, health care, travel, leisure, dieting, policies, etc. Although the concept of McDonaldisation has been related to a critique of consumer culture, it does, however, suit the interpretation of the cultural diversification as well. In the case of Poland, and other post-communist countries the rationality of McDonald's – as a specific organisational method of human agency – stands in contrast to the irrationalities of former communist management strategies, and its remnants. Indicators of the implementation of this organisational model in these countries may be traced in a whole spectrum of economic and social fields such as the housing and trade sectors, in the food industry and mass tourism.

Secondly, the same rule of dissemination pertains to consumption habits and patterns brought in and developed by the newcomers. As one author observes:

> A pattern of consumption which has its roots among an ethnic group, and which helps its members to create a sense of identity, may become partially adopted by some other groups in the wider society. Chinese, Indian, Greek and Turkish Cypriot restaurants, for instance, have had something of this pattern in their history in Britain.
>
> (Bocock 1993: 57)

It also happens that the entrepreneurial immigrants who operate, for example, in the trade or food industry introducing and advertising new products or services may well shape new consumption habits among the indigenous population. This is, for instance, the case of Vietnamese businessmen opening their restaurants and fast-food kiosks all over Poland, attracting and pulling in local clientele, and thus successfully competing with the Polish ethnic businesses. Needless to say, before the mass immigration of Vietnamese entrepreneurs, Oriental restaurants and fast-food kiosks were rare in the country.

Another dimension of the impact of migration on economic culture provides the diffusion of new consumption patterns acquired by migrants abroad, brought back upon their return, and 'implemented' by means of remittances. This time, the direction of the diffusion goes from the host country into the out-migration region *via* the return migrants and their families. The imitation in the home region of consumption patterns obtained abroad reveals a strategy of *postponed consumption* as opposed to *immediate consumption*, occurring in the host country (Romaniszyn 2000b: 140). The former one takes place in the hometown or village upon the migrants' return or, in the meantime, by use of the remittances and serves to raise the migrants' standard of living, and to tighten social relationships due to the sharing of goods (ibid.). It also sets or adds to the shape of the local standards of consumption in the out-migration region which are clear copies or 'mutations' of the patterns perceived in the immigration country. For instance, in Podlasie, which is an out-migration region in north-eastern Poland, those returning from the Benelux countries, the destination for local labour migrants, imitate middle-class housing standards observed abroad. Heading mostly for Brussels and surrounding places these migrants take up jobs as cleaning ladies (women) and construction workers (men), and thus exploit the opportunity to study the patterns of house architecture, decoration, landscaping, etc. Back in the home they copy those patterns utilising acquired means. Visible results of the consumption patterns' diffusion brought about by this labour migration are, for instance, suburban neighbourhoods near the small town of Siemiatycze where comfortable houses with swimming pools mushroom, supplemented with garages equipped with automatic doors (Romaniszyn 1999a: 94). The observed phenomenon is far from being modern or unique, the evidences of 'dissemination' of work, housing, or dress patterns, etc., from the receiving to the sending regions as a result of return migration have been reported in literature (Gabaccia 1994). For instance, at the turn of nineteenth and twentieth centuries 'baggage from America consisted not only of money, or tools, or seeds but also of ideas', as well as clothes, food, and new customs and words (Wyman 1993: 150, 182). In effect, 'the "American houses" . . . sprang up like mushrooms after a rain', 'seeds carried back . . . produced plants that were new and impressive to neighbors . . . so tobacco plants thrived in Norwegian soil, tomatoes in Finland, and lettuce in Ireland' (ibid. 128, 141). Today, of course, the diffusion of consumption, and other cultural patterns does not result from immigration basically and exclusively, but tourism and mass media also significantly add to 'the migration' of lifestyles, the styles of consumption or new ideas. As shown by the examples discussed, the impact of the immigrant entrepreneurs, the 'inflow' of a new organisational culture brought in by the newcomers, and the importation of foreign consumption patterns by returning migrants, altogether influence and reshape the economic culture of the society involved, diversifying this sphere.

Also, the social culture, understood as a realm of social relations, roles and statuses, does not remain 'immune' to the influences stemming from the international migration. First, changes can be traced in the sphere of interpersonal contacts between the newcomers and the host society's members. Immigrants who stay and work in the recipient country come into contact with its citizens and institutions. The interpersonal contacts between the newcomers and the indigenous people sometimes dismantle barriers of ignorance and indifference, bring the members of the two societies and cultures closer together, and, hence, link the involved societies (Romaniszyn 1999b: 127). In fact these people take on the role of contact-builders between the sending and receiving societies, who create and maintain social ties across boundaries with persons met in the migration country. This not only broadens the landscapes (Schama 1995) rendered familiar to immigrants, but also works towards bridging the gap between the sending and the receiving communities involved. Furthermore, these interpersonal contacts may further support the establishment or development of the migratory networks that augment, direct, and structure the subsequent inflows (as mentioned earlier).

Second, international migration may affect the role and status changes within the migrant family, sending community, and even wider society. An excellent example is provided by recent, intensified migration of women.[5] It has the potential to improve migrant women's status within the household, and within the wider society by providing them with opportunities to earn their own income, and by weakening traditional patriarchal authority. To some extent this potential advantage of migration may be hindered by the nature of the work in which the migrant women are engaged. When that work is low paid and involves poor working conditions with little prospect of upward mobility, it is unlikely to lead to an improvement in the status of women either within the household or in society at large (Bilsborrow and Zlotnik 1992: 140). This, however, is true only in the case of immigrants who have settled in a host country. Those migrant women who just work abroad providing their families with remittances, and take over the role of family bread-winners, by this very fact improve their status within the household back in the home country regardless of their job. Employed as domestic servants, migrant women also help the professional career of their female employers by undertaking the domestic duties of the latter. Indeed, the career of the middle-class women in the host societies has been augmented by the employment of foreign women servants undertaking their patrons' housewife duties. Thus, in the long run, female migration affects gender relations within migrant families by improving these women's status, and within the recipient families by easing the professional careers of wives and mothers.

Third, migration may well reshape, or develop new patterns of accepted behaviour. For example, the widespread approval of migration in the sending country or just in its out-migration regions – when it occurs – reveals the devel-opment of a new social norm of proper behaviour in these regions. According to this norm, migration is collectively perceived as a sound and workable life strategy. In turn, the social acceptance of a migratory life further accelerates migration, which may even be treated as a rite of passage – one means by which people make their transition into adulthood and social prestige depicted, for instance, in numerous local communities in the west of Ireland (Gmelch 1987: 266ff.). The emerging and functioning of this norm builds the local culture of migration. A rise in the social status of the migrant households, basically due to remittances and enhanced consumption ability, is one indicator of this culture.

Fourth, international inflows leading to concentration and settlement of the newcomers from numerous countries in particular districts or residential areas result in a qualitative change of the 'affected' local communities. The reason for this is that the new residents originating from various nations have their meaningful social relations not with the immediate neighbours, as used to happen, but entirely outside the local community and across the globe (Albrow 1997: 53). The effect of this novel pattern of behaviour and settlement is twofold: first, the newcomers do not assimilate into the local community and its culture; second, their 'semi-presence' changes the local community so that it gradually loses its specific culture. In such instances, locality parts with community. This crucial change obviously does not pertain to all local communities inhabited by immigrants nor to all local communities in the target countries, which means a diversification also in this social sphere.

The influence of international migration is to be traced also in the sphere of symbolic culture, in the spread of new values, norms and ideas, including religious norms and values. Again, migration is not the only or the chief source of the dis-semination of new ideas in contemporary societies: the mass media communicates and spreads them on a global scale. Nevertheless, migrants themselves and their communities may effectively import new ideas, norms and values, or help to revive old and muted ones in the host society. The former instance may be observed in

Poland and other newly 'opened' societies of the region, where migratory inflows augment the spread of new, foreign religious movements and sects. In Polish society, thus far predominantly Catholic, these movements find their adherents, proving that importation of new ideas by the 'addicted' newcomers effectively diversifies life-styles and beliefs in the country. Another prominent example is provided by converts to Islam in some Western European societies. Research on Dutch female converts to Islam reveals that in the Netherlands, in as early as 1993, the number of these women was estimated at between 3000 and 4000 (Nieuwkerk 2000: 2). While most of these women were first married to Muslim partners and then eventually converted to Islam, others 'found their way to Islam and afterwards married Muslims' (ibid.), and similar cases had been reported from Norway and France. This conversion is very symptomatic. It occurs in the receiving states which contain substantial Muslim communities, proving that the neighbour-hood, personal contacts, created interpersonal ties, and daily observed patterns of behaviour may effectively influence beliefs and change religious identity of some members of the host society.

The two examples given show that new ideas imported by the newcomers both add to the existing cultural mosaic of ideas and values, diversifying the sphere of religion, and find their adherents among the indigenous society. The latter instance reveals a crucial fact, namely that 'the symbolic importation' may effectively compete with a set, traditional creed, and win over a number of its former followers. On the other hand, numerous conversions to Islam may prompt and augment the social discussion on the national creed and the uniqueness of European civilization, and compel individuals to rethink and reconsider their national and cultural identity vis-à-vis distant cultures. In other words, they may prompt the re-examination of both the collective and personal identity in the recipient society.

As mentioned above, mass international inflows may well help the revival of forgotten or muted ideas, a good example here is racism. Intolerance towards the 'other' has a long tradition in Europe; nevertheless, it has been muted, and disappeared from public life for decades after the Second World War. In recent decades, however, the negative image of the newcomers portrayed as 'the alien dangerous invaders' has seemed to increase significantly. Racism in contemporary Europe is taking on forms of ideologies, movements, and every-day practices, attitudes, and prejudice based on phenotypical, or cultural characteristics seen as fixed, naturalised and inherently different (Rath 1993: 231). Contacts between immigrants and the host society members enter into negative effect when attitudes and practices directed towards the newcomers are based on their phenotypical characteristics or cultural identity imposed upon them and then utilised as a marker of their inherent difference. The latter case, when the 'immigrant-other' is considered as an inherently different and inferior 'cultural being', equates to 'cultural racism' symptomatic of the 'new' or contemporary racism. The revival of these attitudes constitutes a disturbing and potentially explosive aspect of the ongoing cultural change in Western recipient countries (Romaniszyn 2001). The intensification of anti-foreign sentiments, intolerance, and xenophobia, which began in the 1980s and forms a part of cultural change seems to be an immediate consequence of socio-economic transformation, the numerous newcomers just provide an easy object of the already existing evil feelings. A thesis as to the close links between transformation and the development of racism directed against ethnic minorities and immigrants is propounded by numerous authors (Castles 1993; Solomos and Wrench 1993; Wieviorka 1994). They all acknowledge that the alteration of the social structure is a particularly important change, which results in the polarisation of society between the well off and the marginalised. The new social stratification makes for the growth of social inequality and the feeling of insecurity on the part of those who have found themselves at the bottom of the emerging social hierarchy. The excluded attribute the costs of transformation they are to bear to immigrants blamed as a burden on the welfare system, considered as competitors in the labour market, and accused of driving down wages, even if they themselves share the same experience of marginalisation. Numerous reports and studies demonstrate that racial expressions and practices focusing on immigrants have already occurred.

For instance, surveys carried out in 1987 and 1993 in Finland detect a considerable change in attitudes toward refugees and other immigrants. On the whole they became negative, which 'pertains to all age, gender, and social groups in both rural and urban areas' and induces 'negative attitudes to social interaction with foreign people' (Jaakkola 1995: 3, 11). Characteristically, 'Simultaneously, the number of asylum seekers and other immigrants has increased, and the economic recession has deepened' (ibid.: 3). A study on the media's descriptions of aliens in the Federal Republic of Germany in the 1980s and 1990s reveals the continuous 'negative coverage of immigrants and the depiction of them as a source of danger and threat' (Brady 1997: 1). In the Netherlands the south Asian and the Caribbean migrant workers are constructed as a specific race, distinguished from the white race of the natives, and their presence in the society is seen as a problem (Rath 1993: 218). 'The consequence . . . is the ranking of these specific categories of migrant workers and their offspring among the lower positions in the social hierarchy' (ibid.). In Norway and Denmark the anti-immigration movement claims to be the new resistance movement fighting against 'the Muslim invasion' and its national supporters (Bjorgo 1997: 56). Available research on attitudes towards migrants and ethnic minorities in Central and Eastern Europe also arrives at interesting findings (Haerpfer and Wallace 1997).[6] Based on an annual survey that began in 1992, it reveals that, in most countries studied, a 'fear of ethnic minorities and migrants has fallen rather than risen since 1992 and this means that seeing post-Communist Central Europe as seething with ethnic strife and xenophobia is not an accurate portrayal. Most people don't care about either migrants or minorities' (ibid.: 24).

There are numerous examples to support the thesis presented, that international inflows influence symbolic culture of the host society, and among others may add to the revival of the old, long muted, ideas. One may comment on the instances of racialisation in contemporary Europe with an assessment offered by Leszek Kołakowski (1990) in his essay on the intrinsic characteristics of European culture. Kołakowski noticed that European culture possesses an ability to watch itself in the mirror of other cultures, to contest itself, and the European universalism implies a persistent habit of introspection. The discussion and monitoring of contemporary racism going on in Europe prove this assumption correct.

In Western European host countries, racist attitudes followed by social exclusion has been condemned for breeding ethnic minority enclaves (Castles 1993: 28).[7] They, in turn, augment exclusionary practices and maintain marginalised ethnic communities whose members are feared and excluded (Riggs 1991: 449).[8] The persistence of migrant enclaves is further augmented by the 'structural discrimination' that is neither deliberate, nor directed against individuals (Entzinger 1990: 281). It results from the fact that all major social institutions are governed, formally or informally, by habits, rules, and regulations derived from the dominant culture. Familiarity with these rules and regulations permit access to those institutions. It follows that migrant ethnic enclaves may be perceived as persisting 'peripheral cultures' vis-à-vis a cultural centre. The establishment of migrant enclaves has a considerable, direct impact on the recipient country's culture as they *expose* its dominant position, and often question it. This is related to the issue of the management of ethnic and cultural pluralism that results from international inflows addressed in the next section.

International inflows have yet another impact on symbolic culture resulting from the contacts between the newcomers and the members of the host society as they perpetuate, or assist the creation of new ethnic stereotypes. These developments influence the collective and individual identity of both parties. Research on the political discourse on immigration in Greece and Italy reveals that in Greece the image of immigrants has been shaped by a presumed national character of the nation from which they originate. For instance, 'according to some of the people interviewed, Poles have "a different attitude" . . . "they impose themselves"' (Triandafyllidou 2000: 197). Confronting this with the research on undocumented Polish migrants, carried out in Greece in 1993, one discovers the development of a counter-stereotype about Greeks amidst Poles, who 'frequently expressed – seemingly an already common belief among the Polish undocumented – that 'Greeks are difficult to put up with' (Romaniszyn 2000b: 128). Importantly, such a stereotype had not been found in Polish culture before the era of massive labour migration to Greece. The two independently carried-out studies register the two aspects of the same phenomenon, both parties – the indigenous people as well as the newcomers – are prone to perceive each other through the spectacles of stereotypes, already existing or just being developed. The fact that political discourse on immigration draws upon collective identity poses the issue of this identity stimulation so that it 'immunises' itself against intolerance. Otherwise, left to themselves the two sides of the encounter – the immigrants and the indigenous people – may breed ill feelings of mutual intolerance. The more so as the intensification of contacts between people of different cultural backgrounds, forced by mass international migration, tends to result in intolerance and negative stereotyping.

The analysis presented validates the initial thesis that international migration has a considerable impact on the culture of the societies involved, leading to their (further) diversification. The analysis does not pretend to completeness as there are very probably other dimensions of cultural diversification brought about by the inflows that have not been addressed here and are to be searched for. It rather promotes the novel subject in the research on migration, and on cultural change ongoing in the European nation-states, and thus supplements the analysis of the Europeanisation process set in motion by European integration.

## Cultural pluralism – dilemmas with governance

Cultural diversification brought about by international migration reveals itself in the above-mentioned pluralisation of all spheres of the affected culture, and the differentiation of the recipient state's ethnic structure. The latter instance poses the problem of the management of ethnic pluralism that has become a constant characteristic of the European receiving nation-states. It shapes the new Europe along with the progressive consolidation and unification of the European nation-states, stemming from the European Union enlargement process, further intensified by the collapse of the Soviet bloc. Thus, the twofold inner cultural *diversification* of the European nation-states, resulting from the admission of the newcomers, forms a context for the opposite process: *the* Europeanisation.

The permanence of immigrant residence and the development of their ethnic enclaves call for the implementation of the effective measures promoting the peaceful co-existence of numerous ethnic minorities within a nation-state. A crucial issue regarding the management of ethnic, and subsequent cultural, pluralism within nation-states is summed up in the following questions: to what extent must a national culture change in order to integrate minorities? What is the status of minorities' culture, including religion vis-à-vis the dominant culture? Roughly, the debates on the management of ethnic and cultural pluralism focus either on the interests of the nation-state and its dominant culture, or on civil society as a remedy to ethnicity. As one party thinks of protecting, by skilled management, the cultural centre (core) against the alien cultures, the other calculates on dismantling the nation-state. The ultimate aim of the former strategy is the full integration of immigrants and their offspring, who are expected to reconcile their cultural heritage with the dominant culture. Cultural homogeneity is perceived as the basis for the politically centralised nation-state. In the latter case, the usually unspoken ideal, matching the development of a modern liberal creed, seems to be the 'post-nation' state. In both cases, despite the differences between them, ethnic cultures are expected to adjust to the model of co-existence set by the dominant culture that preserves dominant status for itself.

A good start to a discussion of this issue is provided by the ideal types of response to ethnic diversity, set out by Modood (1997: 21ff.). The first two, 'the decentred self' and the 'liberal state' solutions offer politically constituted multiculturalism where individuals relate to the state as citizens, not as members of any groups, ethnic ones included. Such a state is 'group-blind, it cannot "see" colour, gender, ethnicity, religion or even nationality' which remain private to individuals (ibid.: 22). The 'republic' remedy also does not recognise groups and relates to each citizen as an individual, but it seeks to make the individuals the members of a civic community. The 'federation of communities' option perceives communities as primary units of public life since individuals belong to and are shaped by communities. The 'plural state' recognises both rights for all individuals as well as groups and institutions, the latter being 'active public players and forums for political discussion' (ibid.: 23).

> For the plural state the challenge of the new multiculturalism is about the integration of transplanted cultures . . . into long-established, ongoing, historic, national cultures . . . it is about extending, reforming and syncretizing in new ways existing forms of public culture and citizenship. It is not about decentring society or deconstructing the nation-state, but about integrating difference by remaking the nation-state.
>
> (Modood 1997: 24)

These are ideal, in the Weberian sense, types of responses that may be utilised as an analytical tool for the interpretation of particular responses.

Currently the restrictive policies concerning the entry of potential immigrants adopted by most European countries have been balanced with more attention given to the social, economic, and political *incorporation* of those already admitted. In the political domain this general option ranges from expectations that immigrants will adopt civic principles, to the conviction that interaction between the newcomers and indigenous people should aim at the construction of a shared political culture. Under conditions of ethnic and cultural pluralism a shared political culture – that adds up to a common political language and conventions of conduct – has been perceived as a 'common space' to be constructed through the political action of all citizens (Habermas).[9] Thus it seems that both 'the liberal state' and the 'republic' ideals inspire the multicultural policy adopted by the European governments. They perceive the multi-ethnic and multicultural state as 'a political community, based on a constitution, laws and citizenship, with the possibility of admitting newcomers . . . providing they adhere to the political rules, while at the same time accepting cultural difference and the formation of ethnic communities' (Castles and Miller 1993: 39). The approved model seeks a united political community while cultural diversity is restricted to a private sphere. The public domain, which extends to law, politics, economics, and welfare policy is to provide equal opportunity and uniform treatment to everybody.[10] However, the point is that 'the public domain' and 'the political culture' are *embedded* in, and constitute a *part* of national culture, thus reflect its values and norms that may still or constantly be alien to the newcomers. Besides, a purely civil society where everybody can feel at home regardless of creed, or language does not, yet, exist. There is little doubt that the governments' responses to ethnic and cultural pluralism do not lead to a 'plural state' ideal but even setting up the 'liberal state' and 'republic' ideals encounter serious obstacles.

First, the naturalisation proceedings and the voting-rights issues provoke controversy. The argument of the immigrant rights' advocates that 'Immigrant demands . . . will not be taken seriously unless local political parties depend on their votes' has been rebutted by the nation-state defenders, arguing that 'only citizens should enjoy full political rights . . . [as] voting rights usually assume literacy and some knowledge of and sympathy for the country and its institutions' (Coleman 1994: 60). In one view, the voting-rights issue represents a challenge to the future of Western legal civilization,[11] according to another, 'citizenship . . . is the modern equivalent of feudal privilege, an inherited status that greatly enhances one's life chances' (Carens 1987: 252). Undoubtedly, the idea of mass participation in the public domain amounts to wishful thinking when immigrants are deprived of the voting rights or citizenship.

Second, the newcomers – the potential partners in constructing a shared political culture – are often economically, politically and educationally disadvantaged over generations. The analyses show that on the whole, in European recipient states, unemployment among immigrants and their offspring has been getting worse in the 1990s, and is often higher than in the host population. The second generation's school underachievement adds to the problem, decreasing job opportunities for ethnic youth. A concentration of immigrant settlement in poor districts, along with a right to preserve their traditional society and culture, may actually lead to the creation of inner city ghettos, already familiar from the American metropolises. Paradoxically, the state support received by immigrants may also hinder their integration. For instance, setting up ethnic schools may lessen a good command of the official language and general knowledge of the dominant culture, the two necessary preconditions for upward social mobility. It follows that full exercise of the proffered rights may strengthen structural discrimination (see below) leading to social and economic marginalisation of immigrants, at least in the short term. The implementation of multicultural curricula, aimed at acquainting students with the diversity and wealth of the cultures represented in the society, and at inculcating them with respect for the 'other' also faces various obstacles. For instance, some Muslim minorities demand separate education for girls or even separate Muslim schools, while some white parents remove their children from schools where ethnic minority pupils predominate, and where a multicultural curriculum has been enforced (Coleman 1994: 58, 62).

This brings us to the issue of immigrant responses to state policy. Generally, and obviously, they either withdraw from, or try to enhance their participation in a wider society. The latter attitude most likely evokes the expectation of 'mutual respect', and replaces a demand for 'rights' or 'equality' (Modood 1997: 6).[12] Such an attitude indicates an effort on the part of the immigrants involved to shift from a client-status to a partner one, suggesting that at least the socially active cohort of immigrants has ceased to perceive themselves as clients of the recipient state (Romaniszyn 2002).[13] An attempt to overcome a patron–client relationship between the host state and immigrants should be regarded as a crucial qualitative change which paves the way to a conscious citizenship of the newcomers, providing the immigrants cease to be perceived by the host state as the passive clients. This seems to be one necessary precondition for both the participation in construction, and utilisation of 'the common sphere' by immigrants, and hence for achieving any of the ideal types of response to ethnic diversity presented by Modood.

On the other hand, immigrants especially those from a rural background, may cling to their traditionalism, tend to form an ethnic enclave in the receiving society, and alienate themselves from both the host and the home country.[14] A good example is provided by the Turkish neighbourhood in Vienna where a traditional community has been established in one building: 'At the entrance level . . . there was an all-men's coffee house, and below the ground level was the mosque. The life in this building was like a "squeezed village life"' (Erman and Turan 1997: 8–9).[15] More importantly, the community persuaded its female members to *start* covering their bodies and hair, a practice which had been abandoned back in the home village!

This instance relates to a broader issue of the deliberate rejection expressed by some ethnic communities of the liberal principles: the rule of secular law, the separation of church and state, universal education, the emancipation of women, freedom of speech, etc., that underpin modern democracies. For instance, some Muslim immigrants insist upon organising their life according to *their* laws that endorse the seclusion of women, daily prayer, etc., and collide with the secular, liberal principles governing the social and political life of Western democracies. Indeed, the reaction of immigrants who are followers of orthodox Islam reveals the limits to the rhetoric on incorporation of migrants, at least some of them.

Furthermore, the reception of Islam in Western democracies is double-edged. On the one hand, several Western European states are working to allow some space for Islam within national symbols and national institutions (Modood 1997). In some of them Islam is also given high status, for instance in Belgium, Islam was recognised as one of the official state religions as early as 1974. Nevertheless, this religion happens to be perceived as the main threat to what is conceived of as Western civilization, and Muslims happen to be portrayed as 'invaders' or alien 'others' also by 'the commentators in the quality media and many social scientists' (Rex 1996).[16] This indicates that, despite incorporation efforts, Islam remains an alien set of ideas within Western receiving societies. However, 'At least in Britain, committed Christians are less likely to express prejudice against Muslims than are nominal Christians and agnostics/atheists' (ibid.). Thus the alienation does not stem from rejection by other believers, i.e. Christians, it is rather a reaction to the orthodox Muslims' will and attempt to organise the whole, not only private, life according to Islam's prescriptions that clashes with the liberal principles of the secular state. On the other hand, the committed advocates of these principles tend to perceive them as a 'secular religion' while remaining intolerant of any religion in the public sphere. Actually, the inflows of alien cultures have taken place 'at a time when industrial countries have lost confidence in the values of their own societies, the worth of their own nation or the truths of their own religion' (Coleman 1994: 43). Another aspect of this profound cultural change has been a development of a civil society founded upon liberal principles, and this transformation has not eased the concurrent integration of the bearers of distant cultures. The liberal principles of the 'open society' agreed upon as the modern creed of secularised democracies that are to be accepted by the newcomers *collide* with traditional values safeguarded by a number of migrant communities. The latter praise their non-Christian religion and traditional principles of conduct, and openly oppose the liberal, secularised, and 'post-Christian' culture of modern democracies. It follows that the modern creed of liberal democracies and the liberal political culture alone may not be able to bind multi-ethnic and multicultural states together, particularly when faced with the various forms of religious fundamentalism.

Currently however, a desire to *remake* secular societies in order to integrate cultural differences, especially the religious ones, according to 'the plural state' ideal prescription, is hardly visible. On the contrary, very recently a hint appears suggesting a swift withdrawal from the multicultural policy, as one British Minister said 'it was time to go "beyond multiculturalism" for a debate on essential British values' (Ahmed *et al.* 2001: 7). Nevertheless, the conceivable abandonment of multicultural policy will not change a well-established fact of ethnic and cultural pluralism of British and other European receiving societies. Indeed, the end result of the 'multicultural experiment' remains unforeseen. Besides, dilemmas with the governance of ethnic and cultural pluralism pose a challenge to the Europeanisation process, understood as a search for a common, unique European creed. The evolution of policy aiming at exposing and elevating the national values and creed vis-à-vis distant cultures will very probably affect the Europeanisation process. Whether it will obstruct or work in accordance with the process relates to our construction of Europeanness, specifically it depends on the space allowed for national creeds.

## Migration – cultural diversification – Europeanisation

The socio-cultural consequences of international migration present a real not imaginary challenge to the European nation-states that are simultaneously undergoing the process of integration. It pertains to cultural coherence, national identity, the democratic system, and due to the threat of global terrorism, to the security of the receiving nation-states. The shared intense concern underpins the development of a common European Union immigration and asylum regime, along with the decrease in internal border controls; it makes EU partners inter-dependent and united against outside intruders. This strategy and policy materialises the 'Fortress Europe' metaphor, having its continuation and supplement in a xenophobic mentality that reveals itself in portraying immigrants as cultural or racial 'others'. However, the 'othering', marginalisation, and racialisation practices do not relate to migrants from the European Union member states but to the newcomers from outside the EU whose inflows intensify. Indirectly, the practices of 'othering' or racialisation of immigrants from distant cultures suggests that their presence serves to reconstruct and explicate national identity vis-à-vis the 'aliens' (that corresponds with the change in multicultural policy, mentioned above). But the very fact that these practices do not relate to migrants from the EU member states indicate that they also involve the discovering of European identity vis-à-vis non-European immigrants, and perhaps migrants from the other parts of Europe seen as inferior to 'the West' or 'Europe'. It follows that the international inflows may help establish European identity or the Western European identity and hence, augment the Europeanisation process.

Academic commentary seems to arrive at the consensus that the European Union should be viewed as transnational regime that locates itself in between a confederation of states and a federal state. This involves a problem of the modes and degrees of the Europeanisation of the nation-states and national identities, that is, the European system of nation-states reorganisation, and the redefinition of national identities. Europeanness, both as an ideal to be matched and the emerging reality that manifests itself on an identity level, has been defined in a number of ways. It has been seen as either an additional or a secondary layer to the basic or primary national identity, or as a new layer that replaces the pre-existing national identities. The third assessment, probably the closest to reality and hence the more accurate, holds that Europeanness will be an ever-developing hybrid or configuration of European and national components. In this context, an argument about the plurality of identities (Burke 1992) seems particularly valid.

> The term 'identity' should be used in the plural. Popular identities included a sense of membership in a nation, a region, a town or village, a craft, and finally a class. . . . I would prefer to argue that identities are multiple and fluid or "negotiable" and that the same individual or group may privilege one identity over another according to the situation and the moment.
>
> (Burke 1992: 305)

As seen, the proposed interpretation views an identity actually as a 'kit' of identities, any of which may be used for different purposes and at different, suitable situations. If accepted, this approach recognises Europeanness as just a new item in the 'kit', coexisting alongside other identities, not a dominant identity that embeds or constitutes a frame of reference for other identities (class, national, etc.). In turn, Europeanisation viewed from this perspective appears as a process that enhances the enlargement, without causing a *thorough* reconfiguration of national identity. In other words, Europeanisation works towards the diversification of national identity, enriching the existing identity with a new component – the European identity. The process coincides with the merits of the two current transnational processes: European integration and international migration that restore the structural and cultural pluralism of European civilization.

This chapter has investigated the ways in which international inflows have reshaped the European receiving nation-states by bringing about cultural diversification. As presented in previous sections, international inflows diversify the receiving and sending nations' culture in two basic ways, making them more heterogeneous, less coherent, and less unique. First, they bring about the coexistence of ethnic groups and cultures within a nation-state; second they cause a meshing of cultures, or viewed from another angle, a pluralisation of the host's or the receiving society's culture. Obviously also the latter instance relates to the Europeanisation process which has been discussed.

The appearance of ethnic restaurants, the ethnic forms of entrepreneurship (e.g. bazaars), ethnic schools, societies, districts, etc., that shape the landscape of our cities poses the question of whether all these ethnic artefacts are 'ours'? That is, whether they are part and parcel of our European, German, Greek, etc., society? Any answer requires justification that cannot be offered without referring to the national and European identities. The revival of racist prejudice directed towards immigrants confronts members of the receiving society with uneasy questions that also involve reference to collective identity: Do we agree with it? Are we racists? What are we to undertake to avoid it? The conversions to Islam pose another issue: whether the converts still belong to 'us' or whether they have become alien because of the religious conversion. Hence, who are we? Acceptance and inclusion of the converts can be equated to a 'domestication' of their new denomination, that is with admitting that the French (Dutch, Danish, etc.) and generally the European may be Muslim. Their exclusion necessitates justification, again, impossible without direct reference to the national and European identities, and to the national and European creed(s). Even the explicit discounting of any religion as marginal or not valid for modern national and European identities requires allusion to these identities. Needless to say, as all the stated examples call for reference to national and European identities, they may also imply their rethinking and possibly reformulation.

Cultural diversification resulting from international inflows, among others, adding the new, alien ingredients, such as Islam, into receiving societies, and augmenting the revival of fallacious ideas such as 'the new racism', prompts the explicit formulation and explication of the European creed. A confrontation with the alien values and our own fallacious ideas necessitates the clarification of this creed that would form a content of the European identity, and a point of reference for national identities. It raises the issue of the tradition and heritage of European civilization. No other issue is more fundamental than the recollection of the European humanism – that implies liberal principles, but not the other way around – and its philosophical and ethical background. The liberal principles extracted from European humanism that organise the political, economic and social realms of secularised European democracies, do not, by themselves, stand for European humanism nor the European civilization creed. Undoubtedly, the future of European civilization – confronted on its own grounds by distant cultures – depends upon the kind of response given to this issue, that also forms the chief aspect of the Europeanness as broadly discussed and Europeanisation processes.

## Notes

1 In this text I adopt the understanding, well established in social anthropology, of 'culture' as composed of material, social and symbolic aspects.
2 'The following . . . types of migration flows moving across the new migratory space of the CEE region have been distinguished: westward directed transit migrations, legal and illegal; westward directed labour migrations, legal and illegal; westward directed emigration; westward directed involuntary migration of refugees and asylum seekers; the regional petty-trade mobility, generally illegal; the regional labour migration, both legal and undocumented; the eastward petty-trade mobility; and the eastward labour movements' (Romaniszyn 1997: 27–8).
3 By 'economic culture' I understand organisation and work patterns, style of consumption and management.

4 For instance, for the year 1997, the turnover at the Białystok bazaar was circa 550 million Polish złoty, at the Warsaw bazaar it was 1.9 billion, and at the Łódź bazaar 3.4 billion (Romaniszyn 2000a: 99). Since 1998, due to the economic turbulence in Russia and the visa requirement introduced by Polish authorities, trade at the bazaars has radically declined.

5 It is agreed that women's migration has intensified in the last decades which compels some authors to assert the 'feminisation' of the recent international inflows. Already in 1984 there were about 3 million women in Europe born outside the frontiers of their present country of residence.

6 This was carried out in Poland, the Czech and Slovak Republics, Hungary, Bulgaria, Romania, Slovenia, Croatia, Byelorussia and Ukraine.

7 'The transformation of immigrant groups into new ethnic minorities is not inevitable. . . . But the experience of discrimination and racism in western European countries forced immigrants to constitute their own communities and to define their group boundaries in cultural terms' (Castles 1993: 28).

8 Other categories of ethnic communities distinguished by Riggs (1991: 449) are the minority ethnic community, majority ethnic community, and dominant ethnic community.

9 J. Habermas, *Die Einbeziehung des Anderen: Studien zur politishen Theorie*, Frankfurt/Main, 1996, as quoted in John Brady (1997: 8–9).

10 An interpretation offered by J. Rex as noted in Modood (1997: 16).

11 'Denial of equal rights constitutes a challenge for democracy, if one takes into account also the restrictive naturalization policies, that do not allow a considerable part of the actual population to have his voice over the public issues' (Katrougalos 1997: 14–15).

12 It is worth noticing that such a language and way of portraying ethnic minorities was introduced in Canada in the 1970s when the Canadian multicultural ideology and policy was implemented.

13 As I have stated elsewhere, a patron–client relationship may well be applied to the interpretation of the immigrant–host state relation (Romaniszyn 2002). It denotes expectations on the part of immigrants of services from the host state, and the conviction, on the part of the recipient country, that these expectations are to be fulfilled.

14 This is likely to happen when migration links a traditional society, with its principles and rules, with those of a modern post-industrial one (Coleman 1994: 71).

15 The cited research was carried out in Vienna in the mid-1990s.

16 As quoted in Modood (1997: 4).

# References

Ahmed, K., Hinsliff G. and Morgan, O. (2001) 'Plan to end forced marriages', *Guardian Weekly*, 8–14 November.

Albrow, M. (1997) 'Travelling beyond local cultures', in J. Eade (ed.) *Living the Global City: Globalization as a Local Process*, London: Routledge.

Bilsborrow, R. and Zlotnik, H. (1992) 'Preliminary report of the United Nations Expert Group meeting on the feminization of international migration', *International Migration Review* 26, 1.

Bjorgo, T. (1997) '"The invaders", "the traitors" and "the resistance movement": the extreme Right's conceptualisation of opponents and self in Scandinavia', in T. Modood and P. Werbner (eds) *The Politics of Multiculturalism in the New Europe: Racism, Identity and Community*, London and New York: Zed Books.

Bocock, R. (1993) *Consumption*, London: Routledge.

Boyd, M. (1989) 'Family and personal networks in international migration: recent developments and new agendas', *International Migration Review* 23, 3.

Brady, J. (1997) 'Dangerous foreigners: the discourse of threat and the German–immigrant public sphere in Berlin', paper presented to the ESA conference on 'Inclusions – exclusions', 27–30 August, Essex, UK.

Burke, P. (1992) 'We, the people: popular culture and popular identity in modern Europe', in S. Lash and J. Friedman (eds) *Modernity and Identity*, Oxford: Blackwell.

Carens, J. (1987) 'Aliens and citizens: the case for open borders', *The Review of Politics* 47.

Castles, S. (1993) 'Migrations and minorities in Europe. Perspectives for the 1990s: eleven hypotheses', in J. Solomos and J. Wrench (eds) *Racism and Migration in Western Europe*, Oxford: Berg.

Castles, S. and Miller, M. (1993) *The Age of Migration: International Population Movements in the Modern World*, London: Macmillan.

Cohen, R. (1991) 'East–West and European migration in a global context', *New Community* 18, 1.

Coleman, D. (1994) 'International migrants in Europe: adjustment and integration processes and responses', in M. Macura and D. Coleman (eds) *International Migration: Regional Processes and Responses*, Economic Studies no. 7, New York and Geneva: UN.

Daly, F. and Barot, R. (1999) 'Economic migration and social exclusion: the case of Tunisians in Italy in the 1980s and 1990s', in F. Anthias and G. Lazaridis (eds) *Into the Margins: Migration and Exclusion in Southern Europe*, Aldershot and Brookfield, USA: Ashgate.

Entzinger, H. (1990) 'The lure of integration', *Journal a Plusieurs Voix* 4.

Erman, T. and Turan, N. (1997) 'The role of the neighborhood in the inclusion/exclusion of (im)migrants', paper presented to the conference on 'Inclusion – exclusion', 27–30 August, Essex, UK.

European Commission (1997) *Eurobarometer: Racism and Xenophobia in Europe*, Luxembourg: Office for the Official Publications of the European Communities.

Fassmann, H. and Munz, R. (1994) 'European East–West migration, 1945–1992', *International Migration Review* 28, 3.

Gabaccia, D. (1994) *From the Other Side: Women, Gender, and Immigrant Life in the U.S. 1820–1990*, Bloomington and Indianapolis: Indiana University Press.

Gmelch, G. (1987) 'Return migration to rural Ireland', in H. Buechler and J. Buechler (eds) *Migrants in Europe: The Role of Family Labour and Politics*, New York: Greenwood Press.

Haerpfer, C. and Wallace, C. (1997) 'Changing attitudes to migrants and ethnic minorities in East-Central Europe', paper presented to the conference on 'Migration from Middle and East to West European countries/Migration between Middle and East European countries', Frankfurt/Oder, September.

Hannerz, U. (1990) 'Cosmopolitans and locals in world culture', in M. Featherstone (ed.) *Global Culture*, London: Sage Publications.

Jaakkola, M. (1995) 'Polarization of Finns' attitudes to refugees and other immigrants', paper presented to the ESA conference on 'European societies: fusion or fission?', Budapest, 30 August–2 September.

Joly, D. (1996) *Haven or Hell? Asylum Policies and Refugees in Europe*, London: Macmillan.

Katrougalos, G. (1997) 'Refugees, illegal immigrants and citizenship rights in the European south', paper presented to the conference on 'Non-military aspects of security in southern Europe: migration, employment and labour market', 19–21 September, Santorini, Greece.

Kołakowski, L. (1990) *Cywilizacja na ławie oskarżonych, Warsaw: Res Publica*.

Kuijsten, A. (1994) 'International migration in Europe: patterns and implications for receiving countries', in M. Macura and D. Coleman (eds) *International Migration: Regional Processes and Responses*, Economic Studies no. 7, New York and Geneva: UN.

Kurti, L. (1997) 'Globalisation and the Discourse of Otherness in the "New" Eastern and Central Europe', in T. Modood and P. Werbner (eds) *The Politics of Multiculturalism in the New Europe: Racism, Identity and Community*, London and New York: Zed Books.

Macura, M. (1994) 'Overview', in M. Macura, and D. Coleman (eds) *International Migration: Regional Processes and Responses*, Economic Studies no. 7, New York and Geneva: UN.

Macura, M. and Coleman, D. (eds) (1994) *International Migration: Regional Processes and Responses*, Economic Studies no. 7, New York and Geneva: UN.

Modood, T. (1997) 'Introduction: the politics of multiculturalism in the New Europe', in T. Modood and P. Werbner (eds) *The Politics of Multiculturalism in the New Europe: Racism, Identity and Community*, London and New York: Zed Books.

Morokvasic, M. (1984) 'Birds of passage are also women', *International Migration Review* 18, 4.

Nieuwkerk, K. van (2000) 'Symbolic migrants: Dutch female converts to Islam', a paper presented to the EASA conference on: 'Crossing categorical boundaries: religion as politics/politics as religion', 26–9 July, Kraków, Poland.

Okólski, M. (1999) 'Migration pressures on Europe', in D.J. van de Kaa, H. Leridon, G. Gesano and M. Okólski (eds) *European Populations: Unity in Diversity*, Dordrecht: Kluwer Academic Publishers.

—— (2000) 'Recent trends and major issues in international migration: Central and East European perspectives', *International Social Science Journal* 165, 3.

Pike, K. (1967) *Language in Relation to a Unified Theory of the Structure of Human Nature*, The Hague: Mouton & Co.

Rath, J. (1993) 'The ideological representation of migrant workers in Europe: a matter of racialisation?', in J. Solomos and J. Wrench (eds) *Racism and Migration in Western Europe*, Oxford: Berg.

Rex, J. (1996) *Ethnic Minorities in the Modern State*, London: Macmillan.

Riggs, F. (1991) 'Ethnicity, nationalism, race, minority: a semantic/onomantic exercise (part two)', *International Sociology* 6, 4.

Ritzer, G. (1996) *The McDonaldization of Society*, Thousand Oaks: Pine Forge Press.

Romaniszyn, K. (1997) 'Current migration in Central and Eastern Europe', Working Paper no. 15, Warsaw: ISS Warsaw University.

—— (1999a) 'Cultural implications of modern international migrations – an outline', *Studia Polonijne* 20.

—— (1999b) 'The presence of the Polish undocumented in Greece in the perspective of European unification', in F. Anthias and G. Lazaridis (eds) *Into the Margins: Migration and Exclusion in Southern Europe*, Aldershot and Brookfield, USA: Ashgate.

—— (2000a) 'Towards cultural diversification in Poland: the effects of transition from "closed" to "open" society', in J. Dacyl and C. Westin (eds) *Governance of Cultural Diversity: Selected Aspects*, Stockholm: UNESCO/CEIFO.

—— (2000b) 'Clandestine labour migration from Poland to Greece, Spain and Italy: anthropological perspectives', in R. King, G. Lazaridis and C. Tsardanidis (eds) *Eldorado or Fortress? Migration in Southern Europe*, London: Macmillan Press.

—— (2001) 'International migration as a challenge to "the cultural status quo" of the receiving societies', in J. Dacyl (ed.) *Between Universal Values and Unbounded Diversity*, Stockholm: UNESCO/CEIFO.

Rycke, L. de, Swyngedouw, M. and Phalet, K. (1997) 'The subjective experience of discrimination of Moroccan and Turkish immigrants in Brussels', paper presented to the ESA conference on 'Inclusions – exclusions', 27–30 August, Essex, UK.

Schama, S. (1995) *Landscape and Memory*, New York: Alfred A. Knopf.

Solomos, J. and Wrench, J. (1993) 'Race and racism in contemporary Europe', in J. Solomos and J. Wrench (eds) *Racism and Migration in Western Europe*, Oxford: Berg.

Triandafyllidou, A. (2000) 'Racists? Us? Are you joking?' in R. King, G. Lazaridis and C. Tsardenidis (eds) *Eldorado or Fortress? Migration in Southern Europe*, London: Macmillan Press.

Wieviorka, M. (1994) 'Racism in Europe: unity and diversity', in A. Rattansi and S. Westwood (eds) *Racism, Modernity and Identity: On the Western Front*, Cambridge: Polity Press.

Wyman, M. (1993) *Round-Trip to America: The Immigrants Return to Europe, 1880–1930*, Ithaca and London: Cornell University Press.

# Part II

# Europeanisation, nations and collective identities

# 7 European East–West integration, nation-building and national identities

## The reconstruction of German–Polish relations

*Willfried Spohn*

## Introduction

Since the collapse of the Soviet Empire and the communist regimes in Central and Eastern Europe German–Polish relations have experienced an enormous improvement and represent a cornerstone of the progressive process of European East–West integration and the evolving Eastern enlargement of the European Union.[1] The recognition of the Western Polish Odra–Neisse border by the German government, initiated by the new *Ostpolitik* of the West German Chancellor Willy Brandt and followed and finalised by Helmut Kohl, was one of the crucial pre-conditions for German unification in 1990 and conversely opened the door for the support of German unification by the new democratic government under Lech Walesa of independent Poland. On this basis, a 'special partnership' between Germany and Poland has developed. United Germany has promoted itself as the foremost advocate for Poland's accession to the European Union, whereas Poland has learned to accept Germany as the most important gateway to its return to Europe. The planned accession of Poland to the European Union in 2004 will finally complete the common integration of both Germany and Poland in a uniting Europe.

From the perspective of the long-term asymmetric, conflictive and finally destructive history between the two nations, this change in German–Polish relations can be seen as an almost miraculous achievement. But after the particularly ruinous destruction of Poland by Nazi Germany and the following loss of the Eastern German territories through the Western relocation of Poland, coming to terms with this traumatic history on both sides was one of the main moral forces in the renewal of German–Polish relations.[2] The reconciliation between the two nations was initiated by small circles of German and Polish religious and cultural intellectuals. It found increasing resonance within the political leaders and broader strata of the populations and had an important impact on the reconstruction of both countries as independent nation-states. However, it should not be overlooked that the preparation and building of new bilateral relations have been primarily promoted by parts of the elites, whereas other parts of the elites and still broader parts of the populations on both sides are still hesitant or even afraid to accept the enormous geopolitical changes.

In Germany, only one third of the population supports the Eastern enlargement, whereas one half is concerned about increasing economic competition and immigration pressure, particularly from Poland. In Poland also, there is a rising tide against accession to the European Union, with declining levels of support, close to 50 per cent, and rising levels of rejection, close to one third, based on fears of a new domination by Western Europe and particularly by a powerful Germany, and also fears a return of Germans to Polish lands.[3] These concerns and fears on both sides reflect not only the traumas of the recent history between the two nations. They also reflect the reconstruction of traditional centre–periphery relations between Western and Eastern Europe and also between Germany and Poland. Despite the successful reconstruction of the Polish post-communist economy and consolidation of Polish democracy, the traditional economical and political asymmetries and inequalities between Western Europe, Germany and Poland persist. They correspond to a considerable growth of East–West migration of Polish migrant workers, particularly to Germany, which has reached similar proportions to those at the turn to the last century. These political and economic hierarchies also go hand in hand with continuing cultural asymmetries, of feelings of superiority and inferiority complexes and related ethno-national stereotypes.

The Eastern enlargement of the European Union is planned to counteract these structural and cultural asymmetries between Western and Eastern Europe and it should also have an impact on the future development of German–Polish relations. Thus, it can be expected that the Eastern enlargement will diminish the socio-economic inequality between Germany and Poland, reduce the political power hierarchy between the two states and also promote a better cultural understanding between the two nations. However, it is far from clear to what degree the Eastern enlargement will progress as planned or rather involve major economic and social disruptions with negative political and cultural repercussions. Under such unfavourable conditions, there is always the possibility of remobilising traditional ethno-nationalist sentiments on the basis of still persisting centre–periphery structures between the two nations – unless a conscious effort is made to transform the nationalistic sentiments and national identities on both sides in a more transnational and European direction.

In order to assess the actual and potential impact of the persisting centre–periphery structures between Germany and Poland on the development of German–Polish relations in the context of the Eastern enlargement of the European Union, the following contribution will first outline the historical foundations of the two forms of unequal and conflictive types of nation-building and national-identity formation until 1944/5, then characterise the reconstruction of both the German and Polish nation and national identities after the Second World War until 1989/90 and finally analyse the recurrent structural and cultural inequalities in German–Polish relations as challenges to and tasks for the Europeanisation of both nations and national identities in the context of the emerging Eastern enlargement of the European Union.

## Asymmetries and conflicts in two processes of nation-building and national identity formation: historical foundations 1772–1939/45

Within a European typology of state formation and nation-building, Germany and Poland can not only be contrasted to Western Europe but also represent quite opposite types.[4] Whereas in Western Europe the processes of nation-building followed the early formation of states and thus early on enabled a basic congruency between both processes, in Germany and Poland nation-states were formed relatively late and only with considerable discrepancies between state formation and nation-building. In both cases, former Empires predated the formation of nation-states. The first unified German nation-state in 1870/1 was built on the basis of the former Holy Roman Empire of the German Nation consisting of a polycentric form of German-speaking ethnic groups, a fragmented and later centralised form of dynastical territorial states as well as an overarching high culture.[5] After its dissolution in 1803 under the impact of the French revolution and Napoleonic warfare, the formation of the German nation-state developed in a combination of the German Federation under the leadership of the rising Prussian state and an evolving unifying nationalism oscillating between a great-German imperial and small-German national solution. The then found 'small-German' solution of a nation-state materialised by Bismarck, however, comprised German speaking territories under the exclusion of Habsburg Germans and considerable national minorities such as Polish, French and Danish populations and thus still contained an imperial extension. The resulting tensions and conflicts between German imperial nationalism including Habsburg German irredentism and the separating nationalisms of the national minorities within Germany thus remained substantial during the *Kaiserreich* and contributed decisively to the destabilisation of the Weimar Republic and the rise of the Nazi Third Reich.[6]

Also in the Polish case the imperial framework of the early modern Jagiellonian Polish–Lithuanian Commonwealth predated the formation of a Polish nation-state (Davies 1981, 1984). As a multi-national Empire under the leadership of the Polish-speaking aristocracy it included considerable ethnic minorities such as Germans, Jews, White Russians, Ruthenians and Ukrainians. However, through the three partitions in 1772, 1793 and 1795 by the surrounding imperial powers of Prussia, Habsburg and Russia, the Polish–Lithuanian Commonwealth was dissolved and lost its state sovereignty with the short exception of the Warsaw principality in the Napoleonic era between 1806 and 1815. Under imperial domination and deprived of any state institutions, the Polish nation formed on the ruins of the Jagiellonian Empire and in emulation of the Western European nation-states, but due to the suppression of the uprisings in 1831 and 1863, was unable to regain national sovereignty. The foundation of an independent Polish nation-state in 1918 became only possible with the collapse of the three partition powers in the First World War. But also in the Polish case, the imperial legacies renewed in the victory over Soviet Russia in 1920 resulted in a territorial extension beyond a politically limited 'small-Polish' solution and the resulting ethnic and cultural diversity stood in sharp contrast to a culturally more homogeneous and politically more stable nation-state (Krzeminski 1991; Tomaszewski 1993).

As neighbouring countries and with considerably overlapping populations, the construction of culturally homogenous nation-states in Germany as well as Poland included structural problems that became manifest in constant German–Polish tensions and conflicts throughout the nineteenth century and culminated finally in the catastrophe of the twentieth century (Kobylinska *et al.* 1992). These tensions and conflicts did not however develop on equal terms, but were characterised by growing structural asymmetries between the two evolving nations. The annexation of Polish lands by Prussia and Habsburg Austria was the crucial starting point of these asymmetries. But in addition, these asymmetries were sharpened over time by the growing East–Western European socio-economic and political unevenness. This was particularly true for the relationship between Prussia and Polish lands. After the dissolution of the German-Roman Empire, it was precisely Prussia that evolved as the most powerful territorial state in the German regions and became the new political leader for German unification by replacing the traditional Habsburg centre. This political leadership was based not only on the Western extension of Prussia into Germany with the Vienna peace treaty in 1815, but also on the specific modernity of the Prussian state, combining an enlightened absolutism, a centralised state bureaucracy and a modernising reform policy that promoted economic development and capitalist industrialisation and on this basis was able to increase its military and political power (Nipperdey 1987, 1991; Wehler 1987, 1995). This growing power of the Prussian state, on the one hand, enabled the unification of Germany. But on the other, the Polish regions were thus dominated and confronted with an increasingly powerful centre that made any political resistance to it correspondingly impossible.

One of the crucial factors of this evolving military and political power hierarchy between German and Polish lands was the economic development of Germany from a moderately backward economy to a leading economic core in Europe during the nineteenth century. Again, it was the mercantilist developmental policy of the Prussian state – created under the conditions of the particular backwardness of the Prussian lands – that served as a major mechanism of German catching-up modernisation (Spohn 1995). Germany then even overtook first France (with the war won in 1870/71 and the annexation of Alsace-Lorraine), but later also Great Britain at the turn of the century on the basis of the growing economic potential of the new big industries. The Polish lands, particularly in the Prussian zone, participated to a certain degree in this German–Prussian growth dynamic, but more in traditional textile and agrarian than in modern industrial production. As a consequence, the Polish regions – not much less developed at the times of their partition than the Prussian lands – became more and more a backyard of the European and particularly German economy (Berend and Ranki 1982; Berend 1995: 129–50). The economic asymmetry between Germany and Polish lands grew continuously throughout the long nineteenth century and diminished only slightly in the inter-war period in the first half in the twentieth century.

To these political and economic asymmetries should be added the religious and cultural differences and oppositions between Prussian-German and Polish societies (Spohn forthcoming). Of particular importance were the diverging religious developments of both countries with the Protestant Reformation and the Catholic (Counter)Reformation. In Germany, after the forces of the Protestant Reformation and the counterforces of the Catholic Reformation and the resulting European religious wars had found an equilibrium in the Westphalian peace treaty of 1648, a confessional dualism roughly equal in size was established (Evans 1982; Nowak 1995). Following the principle *cuius regio eius religio*, Northern and Eastern Germany became predominantly Protestant, primarily Lutheran and secondarily Calvinist-Reform, whereas Southern and Western Germany remained predominantly Catholic. Many regions were still mixed and became more homogenised only with the rise of regional absolutism. However, Brandenburg/Prussia as well as Saxony as the two adjacent states to Poland turned into almost homogenous Lutheran-Protestant regions. Also in Poland the Protestant Reformation made some inroads insofar as parts of the aristocracy converted to Calvinism and the German minority to Lutheranism (Tazbir 1994: 168–80). But with the escalating conflicts and wars with Protestant Sweden and Brandenburg/Prussia, the partial conversion of the Polish aristocracy to Protestantism came to a halt and the Protestant aristocratic elite reconverted to Catholicism. Thus, at the time of the first partition in 1772, the Polish–Lithuanian Commonwealth consisted of 43 per cent Roman Catholics, 33 per cent Greek Catholics, 10 per cent Christian Orthodox, 9 per cent Jews and 4 per cent Protestant – roughly identical to ethnic divisions (Davies 1981, vol. 1: 162). As a consequence of the partition, however, the multi-religious Polish–Lithuanian Commonwealth was reduced to a primarily Catholic Polish society.

Interwoven with nation-building during the nineteenth century, the resulting religious divergence between Protestant Prussia and Catholic Poland developed into increasing religious and cultural oppositions. In Germany, as a result of national unification under the leadership of Protestant Prussia and the exclusion of Catholic Austria, the previously balanced Catholic–Protestant dualism in German society turned into a Protestant-Lutheran hegemony over minority Catholicism (Spohn 1994: 173–90). This implied, on the one hand, a shifting confessional relation: taking the numbers in 1913, almost two thirds of the German society was Protestant (62 per cent), slightly more than one third was Catholic (35 per cent) and a small minority was Jewish (1 per cent) (Spohn 1994: 181). This meant, on the other, a predominantly Protestant, religious as well as secularised, shape to the German nation-state, with a corresponding discrimination against the less secularised Catholic minority. On the other side, in the Prussian-Polish regions the lack of independent statehood reduced the forces of religious differentiation and secularisation and instead strengthened Catholic integralism (Kriedte 1997: 249–74). In addition, the aristocracy, as the carrier of a state-led and rather secular and enlightened liberal nationalism, became weakened and the Catholic church, as a carrier of a more organic nationalism, became strengthened. The result was a sharp structural as well as cultural opposition between the predominantly

Protestant–secular German state-nation and the state-aspiring Catholic–integralist nation.

The German–Polish ethno-national opposition on the basis of the overlapping settlement structure was thus aggravated by three structural asymmetries between the emerging German and Polish nations: the growing power imbalance between the Prussian-German state and Polish society, the increasing core–periphery relation between the German and Polish economy, and the religious divergence between Protestant Prussia and Catholic Poland. These structural asymmetries also shaped the formation of national identities as well as the self-perception and construction of the other on both sides. From the German perspective, the growing social power and political superiority was based on virtues such as discipline, work and order combined with loyal obedience, cultural education and rational enlightenment. These German self-images corresponded with images of the Polish 'other' such as lack of discipline, laziness, chaos, cultural barbarity and superstitious irrationalism. From the Polish perspective, the Germans represented lack of freedom, personal repression and bureaucratic rule-making, blind obedience, cultural arrogance and amoral rationalism – German images that contrasted to the Polish virtues of freedom, heroism, sacrifice as well as a culture of the heart and religiosity. These cultural binary construction reflected particularly the Protestant–Catholic oppositions.[7] The German-Prussian values represented variations of a Lutheran pietist ethic centring on an inward-directed world piety combining a sense of duty and obedience toward the spheres of work and state. Through these lenses Polish Catholicism represented a clerical, papist, emotional and superstitious popular religion. On the other side, the Polish values formed a variation of a Catholic ethic combining a pragmatic work ethos with marianic expressive symbolism and church-oriented piety. In Polish eyes, German Protestantism appeared heartless, secular and individualistic.

Yet, these religious and cultural perceptions and identities became only mobilised with nation-building and national identity formation (see Hoffmann 1997). In the period from the partition to the French revolution, they were only shared by few members of the aristocratic and middle-class elites, but did not yet have any wider or even nationalistic meaning. In the Napoleonic era, the reorganisation of Germany and the short-lived foundation of the duchy of Warsaw interrupted the crystallising asymmetries. In the restoration era, the religious and cultural oppositions revived, but at the same time, the emerging liberal national movements on both sides also strengthened a sense of equality between the two peoples. The Polish uprising in 1830/1 was accompanied by wide-spread sympathies on the German side, the spring of peoples and the 1848 revolution renewed the mutual support. At the same time, it also revealed the first tensions between the German and Polish and other Slavic national movements and aspirations regarding the future boundaries of the imagined democratic nation-states. But the Polish uprising in 1863, despite the anti-Polish cooperation between Bismarck and Russia, was still followed with positive German sentiments. However, with the foundation of the German Empire these pro-Polish sentiments changed decisively. Now, the Catholics in Germany and the Polish Catholics in particular were increasingly perceived as an internal threat to the newly founded German nation-state. The discrimination against Catholics affected the Polish population in particular and was soon complemented by an intensifying missionising Germanisation policy. This fuelled, on the other side, rising anti-German Polish national sentiments (Hagen 1982; Smith 1995). After the failure of Polish heroic-romantic aristocratic nationalism, however, these Polish national sentiments were increasingly shaped by an organic conception of nation-building in which the Catholic church and Catholic religiosity played a constitutive role.

The defeat of Imperial Germany and the Habsburg Empire in the First World War changed decisively the geopolitical conditions in East Central Europe by (re-)creating an independent Polish nation-state. However, on the basis of the ethnic–national oppositions which had been formed and out-breaking territorial conflicts, the geopolitical changes remained fragile (Winkler 1992: 95–103). On the German side, independent Poland was now primarily seen in purely strategic terms, as a buffer zone against the newly founded Soviet Union, but at the same time the loss of former German, though predominantly Polish-settled, territory particularly contributed to the sense of national humiliation and fuelled feelings of national resentment against Poland.[8] On the other side, the newly independent Polish nation-state used the occasion to claim as in the case of Gdansk/Danzig or Pomerania ancient Polish territory even with a majority of German-speaking or feeling populations. Thus, although most of the territorial disputes were finally solved by referenda, the dominating nationalisms on both sides were not able to compromise. With it, despite the geopolitical changes, the structural and cultural asymmetries between Germany and Poland contributed to the radicalisation of two forms of integral nationalism. On the German side, the rise of national-socialism was accompanied by the change of the traditional cultural asymmetries into racist conceptions of German superiority against Slavic and Polish inferiority. On the Polish side, the rise of an integral cultural nationalism aiming at homogenising the Polish nation and with it Polonising ethnic minorities also contributed to the rise of ethno-national conflicts in the German–Polish border regions (Davies 1981, vol 2: 393–434). In the end, the Hitler–Stalin pact sealed the fate of independent Poland, aiming to recreate the former partition of the Polish state by annihilating the Polish nation.

## Deconstructions and reconstructions of two nations and national identities 1944/5–2000

The Second World War had catastrophic consequences particularly for Poland. After the war the Eastern German regions were transferred to Poland and the Eastern Polish regions occupied by the Soviet Union were annexed. Thus, the war resulted in enormous territorial shifts. The Western relocation of Poland included the loss of about one third of its former territory to the East to the Soviet Union (i.e. Ukraine, Belarus and Lithuania) and compensated for by about one third of its territory from the former Eastern German regions. With this compensation, Germany also lost almost one third of its former pre-war territory. At the same time, the war resulted in monstrous population losses and movements. During the war about 6 million Poles, 3 million ethnic Poles and 3 million Polish Jews, lost their lives. The death toll disproportionately affected the Polish elites, because Nazi Germany and the Soviet Union especially aimed to erase the leadership of the Polish nation. After the war almost 2 million Poles were expelled from the Eastern territories and resettled in the Western Polish former Eastern German regions. According to German and Polish numbers (which still conflict), of the 10 million former German inhabitants of these regions about 7 million fled or were expelled, of whom about one half were refugees escaping the Red Army and the other half expelled by the Polish administration; 2 million were killed, about 1.6 million of whom during expulsion; and about 1 million (though then diminishing) stayed as 'autochthonous' citizens within post-war Poland.[9]

These enormous territorial and demographic changes had two major interrelated structural implications for the post-war reconstruction of both nations. The first implication was that two nations historically overlapping in their ethnic settlement structures and conflictively entangled in the process of nation-building became finally separated. Though this national disentanglement included enormous suffering and caused lasting traumas on both sides, this separation also opened the long-term possibility to reconstruct both nations and the relations between them in new ways.[10] At the same time, the emerging bloc confrontation between the victorious allies over defeated Nazi Germany defined specific international conditions under which the reconstructions of both nations and their mutual relations took place. The two nations did not develop in the form of two independent states, but under the respective hegemony of the Western and Eastern bloc. Germany deprived of its independent nationhood became divided in two parts, West Germany in close international integration with and under more indirect supervision by the Western allies, and East Germany under direct military control by the Soviet Union. Poland, despite its belonging to the victorious alliance, also lost its independent nationhood, became subjected to the Soviet Union and forced to be a partner of East Germany in the Soviet interstate system. Under these international conditions, West Germany, defining itself as the legal successor state of the Third Reich and the major recipient of the Eastern refugees and expellees, did not officially recognise and only gradually accepted the loss of its Eastern territories. By contrast, East Germany was forced by the Soviet Union to recognise the Odra–Neisse border but was reluctant to accept it. Poland, in recompense for the enormous losses, took possession of the former Eastern German regions, but at the same time remained basically insecure in its national territory as long as West Germany did not recognise its international legality. This national insecurity made Poland inversely dependent on the 'protection' by the Soviet Union.

The second implication of these territorial and demographic changes was that each nation became basically congruent with the emerging political state structures. In the case of Germany, the loss of the Eastern territories as well as the flight and expulsion of the German populations from their Eastern German and Eastern European homelands, implied a decisive break with its former pattern of nation-building. For the first time in German history, the settlement structure of the German-speaking population found itself in a basic congruence with territorial and political boundaries. Through the resettlement of most Germans from Eastern Europe to the West and their integration into the three successor states of the Nazi-German Empire, the Federal Republic, the GDR and Austria, any extraterritorial lands with potentially irredentist German populations were gone. As a consequence, the past imperial oscillations of a German nation-state between a political and territorial limitation and an imperial extension had lost its social basis. This also entailed a solution to the past contradictions between the German *Kulturnation*, which aimed at the political inclusion of all German-speaking populations, and a German political nation restrained to a civic–political inclusion within the limitations of a German state.[11] In the Polish case also, the shift of the Polish settlement space to the West, the loss of the Eastern Polish mixed areas and the expulsion of Germans in the Western regions, resulted in a basic correspondence between nation and state. As in the German case, a final break with the imperial legacies through the outcomes of the Second World War had materialised, even though some problem zones of ethno-national conflicts still affected Polish post-war history (Davies 1981, vol. 2: 556–633). So the Polish minority in Lithuania created some irritations between Poland and Lithuania. More troublesome were the postwar ethnic cleansing and repression of Ukrainians in South-Eastern Poland. And also the remaining German minority faced continuing discrimination and assimilation pressure.

Separated by the population resettlements, cut off by the iron curtain between East and West, and in addition with a tightly controlled border between East Germany and Poland, the two nations underwent their reconstruction along two isolated paths. The reconstruction of the German nation-state proceeded for over 40 years in a divided form of two states, two asymmetric democratisation processes and two partial collective identities without, however, dissolving the inherited common nation. In West Germany, a democratic constitutional political system became institutionalised, overcoming the past authoritarian and totalitarian forms of state centralism by a pluralistic, federal and increasingly participatory structure.[12] With it, the authoritarian and collectivist nationalism of the past was transformed into a civic and pluralist form of political identity and the inherited cultural nationalism became increasingly replaced by a moral consciousness to come to terms with the past. In East Germany, by contrast, the Soviet communist system reproduced the authoritarian and totalitarian state structures of the past in a new form.[13] With it, also authoritarian and collectivist forms of nationalism and political identity were reproduced, but at the same time dissident-socialist and liberal-democratic attitudes oriented to West Germany developed as a *niche* counterculture. In a parallel movement, the inherited cultural nationalism became divided between the predominant affirmative antifascist claim to have overcome the past and the subterranean critical consciousness that the socialist system had only partially fulfilled that claim. The democratic-national revolution of the GDR made the socialist system finally collapse and the unification of Germany replaced it with the West German constitutional and federal democratic institutions. On this basis, the two political identities started to fuse with each other in a more pluralist national identity, even though still marked by remaining East–West distinctions.

The reconstruction of the Polish nation-state under the communist regime imposed by the Soviet Union renewed, in a sense, the peripheral and dependent situation of the Polish nation before the First World War. But this time, the Polish nation was not partitioned, the Soviet Union acknowledged the existence of Polish nationhood, and the communist regime allowed for the construction of a Polish state with its own administrative bureaucracy, legal system as well as police and army forces.[14] Still, the Polish communist regime only came into existence due to Soviet military occupation, the non-recognition of the Polish exile government, the repression of the independent Polish national movement and resistance army and the instrumentalisation of the Polish communist party. As a consequence, the Polish state developed in a deep rift, estranged from Polish society and the nation, even though the communists, alarmed by continuing resistance and upheaval, accommodated the Polish nation and Polish nationalism. The most important counterpower to the communist regime became the Polish Catholic Church, forcing the ruling communists to make important concessions in economic, social and religious matters and thus preserving a certain, even though limited, social space for an independent civil society (Morawska 1987). Under its protection, there also developed the Social Catholic *Solidarność* movement, combining an independent workers' movement and organisation with dissident and liberal currents of intellectuals. As an uncontrollable and widening mass movement, it substantially contributed to the erosion of the downfall of the Soviet communist bloc as well as to the transition to democracy in Poland itself. At the same time, it also contributed to the specific shape of the post-communist Polish democratic system: a still wide-spread identification with the Polish nation and civil society and a continuing distrust of the Polish state and political establishment.

The separated reconstruction of the two nation-states also included a separated development of the German and Polish economies. On the one hand, West Germany with its post-war 'economic miracle' very quickly resumed the former German position of relative economic dominance compared to other West European economies. This was aided particularly by the fact that the major part of the former German industrial economy (still relatively intact) belonged to West Germany, that most of the refugees and expellees settled in West Germany and that the West German economy could develop in competitive interconnection with European and world markets. In contrast, the East German economy, cut off from its former markets and drained by continuing labour emigration, started with considerable disadvantages. After closing its borders, however, the GDR state's centralised economy advanced to become one of the most developed economies within the Soviet bloc (Berghahn 1987; Spohn 1995). On the other hand, the Polish economy had suffered most by the destruction of the Second World War and its economic reconstruction and development lagged behind the East German economy. At the same time, Poland supported by the state's centralised economic policy experienced a leap forward in industrialisation and urbanisation (Hoensch 1990: 300–57). With the collapse of Soviet communism, the East German and Polish state centralised economies also collapsed, unable to compete with the developed Western post-industrial economies. The East German economy now became a highly subsidised neo-mercantilist annex of the West German and European economy, whereas Poland managed a rather neo-liberal transformation to a capitalist market economy (Poznanski 1993).

The separated course of the two nations implied, moreover, a considerable change in their religious and cultural structures. In West Germany, on the one hand, the former Protestant hegemony over the Catholic minority became transformed to a balanced dualism between Protestantism and Catholicism. To this contributed not only the separation from East Germany with its overwhelmingly Protestant regions but also the progressive secularisation process, weakening the former religious oppositions within German society, and in addition, as a reaction to the Nazi catastrophe, a strengthening ecumenical orientation of both confessions in the desire to overcome the former ideological and religious conflicts (Daiber 1995). In East Germany, by contrast, there remained primarily Protestant regions, reducing the former opposition to Catholicism to an irrelevance. At the same time, the secularisation process was particularly strong, due not only to the enforced secularisation from above but also to the pronounced proclivity of German Protestantism to secular state socialism (Pollack 1994). On the other hand, in Poland, Catholicism became even strengthened due to the national resistance of the Catholic Church to the imposed atheistic secularism (Luks 1997: 234–48; Morawska 1995: 47–75). As a consequence, the secularisation process characteristic for industrialising Catholic countries in Europe remained extremely weak. As a result, with the collapse of communism, unified Germany had turned into a rather secular and ecumenical society with a considerably weakened anti-Catholicism, whereas Poland remained a Catholic country with high religiosity, but at the same time with less virulent anti-Protestantism.

After the traumatic separation of the German and Polish nation and with their isolated reconstruction as nation-states, economies and cultures, the German–Polish post-war relations re-emerged in rather hesitant and ambiguous ways (Jakobsen 1992: 395–401; Rosenthal 1976). The first post-war decades until the 1960s were still overshadowed by the ethnic and nationalistic conflicts of the Second World War and its aftermath. The West German Christian-Democratic led governments under Adenauer, Erhard and Kiesinger still upheld the borders of the German Reich of 1937, nourished German claims to the lost East German territories and defined their legal status against the Western and Soviet views as under provisional and temporary Polish administration. They were influenced particularly by the vocal expellee organisations and their declared aim to regain their lost homelands. In addition, in East Germany, despite the official recognition of the Odra–Neisse border, these attitudes remained influential and were supported by continuing border conflicts. On the Polish side, the official West German position enhanced the fears of losing the former East German territories, invigorated the legitimacy claims that Poland had regained its Western ancient Piast territories, and inflamed the accusations of German imperialist revanchism.

These official positions were however gradually undermined by a moral reassessment of the past, the guilt feelings on both sides and the wish to overcome the past conflicts and atrocities. In Germany, the guilt declaration of both Churches created an opening and the emerging Holocaust debate and policy of recompensation also opened the way for a moral reassessment of German relations to Eastern Europe and particularly Poland. In Poland, the request for forgiveness by the Catholic Church broke the official silence. Bi-national networks such as *Aktion Sühnezeichen* built bridges over the abyss between both peoples. On this basis, in the decades from 1970 to 1990, the new *Ostpolitik* of the Social Democratic government – symbolised in Brandt's kneeling in front of the Warsaw ghetto memorial – emerged, opened the official acknowledgement of the German–Polish Odra–Neisse border, and found its conclusion in Chancellor Kohl's official recognition of this border with German unification. And inversely, the Polish government under Gierek and Jaruzelski began new relations with the West German government, leading to intergovernmental contacts, trade and cultural agreements and so prepared the support for German unification with the collapse of communism.

## European East–West integration and the transformation of German–Polish relations, 1990–2002 and beyond

The collapse of communism in Central and Eastern Europe did not only mean the reconstruction of independent nation-states, the transition to democratic regimes and the development of market societies. It also meant a geopolitical sea-change reconnecting and reintegrating Western and Eastern Europe through the progressive reconstitution of a common European market economy, a European pluralistic inter-state system and a multiple European culture. A major vehicle of this European East–West integration is and will be the extension of the West European integration project to the East. Within this geopolitical context, the isolated reconstruction of state and nation in Germany and Poland came to an end and a growing interconnection of both societies developed. At the same time, along with this growing inter-societal and inter-cultural interweaving, the critical question arises to what degree the traditional structural and cultural asymmetries between the two societies have also become reconstituted, to what extent they have been changed through the social and cultural developments in the second half of the twentieth century and particularly in the last decade, and what potential impact the Eastern enlargement of the European Union will have on the still existing asymmetries?

On the basis of the first mutual reconciliation moves and the final recognition between Germany and Poland, the German Polish relations have developed during the decade into a so-called 'special relationship' (Bingen 1997). After the atrocities of the past, the evolution of this special German–Polish relationship is one of the miraculous twists in twentieth century Europe. Since 1990, bi-lateral visits between the two governments have been made on a regular basis. They were accompanied by important symbolic gestures such as the visit of President Herzog to the fiftieth anniversary of the Warsaw uprising or the invitation of foreign minister Bartoszewski to the German parliament at the fiftieth anniversary of the end of the Second World War. Military and police cooperation, common manoeuvres of the two armies and common training of police units from both sides were carried out. Economic cooperation, technical and financial aid as well as the creation of a special Odra–Neisse border region accompanied the growing economic liberalisation and interconnection between the two countries. There also evolved a new cultural exchange in the form of contacts between intellectuals and artists, cooperation between academic and cultural institutions as well as expanding visits and tourism. On this basis, the German government offered special support for Poland's accession to the European Union and conversely also the Polish government accepted Germany as its major partner on its way to European Union membership.

Underneath this governmental policy level, there evolved an increasing inter-connection between both societies through growing economic exchange in commercial trade, capital flows and labour migration. One indicator of the growing economic exchange between Germany and Poland is the evolving import/export structure of the Polish economy. In 2000, Polish overall imports reached a total of $48.9 billion, concentrating primarily on machine tools, electrical goods and automobiles (38.4 per cent) as well as chemicals and chemical products (17.5 per cent), whereas Polish exports consisted of $31.7 billion, focusing also on machine tools, electrical goods and automobiles (30.4 per cent) as well as leather goods and textiles (12.7 per cent) and metal goods (12.7 per cent), whereby the import share from Germany with 23.9 per cent and the export share to Germany with 34.9 per cent, was by far the highest as compared to other European countries (von Baratta 2002: 642). These figures show a certain asymmetry regarding the export/import ratio as well as the composition of goods. This economic asymmetry is even more marked regarding the flows of foreign capital investments with $10.8 billion, whereby US capital is leading in corporate firm investments and German capital in middle-sized firm investments.[15] Foreign capital is particularly attracted by qualified and less expensive labour, as well as by the expanding Eastern European markets. And inversely, Polish labour migration has resumed to pre-First World War levels of about 1 million, of which 200,000 are in the form of legal contracts and the rest undocumented, attracted by considerably higher German wage levels (Morawska and Spohn 1997). Taken together, these economic asymmetries reconstitute the classical core–periphery pattern. The per-capita income of United Germany in 1992 was, with 24,400 US dollars, about 11 times higher than Poland, with 2,200 US dollars; in addition, the wage level in Germany was about 10 times higher than in Poland.[16] These economic differences were reduced by 1999, to a ratio of 6 in per-capita income between Germany, with 25,600 US dollars and Poland with 4,070 US dollars, and to a ratio of 7 in wage differences between Germany and Poland.[17] This reduction reveals the relative success of the Polish economic transformation, with a considerably higher growth rate, of 4.7 per cent, than the German rate of 1.2 per cent on average from 1990 to 1998 (von Barata 2002: 182 and 642). However, since the Polish economic growth rate is expected to decrease, the marked economic inequality between the German and Polish economy will continue for the foreseeable future.

Thus, although the developmental discrepancy between the German and Polish economies has been somewhat reduced, there is still a marked socioeconomic gap and core–periphery asymmetry between both countries.[18] This economic asymmetry is also the social basis of a parallel asymmetry in the power balance between the two countries. Unified Germany with a population over 80 million, as compared to the other large states in Western Europe such as France, Italy and the UK, all with over 50 million, has won not only more population weight, but also more political weight within and outside the European Union. This increased German weight in international politics has been demonstrated in the new political and military role in the break-up process of Yugoslavia; the decisive support for enhancing European economic integration with the introduction of the Euro; the leading role in promoting the Eastern enlargement of the European Union; the integrative function in reforming the institutional structure of the European Union; the particular relation to post-Soviet Russia as well as the stronger activity in world politics. In contrast, Poland despite its population of almost 40 million and against its self-definition as a crucial nation for the new European architecture, is considered rather as a small state. To be sure, Poland has played an active role towards Lithuania, Byelarus, Ukraine and particularly Russia. But at the same time, the European Union pressures Poland to comply with the Copenhagen criteria as a prerequisite for accession. In this situation, Germany's special support for Poland in the European Union is crucial, but at the same time this increases the dependence of Poland on Germany in its accession to the European Union. However, this renewed power asymmetry between Germany and Poland is not equivalent to the dependent and volatile buffer zone position of inter-war Poland between Weimar Germany and Soviet Russia. Contemporary Germany, even if relatively predominant in its economic and political weight, is tamed by its integration into the European institutional framework and Poland, even if economically still relatively backward and politically merely a small state, has gained its security as a part of the Euro-Atlantic bloc.

Despite the substantially changed European geopolitical structure, however, the re-emerging economic and political power asymmetry between Germany and Poland also contributes to a renewed cultural asymmetry between the two nations. On the German side, the reconstruction of its European core position of relative economic dominance went hand in hand with a cultural self-definition of Germany as the economic model for Europe and the economic locomotive of European integration; this self-image now merges with its special economic modernisation role for Eastern Europe. In a parallel development, the political integration into the European Community was originally defined as a self-protection against Germany's potential renewal as a nationalistic hegemonic power, but this has now changed into an increasing assertion of a leadership function for shaping the European Union and its enlargement to the East. These new aspirations for a European economic and political leadership role are inextricably intertwined with a new self-conscious posture of having come to terms with the past and this moral reassurance also supports the specific reconciliatory mission towards Eastern Europe. With regard to Poland, these German self-images of a remoralised, economic and political model for Europe revitalise the traditional counter-image of Poland as a rather economically backward, politically still unstable and culturally unenlightened society. On the basis of the increased Polish labour migration to Germany, in addition, these images are linked to renewed German stereotypes of the Poles as uncultured and cheap workers and sometimes even as criminals and thieves.[19] Due to the lack of an ethnic and nationalistic conflict as in the past, however, these revived images and stereotypes are less widespread, less powerful, more fluid and also counteracted by more sympathetic and egalitarian images and views.

On the Polish side, the successful role of the *Solidarność* movement, its sacrifice for the Polish nation and its contribution to the fall of communism in Poland and Eastern Europe was accompanied by a revival of Polish heroic-romantic nationalism and its core image of Poland's special mission for Europe. But this important current within Polish national identity was soon eroded along with the crisis-prone economic transformation process, the disintegration of *Solidarność* and the political come-back of the post-communists on the road to a consolidated democracy, the declining role of the intelligentsia and the rejection of the too powerful influence of the Catholic church. In addition, the imagined European mission soon conflicted with the requirement to adopt the *acquis communautaire* of the European Union. Moreover, the highly emotional public debate on *Jedwabne* destroyed the self-image of a solely benign and victimised Polish nation. With all this, the heroic-romantic character traits of Polish identity with its imagined cultural superiority of the Polish nation were substituted by more pragmatic orientations but also a renewed sense of cultural inferiority. This swing of the social psychological pendulum also affected the changing attitudes towards Germany.[20] On the one hand, Germany was accepted and also to a certain extent appreciated as the gateway to Europe and also seen as the model of an economically and politically modern Europe. On the other hand, this also mobilised traditional stereotypes of the conquering and dominating Germans aiming to return to their former lands, sell out Polish farmers, invade Poland by their economic power and use Brussels for these purposes (see Lang 2000). The revival of these traditional stereotypes were in addition supported by the rise of German neo-nationalist xenophobia and the frequent experiences of discrimination of Polish migrant workers in Germany. Still, taking together these positive and negative attitudes, the Polish levels of sympathy for the Germans have risen from marked antipathy in the early 1990s to medium sympathy at the end of the decade (CBOS 2000).

In summarising this complex relational matrix between German and Polish society, it can generally be stated that the historical, structural and cultural asymmetries between the two societies have reappeared to a certain extent, but at the same time they have been crystallising in considerably changed forms. First, the economic core–periphery relation has been revived, but the Europeanisation of the German economy and the expanding dynamics of the Polish economy have changed and diminished the traditional socio-economic inequalities and dependencies. Second, the political power hierarchy has been reconstituted, but the ethnic demographic separation of the two societies, the mutual acknowledgment and again the European mediation of German political hegemony have considerably eroded the former hierarchical nationalistic oppositions. And third, cultural asymmetries have reappeared, but the former religious Protestant–Catholic dualism interwoven with nationalistic missions have lost their force. As a corollary, the revived traditional stereotypes have also remained limited in scope and in addition are counteracted by the political and cultural elites in both countries and their positive relationship to each other. Let us finally ask: how does this inter-societal matrix between Germany and Poland affect the extension of European integration to the East and how will the extending Eastern enlargement of the European Union impact on the further development of this German–Polish relational matrix?

The evolving Eastern enlargement of the European Union is motivated by a variety of imperatives shared by the Western European and Eastern European elites (Spohn 2000). It is supposed to accelerate the reconnection between the two parts of the continent; support an overarching pan-European peace and security zone; create a pan-European economy in order to level down the traditional socio-economic gap; extend the transnational political and legal institutional order of the European Union in order to stabilise the consolidation of the new democracies in Central and Eastern Europe; and improve the cultural understanding between the multiple ethnic and national cultures and identities in Europe. For the actual development and shape of the Eastern enlargement process not only do these guiding imperatives, but also complex structural conditions come into play: the political and economic interests of each country; the reform capacity of the European Union to take in tendentially double as many member states; and the adaptation capacity of the Central and Eastern European accession candidates to comply with the entrance criteria to the European Union. In this overall context of the Eastern enlargement, the German–Polish relations have played a crucial role. Germany as the country directly neighbouring to Central and Eastern Europe has a vital geopolitical and economic interest to integrate these countries in the common European institutional framework. Poland as the biggest East-Central country represents a sort of litmus test of whether or not the Eastern enlargement of the European Union will work.

These converging geopolitical interests also determine the attitudes of the elites to the Eastern enlargement on both sides. A recent survey analysis of German and Polish elite attitudes to the Eastern enlargement of the European Union reveals a considerable degree of convergence, with some characteristic differences (Eberwein and Ecker-Erhardt 2001). On the part of the German elite, 85 per cent support the accession of Poland to the European Union, 11.5 per cent are undecided and only 3.5 per cent are against. On the part of the Polish elite, even 95.2 per cent are in favour of Poland's integration into the European Union and only 1.6 per cent are against, with 3.2 per cent undecided (Eberwein and Ecker-Erhardt 2001: 52). Regarding the potential gains and losses for Poland resulting from the Eastern enlargement, the German and the Polish sides share the expectation that Poland will be recognised fully as part of Europe and will be protected from Russia. But the Polish side sets more hope in influencing European culture and improving Polish living standards; whereas the German side emphasises more the considerable support for Poland from EU funds. Regarding the gains and losses for Germany, both sides agree that Germany will win new Eastern European markets, but the Polish side emphasises more that Germany will win more security at its Eastern border and will gain more political influence in Eastern Europe. And regarding the evaluation of converging European policy domains, both sides support mainly a common security policy, a common currency, a common economic policy, a common immigration policy, a common environmental policy and even a common army, but less a common police force and common citizenship. Yet, the Polish side is more sceptical about a common foreign policy and a common financial policy; whereas the German side is less in favour of a common social policy. On the whole, this study reveals the high convergence of the German and Polish elites regarding their common support for the Eastern enlargement in its general direction and in particular policy issues. The differences are characteristically related to the importance of national culture on the Polish side and its potential threat from West European and German secular culture, and to the importance of economic interests on the German side regarding the expected socio-economic and financial costs of the Eastern enlargement.

These differences at the elite level also reflect the considerable differences and divergences in the attitudes towards the Eastern enlargement between the German and Polish society, among the mass public (Spohn 2000b). On the German side, the general support for the Eastern enlargement, with 36 per cent of the population in 2000, is rather low and the general rejection level, at 43 per cent, rather high as compared to the EU average support of 44 per cent and the rejection rate of 35 per cent (European Commission 2001). These public attitudes reflect particularly the fear of rising immigration, higher unemployment rates, higher financial burdens and the loss of EU subsidies. The German support for Poland follows the general level of support for the Eastern enlargement: in 2000 37 per cent of the German population were for and 46 per cent on average against Poland's accession (European Commission 2001). But there is also a characteristic difference between West and East Germany: only 36 per cent of West Germans, but 42 per cent of East Germans supported Poland's accession; whereas 49 per cent of West Germans, but only 40 per cent of East Germans rejected Poland's accession to the European Union. This difference is related to the stronger persistence of traditional Polish stereotypes in West Germany and the weakening of these stereotypes in East Germany, due to the common communist past. On the Polish side, there was very high general support for the Eastern enlargement throughout the 1990s, with levels above 70 per cent of the population, but the closer the actual accession has been approaching, the more the levels of support have fallen, to as low as 50 per cent, and the rejection levels have been rising up to over 20 per cent.[21] Accession to the EU is particularly supported by the more well-to-do, the new middle class, the educated strata and the younger generation, whereas the peasants, the old working class, the less educated and the older generation have rising fears about the consequences of Poland's accession. At the centre of these public fears are the loss of national independence, the erosion of Catholic values by Western European secularism, the rising economic competition and its negative social consequences. Of importance in these public fears is also the imagined role of a new hegemony of Germany over Poland through the Eastern enlargement of the European Union (Lang 2000).

The consequence of these stereotypical fears on both sides is that the accession of Poland to the European Union – in all probability in 2004 – will be accompanied, at the request of the German and Polish governments, by a transition period of about four to seven years in which Poles will have only limited access to the Western European labour market and foreigners will be restricted in buying Polish land. Yet, these delaying measures will apply only temporarily and the full accession of Poland will prove that the stereotypical fears on the German and the Polish sides are grossly exaggerated. It is not the case that Poles, who will find growing opportunities in their own country, will be motivated to emigrate in growing numbers to Germany, nor are the Germans, who are only to a very small degree still farmers, particularly interested in Polish land. On the contrary, the Eastern enlargement will accelerate the economic exchange and interconnection between both countries, continuing – but with a diminishing power hierarchy – a West–East German–Polish gradient. In addition, the membership by the East Central European countries of the European Union will even more than now counterbalance the political weight of the large Western European states by the many small states. With it also, the still existing power hierarchy between Germany and Poland will be further reduced. Finally, the accession of Poland to the European Union will also offer more opportunities for an increased cultural exchange between the two countries. Even if these opportunities are taken up, this will probably not mean a complete reversal of the cultural hierarchy between the two countries: the high level of interest by Poles in German and Western cultures and languages and the low interest of Germans in Polish culture and language. But an increasing cultural exchange would be the only way to further reduce the still present and often unconscious national missionary overtones and stereotypical fears in both nations by a common participation in a multiple European culture.

## Notes

1 For a political study see Bingen 1997; for a critical analysis, Krzeminski 2001.
2 For political-sociological studies see Hanson and Spohn 1995; Katzenstein 1977, 1998; and Markovits and Reich 1997.
3 For an overview see Spohn 2000a.
4 European historical-comparative approaches are Schieder 1992; Schulze 1994; and Smith 1986.
5 Amongst others see particularly Conze 1992; Dann 1993.
6 See with extensive literature Spohn 1995.
7 This is my central thesis in Spohn forthcoming.
8 For a study on the Eastern German border regions, see Baranowski 1995.
9 The following figures are based on Benz 1992: 413–19; Dimitrow 1992: 420–7.
10 On post-Second World War German–Polish relations see Rosenthal 1976.
11 As a recent interpretation of German history after 1945 see Winkler 2001.
12 Among others see particularly Berghahn 1987; Conze and Lepsius 1984; Dahrendorf 1965.
13 See, among others Childs 1988; Glaeßner 1989; Kaelble and Kocka 1994.
14 See particularly Davies 1981: 556–663; Hoensch 1990; Krzeminski 1991.
15 Bingen 1999: 175–6. The Polish GDP/FDI ratio is however considerably lower than the Hungarian one; see Greskovits and Bohle 2001: 3–27.

16  I have taken these figures from Bingen 1999: 169.
17  See the tables in von Barrata 2002: 31–4 and 43–6.
18  An excellent, though too pessimistic, study of the general West–East European core–periphery relations is Berend 1996.
19  These images are revitalised particularly in crisis situations like the Odra flood in 1997. On the evolution of German–Polish mutual perceptions and stereotypes, see also Grathoff and Kloskowska 1994.
20  See the sensitive essays of Krzeminski 2001
21  European Commission, *Eurobarometer 50*, 1999: B 62 and Miroslava Marody's chapter in this volume.

# References

Baranowski, S. (1995) *The Sanctity of Rural Life: Nobility, Protestantism and Nazism in Weimar Prussia*, Oxford/New York: Oxford University Press.

Benz, W. (1992) 'Flucht – Vertreibung – Zwangsaussiedlung', in E. Kobylinska, A. Lawaty and R. Stephan (eds) *Deutsche und Polen: 100 Schlüsselbegriffe*, Munich: Piper.

Berend, I. (1995) 'German Economic Penetration in East-Central Europe in Historical Perspective', in S. Hanson and W. Spohn (eds) *Can Europe Work? Germany and the Reconstruction of Postcommunist Societies*, Seattle: University of Washington Press.

—— (1996) *Central and Eastern Europe, 1944–1993: Detour from Periphery to Periphery*, Cambridge: Cambridge University Press.

Berend, I. and Ranki, G. (1982) *The European Periphery and Industrialization, 1780–1914*, Cambridge: Cambridge University Press.

Berghahn, V. (1987) *Modern Germany: Society, Economy and Politics*, Cambridge: Cambridge University Press.

Bingen, D. (1997) 'Die Entwicklung der deutsch–polnischen Beziehungen seit 1991', *Berichte des Bundesinstituts für ostwissenschaftliche und internationale Studien* 52, Cologne.

—— (1999) *Die Republik Polen*, Munich: Olzog.

CBOS (Centrum Badania Opinii Spolecznej) (2000) Report, Warsaw: CBOS.

Childs, D. (1998) *The GDR: Moscow's German Ally*, London: Unwin.

Conze, W. (1992) *Nation, Staat, Gesellschaft*, Göttingen; Vandenhoek and Ruprecht.

Conze, W. and Lepsius, R. (1984) (eds) *Sozialgeschichte der Bundesrepublik Deutschland*, Stuttgart: Klett and Cotta.

Dahrendorf, R. (1965) *Gesellschaft und Freiheit in Deutschland*, Munich: Piper.

Daiber, K.-F. (1995) *Religion unter den Bedingungen der Moderne: Die Situation der Bundesrepublik Deutschland*, Marburg: Diagonal.

Dann, O. (1993) *Nation and Nationalismus in Deutschland 1770–1990*, Munich: Beck.

Davies, N. (1981) *God's Playground: A History of Poland*, 2 vols, Oxford: Clarendon Press 1981.

—— (1984) *Heart of Europe: A Short History of Poland*, Oxford: Clarendon Press.

Dimitrow, E. (1992) 'Flucht -Vertreibung – Zwangsaussiedlung', in E. Kobylinska, A. Lawaty and R. Stephan (eds) *Deutsche und Polen: 100 Schlüsselbegriffe*, Munich: Piper.

Eberwein, W.-D. and Ecker-Erhardt, M. (2001) *Deutschland und Polen: Eine Werte- und Interessengemeinschaft? Die Elitenperspektive*, Opladen: Leske & Budrich.

European Commission (1999) *Eurobarometer 50*, Luxembourg: Office for the Official Publications of the European Community.

—— (2001) *Eurobarometer 54*, Luxembourg: Office for the Official Publications of the European Community.

Evans, R. (1982) (ed.) 'Religion and society in modern Germany', *European Studies Review* 12, 3.

Glaeßner, G.-J. (1989) *Die andere Republik*, Opladen: Westdeutscher Verlag.

Grathoff, R. and Kloskowska, A. (1994) (eds) *The Neighborhood of Cultures*, Warsaw: Instytut Studiow Politycznych.

Greskovits, B. and Bohle, D. (2001) 'Developmental paths on Europe's periphery: Hungary's and Poland's return to Europe compared', *Polish Sociological Review* 1: 3–27.

Hagen, W. (1982) *The Nationality Conflict in the Prussian East, 1772–1914*, Chicago: Chicago University Press.

Hanson, S. and Spohn, W. (1995) (eds) *Can Europe Work? Germany and the Reconstruction of Postcommunist Societies*, Seattle: University of Washington Press.

Hoensch, J. (1990) *Geschichte Polens*, Stuttgart: Ulmer.

Hoffmann, J. (1997) (ed.) *'Nachbarn sind der Rede wert': Bilder der Deutschen von Polen und der Polen von Deutschen in der Neuzeit*, Dortmund: Forschungsstelle Ostmitteleuropa.

Jakobsen, H.-A. (1992) *Deutsche und Polen 1945–1991*, in E. Kobylinska, A. Lawaty and R. Stephan (eds) *Deutsche und Polen: 100 Schlüsselbegriffe*, Munich: Piper.

Kaelble, H. and Kocka, J. (1994) (eds) *Sozialgeschichte der DDR*, Göttingen: Vandenhoek and Ruprecht.

Katzenstein, P. (1977) *Tamed Power*, Ithaca, NY: Cornell University Press.

—— (1998) (ed.) *Mitteleuropa: Between Europe and Germany*, Oxford: Berghahn Books.

Kobylinska, E., Lawaty, A., and Stephan, R. (1992) (eds) *Deutsche und Polen: 100 Schlüsselbegriffe*, Munich: Piper.

Kriedte, P. (1997) 'Katholizismus, Nationbildung und verzögerte Säkularisierung in Polen', in H. Lehmann (ed.) *Säkularisierung, Dechristianisierung, Rechristianisierung im neuzeitlichen Europa*, Göttingen: Vandenhoek and Ruprecht.

Krzeminski, A. (1991) *Geschichte Polens im 20. Jahrhundert*, Munich: Beck.

—— (2001) *Deutsch–Polnische Verspiegelungen*, Vienna: Holzhausen Verlag.

Lang, K.-O. (2000) *Polens Katholizismus und die europäische Integration*, Berichte des Bundesinstituts für ostwissenschaftliche und internationale Studien 14, Cologne.

Luks, L. (1997) 'Der "Sonderweg" des polnischen Katholizismus', in H. Lehmann (ed.) *Säkularisierung, Dechristianisierung, Rechristianisierung im neuzeitlichen Europa*, Göttingen: Vandenhoek and Ruprecht.

Markovits, A. and Reich, S. (1997) *The German Predicament*, Ithaca, NY: Cornell University Press.

Morawska, E. (1987) 'Civil Religion vs. State Power in Poland', in T. Robbins and R. Robertson (eds) *Church–State Relations: Tensions and Transitions*, New Brunswick: Transaction Books.

—— (1995) 'The Polish Roman Church unbound: change of face or change of context?', in S. Hanson and W. Spohn, (eds) *Can Europe Work? Germany and the Reconstruction of Postcommunist Societies*, Seattle: University of Washington Press.

Morawska, E. and Spohn, W. (1997) 'Moving Europeans in the globalizing world', in W. Gungwu (ed.) *Global History and Migrations*, Boulder, CO: Westview Press.

Nipperdey, T. (1987, 1991) *German History 1800–1866 and 1866–1918*, 3 vols, Munich: Beck.

Nowak, K. (1995) *Geschichte des Christentums in Deutschland*, Munich: Beck.

Pollack, D. (1994) *Kirche in der Organisationsgesellschaft*, Stuttgart: Kohlhammer.

Poznanski, K. (1993) (ed.) *Stabilization and Privatization in Poland: The Economic Analysis of Shock Therapy*, Boston: Kluwer Academic Press.

Rosenthal, H.K. (1976) *German and Pole: National Conflict and Modern Myth*, Gainsville: University Presses of Florida.

Schieder, T. (1992) 'Typologie und Erscheinungsformen des Nationalstaats in Europa', in *Nationalstaat und Nationalismus*, Göttingen: Vandenhoek and Ruprecht.

Schulze, H. (1994) *Staat und Nation in der europäischen Geschichte*, Munich: Beck.

Seton-Watson, H. (1977) *Nations and States*, Boulder, CO: Westview Press.

Smith, A. (1986) *The Ethnic Origins of Nations*, Cambridge: Cambridge University Press

Smith, H.W. (1995) *German Nationalism and Religious Conflict, 1870–1914*, Princeton, NJ: Princeton University Press.

Spohn, W. (1994) 'Protestantism, secularization and politics in nineteenth-century Germany', in Sabrina Ramet (ed.) *Render Unto Caesar*, Boulder, CO: Westview Press.

—— (1995) 'United Germany as the renewed core in Europe', in S. Hanson and W. Spohn (eds) *Can Europe Work? Germany and the Reconstruction of Postcommunist Societies*, Seattle: University of Washington Press.

—— (2000a) 'The Eastern enlargement of the European Union and changes in collective identities: a Western and Eastern European comparison', EUI working paper, Florence.

—— (2000b) 'The Eastern enlargement and the role of collective identities: a Western and Eastern European comparison', paper presented at the European Sociological Association, Helsinki.

—— (forthcoming) 'Religion und Nationbildung: Deutschland und Polen im transnationalen Vergleich', in *Modernisierung, Religion und kollektive Identität: Deutschland zwischen West- und Osteuropa*.

Tazbir, J. (1994) 'Poland', in B. Scribner, R. Porter and M. Teich (eds) *The Reformation in National Context*, Cambridge: Cambridge University Press.

Thränhard, D. (1987) *Geschichte der Bundesrepublik Deutschland*, Frankfurt am Main: Neuausgabe.

Tomaszewski, J. (1993) 'The national question in Poland in the twentieth century', in M. Teich and R. Porter (eds) *The National Question in Europe in Historical Context*, Cambridge: Cambridge University Press.

von Baratta, M. (ed.) (2002) *Fischer Weltalmanach 2002*, Frankfurt am Main: Fischer.

Wehler, H.-U. (1987, 1995) *Deutsche Gesellschaftsgeschichte 1815–1848/49 and 1849–1914*, 3 vols, Munich: Beck.

Winkler, H.A. (1992) 'Im Schatten von Versailles: Das deutsch–polnische Verhältnis während der Weimarer Republik', in E. Kobylinska, A. Lawaty and R. Stephan (eds) *Deutsche und Polen: 100 Schlüsselbegriffe*, Munich: Piper.

—— (2001) *Der lange Weg nach Westen: Deutsche Geschichte vom "Dritten Reich" bis zur Wiedervereinigung*, Munich: Beck.

# 8  Polish identity in the process of Europeanisation*

*Miroslava Marody*

## Introduction

Poland was one of the first countries to begin a process of economic and political transition in the post-1989 period. The 1989 crisis of the Communist regimes in Central and Eastern Europe opened the way for a re-orientation in Polish politics. When the Solidarity movement leadership came into power, it launched a policy of close cooperation with Western European institutions. The 'return to Europe' concept became the leitmotiv of Polish foreign policy. This term was put in quotation marks since Poles believe that they have always been an integral part of this cultural circle. The integration with Western European institutions of economic and political cooperation is connected, however, to a high social cost that must be paid whenever adoption of certain legal and economic criteria of European Union (EU) membership is involved. The benefits are said to be forthcoming, but the cost of adoption has to be paid now – as many Poles believe.

This chapter focuses on the question of how the ongoing – economic and cultural – processes of European integration influence the national identity of Poles and how, in turn, the latter may influence the further processes of integration. Starting with Jacobson-Widding's division into the 'sameness' and 'distinctiveness' aspects of identity and using data from empirical studies, the author shows how some historical processes have influenced existing features of Polish national identity and how Poles now perceive their place among other European nations.

## Attitudes towards Poland's accession to the European Union

In Poland public support for integration into the European Union was highest in 1996, when it reached 80 per cent. Since then we have observed a visible decline of Poles' readiness to vote for joining the European Union. At the end of 1999 only 59 per cent of respondents declared that they would vote for Poland's entry into the EU, if a referendum on this issue were held today (see Table 8.1). It means a fall of one quarter during the three years. And with a relatively stable percentage of those who do not have an opinion on this issue, it also means an increase in those opposing, to one quarter of the population.

*Table 8.1* Changes in the level of support for Poland's integration into the European
Union

| If a referendum on joining the European Union were held today, would you vote: | Responses according to date of research (in %) | | | | | | | |
|---|---|---|---|---|---|---|---|---|
| | June 1994 | May 1995 | May 1996 | Apr. 1997 | May 1998 | Aug. 1998 | May 1999 | Nov. 1999 |
| For entry | 77 | 72 | 80 | 72 | 66 | 63 | 55 | 59 |
| Against entry | 6 | 9 | 7 | 11 | 19 | 19 | 26 | 26 |
| Don't know | 17 | 19 | 13 | 18 | 15 | 18 | 19 | 15 |

Source: CBOS 'Current problems and events' research (114), 10–15 November 1999, on a random
representative sample of adult Poles (N=1089).

An insight into the hidden reasons behind those answers is provided by responses
to another question regularly asked in the CBOS (Center for Social Opinion
Research) research (see Table 8.2). It shows a steady increase in the number of
respondents who are of the opinion that Poland should improve and modernise its
economy first, and then apply for the entry into the European Union. Since 1997
there has also been a steady fall in the percentage of respondents who believe that
joining the EU as quickly as possible would help us to improve and modernise our
economy.

It suggests that the respondents who are opposed to integration into the EU, as
well as at least some of those who are for it, believe that Poland is now economically
too weak to stand up to the competition within the common European market.
Such an interpretation is in accordance with the findings of CBOS research which
show that attitudes towards integration are influenced by an individual's assessment
of the country's economic situation and the economic well-being of his or her family

*Table 8.2* Changes in opinion on the desired pace of Poland's integration into the
European Union

| In your opinion: | Responses according to date of research (in %) | | | | |
|---|---|---|---|---|---|
| | Apr. 1997 | Aug. 1997 | Dec. 1998 | May 1999 | Nov. 1999 |
| Poland should improve and modernise its economy first, and then apply for the entry into the European Union | 48 | 43 | 50 | 58 | 62 |
| Poland should try to join the EU as quickly as possible, since it will help to improve and modernise its economy | 40 | 39 | 34 | 26 | 27 |
| Difficult to say | 12 | 19 | 16 | 16 | 11 |

Source: CBOS 'Current problems and events' research (114), 10–15 November 1999, on a random
representative sample of adult Poles (N=1089).

at the time of the study. In other words, there are current Polish issues and problems that matter when people are making decisions about their voting intention, for or against European integration.

It is clearly visible when, instead of asking them about voting for or against Poland's integration into the EU, we asked people more direct questions about their hopes and fears connected with Poland's accession to the EU. Such a question was introduced into a study conducted by my colleagues in 1998 (see Table 8.3). We can see that the expectation that integration will help Poland to develop economically is shared by 78 per cent of respondents, the highest percentage for any answer. The pattern of answers also shows that positive feelings connected with the future integration of Poland into the EU prevail over the negative ones.

This pattern seemingly contradicts the findings from CBOS research included in Table 8.2. One of the possible ways to integrate findings from both studies is offered by Claus Offe's (1998) conception of the instrumental use of identity symbols.

Offe points to the fact that, 'the politics of identity-based differences is an increasingly prominent feature of increasing segments of the contemporary world, developed and developing alike' (1998: 122). The instrumental use of identity

*Table 8.3* Hopes and fears accompanying the idea of Poland's integration into the European Union

| *When you think about the possible accession of Poland into the EU, do you:* | *Yes* | *No* | *Don't know* |
|---|---|---|---|
| Hope that it will open up Poland's prospects for economic development | 78 | 10 | 12 |
| Feel satisfied that Poland will be safe | 77 | 11 | 12 |
| Feel satisfied that Poland will have the same laws and regulations as the European Union | 70 | 13 | 16 |
| Feel satisfaction that Poland will regain its due place amongst other European countries | 66 | 19 | 15 |
| Fear that Poland will not be free to decide about its own problems | 61 | 26 | 13 |
| Feel uncertain whether Poland will manage in the European Union | 58 | 25 | 17 |
| Feel an anxiety that it will cause Poland enemies on the East | 54 | 32 | 14 |
| Fear that Poland will stop being 'familiar' and as it always used to be | 46 | 39 | 15 |

Source: Research 'European identity of Poles in the perspective of integration with the European Union', conducted by M. Grabowska, K. Koseła and T. Szawiel, 20–24 March 1998, on a random representative sample of adult Poles (N=1107).

symbols becomes a device for establishing economic privileges, acquiring group-specific protection, promoting the acquisition of additional rights and the exemption from common duties.

According to Offe, this phenomenon is connected with fundamental features of the democratic political order. In constitutional democracies, says Offe, identity conflicts used to be solved by granting group rights to some unjustly oppressed structural minorities. Recently, however, not only has answering the question of the basis on which the minority is a minority become more difficult, but we also observe more and more often the intentional attempts to *construct* minorities on the basis of some social identities in order to gain some additional social benefits. This is facilitated by the fact that the contours of the 'oppressed minority' concept can be easily blurred, as the vast majority of society – 'everyone but [the] relatively well-off, relatively young, able-bodied, heterosexual white male' as Kymlicka (1995) formulates it – can arguably be included, or in good conscience include him or herself, into a giant rainbow-coalition of oppressed minorities. Hence, even if in the contemporary world the significance of differences is decreasing in the cultural dimension, it gains a new importance in the political one.

The hypothesis that, partly at least, we are dealing with the case of instrumental use of identity in the answers to the questions about Poland's integration into the EU, can be supported by pointing to three facts. First, in public discourse, Polish national identity is most often recalled in the context of the threat that integration into the EU creates to the interests of specific social groups. It is argued that the government should defend not simply peasants, steelworkers, or workers in sugar factories, but *Polish* peasants, *Polish* steelworkers, *Polish* sugar-factory workers. A given social group is presented in public discourse as a minority unjustly oppressed within the European common market only because it is Polish. Second, the decline in public support for the idea of Poland's integration into the EU is accompanied by an increase in support for the opinion that, hitherto, relations between Poland and the EU have brought more benefits to the EU states (see Table 8.4). An unequal share in benefits following from social cooperation is prototypical for the minority argument. Third, when asked about their attitudes towards such a symbolic marker of national identity as the passport, Poles turn out to be quite eager to replace the passport of a citizen of the Polish Republic, with a passport of the European Union citizen (see Table 8.5).

The instrumental use of national identity in the discourse concerning European integration does not rule out the importance of this type of identity for Poles. Rather, it calls for a change of perspective from which the issue is discussed. The problem of European integration is usually analysed from the perspective of formal accession. Therefore, questions most often asked in public opinion surveys are whether Poles want to join the EU as quickly as possible or not. From such a perspective an emphasis put by Poles on their national identity, national interests and national values has to be regarded as one of the obstacles to effective integration.

However, one can argue that the process of integration – in the sense of the opening-up of the economy and an intense flow of goods, capital, services, and also increasing mobility of people – is already taking place. From this perspective the

*Table 8.4* Changes in the acceptance of opinions about relations between Poland and the European Union

| How do you assess the previous relations between Poland and the European Union? Who benefits more from them? | Responses according to date of research (in %) | | | | | | | |
|---|---|---|---|---|---|---|---|---|
| | July 1993 | Mar. 1994 | May 1995 | May 1996 | Aug. 1997 | Aug. 1998 | May 1999 | Nov. 1999 |
| The EU states | 41 | 38 | 31 | 19 | 28 | 39 | 39 | 47 |
| Poland | 5 | 8 | 11 | 11 | 11 | 7 | 8 | 8 |
| Equally – Poland and EU states | 27 | 26 | 33 | 46 | 35 | 30 | 30 | 27 |
| Difficult to say | 27 | 27 | 26 | 24 | 27 | 24 | 23 | 18 |

Source: CBOS 'Current problems and events' research (114), 10–15 November 1999, on a random representative sample of adult Poles (N=1089).

*Table 8.5* The acceptance of some effects of Poland's integration with the European Union

| Would you accept: | Yes | No | Don't know |
|---|---|---|---|
| The replacement of Polish Republic passports with passports of the European Union | 63 | 22 | 15 |
| The replacement of Polish złoty with European euro | 58 | 29 | 13 |
| Using symbols of the European Union side by side with Polish flag and emblem | 50 | 39 | 11 |
| The label 'Made in EU' instead of 'Made in Poland' on goods produced in Poland | 36 | 51 | 13 |
| A foreigner who hardly speaks Polish as your boss | 23 | 63 | 14 |

Source: Research 'European identity of Poles in the perspective of integration with the European Union', conducted by M. Grabowska, K. Koseła and T. Szawiel, 20–24 March 1998, on a random representative sample of adult Poles (N=1107).

most important problem becomes the question of how this ongoing processes of integration influences the national identity of Poles and how, in turn, the latter may influence the processes of integration.

## Polish national identity in the process of European integration

The concept of identity has two different, though interrelated, aspects. First, an answer to the question, 'Who am I?' stresses the elements of continuity, permanence, the feeling of 'being the same'. But by its very nature this answer also implicitly contains the answer to the question, 'Who am I not?', pointing to the distinction between ingroup and outgroup, between 'us' and 'them' (Jacobson-Widding 1983). Anita Jacobson-Widding calls these two aspects of identity, correspondingly, the 'sameness' and 'distinctiveness'. In the case of national identity, the 'sameness' is shaped by the totality of national history, by unique experiences of the nation, transmitted from one generation to another. The sense of 'distinctiveness', on the other hand, can be analysed as a complex product of contacts and interactions, cooperation and conflicts with the representatives of other nations.

As Zbigniew Bokszański (1999) points out, an important characteristic of Polish national identity in the pre-transformation times was its focus on the aspect of 'sameness' with a relative neglect of the 'distinctiveness' aspect. It can be explained by pointing to the fact that for a long period of its history, the Polish nation was deprived of the organisational frames of its own state and divided into three parts, existing under foreign regimes. Under such circumstances, the concentration on finding constant elements of 'being a Pole', even if not living in a 'Polish' institutional environment, was quite natural. However, the same factors which help us to understand the focus on the continuity aspects, on 'being the same' issue, have also influenced the content of this 'sameness'. I would like to stress here two of its specific features.

First, there is the relative unimportance of institutional and group symbols of identity. Not having their own national institutions for a long time, Polish people attach more significance to moral and spiritual characteristics of 'being a Pole'. This could explain the distribution of answers within Table 8.5 – on one hand, readiness to accept EU passports, currency and emblems, and on the other, a resistance to labels which would, perhaps, hide national inventiveness and skilfulness. Jasińska-Kania (1996) has showed that even in the 1970s and the 1980s, irrespective of whether the self-image constructed by Poles was more positive or more negative (which was closely related to the actual political and economic situation in the country), it always contained an element of moral superiority and exceptionality. Even our faults were exceptional.

Second, focus on the 'sameness' aspect of identity has also resulted in a transference of the possible divisions between 'us' and 'them' into the boundaries of the Polish nation. One can say without much exaggeration that for the last 200 years Poles have been occupied with attempts to refine the concept of a 'true Pole'. There are a lot of descriptions in Polish phraseology – starting with a 'Pole-catholic', through 'Commies', to one of the most recent inventions: 'newspaper using the Polish language' that is used instead of the title of the leading Polish daily 'Gazeta Wyborcza' – whose main function is to stress the difference between a 'genuine Pole' and somebody who only pretends being a Pole or even disguises his real identity.

There were of course also some demarcation lines between 'us' and 'them' which included a division between the Polish nation and some other nations. Traditionally, 'them' referred to the Germans, who in Polish history have been the personification of an 'Alien' and always played the role of the main enemy of Poland. For many years, in public opinion studies, Germans were placed in first position among nationalities that Polish respondents disliked for different reasons and whom they did not trust. As to the second neighbour of Poland, i.e. the Russians, their position was ambiguous, since on the one hand, they were identified with the unwanted Communist regime, which was imposed by force on the Polish nation, and as a result the very word 'Russians' had and still has a strong negative connotation in everyday Polish language.

On the other hand, in the 1970s Russians as people were among those nations whom Poles liked most, including Hungarians, French, Slovaks, Czechs, Americans, Italians, Vietnamese and Bulgarians. In the second half of the 1980s, sympathy of Poles towards nations belonging to the 'Communist camp' started to decrease. The most radical was a change of attitude towards Russians: from +31 in 1985, to +8 in 1989, and –16 in 1991 (Jasińska-Kania 1996; the quoted numbers are differences between the percentage of respondents with positive and negative attitudes).

Partly at least, these changes in attitudes towards Russians were an effect of political changes and a freedom in expressing one's ideas and feelings. However, it was not the only factor, since these changes went hand in hand with not so much radical but, nevertheless, clearly visible changes in attitudes towards Germans. In the second half of the 1980s, the negative attitudes towards Germans were slowly but steadily falling and recently they have been on the verge of changing into slightly positive attitudes. In a study conducted by CBOS in October 1999, on a 7-point scale of 'like–dislike' opinions (from –3 to +3), Germans scored –0.15, whereas Russians scored –0.84. At the negative end of the scale were placed Gypsies (Roma, –1.20) and Romanians (–1.08), while at the positive end were Americans (+0.90) and Italians (+0.85). It is worth mentioning that between 1998 and 1999 there was a small decrease in negative feelings towards all the 11 nations that were the subject of negative attitudes in Poland, with only one exception: feelings towards Russians (–0.79 in 1998 and –0.84 in 1999).

The changes in attitudes towards Russians and Germans bear witness to a change of general identity-orientations. Such an interpretation is supported by findings from the earlier quoted study on European identity (Figure 8.1). They illustrate

*Figure 8.1* Location of some subjects on a scale of 'Europeanity'.
Source: Research 'European identity of Poles in the perspective of integration with the European Union', conducted by M. Grabowska, K. Koseła and T. Szawiel, 20–24 March 1998, on a random representative sample of adult Poles (N=1107).

both some peculiarities of the 'sameness' aspect of Polish identity discussed above, as well as changing orientation of 'distinctiveness'. As one can see from Figure 8.1, Polish respondents perceive themselves as a little bit more 'European' than other Poles, and Poland as more 'European' than they are. One can also notice that a distance between Poland and the more 'European' Germany is shorter than distance between Poland and the less 'European' Russia (1.90 and 2.72, correspondingly).

The 'sameness' and 'distinctiveness' aspects of the identity concept can, of course, be differentiated only analytically. They are actually interrelated, and the changes in the 'distinctiveness' dimension also influence what is meant by 'being a Pole'. It is interesting that this change in the frame of reference, or rather one should say, the re-emergence of the European frame of reference, results in a very humble self-portrait of Poles (see Table 8.6). Taking into account that the list of features in Table 8.6 contains only positive ones, one can say that Poles see themselves as better only in the case of four categories out of the 18 under question. They perceive themselves as more family-oriented, more religious, more patriotic, and more helpful to others than an average European. The most striking is the lack of confidence, the feeling of being lost, which turned out to be the most often mentioned psychological 'deficit' in this self-portrait of Poles.

*Table 8.6* Opinions about a typical Pole and typical European

| Feature | Percentage of the answers 'has a given feature' | | |
|---|---|---|---|
| | *A Pole* (1) | *A European* (2) | *Difference* (1–2) |
| kind | 73 | 84 | −11 |
| open to others | 66 | 69 | −3 |
| patriotic | 84 | 67 | +17 |
| educated | 69 | 94 | −25 |
| well-behaved | 66 | 85 | −19 |
| religious | 93 | 47 | +46 |
| resourceful | 77 | 88 | −11 |
| self-confident | 40 | 91 | −51 |
| thrifty | 48 | 82 | −34 |
| honest | 60 | 78 | −18 |
| success-oriented | 57 | 88 | −31 |
| living modestly | 74 | 57 | +14 |
| good worker | 70 | 93 | −23 |
| good standards of living | 23 | 77 | −54 |
| respects his work | 63 | 90 | −27 |
| in difficult situations unites with others in joint actions | 77 | 80 | −3 |
| helps others | 55 | 40 | +15 |
| family is for him more important than work | 80 | 32 | +48 |

Source: CBOS 'Current problems and events' research (114), 10–15 August 1996, on a random representative sample of adult Poles (N=1089).

One could say, that in the case of an individual such a self-concept would have devastating effects on his or her self-esteem and functioning. In the case of the nation, it serves rather as a tool of measuring a distance which most Poles would like to shorten.

## Note

* Paper supported by grant from the Institute of Sociology, University of Warsaw.

## References

Bokszański, Z. (1999) 'Tożsamość narodowa w perspektywie transformacji systemowej' [National identity in the perspective of systemic transformation], in J. Mucha (ed.) Społeczeństwo polskie w perspektywie członkostwa w Unii Europejskiej, Warsaw: Wydawnictwo IFiS PAN.

CBOS (Centrum Badania Opinii Spolecznej) (1999) *Sympatia i niechęć do innych narodów* [Sympathy and dislike of other nations], Research Report No. 173, Warsaw: CBOS.

Grabowska, M., Koseła, K., and Szawiel, T. (1998) *Europejska tożsamość Polaków w perspektywie zjednoczenia z UE* [European Identity of Poles in the Perspective of integration with the European Union], Warsaw: Instytut Badań nad Podstawami Demokracji.

Jacobson-Widding, A. (1983) (ed.) *Identity: Personal and Sociocultural*, Uppsala: University of Uppsala.

Jasińska-Kania, A. (1996) 'Stereotypowe wyobrażenia Polaków o sobie i innych narodach' [Polish self-stereotype and stereotypes of other nations], in M. Marody and E. Gucwa-Leśny (eds) *Podstawy życia społecznego w Polsce*, Warsaw: ISS UW.

Kymlicka, W. (1995) *Multicultural Citizenship*, Oxford: Clarendon Press.

Offe, C. (1998) ' "Homogeneity" and constitutional democracy: coping with identity conflicts through group rights', *The Journal of Political Philosophy* 6, 2: 113–41.

# 9 Russian perspectives on Germany and Russian self-definitions

*Erhard Stölting*

In 1997, the now vanished President Yeltsin invited the Russians to participate in a competition: a large sum of money was to be given to anybody who could develop a new 'Russian idea' suitable to be the new official ideology of the Russian state (McDaniel 1998: 162–73). After the disintegration of the Soviet Union and the evaporation of its socialist ideology it was felt that the Russian nation needed a binding new philosophy. The underlying assumption was that any stable society must be held together by a common system of beliefs and values.

Unfortunately, the competition for a 'new Russian idea' came to nothing. The issue was simply dropped. Evidently nobody was able to invent a new ideology. Collective identities may be invented but the process of their elaboration and their taking root in society is slightly more complicated than was supposed in the competition (Anderson 1983). But the very idea of conceiving this competition can be attributed to a specific previously existing image of political society in general. According to this image, society is shaped and organised by political authority; order and cohesion has to be imposed from above. Any autonomous developments inside society are thought to be either impossible because a society which is not shaped by authority is amorphous and passive; or any society which is not held together by a binding altruistic ideology and a strong ruler will explode into chaotic disorder as a result of the diverging egoistic and amoral striving of its constituent individuals. The idea of the competition reflected a specific perception of actual Russian society.

The idea that society has to be integrated by values has been central to the sociological tradition since its initial stages and up to Talcott Parsons (Levine 1995: 35–58). The fear of an anarchic dissolution of society and the unrestrained and amoral struggle of egoistic individualist interests is not only part of a Russian political heritage which used to legitimise authoritarian rule. It is part of the European conservative tradition in general. And to conceive of society as inherently passive and needing stimulating inspiration from outside has been constitutive for political ideas which stress mobilisation by political ideology and/or charismatic leaders (Stölting 1990: 139–53).

Although the underlying concept of society can, in this way, be thought of as a part of the European intellectual tradition it can also be seen, as specifically Russian. The intention of creating a 'new Russian idea' was in line with Russian political thought since the emergence of Slavophilism in the nineteenth century (Walicki 1989: 421–58). It has been and still is very much alive even if the deep political and societal crisis has led to widespread emotional and moral insecurity or political apathy. But the post-Soviet moral and political crisis can be seen as defined by traditional Russian thinking because even unhappiness is shaped by traditional preconceptions. Thus, the traditional Russian idea determines the perception of the present crisis. The lack of binding moral values demands a solution for perceived shortcomings. The new binding ideology will resemble the old one.

Yet, still another phenomenon can be detected in the competition for a new moral system and a common world view. The present crisis is defined at least in part as a result of the crumbling Soviet system which had been held together by Marxist-Leninist ideology. The value system and the common world view is, thus, seen in analogy to this ideology. The underlying political approach is functionalist insofar as the criterion for the acceptability of the intended new ideology is not some inherent truth but its ability to enforce order and to stabilise and invigorate society.

However, the functionalist approach contains a dilemma which elsewhere has been described as the 'dilemma of conservatism' (Greiffenhagen 1971). An altruistic value system can only be effective if people believe in its unconditional truth and legitimacy. But no functionalist argument can prove the unconditional truth of any value. On the contrary, arguing rationally for the usefulness and hence the acceptability of values destroys their pretence to unconditional authority. The inherent authoritarianism of classical functionalist thinking thus becomes apparent. The ruling elite may rationally discuss the usefulness of one value or another. But it has to shield this discussion from the wider public, because the bulk of society has to believe and to obey.

The very call for a new binding ideology can be seen as being part of an authoritarian political tradition. In this way, the intended competition has proven its uselessness. The new 'Russian idea' was conceived in the spirit of the old one (Berdiaev 1979; McDaniel 1998: 162–73).

This 'Russian idea' was to be more than functional in the moral cohesion of Russian society. It had to be the essence of a historically specific collective individuality.

## Collective identities and Russian identity

Collective identities are supposed to encompass the characteristics of certain societal entities defined as a nation, a profession, a religion, etc. As a rule, it is supposed that these identities form a coherent whole; but in most cases this presupposition can be falsified on close scrutiny. Hidden under the strong conviction of the collective as an integrated whole, different images and beliefs can be found which sometimes are even contradictory and often have rather heterogeneous roots. Therefore not all aspects of a constructed collected identity will be used at the same time. Different images are stored up in a kind of arsenal and kept ready for future use under diverse conditions and with diverse aims. Some may be chosen in appropriate circumstances while others are rejected if they do not fit this specific situation; they have to wait for an opportunity in which they can be used as an argument. Indeed, the availability of the different images presupposes that the contents of this arsenal are not forgotten altogether during the time in which specific images are not used. They have to be kept in use or revived by way of quotations, even if intermittently. The contents of the identity arsenal may be compared to the jumble of an antique shop, assembling meaningful ugly or pretty objects of different origins, epochs, and values. These objects are waiting to be individually rearranged in some apartment in which they may help its owner to recreate some attractive identity.

Normally, the images used in identity constructions consist of contrasting, paired concepts which define each other negatively. A characterisation of a specific opposite social unit is always a self-characterisation of the own unit as well. In this way, the other side defines the own side and vice versa: if the others to which the image refers are 'bad', then we are 'good', if they are 'ugly', we are 'beautiful', if they are 'dishonest' we are 'honest' and vice versa. Therefore, the concepts used in the construction of a self-image depend on those concepts which are used in the description of others. Different images can be seen as traces of historical conflicts or constellations which are kept alive in order to be used in self-identifications under specific circumstances.

Like others, the arsenal of Russian identity constructions consists of widely varying images. They define 'Russia' or 'Russian culture' by evoking contrasting images of others. If Russian identity is contrasted with the Islamic cultures of central Asia it differs completely from the Russian identity which emerges when contrasted with the West.

The image of Germany has been of special importance for Russian self-definition in the nineteenth and twentieth centuries. It doesn't mean that relationships to other images are unimportant. For example, the definition of the United States in the Russian tradition would merit special attention; it is even impossible to reconstruct Russian conceptions of modernity without taking into consideration the ambivalent Russian reflection of American developments. This has been true even in socialist times. The concept of socialist Soviet society is inexplicable without its reflection of perceived American modernism (Gaddis 1978). At present, Europe is largely seen in Russia as a prospering annex of the US. If it is thought to be important economically and politically, it is seen as being dull and dependent in a cultural sense. Today, the US is considered the main source for innovation and inspiration.

For this reason, the role of Germany is a largely historical one in this context. But it is important in this historical sense. Cultural and intellectual relations between Germany and Russia have been very close although not continuously friendly (Laqueur 1990). And these relationships have lasted for more than just one hundred years.

## East and West

From a Russian perspective, Germany was seen as a part of the West not only in a geographical sense. To begin with, the difference between East and West encompassed the difference between Russia and Germany. Second, this dichotomic construction reveals a further specific trait of identity constructions.

The dichotomic opposition of East and West has, indeed, been of paramount importance for cultural life in Russia. But this contrast consists of quite diverse elements which are still stored up in the arsenal of ideas to be used in intellectual and political debates and in the construction of self-identifications. I would like to concentrate on the most important elements which have been in use since the nineteenth century.

As a rule, they contain a strong normative element: either we are good and they are bad, or they are good and we are bad. But these normative ascriptions may exist independently of their descriptive contents. The value judgements can be reversed while at the same time their descriptive basis remains recognisable. In the Russian case, the distinction between an evil West and a good East which characterised the Slavophile tradition could be inverted by representatives of Westernism, as the example of Pëtr Čaadaev shows most impressively (Čaadaev 1991: 546–9). On a basic descriptive level the differences appear to be very similar – as seen, for example, in the opposition of rationality and feeling, of legal constitution and spiritual unity, etc. (Stölting 2000: 23–38).

If value judgements can be inverted without changing the descriptive content to which they refer, they are only rarely held in an equilibrium. More often than not it is possible to distinguish dominant and minority tendencies and traditions. In this way Russian culture and self-identifications have been under the influences of 'Westernising' social and intellectual ideas at least since the end of the eighteenth century, although the orthodox Slavophilism seems to have had the upper hand in most times. Both traditions continued to coexist although they were not equal in strength.

One of the most important historical elements used in the construction of Russian self-definitions is the 'Tatar yoke' and the alleged liberation by the princes of Moscow who later were to become Czars (Beevor 1998; Werth 1964: 441–564). This tartar yoke has been used in quite diverse ways:

1   It was used as one of the founding myths of the Russian state and empire. According to it, the oppressed Russian nation freed itself under the guidance of its hereditary leaders. In this way the insurrection against Tatar rule served to characterise the Russian people as one of freedom-loving and valiant warriors.

2   Slavophile and Westernisers alike have defined the Tatar yoke as responsible for the economic backwardness of Russia and even the alleged political submissiveness and apathy of the Russian populations.

3   Westernisers have also used the Tatar yoke to characterise some of the special Russian characteristics beside submissiveness, as for example Russian excessive despotism and bureaucracy. The non-Russian qualities of the Tatars revealed during the time of their rule over the Russian lands were those of backwardness, cruelty, and ignorance. If Russians were backward by comparison to the West, they were so because of the Tartar yoke. In principle, and by comparison with the Tatars, Russians were progressive, civilised and intelligent.

4    The perceived Tatar qualities were used to characterise not only the Tatars of the Volga and of Crimea but Muslim peoples in general who came under the sway of Russia since the end of the eighteenth century. 'Tatar' merged with the concept of 'Asian' in contrast to 'European'.

5    But the Asian qualities of Russia could also be seen in a positive way. Some Russian intellectuals did identify themselves as partly 'Asian'. To be 'Asian' meant to be young, vital, not yet decadent if uncouth, cruel but honest. In opposing the West, this Tatar–Asian image could be used as a threat against the West. This was the case in 'Eurasianism' which was revived in the 1990s (Isaev 1992: 3–26).

These Russian self-descriptions of the effects of the 'Tatar yoke' corresponded to Western descriptions of Russia. Accordingly, Russia was characterised as 'Asian', non-European, as a political and military threat which had to be fenced off in order to protect Europe from barbarity. In this perspective Russians were equated with the wild invaders of past centuries like the Huns or the Mongols. Obviously, Russian historians and intellectuals were readers of these Western interpretations as well.

The arguments underlying the concept of the 'Tatar yoke' were extended to the Muslims of Central Asia, homeland of legendary cruel Asian despots like Genghis Khan or Timurlane. It was extended to the wild tribes of the Caucasus mountains as well, who had stubbornly opposed Russian rule in the nineteenth and twentieth centuries, especially the Chechens as the incarnation of the wild, unruly and predatory '*gorec*'. In this context the Chechens had played a dominant role in Russian fiction and poetry of the nineteenth century. The anti-Chechen stereotypes of today, brutal kidnappers who like to maim their victims, mafiosi of the mountains and the big Russian cities, reflect an attitude which had already been largely accepted in the nineteenth century (Dunlop 1998; Gammer 1994; Seely 2001). In Russian and later in Soviet historiography they could be contrasted with more civilised peoples of the Caucasus region like the Georgians, who allegedly submitted voluntarily to Russian rule and hereby had proved their high culture.

Even in this case, it is possible to notice the underlying ambivalence in characterising the wild and unruly inhabitants of the Caucasus mountains, the '*gorcy*'. In Russian literature, even the Chechens could be depicted as noble savages whose manners were characterised by hospitality, magnanimity and friendliness, even if everybody had to be aware of their vengefulness.

In their confrontation with 'Asia' the Russian self-image could be European in the emphatic sense of the word. According to this perspective Russia had a civilising mission for the Eastern, Muslim and Asian peoples. It was an outpost of Western, European civilization. This self-definition has constantly been enacted in Russian and Soviet policies in the face of Central Asia and the Caucasus. It was and still is, in this sense, a core element of Russian identity-construction.

This perspective and its reflections in actual political attitudes has often been underestimated in the West. The astonishing phenomenon that the ongoing war in Chechnya has won the support of a majority of the Russian population and that even many Russian intellectuals do not understand Western objections to human rights violations in this case, can be explained by the assumption that Russia is protecting Europe and European civilization against the menace of barbaric disorder. The Russian view on Chechnya resembles the Western view on Russia.

It is for this reason that Western criticism of warfare in Chechnya has always been perceived as an offence: the West was seen as rebuffing Russia at a moment when it was defending Western civilization. Similar responses to Western ignorance can be found throughout the political and cultural history of Russia.

The 'Tatar' and 'Asian' types of argument occupy important parts of the conceptual arsenal of Russian identity constructions. They can be combined with an imperial perspective in the strict sense. The awareness that by any standards Russia and the Soviet Union were and are very large and the corresponding pride have been central to Russian self-esteem at least since the nineteenth century. Even today this pride is reflected in the aspiration that Russia, in principle, is a superpower which has the right to be treated on an equal level with the United States. To deny this status is felt as an offence. If Russia is not in a position to realise its position as a superpower the reason must be either Western perfidy or treason in Russia, for which politicians like Gorbachev or Yeltsin have been responsible.

Apparently, the topic of the overwhelming size of a country and the pride it can inspire is neither inherently Western or Eastern. But it can be combined with other images and, like these, be differently valued. The problems Russia is confronted with can be seen to be as large as the country itself. But alternatively, Russia can be seen as possessing a natural right to centrality and dominance. Historical distress results wherever actual capabilities do not match justified claims.

The idea of a strong and centralised Russian state can be identified with the idea of a strong ruler. It corresponds to the Byzantine imperial concept which has been the official ideology since Ivan III (1440–1505). According to this doctrine, the Ottoman conquest of Constantinople in 1453 made Moscow the centre of the Christian universe, the 'Third Rome'. The prince of Moscow was now legally the emperor (Czar). The Byzantine double eagle became the Russian state emblem, Byzantine court ceremonials were adapted in the Kremlin of Moscow certifying that it had become the legitimate centre of the universe (Rimscha 1983: 152ff).

This official ideology put an end to previous self-conceptions which defined the Russian princes as being culturally and religiously dependent on the Byzantine empire. Moscow assumed the political and religious claim for universal leadership. This claim defined the heathens of the East as people to be brought under the firm, benevolent, and civilising rule of the Czar. At the same time it prefigured the contrast to the Latin West: as the Western Christian churches did not recognize true – orthodox – Christianity it was by definition heretic. The West was evil and treacherous because it rejected true faith.

## Russia and Germany

Seen from Russia, Germany lies in the West. But the mutual perceptions between Russia and Germany were more complicated and specific; they had been intense for long and created several ambivalent conceptual types.

These types can be traced back to historical experiences or rather to images of them.

1   One of these experiences were contacts with Germans living in Russia, especially urban Germans living there as artisans and merchants (Stricker 1997). One of the formative influences on young Peter I were the Germans of the German Quarter, the '*Nemeckaya Sloboda*' in Moscow.

2   After the annexation of the formerly Swedish provinces of Estonia, Livonia and Latvia by Peter I, another type of German emerged in Russian history. The urban German populations of the Baltic towns resembled those inside Russia. The towns of the new Baltic provinces looked like other German towns on the coasts of the Baltic sea. They strengthened the former image of Germans as modern artisans and merchants.

3   Quite a different impression was produced by the German aristocracy in the new Baltic provinces. This aristocracy became an important element in the Russian army and in state bureaucracy, an element which was loyal to the Czars even in times of rising Russian ethnic nationalism at the end of the nineteenth century. Unlike the Poles, the Baltic German subjects were very loyal Russian subjects, at least until the end of the nineteenth century.

4   German idealistic philosophy was a third formative influence of the first half of the nineteenth century. Russian students flocked in great numbers to German universities, especially to the university of Berlin. The influence of Hegel, Schelling, and more generally of Romanticism, was to have considerable impact on the development of Russian thought. This accounts for the similarity of German Romantic ideas and Slavophile thought.

5   The influence of German social democracy, which was very important at the end of the nineteenth century, is negligible as far as the present situation is concerned. As far as they have survived, socialist ideals have been blended with nationalist thinking among the political left in Russia.

6   If during most of the nineteenth century Prussia was a largely dependent ally of the Russian Empire it came into a very conflicting relationship after the dismissal of Bismarck. Anti-German feelings ran high during the First World War. Wherever possible, traces of German cultural presence were removed. Understandably, anti-German hostility culminated with the 'Great Patriotic war of the Soviet Union' because of the atrocities committed by the German forces and their final defeat (Laqueur 1990: 188ff).

This variety of contacts resulted in different images of the Germans. As a consequence of the first type, Germans acquired a reputation for being thrifty, skilful at the trades, not completely honest but, on the whole, reliable. In general, the image was positive. The contrasting Russian self-ascription follows out of this rather positive reputation of the Germans: accordingly, Russians were lazy, dirty, sloppy, ignorant, and xenophobic. The task of the Russian Czar who took the same negative view of his Russian subjects was, then, to educate them like a stern father. He had to gradually make them more German in order to make his own empire prosperous and powerful. The idea of a Russian people consisting of a mass of Calibans remained a topic in ensuing times, and with it the idea of mass education. It was especially virulent in early socialist and Stalinist times. Taking a pessimistic outlook, it could be thought that any educational effort to introduce discipline, assiduity, and thrift to the Russian nation would ultimately prove futile. This view could merge with a traditionally russophobic position or – if twisted in a positive way – could point to the sympathetic generosity of the Russian national character.

Of course this first type of German image did not predate Peter I. Before that time Germans had just been infidels, non-Christians, worse than heathen in Russian eyes, people who lacked the right religion (orthodoxy, *pravoslavije*). These people, who brought merchandise and were skilful at the trades only partially resembled real human beings. As long as they knew their place they could perhaps be tolerated. In times in which Russians did not identify themselves as Russian, differences between Western heretics such as the Dutch, English, Italians or Germans were negligible.

But the first type of Westerner was shaped according in the image of the Germans, since they were the most numerous. They were only gradually superseded by other influences during the eighteenth century. As in the rest of Europe, absolutism stood culturally under the dominance of French court culture, manners, and language, the French language having become the preferred means of cultured communication among aristocrats.

In contrast to the French, the typical German was now a person apt at bureaucracy and the trades but at the same time intellectually narrow and simple-minded. In contrast to the brilliant French *esprit* and English abilities for commerce, Germans represented the Philistine, honest but boring middle-classes. If Germans were perceived as possessing higher civilization in a technical sense and a better popular education they still were seen as insipid and heartless, industrious but selfish pedants. At their best they might be unworldly bookworms, musicians or dreaming cranks. Yet German influence, especially Baltic German influence, still continued in the state bureaucracy and the army.

German stereotypes were constructed correspondingly. The spectrum of images of Russia ranged from very positive to very negative at the end of the eighteenth century. Russia was seen as a sleeping giant with a submissive, sloppy and uneducated population. If taken in the hands of a strong ruler this country might become either great or extremely dangerous, threatening to unleash their dangerous hordes on a peaceful, cultured and industrious West.

Joseph von Görres (1776–1848), who wrote extensively about Russia, was originally a radical democrat who became a monarchist catholic but nevertheless he upheld his negative conception of Russia. According to him, Russians were a passive object of the political will of the ruler (Tschižewskij and Groh 1969: 41–3). If there was no ruler, they still were passive except for some outbreaks of senseless and destructive violence. It was necessary to bind these people by fear. Perhaps after a long period of autocratic rule, Russians would mature to freedom.

The contrasting conception was held by August von Kotzebue (1761–1819). He was German by culture and Russian by heart, and reflected the anti-German mood in the Russian officer corps at the beginning of the nineteenth century (Kopelew

1987: 11–37). Indeed, both Kotzebue and Görres reflected views which were to be found in the ample German literature on Russia of the time (Fissahn 1987: 136–52). This image based on descriptions and travel literature of the sixteenth and seventeenth centuries was constantly amended. But although new elements were added in subsequent times, it didn't undergo fundamental changes.

Influences of quite another type came with the Russian students of the German Idealist philosophers of the early nineteenth century (Müller 1966, 1993: 106–45; Peskov 1993: 53–94). Many of the then leading Slavophiles had studied in Germany even if they later explicitly denied any German influence. Although the Slavophile movement was extremely variegated the opposition of Eastern and Western spirit and history remained the same in broad lines (Garrigue Masaryk 1992 (1913): 206–92; Goerdt 1995: 262–315; Walicki 1989: 421–58).

At least with the end of the eighteenth century German identity had been constructed in opposition to French civilization (Elias 1989; Plessner 1959). French culture was largely identified with the civilization of European aristocracy and the Absolutist courts the model of which, indeed, was Versailles. German honesty was contrasted to the treacherousness and the intrigues of the courts, German poetic feeling to the cold rationalism of the French, German family honour to French moral dissolution, German frugality to French luxury. Romanticism applied these conceptual oppositions to the difference between Germany and the West. This contrast would later be differentiated in a specific opposition to the British mercantile spirit and dishonesty (Sombart 1915).

Correspondences between the Russian Slavophile tradition of establishing an East–West difference and its German counterpart are obvious. In both cases the differences were used to construct some crucial traits of a national identity. On the German side this has created its own ambivalence toward Russia. On the one hand, the old negative tradition was upheld, on the other hand it was constantly reformulated since the times of the German travellers and of Astolphe Custine. In this perspective, Russia continued to be a country with an uncivilised population barely held together by a despotic government. In contrast to this perspective, Germans were a very civilised, industrious and politically mature Western nation. In its most extreme formulation this perspective culminated in the concept of 'Slavic subhumans'.

The correspondence of German and Russian anti-Westernism was striking even at the end of the nineteenth century. It was at this time that, for some parts of the intellectual and artistic milieus of Germany, Russian thinking became extremely popular. Dostoyevskyi and Tolstoy were widely read and venerated. Many works of conservative and idealistic Russian thought were translated and were successful on the German market: Merežkovskyi, Berdiaev, Florenskyi, Bulgakov, or Solov'ëv were bestsellers or at least widely read by intellectuals (Šestakov 1993: 280–306). This fashion was but the peak of even broader mutual influences (Davydov and Gaidenko 1995). Russian poetry, too, was very popular. The famous Austrian poet Rainer Maria Rilke even wrote some poems in Russian and wore a Russian blouse like Tolstoy or Gor'kyi. Many Germans liked to identify with Russia as it was defined by its 'Asiatic', non-Western traits.

In general, this kind of Russophilia indicated an anti-Western attitude in the German context. It either symbolised the wish to dissociate from a Germany which had become too modern and too westernised, or it symbolised the idea of the basically Eastern character of Germany as opposed to the West; Russia and Germany were seen as twin nations.

The situation in Russia was quite different. As romantic anti-Westernism was claimed as something essentially Russian, it could not be German. So even the early impression made by Schelling or Hegel was subsequently kept secret or denied. It was said that nobody in the West, including German Romantics, was able to penetrate or understand the deep Russian mind. The dominant image of Germany remained that of a Western nation. The Russian mind was unfathomable.

The situation was different with Russian Westernisers. As can be exemplified with Herzen, they no longer tended to identify with Germany, but with France or Britain. According to an older image, Germany was the cold and philistine nation in contrast to magnanimous and sparkling France or solidly cosmopolitan Britain, the identification with the West going as far as contempt for Germans, and especially its émigré community (Gertsen 1973: 130–54, 397–400).

## The Soviet Union and the Great Patriotic War

In many respects Soviet self-definitions preserved the great Russian idea in Marxist-Leninist disguise. In the public rituals, in the veneration of strong leaders, in the enforcement of unconditional submission and in the authoritarian power structures, the Byzantine tradition was alive although it was veiled by Marxist-Leninist and internationalist rhetoric in the Soviet Union.

But ever since Stalin rose to absolute power at the end of the 1920s, official Communist ideology cannot be seen as a continuation of Westernising aspects of the Russian tradition alone. With the Third International, Moscow became the focal point of world history. If for Trotsky and many of the elder Bolsheviks the Revolution had to take place on a global scale or at least in the developed world, the end of the 'Permanent Revolution' marked a shift from ubiquity to a geographical centre. Moscow became the focal point of world history once more as it had in the ideology of the Russian empire.

Until the Second World War, Germany was held in high esteem. It was the country of birth of Marx, Engels and also of minor socialist theorists like Rosa Luxemburg and Karl Kautsky. It was the country which until the outbreak of the First World War had had a particularly strong and disciplined socialist movement. It was even expected for some time that Germany should be the second country in which a socialist revolution would be successful. But support for the German government by the majority of the Social Democrats at the outbreak of the war and the role they played in the crushing the Spartakus rebellion of November 1918 in Berlin could be integrated into a grand historical tale: the leadership of the global socialist movement had passed from Germany to Russia. Moscow had become the Third Rome of socialism. Indeed, since 1929 Stalin himself had become the living incarnation of socialism and was ascribed a charismatic position which no Czar had ever reached in previous times (Stölting 1997: 45–74).

In this context, in which Russian and socialist historical narrations merged, the Second World War redefined German–Russian perceptions and with them Russian self-definitions.

Outside the Soviet Union, in Eastern and Central Europe, the German invasions and the German atrocities were experienced as a terrible disaster. The German nation which had committed these crimes had to be punished. National history was seen as a national catastrophe in each country, although the Holocaust was not central to public memory, the fact that Nazi Germany had lost the war was not a reason for triumph since the losses had been terrible. Victory was the just end of a period of horror.

In East Germany, the history of the Second World War was told in a slightly different way. Here, Nazi atrocities were seen as committed primarily on communists and democrats; the East European peoples being the second group of victims, the Holocaust not central to public memory. In consequence, according to official GDR history writing, the perpetrators were not the Germans but the Fascists. The good Germans were victims of the bad Germans as had been all the others. Since the German Democratic Republic was the state of the good Germans inheriting the democratic and socialist traditions of that country, East Germany had not lost the war in 1945, it had been liberated by the Soviet Union (Fulbrook 1992: 221–43, 291–317).

The same history had a different plot in the Soviet Union. Nazi Germany was a terrible and ruthless enemy which had attacked an unsuspecting and peaceful Soviet Union that had concentrated on its efforts on building a Socialist society. With these actions, Germany was the incarnation of historical evil, and its fascism was the culmination of the fight of reactionary capitalist forces against the bright hopes of humankind (Felice 1995: 51–81). The strength, the cunning, and the cruelty of the Germans represented the old spirit which fought its last battle against socialist revolution.

There was a slightly different version which was told during the war and which far better fitted into national Russian history telling. It was the story of the eternal battle of a cruel, greedy and decadent West against a hopeful, valiant and honest East as shown in Eisenstein's film 'Aleksander Nevskyi'. The Russian victory over the German knights was one of brave humans against the forces of evil. The people of Novgorod who dismantled its corrupt democratic institutions in order to submit to the stern but benevolent autocratic rule of Aleksander were the same Russian people who put their fate into the strong hands of Stalin.

Therefore, Soviet victory over Nazi Germany signified the triumph of the historical hopes of mankind over the forces of evil – a decisive step in world history. The ruthlessness and cruelty of the Germans or the Fascists, their terrible and evil power, was needed in order to demonstrate the greatness of the Soviet victory. Hence, the history of the 'Great Patriotic War' did not simply consist in terror and destruction but in terror and destruction followed by triumph. After the war, this definition of history was celebrated in innumerable monuments all over the Soviet Union. The symbolism of two events may illustrate this meaning: the battle of Stalingrad and the final conquest of Berlin (Glantz and House 1995: 129–78; Overy 1998).

Even before the war, Stalingrad had been one of the central symbolic places of Soviet mythology. In Stalinist historiography the history of the Revolution and of the Civil war had gradually been re-written in order to install Stalin as the man who had organised both events. In this new historiography, the old Tsaritsyn became the place where during the Civil War Stalin allegedly had obtained the decisive victory over the White armies. For this reason it was renamed in honour of the great leader of the Soviet peoples. Stalingrad had been a holy place even before the war.

Therefore, it was no accident that in the Soviet perspective Stalingrad became the focal point of the Second World War. The same was true for the German side. In a military context the battle of Stalingrad made little sense. The Germans could have saved their Seventh Army and used it in other places had they retreated in time. The Soviet army could have easily by-passed the German army and proceeded westward, cutting the enemy off from its supplies. Soviet losses would have been considerably smaller. Here symbolic reasons were a driving motive, too. Apparently Hitler was cognisant of the symbolic importance of Stalin's city, and Stalin wanted to repeat his triumph where his historians had located his decisive triumph of the Civil war (Conquest 1991: Chapters 1–2; Ward 1993: 151–87).

This battle testifies to the historical force of symbols, even if they are based on invented history. Although in strategic military terms the battles on the outskirts of Moscow, the defence of beleaguered Leningrad and the battle of Kursk were far more important, it was Stalingrad, which was seen as the turning point of the war. As seen in its triumphant memory, it was a battle of eschatological dimensions.

The conquest of Berlin has an astonishing symbolism of its own. In Soviet imagery it was not the take-over of Hitler's Chancellery, his headquarters, which symbolically marked the end of the war but the occupation of the Reichstag. A famous photograph by Yegenyi Khaldey shows two Soviet soldiers raising the Soviet flag on top of the destroyed building. The ideological context in which this concentration on the Reichstag makes sense was the Marxist-Leninist conception of German fascism. Since fascism was thought to be the final stage of capitalist society Soviet victory was not only a victory over Germany but over capitalism in its most aggressive form. The Reichstag was the abode of the German parliament, and a bourgeois parliament was an instrument of class oppression. Therefore, the conquest of the German parliament was in essence a historical triumph over capitalism in general. By contrast the fact that the Reichstag had already been burned down in 1933 and that the parliament had altogether disappeared in Nazi Germany was of no symbolic significance.

For the Soviet public the Great Patriotic War was a kind of second founding myth, comparable to the conquest of Kazan (1552) by Ivan Groznyi (the Terrible) which marked the ultimate end of Tatar rule in Russia, the victory of Poltava (1709) which ended the Swedish incursion and made possible the annexation of the new Baltic provinces, and, finally, the triumph over Napoleon in 1812. By its victory over Nazi Germany the Soviet Union had become a superpower – or, to be more precise, the good superpower as contrasted to the evil one, the USA.

Germany had been dwarfed by this Soviet victory. But historically it was still important. Its historical, military and cultural significance was constantly stressed because the stronger Germany had been, the more impressive the Soviet victory could appear. In this sense Germany was presented less as a deviant and criminal historical phenomenon rather than an evil but immensely astute, disciplined, gifted and nearly invincible enemy who could be overcome only by a very heroic people under the genial leadership of Stalin. In this sense, the Soviet triumph in the Second World War became a cornerstone in the official construction of a Soviet identity which was at least as important as the myth of the October Revolution itself.

As the Second World War had ended in triumph the new political imagery was very successful in Soviet public opinion. Many civic rituals were created in order to instil and reinforce collective pride. It was not necessary to adhere to Marxism-Leninism or to be a convinced communist to take pride in being a citizen of the Soviet Union.

The success of this construction of a collective identity became apparent after the collapse of the Soviet Union and of Communism. Even before that time, the attempt to present Stalin as a criminal and to erase him from Soviet history had proved to be difficult. Stalingrad had become Wolgograd but it was not remembered as such. Now it was nearly impossible to define the Soviet period as a historical aberration and to symbolically return to pre-revolutionary times. Indeed, Leningrad was renamed St Petersburg. If historiography had become free to describe terror as terror, inefficiency as inefficiency and crime as crime, civil rituals and public remembrance would hardly forget the triumph without which the history of the last 70 years would have been a terrible mistake and national identity would collapse. This was the time in which the Russian national anthem was lost for some years until the old Soviet anthem was re-installed with a new national text. It was the moment at which the need for a new Russian idea appears to have been generally felt.

It can be doubted whether society really needs a system of common values and orientations as has been supposed in functionalist thinking. But it is significant that dominant Russian political thinking is convinced of the necessity of a binding political ideology. This ideology can be contradictory or it might contain pure inventions. But it has to deliver a strong emotional message. In this sense, history is part of the collective identity and thus part of it a multitude of contrasting collectivities or even enemies. In the construction of collective identities even crucial experiences may be forgotten as they appear to be unfit to mobilise strong emotions. In this sense, the arsenal of symbolic elements which can be used in different circumstances is not easily changed. If collective identities are inherently contradictory they are nevertheless stable.

# References

Anderson, B.R. (1983) *Imagined Communities: Reflections on the Origin and Spread of Nationalism*, London: Verso.

Beevor, A. (1998) *Stalingrad*, London: Viking

Berdiaev, N. (1979) *The Russian Idea*, Westport, CN: Greenwood Press.

Čaadaev, P.Y. (1991) *Pis'mo iz Ardatova v Pariž*, in: *Polnoe cobranie cočineniy, vol. 1*, Moscow: Nauka.

Conquest, R. (1991) *Stalin: Breaker of Nations*, London: Weidenfeld & Nicolson.

Davydov, J.N. and Gaidenko, P.P. (1995) *Rußland und der Westen: Heidelberger Max Weber-Vorlesungen 1992*, Frankfurt am Main: Suhrkamp.

Dunlop, J.B. (1998) *Russia Confronts Chechnya: Roots of a Separatist Conflict*, Cambridge: Cambridge University Press.

Elias, N. (1989) *Studien über die Deutschen: Machtkämpfe und Habitusentwicklung im 19. und 20. Jahrhundert*, Frankfurt am Main: Suhrkamp.

Felice, R.D. (1995) *Le interpretazioni del fascismo*, Bari: Laterza.

Fissahn, B. (1987) 'Faszination und Erschrecken: die Rußlandberichterstattung der "Europäischen Fama" in der nachpetrinischen Ära', in Mechthild Keller (ed.) *Russen und Rußland aus deutscher Sicht, 18. Jahrhundert: Aufklrärung*, Munich: Fink.

Fulbrook, M. (1992) *The Divided Nation: A History of Germany 1918–1990*, Oxford/New York: Oxford University Press.

Gaddis, J.L. (1978) *Russia, the Soviet Union, and the United States: An Interpretive History*, New York: Wiley.

Gammer, M. (1994) *Muslim Resistance to the Tsar: Shamil and the Conquest of Chechnia and Daghestan*, London: Cass.

Garrigue Masaryk, T. (1992/1913) *Russische Geistes- und Religionsgeschichte, vol. 1*, Frankfurt am Main: Eichborn.

Gertsen, A.I. (1973) *Byloe i dumy vol. III*, Moscow: Khud. Lit.

Glantz, D.M. and House, J.M. (1995) *When Titans Clashed: How the Red Army Stopped Hitler*, Lawrence, KA: University Press of Kansas.

Goerdt, W. (1995) *Russische Philosophie*, Grundlagen, Freiburg: Karl Alber.

Greiffenhagen, M. (1971) *Das Dilemma des Konservatismus in Deutschland*, Munich: Piper.

Isaev, I.A. (1992) 'Utopisty ili providcy?', in Puti Evrazii (ed.) *Russkaya intelligenciya i sud'by Rossii*, Moscow: Russkaya kniga.

Kopelew, L. (1987) 'Neues Verständnis und neue Mißverständnisse, neue Verbinungen und neue Widersprüche: zum Rußlandbild der deutschen Aufklärung', in Mechthild Keller (ed.) *Russen und Rußland aus deutscher Sicht, 18. Jahrhundert: Aufklärung*, Munich: Fink.

Laqueur, W. (1990) *Russia and Germany: A Century of Conflict*, New Brunswick: Transaction.

Levine, D.N. (1995) *Visions of the Sociological Tradition*, Chicago: University of Chicago Press.

McDaniel, T. (1998) *The Agony of the Russian Idea*, Princeton, N.J.: Princeton University Press.

Müller E. (Ėberkhard Myuller) (1966) *Russischer Intellekt in europäischer Krise: Ivan Kireevskij (1806–1856)*, Köln: Böhlau.

—— (1993) 'I.V. Kireevskyi i nemeckaya filosofiya', in A.Ya. Šarov (ed.) *Rossiya i Germaniya: Opyt filosofskogo dialoga*, Moscow: Medium.

Overy, R. (1998) *Russia's War*, Harmondsworth: Penguin.

Peskov, A.M. (1993) 'Germanskyi kompleks slavyanofilov', in A.Ya. Šarov (ed.) *Rossiya i Germaniya: Opyt filosofskogo dialoga*, Moscow: Medium.

Plessner, H. (1959) *Die verspätete Nation: Über die politische Verführbarkeit bürgerlichen Geistes*, Stuttgart: Kohlhammer.

Rimscha, H. v. (1983) *Geschichte Rußlands*, Darmstadt: WB.

Seely, R. (2001) *Russo-Chechen Conflict: 1800–2000; A Deadly Embrace*, London: Cass.

Šestakov, V. (1993) 'Nicše i russkaya mysl', in A.Ya. Šarov (ed.) *Rossiya i Germaniya: Opyt filosofskogo dialoga*, Moscow: Medium.

Sombart, W. (1915) *Händler und Helden: Patriotische Besinnungen*, Munich: Duncker & Humblot.

Stölting, E. (1997) 'Charismatische Aspekte des politischen Führertums: Das Beispiel Stalins', in Richard Faber (ed.) *Politische Religion – religiöse Politik*, Würzburg: Königshausen & Neumann.

—— (1990) 'Massen, charismatische Führer und Industrialismus: Erklärungspotentiale eines Denktypus', in W. Süß (ed.) *Übergänge – Zeitgeschichte zwischen Utopie und Machbarkeit*, Berlin: Duncker & Humblot.

—— (2000) 'The East of Europe: a historical construction', in R. Breckner, D. Kalekin-Fishman and Ingrid Miethe (eds) *Biographies and the Division of Europe: Experience, Action, and Change on "Eastern Side"*, Opladen: Leske & Budrich.

Stricker, G. (1997) (ed.) *Rußland: Deutsche Geschichte im Osten Europas*, Berlin: Siedler.

Tschižewskij, D. and Groh, D. (1969) (eds) *Europa und Rußland: Texte zum Problem des westeuropäischen und russischen Selbstverständnisses*, Darmstadt: WB.

Walicki, A. (1989) *The Savophile Controversy: History of a Conservative Utopia in Nineteenth-Century Russian Thought*, Notre Dame, IN: University of Notre Dame Press.

Ward, C. (1993) *Stalin's Russia*, London: Edward Arnold.

Werth, A. (1964) *Russia at War*, New York: Carrroll & Graf.

# Part III

# Europeanisation, national identities and migration

# 10 National identities of Polish (im)migrants in Berlin

## Four varieties, their correlates and implications

*Ewa Morawska*

## Introduction

An examination of the impact of international migration on the national identities of travellers, specifically recent Polish (im)migrants to Berlin in Germany, is timely for two reasons. Sociologically, because the issues of (im)migrants' assimilation into receiver societies on the one hand, and, on the other, their 'transnationalism' or sustained economic, social, political, and symbolic (identificational) engagements in sender countries have recently become the dominant problem agenda of international migration research. But the forms of these identificational engagements have, thus far, been investigated very little (see Smith and Guarnizo 1998; Vertovec and Cohen 1999).

Such an investigation is also relevant politically because the success of the pending accession of Poland to the European Union depends, at least partly, on the 'contents' of national and civic identities and the world orientations of that country's residents. A long history of subjugation to alien states and the romantic concepts of the Polish nation as an innocent martyr-carrier of spiritual values, heroically resisting oppression (including Soviet rule, commonly perceived as the continuation of foreign impositions) have made Polish nationalism an embodiment of the ethnic-particularistic rather than civic-universalist type, informed by exclusionary us–them symbolic distinctions whereby the nation (us Poles) was counterposed to the state (them–alien oppressors).[1]

If such nation-against-state intransigence was appreciated in the West during the Cold War as supportive of freedom and democracy, it is now viewed as one of the hindrances to Poland's democratic transition (see Liebich 1999; Morawska 2001a). The impact on the transformation of these national identities and orientations of large Polish diasporas in the West (including Germany) that maintain active contact with their home societies and of the continuous back-and-forth movement of migrants between their hometowns and Western receiver countries since the 1990s is certainly worth consideration.

This paper is based on a preliminary study conducted in the summer of 2001 in Berlin, the residence of the largest proportion of 1980s–1990s Polish (im)migrants (see Janusz 1995; Stach 1998; Wolff-Poweska and Schultz 2000; Kaczmarczyk

2001; Rajkiewicz 2000). In that study I personally interviewed or corresponded with twenty religious and organisational leaders of the Berlin Polish community, members of the Polnischer Sozialrat (a local German–Polish organisation assisting contract workers and undocumented migrants), editors of Polish-language newspapers and radio programmes, and authors of studies of Polish (im)migrants in Berlin. The list of my (co)respondents can be found in Appendix II.

I also content-analysed 1992–2001 samples of the monthly *Kurier Berlinski-Polonica* published in Polish and German, and Berlin newspapers *Der Tagesspiegel*, *Die Tageszeitung*, and *Die Berlinerzeitung*, looking for material related to Polish (im)migrant adaptation in Germany and, in particular, their national identities, collective self-representations, and images of 'others', especially Germany/Germans and Europe/Europeans.

The Polish group in Berlin is not homogenous but consists of different waves of immigrants 'moved' by different economic and political mechanisms (the interwar period, the 1960s–1970s, the 1980s, the postcommunist era); different ethnic backgrounds (Polish, ethnic German, Silesian,[2] Jewish); and different socioeconomic positions and legal statuses in Germany. This discussion focuses on four groups. In the category of the so-called *Arbeitstouristen*, or tourist-workers predominantly from the postcommunist wave,[3] who overstay the official three-month visit allowance and work illegally in the informal sector of Berlin's economy,[4] I consider low- and highly-educated migrants separately. The other two groups are represented by middle-class immigrant Polish permanent residents in humanistic and business/technical professions who have settled in Berlin since the 1980s and who display different kinds of national identities and perceptions of 'others'.

I began my study with three hypotheses. (1) Because of Poland's continued economic and political backwardness in relation to Western Europe, in this case, Germany, and Poland's treatment by German public opinion as a semi-periphery whose citizens represent a threat as unwanted aspiring members of the European Union, national identities of Polish (im)migrants who are exposed to these realities in their everyday lives represent an intensified combination of the traditional defensive–offensive syndrome of Polish nationalism containing, on the one hand, a resentful 'civilizational inferiority' vis-à-vis West Europeans and, on the other hand, a claim to 'spiritual superiority'. (2) At the same time, during their Western (German) sojourns these ambivalent national identities of immigrants acquire a new, third component, namely, some behavioural habits and a sense of civilizational superiority as residents of a highly developed Western (German) country toward the backwardness at home. (3) These incongruous multidimensional national identities of immigrants are displayed situationally: in Germany, the original defensive– offensive component is dominant; in Poland (after return or during temporary visits), the I-the-Westerner part is played out.

The results of my preliminary study suggest, however, even more complicated patterns – no fewer than four types of national identities among Polish (im)migrants in Berlin. As I discuss each of these types and their generating contexts, I formulate questions for further research.

# Polish *Arbeitstouristen*

## *Unaffected national identities?*

The number of undocumented Polish tourist-workers in Berlin has been estimated at about 100,000 migrants annually. The majority of these migrants are *Pendler/innen*, men and women with elementary and high-school education who move back-and-forth across the border: they either work in the city during the week and return home for the weekends (especially migrants from western parts of Poland) or stay there for a few months, return home for a while after arranging for temporary replacements at their Berlin workplaces, come back to the same or similar jobs, and so on.[5]

Polish *Arbeitstouristen* are concentrated in a few sectors of Berlin's informal labour market. Most men work in construction, predominantly in small firms owned by native Germans, second-generation Italians (children of *Gastarbeiters* from the 1950s–1960s), or longer-established Poles with legal immigrant status, in '*mache alles*' handyman jobs and as helpers in bars and restaurants owned mainly by second-generation German Turks and Yugoslavs. Women find employment mainly in German homes, usually several at the same time, as maids, baby-sitters and caregivers for the elderly, and also in ethnic, especially Turkish, cafés and restaurants, and as prostitutes.[6] From their earnings of 5–7 € per hour these frugal tourist-workers manage to save 70–75% or 400–800 € per month, amounts three to five times higher than the average incomes for men and women in Poland.[7]

These migrants come to the West, in this case, Berlin, '*na saksy*' (this idiom, originally used to refer to customary seasonal employment in Germany of hundreds of thousands of Poles between 1890 and 1914,[8] is still used in contemporary Poland) for the sole purpose of earning additional income for their families. Because of this narrowly defined practical purpose of their Western sojourns and because as *pendel* migrants they remain immersed in everyday affairs at home, Poland and their hometowns there and, of particular concern here, their symbolic worlds, remain the primary reference framework for these tourist-workers.

Long hours of exhausting work during their Berlin sojourns, the only means of realising the goals that brought them there, and unfamiliarity with the German language make social relations with Germans and participation in German culture nearly impossible. In addition, political insecurity related to migrants' undocumented status and their resulting permanent fear of harassment and deportation combined with the hostility or, at best, indifference of German public opinion toward them significantly contribute to the multiple marginalisation of these tourist-workers during their Berlin sojourns.

In the situation of multiple but transitory marginalisation, which does not interfere with their lives in Poland and does not prevent the realisation of their goals in Berlin (unless, of course, they are caught and deported), Polish *Arbeitstouristen*, my respondents believed, 'do not have much curiosity about the world'. Their German sojourns 'do not alter their traditional [home-country] national identities', and 'the idea of Europe and feeling European does not even enter their minds'.[9]

These are sociologically convincing propositions that should be tested in further research. If true, this 'no-effect' effect would represent a case, underinvestigated in (im)migration studies, of migrants' sustained transnational engagements, here economic, without the simultaneous 'transnationalisation' or pluralisation of their national identities.[10] But whether the lack of curiosity about the world and ignorance about Europe are the products of the migrants' situation in Berlin or of their accustomed home-bred dispositions and whether there are any gender differences in this phenomenon deserves examination. In Polish public opinion surveys about one-third of respondents, mainly men and women from less-educated strata employed in manual and lower-level service occupations, expresses no interest and no knowledge about the European Union and Poland's pending accession to this body; the respective proportion among college-educated Poles in professional and managerial occupations is 7 per cent (CBOS reports, 1998–2001). It would be ironic, indeed, if Polish migrants' Western sojourns and, in particular, the circumstances thereof, contributed to the preservation of these inward-turned orientations or even their reinforcement as a defence mechanism or a shield against the hostility of the host German/European society.

According to my respondents, two new elements of tourist-worker self-perceptions evolve over time, however, as the result of their experience in Berlin (see also Cyrus 1995a; Helias 1996; Sakson 2000; Trzcielinska-Polus 2000). One of them is a habit of hard work and frugality, both of which were uncommon orientations in communist Poland that have survived into the new era, particularly among less-educated Poles from poorer economic strata (the absence among citizens of state-socialist regimes of the commitment to and habits of hard work was a staple issue in discussions by social scientists and political critics of the (mal)functioning of the communist system). The other, related orientation is a new sense that it is possible to improve one's life situation by one's own effort that diminishes the habituated *postawy roszczeniowe* (claimant orientations) vis-à-vis the state, which again are still common among lower socioeconomic strata of postcommunist Poland, as the provider of guaranteed employment and other social services.[11]

These new orientations of Polish tourist-workers acquired during their Berlin sojourns have, my respondents believed, a mainly pragmatic, action-oriented character and do not entail 'civilizational superiority' (my original hypothesis) toward fellow countrymen at home simply because these hard-working and marginalised sojourners have no time or opportunity to develop such concepts.

These newly acquired orientations, a commitment to hard work in conditions promising good rewards and an increased sense of self-reliance, become part of Polish tourist-workers' coping strategies in the capitalist world and, over time, an integral component of the 'migration culture' shared with fellow-nationals in the same situation (see Morawska 2001b). Whether and how these attitudes also become part of migrants' self-perceptions as Poles – situationally as Poles abroad or as 'Westernised' Poles at home – and whether they affect other, particularistic-romantic components of their national identities are questions to be addressed in further research.

### New Europeans?

This group of undocumented migrant workers, college students and young professionals, has not, thus far, attracted the attention of students of East–West European international migration, and I did not consider it, either, in my original hypotheses. It constitutes a minority among East European *Arbeitstouristen* in West European countries, but since the mid-1990s, large cities such as Berlin, Paris, Brussels, and Amsterdam have been receiving increasing numbers of such migrants from Poland, the Czech Republic, Hungary, and Slovakia.

They come to earn money, for sure, but this is not the only and for some not even the most important purpose of their sojourns. According to my Berlin informants, Polish college students and young professionals, men and women alike, come to this city either on temporary student visas to learn German or to upgrade their qualifications and undertake undocumented work or to do the same on tourist visas, especially in the summer months. The informal-sector jobs they find and the illegal income they earn are similar to those obtained by their fellow-nationals in the main category of tourist-workers discussed earlier. It is, however, their future projects focused on a time when a successfully transformed Poland will be a member of the European Union that primarily motivates their migrations.

My respondents contrasted this group with typical *Arbeitstouristen*: 'this group is quite different, *swiatla*, cultured or civilized'; 'they are curious about the world'; 'they want to learn the [German] language and gain the [European] experience'.[12] It is a sad way to win their spurs among Europeans but perhaps the best possible for *pauvres cousins* from the antechambers of the European Union.

These are observations of well-positioned local residents. Whether, indeed, these migrants, men and women, are 'civilized cosmopolitans' and aspiring Europeans and, if so, whether their sojourns in Berlin as second-rate, often openly unwelcome, visitors strengthen or weaken these self-perceptions, must be addressed in direct conversations with these people. Universities can be located easily in Poland, so students who recently spent time in Berlin as tourist-workers can be identified and interviewed in their home country (this task would be much more difficult in the case of the typical *Arbeitsouristen*, who come from all over Poland). It would be interesting, too, to investigate interactions (if any) these young and aspiring visitors may have had with different groups of permanent Polish immigrants (see below) and their impact on these sojourners' images of Poland's/Poles' position in Western Europe and, in turn, on their national identities.

### Polish immigrants

In the mid-1990s about 29,000 Polish immigrants lived in Berlin who were either citizens or permanent residents of Germany.[13] The proportionally largest group – and the focus of this discussion – are immigrants who came to Germany in the 1980s and (a lesser number) in the early 1990s (*Polonia w Niemczech* 1995; Stach 1998; Lesiuk and Trzcielinska-Polus 2000; Kaczmarczyk 2001). The majority of them were 35 to 55 years of age. Immigrants who came to Berlin as adults usually experienced some occupational skidding, but most of them subsequently adapted quite well (the sooner they obtained official immigration status, the shorter was the duration of this downslide). Businessmen, managers, and middle-level white-collar employees comprised 40–5 per cent of the total Polish immigrant population in the city in the mid-1990s.[14]

This discussion focuses on this middle-class group because of the economic, political, and cultural role they can be expected to play in forging links between Poland and Germany, and as unofficial mediators in fostering Poland's inclusion into the European Union.

My interviews with Polish organisational leaders and members of the Polnischer Sozialrat, and the content-analysis of the Polish-language press in Berlin suggest that national orientations among Polish immigrants can be classified into two major types. *Trudna polskosc*, or difficult Polishness, as one of the respondents described it, is the identity 'torn' by contradictory, positive and negative emotions toward one's own (Polish) group and by equally opposing attitudes toward 'others,' here, Germany/Germans and Europe/the European Union.

The other orientation represents a combination of post-nationalism and 'implicit multiculturalism' thus far unexamined by (im)migration sociologists whereby the significance of national identity is deliberately underplayed even though immigrants live it, *experience-near* to use Hans Kohut's term for unreflected-upon sentiments, in their everyday activities.[15] This attitude is captured in a reply by a respondent to my inquiries: 'We go back and forth [between Germany and Poland] all the time. We are Polish, we live and work here [in Germany], but it really does not matter much any more'.[16] Both *trudna polskosc* and 'it does not matter anymore' orientations are more complex than the categories of national identities among Polish immigrants in Germany identified in the few existing sociological studies of this problem: Krzysztof Krawat's (1996) distinction between 'national(istic) patriots'[17] and 'European pragmatists', or Kazimierz Woycicki's (2000) concept of cultivated 'dual nationality'.

### Trudna Polskosc

'Difficult Polishness' corresponds to the outcome of Polish immigrants' experience in Germany proposed in my original hypothesis, namely, the intensified combination on both sides of the traditional defensive–offensive syndrome of Polish nationalism containing, on the one hand, a resentful 'civilizational inferiority' vis-à-vis West Europeans – here, Germans – and, on the other hand, a frustrated claim to 'spiritual superiority'. This type of nationalism seems most common among the Polish immigrant intelligentsia, in particular, people employed or otherwise engaged in Polish cultural organisations (newspapers, clubs, educational associations) and events and among leaders representing the Polish group in legal and political bodies of the German administration.

A configuration of factors (more complex than that identified in my original hypothesis) generates this uncomfortable national identity. It is possible that the humanistic education immigrants received in Poland, informed by the Romantic code and a strong emphasis on historical (literary) memory,[18] has imbued them with a sense of traditional Polish nationalism stronger than the 'national average' with its animosities toward powerful and inimical neighbours, including Germany. Ironically, whereas among the Polish intelligentsia in Poland socialised into the same orientations, this traditional offensive–defensive national syndrome and open hostility or suspicion toward Germany/Germans have waned since the 1990s (CBOS reports 1993–2001), among fellow-nationals across the border these attitudes have intensified. The following circumstances have combined to produce these effects.

The particularistic-exclusionary German concept of nationality does not facilitate but hinders the integration of foreign-born residents in general and may actually stimulate mirror-like representations of national identities among them. (On the German concept of nation and national membership, see, e.g., Kohn 1944; Gellner 1983; Brubaker 1992; on its effects on German immigration policies and immigrant integration, see Fijalkowski 1993; Persson 1997; also O'Brien 1988, and Bade 1995.) Antagonism and open discrimination on the part of Germans encountered by Polish immigrants in their everyday lives in Berlin, which reflect this general orientation and, in particular, a long history of Polish–German enmity, has been an important factor in sustaining or even intensifying immigrant perceptions of sharp, us–them group boundaries and feelings of resentful humiliation. When shared with fellow nationals, the offence is generalised into the collective of Polish immigrants/Polish nation. The lack of fluency in the German language common to this group further contributes to immigrants' sense of alienation.[19]

These feelings of anger combine with more aggravating factors. One is the perceived reluctance of the German government to fulfil its obligations as set out in the 1991 Polish–German Tractate about the treatment of national minorities in both countries. Specifically, the German government continues to refuse to recognise Polish immigrants and their descendants as a national minority and has been creating obstacles to providing the agreed on subsidies for Polish-language education and cultural activities. (On the legal status of the Polish group in Germany and controversies around it, see Barcz 1995; Janusz 2000; on the provisions of the Polish–German Tractate of 17 June 1991 and the German government's intransigence, see Mrowka 2000.[20])

Three other factors intensify Polish immigrants' *trudna polskosc*. One is the lack of interest of the German media in the affairs of Poland, especially its culture and accomplishments. Immigrants believe such information could counter the negative image of Poland and its nationals both at home and in Germany. Another is the shared sense of frustration among Polish immigrants caused by a visible absence of their group from the public forums in Germany, especially from local and regional politics, for which they blame the German authorities as well as themselves and, in particular, a 'typically Polish' lack of solidarity and privatism. Indeed, Polish organisations in Germany in general and also in Berlin have been notoriously con-tentious[21] and only a small fraction of immigrants belong to them (see Marchwinski 2000; Sakson 2000). Adding to the discomfort of their difficult Polishness is an appreciation of German respect for the law, good organisation, and effectiveness, not a particular forte of Poles, whose pluck and imagination, however admirable, cannot, as immigrants realise, substitute for these values.[22]

In this situation, the glories of Polish history and culture unrecognised by mainstream German society and Polish immigrants' frustrations stemming from their group's treatment by this society and its institutions and from perceptions of their own failings, all find recognition and expression mainly in immigrant social circles and in the Polish-language press and radio programmes. On the outside, immigrants' *trudna polskosc* assumes a *schildkotenartige Haltung*: like the turtle, they pull into their collective shell believing that in the existing circumstances, a public display might further worsen the Polish group's status in Germany.[23]

This *trudna polskosc* of Polish immigrants has recently acquired another new component, namely, a strongly ambivalent attitude toward Poland joining the European Union. In this matter, Polish immigrants in Berlin differ from their college-educated fellow nationals in Poland whose support for Poland's membership of the European Union has been high (75–80 per cent) and steady over the last decade.[24] My content-analysis of *Kurier Berlinski-Polonica*, the newspaper addressed to and read by Polish intelligentsia in Berlin, has shown the predominance of negative over positive assessments of Polish inclusion, also in reprints from the Polish press in Poland, which presents a generally equal distribution of pro and con positions in this matter. In the context of intensified and 'hurtful' us-othering attitudes among immigrants, especially vis-à-vis Germany, a superpower in the European Union, and the easily generalisable perception in this group of Poles/Poland as unwanted petitioners, their negative-leaning ambivalence is not at all surprising. A combination of factors in this immigrant group's external surroundings and internal structure limits its capacity to forge 'symbolic bridges' between Poland and (West) Europe.

Besides a closer examination of the forces that sustain immigrants' *trudna polskosc*, at least three issues deserve further research. One of them is the forms and 'contents' of this group's assimilation into the German culture and society. Another issue is immigrants' perceptions of Poland's historical membership in the European cultural community (an integral element of Polish national self-representation, particularly emphasised by the Polish Roman Catholic Church during the communist era); this recognition may coexist with suspicion toward the European Union. Third, and underlying these research questions, is the genderedness of the impact of Polish immigrants' experience in Germany on their national identities.

### Does it not matter any more?

Immigrant identities combining declared post-nationalism and implicit multi-culturalism appear to be most common among more established businessmen and co-owners of joint Polish–German ventures, engineers, and members of other technical professions. Because these are predominantly male occupations in Polish Berlin, such a double-pronged identity may be more typical for immigrant men than women.

Immigrants in this group can be called 'pragmatic Europeans' (one of the two identity types among Poles in Germany proposed by Krawat 1996). In contrast to their fellow-nationals burdened with *trudna polskosc*, their support for Poland's membership of the European Union has been unequivocal. For these 'cosmopolitans', as one of my respondents put it, 'the border [between Poland and Germany/Western Europe] does not exist anymore, and, therefore, the nationality issue has lost much of its importance'.[25]

At the same time, however, they live (rather than cultivate) their Polishness by using the Polish language and by 'naturally' observing Polish customs at home and with their Polish friends. Fluent in the German language and engaged in daily professional and social relations with Germans, they also participate in German society and culture. For these immigrants, for that matter, the features noted earlier of the German culture-in-action resentfully admired by the *trudna polskosc* group, are also part of their own outlooks and practices.[26]

A distinction drawn by the Polish sociologist, Stanislaw Ossowski (1967; see also Anderson 1983), between the ideological *Vaterland*, or the imagined community of the encompassing *Patria*, and the *Heimat*, or the local homeland of people's daily activities, may be useful to interpret these apparently contradictory commitments. While the circumstances of immigrants' situations have attenuated the significance of the national *Vaterland*, replacing it with a commitment to the imagined community of Europe, their daily activities sustain the relevance of their two *Heimats* although their attachments to them differ in depth and the emotional hold.

Several superimposed factors responsible for these immigrants' multi-level identities have better prepared them to facilitate not only their own integration into the German society but also, indirectly, the inclusion of their home-country into a 'larger Europe'. Their professions facilitate formal participation in the German society, a form of integration these immigrants promote themselves by participating or even founding bi-national professional organisations, such as Berpol or the Polish–German Club of Businessmen and Industrialists or the Polish–German Club of Engineers. These organisations sponsor well-publicised bi-national events in the city such as the prestigious annual ball organised by the Berpol and attended by prominent German Berliners and diplomats from the Polish Embassy (*Polacy w Berlinie* 1996; *Kurier Berlinski-Polonica* 1997–2001). Immigrants' fluency in German obviously facilitates these activities. Their professional activities and resulting social relations with native Germans mean that Polish immigrants in this group are less exposed to anti-Polish prejudice and discrimination than are their fellow-nationals in the *trudna polskosc* group.

At the same time, the proximity of the border makes frequent travel to Poland a weekly or even daily routine and the absence of a border becomes an experiential reality. As we talked about these back-and-forth movements, one of my respondents informed me that his wife 'just went to dinner to her friends' in Poznan. It's a few hours by car [and] she will be back [in Berlin] tomorrow morning'. Another informant was about to leave for Szczecin because he had 'theatre tickets there for tonight and tomorrow some business to attend'. Many immigrants in this group have apartments in Poland, usually in its western regions that are geographically closest to Berlin.[27] Kazimierz Woycicki (2000) whose research quoted earlier revealed that Polish immigrants have dual national identities, conducted his study in Düsseldorf in western Germany.[28] One of the interesting research questions that await comparative investigation is the effect of proximate (here, Berlin) vs. geographically more distant (Düsseldorf) home and host countries and its implications for the ease and frequency of back-and-forth travels on the composition of immigrants' identities.

Another factor apparently contributing to this identificational configuration is the 'domestication' of or, in sociological terms, anticipatory socialisation into German culture in immigrants' families in the home country. On several occasions during our conversations about this matter, my respondents referred to their backgrounds in Poland's western territories or the former *zabor pruski*, a German division of partitioned Poland (1795–1918) where 'people's habits and outlooks still differ from those in the rest of Poland', to 'respect for the law and order and familiarity with German culture', and to knowledge of [at least some] German maintained in their families.[29]

Finally, there is also a possibility that the emphasis by immigrants in this group on their cosmopolitan (supra-national) orientations represents a form of inner escape from or defence against the low status of the Polish group in Germany. Such escapes into transnational, here, home-country-oriented, identities and engagements by racial minority immigrants in America have been reported in several studies (see, e.g., Waters 1999; Smith and Guarnizo 1998). This case would represent a flight into post-nationalism. I did not pursue this possibility in my preliminary study, but, thus far unexamined in sociological studies, it is certainly worth investigation.

## Conclusion

As the foregoing discussion demonstrates, how the immigrant experience influences the national identities of Berlin Poles depends not only on the particular circumstances they encounter in the host society but also on the home-country cultural capital they bring with them.[30] As a result of this multiplicity, immigrant identities take many forms. Only four have been considered in this chapter. As I discussed each of them, I also pointed out research questions that await further investigation. In conclusion, I return to the two reasons noted in the introduction, which make the study of Polish (and East European) immigrants in Germany (West Europe) worthy of investigation.

The contribution of my Berlin project to the study of immigrant transnationalism has been twofold. A vast literature on immigrant transnationalism[31] that recognises cross-border identities of travellers as a constitutive component of this phenomenon has seldom inquired into the particular forms of these self-representations. I have identified different forms of such identities and circumstances that shape them. My study also repudiates the prevailing view that transnational involvements either de-anchor immigrants from both sender and receiver societies or produce 'bifocal' identities whose social embeddedness in local environments is not elaborated (see, e.g., Vertovec and Cohen 1999; Rouse 1992; and Kearney 1995 for the former approach; Portes 1999 for the latter). As a result, studies of transnationalism and the assimilation of immigrants into a host society have developed in parallel rather than in dialogue with each other.[32] The case of Poles in Berlin demonstrates that immigrants' transnational involvements do not necessarily alter their traditional identities and, if they do, these transnational identities may well coexist with integration into the host society.

Specifically, my study permits the following conclusions. First, the notion of (trans)national identities needs conceptual refinement so that it can capture different kinds or levels of immigrants' identificational engagements. A good starting point for this task can be the distinction proposed here between identifications with the *Vaterland(s)* and with the *Heimats*, which allows for different developments. The circumstances of immigrants' situations in the host society may intensify or weaken their home-country *Vaterland* and *Heimat* identities at the same time; or they may affect these different-level identities in opposite directions enhancing one of them and weakening the other. Likewise, the corresponding host-country identities may remain unaffected or be transformed at both or only one level of commitment. Thus, the transformation of identities of Polish businessmen, managers, and engineers in Berlin represents a diminution of the significance of the national *Vaterland*, which is accompanied by the emergence of a symbolic commitment to Europe (the European Union) as the 'imagined transnational space' and the simultaneous persistence and development, respectively, of (transnational) home- and host-country *Heimat* identifications.

Second, the results of my Berlin study indicate that the economic-only transnational engagements of lower-class migrants whose sojourns abroad are frequent but of short duration, whose political status in the host society is undocumented, and whose income-earning activities do not leave time or energy for the development of any other interests do not 'transnationalise' their accustomed identities. Third, aspiring young 'Europeans' who come to Berlin to earn money illegally and to learn about the outside world suggests that this transnationalisation process may not result, as the immigrant transnationalism argument contends, but actually may precede and even motivate international migration. Fourth, the *trudna polskosc* type of identity indicates that immigrants' transnational/home-country-oriented symbolic commitments can provide, as demonstrated in the transnationalism literature, not only important rewards in personal and group self-esteem in the situation of host-society rejection, but also intensify an embarrassed awareness of the inadequacies of the (home-) national culture compared with that of the hosts. A political significance of the impact of Western, here, German, experience on Polish (im)migrants' national identities derives from the importance of the transformation of the deeply embedded traditional Polish understanding of nation and nationalism as ethnic-particularistic, exclusive categories into civic-inclusive and pluralist concepts for the successful integration of that country into the European community. In this regard, the results of my preliminary study reveal a complicated situation resulting from the different circumstances of different immigrant groups. What is clear, however is that both host and home countries are implicated in the effects of temporary as well as permanent sojourns abroad on (im)migrants' identities. The configuration represented by the identities of Polish immigrant businessmen, managers and engineers in Berlin appears to be the optimal trajectory for the least problematic inclusion of Poland in the European Union. The notion of *Eurolocalisation*, a play on the concept of *glocalisation* (Robertson 1992), or the mixing-and-blending of global influences and local traditions, yielding results that are neither purely global nor exclusively local, may describe the transformation of these immigrants' identities in Germany. The 'Euro' part of the process indicates a reduced symbolic investment in the national ideological community and an increased identification with the European one while the 'local(-isation)' refers to immigrants' sustained, if not identical, engagements in their *Heimats* on both sides of the border/no border.

As noted, however, contingent on multiple socio-economic and cultural requirements, at the present time this kind of identification is a 'luxury' available to a minority of Polish immigrants. But even if it were to become accessible to more Polish travellers, the desirability of weakening commitments to the Polish national *Vaterland* is not unequivocal from the standpoint of Poland's integration into the European Union. Those who recognise Poland's unequal position in the negotiations with the European Union and who project such long-term un-partnerlike relations onto the time it will become part of this body, tend to see a strengthening, not weakening, of Poles' national loyalties at home and abroad as in the best interest of integration. Concentrated efforts to quicken Poland's *perestroika* on the Polish side and, on the Western (German) side, efforts, backed up by practical steps, to appease these Polish anxieties would be the most effective means to make the Eurolocalisation of identities option both feasible and appealing to Polish (im)migrants.

The *trudna polskosc* immigrant identity has been uncomfortable for its bearers and has not facilitated the process of bringing Poland and Poles closer to the European community. Immigrants' accounts, both privately during their visits to Poland and publicly in the Polish media, of their personal experiences with bad treatment of the Polish group and with ignorant negative stereotypes of Poles/Poland in Germany and of their implications for integration into the European Union do not predispose their audiences favourably to this prospect. The role of the host-country, here, German immigration policies, media representation of immigrants and their native country, and German public opinion attitudes and behaviour toward Polish residents, in negatively structuring immigrants' identities is evident in this case, making the direction of desired changes equally obvious. On the Polish side, more active involvement of Poland's government's in supervising the implementation by German authorities of the 1991 Polish–German Tractate – the benchmark for Polish immigrants' complaints about mistreatment of their group in Germany – would also help to diminish frustration and to build up collective self-esteem. To the same effect, Polish immigrants could concentrate on bridging intragroup differences and forming a united 'organisational front' in negotiating their group's interests with the German authorities. The curing of frustrations with national self-image stemming from invidious comparisons of one's own group's failings and others' strengths is a challenge for practical action facing Poles in Poland as well as those abroad.

It would be, undoubtedly, a contribution to Poland's economic transformation 'from below' if the habits of hard work and increased self-reliance acquired by Polish *Arbeitstouristen* during their sojourns in Germany become integral elements of their self-perceptions as new-era Poles and, through the demonstration effect of material improvement in migrant households, also part of the 'cultural tool kits' (Swidler 1986) of the residents in their home-country communities. As my preliminary study indicates, however, this transformation of Polish migrants' practical orientations has not been accompanied by alterations in other elements of their worldviews. In particular, representations of Poland and Poles as part of the European community narrated at home by worldwide returnees could over time influence local residents' orientations. Legalisation of the political status of these tourist-workers in Germany and the improvements of their social and economic situations that would result is a significant challenge to the German government which must consider the strong opposition to such changes by German trade unions and public opinion. Such changes are necessary, however, for these migrants to be able to develop attachments to their local German *Heimats* and, by the same token, to facilitate the broadening of the 'mental horizons' of these visitors through institutionalised opportunities to learn the German language and participate in the German/ European culture, if only through the media. The fulfilment of the European aspirations of a minority group among Polish *Arbeitstouristen* in Berlin, college students and young professionals, would also be more effective – not to mention more humane (as in human rights) – if these migrants either did not have to earn extra income in this way or if their temporary employment abroad were legalised. The realisation of the first condition, increased economic opportunities at home, is the responsibility of Polish society and its leaders, one hopes with the support of the European Union, and it will require considerable time. The second condition, the removal of political obstacles to the temporary employment of Poles, is within the control of the German government and seems easier to fulfil in a shorter period of time.

## Appendix I  Factors affecting (im)migrant national identities (identified in study of Poles in Berlin)

Transportation and communication technology

Geographic proximity

History of home/host-country relations

National factors

| Sending country | Receiving country |
| --- | --- |
| dynamics of economic development | labour market structure and dynamics |
| dominant concepts of nation/nationalism | civic culture/practice of inclusion or exclusion of 'others', in particular racial 'others'* |
| power relations with receiving country | |
| state policies toward and involvement on behalf of immigrant/ethnic groups abroad | government attitudes/behaviour toward (im)migrants |
| | media's depiction of (im)migrants and their home-countries |
| | state policy toward/relations with sending country |

Local factors (receiving country)

| External | Intragroup |
| --- | --- |
| structure and dynamics of the economy | group socio-economic characteristic |
| civic–political culture and practice regarding immigrants particularly from the (specific) country | degree of socio-cultural enclosure of immigrants |
| openness/closure of local political system | sojourn/diasporic collective mentality |
| native perceptions of/behaviour toward immigrants (particularly from the (specific) country) | internal organisation and leadership and representation of group interests in host society's public forums |
| degree of inter-group social exclusion/ inclusion | group sense of civic entitlement in host society |

Individual factors

- cultural capital (education, occupational skills, access to technological resources, advanced acculturation, life goals and values)
- legal (vs. undocumented) status in host society
- employment and prospects of achievement in mainstream host society
- gender

- purpose/circumstances of (e)migration
- experience of prejudice/discrimination on part of host society
- isolation or contact with native Germans (workplace, formal and informal contexts)
- number of years spent in receiving country
- sojourn or permanent (im)migration
- regional origin in home-country
- intensity of attachment to home country
- home-country-centred world (Europe)-oriented outlooks and concerns

## Appendix II  The list of respondents personally contacted by the author

Jacek Barelkowski
Norbert Cyrus
Barbara Erit
Michal Godel
Malgorzata Irek
Witold Kaminski
Jacek Kobink
Joanna Lesniak
Janusz Marchwinski
Wladyslaw Misiak
Leszek Oswiecimski

Grzegorz Pawlak
Maria Pawlak
Aleksandra Proscewicz
Andrzej Sakson
Andrzej Stach
Andrzej Szulczynski
Bogdan Slaski
Ewa Slaska
Tadeusz Sniadecki
Sylwester Wawrzyniak

## Notes

1 On these two traditions of nationalism and the historical circumstances of the emergence of the latter type in Poland and East Europe at large, see Kohn 1944; Walicki 1981; Connor 1994. On the persistence of this concept of nation and nationalism under communist rule in Poland, see Morawska 1987.
2 This is a regional group whose members, viewed as German by Germans and Polish by Poles, tend to identify themselves in terms of their local rather than national membership (see Grabe 2000; Jonczy 2000; Rauzinski 2000; Schmidt 2000).
3 This group also includes (omitted in this chapter) Communist-era contract workers who have stayed on in Berlin and continue to work as illegal immigrants.
4 This group includes an unknown number of Polish contract labourers in Berlin who overstay their temporary visitor permits (see note 14 below) and engage in work in the city's informal economy.
5 Information compiled from Cyrus 1995a, 1997a, 1997c, and his personal communication to this author in September 2001; interview with Witold Kaminski, director of the Polnischer Sozialrat in Berlin, July 2001; *Die Berlinerzeitung* 5 June 1995; Kaminski 1995, 1996; Domaradzka 1996; Miera 1996; Wilpert 1998; see also Kaczmarczyk 2001.
6 The following discussion does not apply to women migrants employed in prostitution. On this group in Berlin, see Cyrus 1997a; Schenk 1993.
7 This and the following information about Polish *pendler/innen*'s goals, earnings, and

savings and about their isolation in Berlin was gathered from interviews with Grzegorz Pawlak, Andrzej Szulczynski, and Witold Kaminski in July 2001; *Der Spiegel* 47, 1994; Cyrus 1995a, 1997a, 1997b; *Der Tagesspiegel*, 29 October 1995, 1 June 1996; Gemende 1996; Miera 1996; Trzcielinska-Polus 2000; this author's ethnographic research in that city in the spring of 2002. On ethnic niches in Berlin's services and industries and their labour force, see Hillmann and Hedwig 1996; Hillmann 1998.

8   See W.I. Thomas and Florian Znaniecki 1918–20; Janowska 1981;  Morawska 1989; *Polonia w Niemczech*, 1995.

9   Interviews with Witold Kaminski, Grzegorz Pawlak, the warden of the Polish parish in Berlin, and Alexandra Proscewicz, the editor of *Kurier Berlinski-Polonica* in July 2001.

10   For the state-of-the-art discussion, supported by empirical studies, of immigrant transnationalism, see Smith and Guarnizo 1998; Gerstle and Mollenkopf 2001. On distinctions between post- and transnationalism and multiculturalism, see note 16 below.

11   On the persistence of these communist-era orientations see, Los 1998; Staniszkis 1999; reportages in the weekly *Polityka*, 1995–2001.

12   Interviews with Andrzej Szulczynski, Witold Kaminski, and Grzegorz Pawlak in July 2001; correspondence to this author from Czarina Wilpert; also *Die Tageszeitung* August 1994, 9–12; *Neues Deutschland* 14 February 1998, 7; Kaczmarczyk 2001.

13   There are several categories of registered (legal) residence in Germany, ranging from citizenship, then *Aufenthaltsberechtigung* (the next most secure status), *Unbefristeten* (unlimited permit to stay), *Befristeten* (residence permit subject to renewal), and *Aufenthaltsbefugnis* or *Duldung* (temporary tolerated status). According to a new law passed in 1998 that abolished the principle of a 1913 law basing citizenship on German blood ties, to obtain German citizenship, immigrants must document continuous residence in Germany for no less than 10 years and give up their native citizenship (dual citizenship is permitted in the case of the Turkish population in Germany on the basis of bilateral agreement between the German and Turkish governments). In practice, a number of Polish immigrants clandestinely retain double citizenship.

14   Estimates compiled from Zietkiewicz 1995; Misiak 1996; and the figures provided to this author by Ewa Slaska, Alexandra Proscewicz, Norbert Cyrus, Andrzej Sakson, and Janusz Marchwinski. According to all these sources there are no reliable exact data on the occupational distribution of the Polish immigrant population in Berlin – yet another indicator, one may argue, of this group's marginal position in the city.

15   The phenomena of *postnationalism* (denoting a shift beyond or, as it were, vertically past or 'post' the traditional state/national memberships and identities toward more encompassing ones such as universal humanity/human rights), *transnationalism* (identities and engagements reaching across and linking people and institutions in two or more nation-states), and *multiculturalism* (understood as either creolisation or mixing-and-blending of cultures, or coexistence of many [sub] cultures in one society) have each their own vast literature. While the affinity between transnationalism and multiculturalism has been recognised in (im)migration studies, a postnationalism–multiculturalism combination has not been elaborated theoretically and to the best of my knowledge not empirically studied, either. For reviews of literature on these three phenomena, see Brubaker 1996; Joppke and Morawska 2002, Introduction; on post-nationalism, see Meyer *et al.* 1997; on transnsationalism, see Smith and Guarnizo 1998; Vertovec and Cohen 1999.

16   Quotes from interviews with Alexandra Proscewicz and Grzegorz Pawlak in July 2001; correspondence from Jacek Kobink.

17   The Polish term *narodowy* characteristically does not distinguish between national and nationalistic.

18   Since the 1960s, trying to enmesh themselves into the Polish nation and its national traditions, the communist regime allowed these representations in school textbooks, film and theatre.

19 This and the following information about the circumstances contributing to Polish immigrants' *trudna polskosc* comes from my interviews with Alexandra Proscewicz, Grzegorz Pawlak and Andrzej Szulczynski in July 2001, content-analysis of *Kurier Berlinski* 1997–2001, from sociological studies of Polish immigrants in Berlin of Wladyslaw Misiak 1995a and Andrzej Sakson 2000, and from my correspondence with these authors. Specifically on prejudice toward and discrimination against Polish residents by Germans, see Kaminski 1995; Meister 1995; Misiak 1995b; Kiwerska 2000; Sakson 2000; Scheven 2000; on the recent rise of xenophobia in German society, see del Fabbro 1995; Rea 1998; Schmidtke 2001.

20 Only three groups: Schlezwig Danes, East Frisians, and Lemkian Serbs have the official minority group status in Germany. The Polish group in Germany partially blames the government of the Polish Republic for giving too many privileges to the German minority in Poland and neglecting the rights of Poles in Germany.

21 Repeated attempts to form one umbrella Polish organisation in Germany, required by the German law for negotiations regarding state subsidies for ethnic activities, have failed because of the refusal of some Polish organisations to join such a body.

22 Quote from the interview with Witold Kaminski, July 2001.

23 The metaphor of a turtle comes from Sakson 2000.

24 CBOS reports 1993–2001.

25 Interview with Andrzej Szulczynski, July 2001.

26 Information from interviews with Grzegorz Pawlak and Andrzej Szulczynski in July 2001; correspondence to this author from Jacek Kobink, Bogdan Slaski and Jacek Barelkowski.

27 Quotes from interviews with Jacek Barelkowski and Andrzej Szulczynski in July 2001; correspondence to this author from Jacek Kobink; on the phenomenon of 'incomplete migration' represented by such back-and-forth cross-border travellers, see Okólski 1998.

28 It should be noted, however, that Woycicki's conclusion is based on interviews with a sample representatives of all post-war 'waves' of Polish immigration to Germany (1956–7 through to the 1980s) – Kazimierz Woycicki's communication to this author, September 2001.

29 Quotes from interviews with Jacek Kobink and Bogdan Slaski.

30 The macro- and macro-level factors in immigrants' home and host countries and their individual characteristics that on the basis of my preliminary study can be identified as directly and indirectly shaping these identities are listed in Appendix I.

31 See note 16 above for the usual understanding of the concept of transnationalism (as distinct from other forms of extra-territorial involvements) in the literature of the subject and for the bibliographic references to studies thereon.

32 For recent exceptions to this tendency that may signal a 'turn' toward simultaneous treatment of these two phenomena, see Hollinger 1995; Smith 1997; Waters 1999; Pessar and Graham forthcoming.

# References

Anderson, B. (1983) *Imagined Communities: Reflections on the Origin and Spread of Nationalism*, London: Verso.

Bade, K. (1995) 'From emigration to immigration: the German experience in the nineteenth and twentieth centuries', *Central European History* 28, 3: 507–35.

Barcz, J. (1995) 'Sytuacja prawna Polakow w Niemczech w swietle Traktatu z z 17 czerwca 1991 roku i prawa krajowego RFN', *Panstwo i Prawo*, No. 5.

Brubaker, R (1992) *Citizenship and Nationhood in France and Germany*, Cambridge, MA: Harvard University Press.

——— (1996) *Nationalism Reframed: Nationhood and the National Question in the New Europe*, New York: Cambridge University Press.

CBOS (Centrum Badania Opinii Spolecznej) (1993–2001) Reports, Warsaw: CBOS.

Connor, W. (1994) *Ethnonationalism: The Quest for Understanding*, Princeton: Princeton University Press.

Cyrus, N. (1995a) 'In Deutschland arbeiten und in Polen leben: was die neuen WanderarbeiterInnen aus Polen bewegt', in *Zwischen Flucht und Arbeit: Neue Migration und Legalisierungs debatte*. Herausgegen von Buro Arbeitschwerpunkt Rassismus und Fluchtlings politik, Hamburg: Verlag Libertore Assoziation.

——— (1995b) *Polnische Pendler/innen in Berlin*, unpublished manuscript.

——— (1997a) 'Zur Situation irregularer polnischer Zuwanderinnen in Berlin,' *Bericht der Berliner Fachkomission 'Frauenhandel'*, Berlin: Senatsverwaltung für Arbeit, Berufliche Bildung und Frauen, pp. 13–19.

——— (1997b) 'Herein!', *Mitbestimmung Festung* 6: 32–38.

——— (1997c) 'Polnisch–deutsche Arbeitsmigration: Skizze eines Systems ausdifferenzierter Pendelmigration' in *Menschen ohne Hoffnung*, Berlin: Rosa-Luxemburg-Verein.

del Fabbro, R. (1995) 'A victory of the street', in B. Baumgartl and A. Favell (eds) *New Xenophobia in Europe*, London: Kluwer Law International.

*Der Spiegel* (1994).

*Der Tagesspiegel* (1992–2000).

*Die Berlinerzeitung* (1994–98).

*Die Tageszeitung* (1992–2000).

Fijalkowski, J. (1993) 'Aggressive nationalism, the problem of immigration: pressure, and asylum policy disputes in today's Germany', *International Migration Review* 27, 4: 850–69.

Gellner, E. (1983) *Nations and Nationalism*, Oxford: Blackwell/Ithaca, N.Y.: Cornell University Press.

Gemende, M. (1996) 'Migranci Zarobkowi z Polski w Niemczech,' *Polityka Spoleczna* 11, 12: 25–7.

Gerstle, G. and Mollenkopf, J. (2001) (eds) *E Pluribus Unum? Contemporary and Historical Perspectives on Immigrant Political Incorporation*, New York: Russell Sage.

Grabe, W. (2000) 'Gornoslascy "Przesiedlency" w Niemczech', in A. Wolff-Poweska and E. Schultz (eds) *Byc Polakiem w Niemczech*, Poznan: Instytut Zachodni.

Gras, A. (2000) 'Pozycja Prawna Polakow w Niemczech', in A. Wolff-Poweska and E. Schultz (eds) *Byc Polakiem w Niemczech*, Poznan: Instytut Zachodni.

Helias, E. (1996) 'Deutsch–polnische Arbeitsmigration auf Basis der legalen Beschaftigungsmoglichkeiten', *Menschen ohne Hoffnung* – papers from a symposium, 18–19 June 1993, Berlin: Rosa-Luxemburg-Verein.

Hillmann, F. (1998) 'A look at the "hidden side": gendered structures in urban labour markets. the case of Berlin', European University Institute Working Paper MIG/32.

Hillmann, F. and Hedwig, R. (1996) 'Jenseits des brain drain: zur Mobilitat westlicher Fach- und Fuhrungskrafte nach Polen', Wissenschaftszentrum Berlin für Social-forschung, Working Paper FS I 96–103.

Hollinger, J. (1995) *Postethnic America*, New York: Basic Books.

Janowska, H. (1981) *Emigracja Zarobkowa z Polski, 1918–1939*, Warsaw: PWN.

Janusz, G. (1995) 'Polonia w Niemczech', in *Polonia w Niemczech*, Warsaw: Elipsa.

——— (2000) 'Mniejszosci Narodowe w Niemczech', in A. Wolff-Poweska and E. Schultz (eds) *Byc Polakiem w Niemczech*, Poznan: Instytut Zachodni.

Jonczy, R. (2000) 'Migracje zarobokowe z regionu opolskiego do Niemiec', in A.

Rajkiewicz (ed.) *Zewnetrzne Migracje Zarobkowe we Wspolczesnej Polsce*, Wloclawek: Wyzsza Szkola Humanistyczno-Ekonomiczna.

Joppke, C. (1998) (ed.) *Challenge to the Nation-State. Immigration in Western Europe and the United States*, Oxford: Oxford University Press.

Joppke, C. and Morawska, E. (eds) (2002) *Toward Assimilation and Citizenship in Liberal Nation-States*, London: Palgrave.

Kaczmarczyk, P. (2001) '"Polski Berlin?" – Uwagi na Temat Najnowszych Migracji Polakow do Stolicy Niemiec', in E. Jazwinska and M. Okolski (eds) *Ludzie na Hustawce: Migracje Miedzy Peryferiami Polski i Zachodu*, Warsaw: Wydawnictwo Naukowe Scholar.

Kaminski, W (1995) 'Na niemieckich papierach', in *Polonia w Niemczech*, Warsaw: Elipsa.

—— (1996) 'Asymilacja czy Integracja', *Dialog*, No. 1.

Kearney, M. (1995) 'The local and the global: the anthropology of globalization and transnationalism', *Annual Review of Anthropology* 24, 2: 547–65.

Kiwerska, J. (2000) 'Postawa Polakow Wobec Panstwa Niemieckieg', in A. Wolff-Poweska and E. Schultz (eds) *Byc Polakiem w Niemczech*, Poznan: Instytut Zachodni.

Kohn, H. (1944) *The Idea of Nationalism*, New York: Collier Books.

Krawat, K. (1996) 'Patriotyzm czy Pragmatyzm', *Dialog*, No. 1.

Kurcz, Z. and Podkanski, W. (1991) 'Emigracja z Polski po 1980 r', in *Nowa Emigracja i Wyjazdy Zarobkowe*, Wroclaw: Wydawnictwo Uniwersytetu Wroclawskiego.

Kurcz, Z. and Wladyslaw, M. (1994) (eds) *Mniejszosc Niemiecka w Polsce i Polacy w Niemczech*, Wroclaw: Wydawnictwo Uniwersytetu Wroclawskiego.

*Kurier Berlinski-Polonica* (1997–2001).

Lesiuk, W. and Trzcielinska-Polus, A. (2000) 'Wokol Definicji Przedmiotu Badan', in A. Wolff-Poweska and E. Schultz (eds) *Byc Polakiem w Niemczech*, Poznan: Instytut Zachodni.

Liebich, A. (1999) 'Pojecie 'Narodu' miedzy Wschodem a Zachodem', *Oboz* 36: 15–33.

Los, M. (1998) '"Virtual" property and post-Communist globalization', *Demokratizatsiya: The Journal of Post-Soviet Democratization* 6, 1: 77–86.

Marchwinski, J. (2000) 'Dostep do Mediow: Doswiadczenia Wlasne', in A. Wolff-Poweska and E. Schultz (eds) *Byc Polakiem w Niemczech*, Poznan: Instytut Zachodni.

Meister, H.P. (1995) 'Polen und statistik', *Polen und wir* 2: 2–9.

Meyer, J., Boli, J., Thomas, G. and Ramirez, F. (1997) 'World society and the nation-state', *American Journal of Sociology* 103, 1: 144–81.

Miera, F. (1996) 'Zuwanderer und Zuwanderinnen aus Polen in Berlin in den 90er Jahren', Wissenschaftszentrum Berlin fur Socialforschung Working Paper FS I, 96–106.

Misiak, W. (1995a) 'Losy i Aktywnosc Polakow w Berlinie (Analiza Wynikow Badan 1994r)', *Slowo*, special issue on Poles in Berlin, Berlin: Polskie Duszpasterstwo Katolickie, 23–65.

—— (1995b) 'Das bittere Wort Exil-uchodzstwo, to brzmi gorzko', in *Polonia w Niemczech*, Warsaw: Elipsa.

—— (1996) 'Etnicznosc w Biznesie', in S. Partycki (ed.) *Spoleczny Wymiar Rynku*, Lublin: Wydawnictwo Uniwersytetu Marii Curie-Sklodowskiej.

Morawska, E. (1987) 'Civil religion v. state power in Poland', in T. Robbins and R. Robertson (eds) *Church–State Relations: Tensions and Transitions*, New Brunswick and London: Transition Books.

—— (1989) 'Labor migrations of Poles in the Atlantic world-economy, 1880–1914' *Comparative Studies in Society and History* 2: 237–72.

—— (2001a) 'International migration and the consolidation of democracy in post-Communist Eastern Europe', in A. Pravda and J. Zielonka (eds) *Democratic Consolidation in Eastern Europe: Domestic and International Factors*, Oxford: Oxford University Press.

—— (2001b) 'Structuring migration: the case of Polish income-seeking travelers to the West', *Theory and Society* 31: 47–80.

Mrowka, H. (2000) 'Organizacje polonijne i ich partnerzy niemieccy', in A. Wolff-Poweska and E. Schultz (eds) *Byc Polakiem w Niemczech*, Poznan: Instytut Zachodni.

*Neues Deutschland* (1996–1998).

O'Brien, P. (1988) 'Continuity and Change in Germany's Treatment of Non-Germans', *International Migration Review*, 22, 3: 109–34.

Okólski, M. (1998) 'Incomplete migration – a new form of international mobility in Central and Eastern Europe: the case of Polish and Ukrainian migrants', paper presented at the conference on International Migration: Challenges for European Populations, Bari, 25–7 June 1998.

Ossowski, S. (1967) 'Analiza Socjologiczna Pojecia Ojczyzny', in S. Ossowski *Z Zagadnien Psychologii Spolecznej*, Warsaw: PWN.

Pallaske, C (ed.) (2001) *Die Migration von Polen nach Deutschland*, Baden-Baden: Nomos.

Persson, H.-A. (1997) 'Foreigners, historical ethnic immigration, and the successful Western German model', in H.-Å. Persson (ed.) *Encounter with Strangers: The European Experience*, Lund: Lund University Press.

Pessar, P. and Graham, P. (forthcoming) 'Dominican New Yorkers: transnational identities and local politics', in Nancy Foner (ed.) *New York's New Immigrants*, New York: Columbia University Press.

*Polacy w Berlinie* (1996) Berlin: Die Auslanderbeauftragte des Senats.

*Polityka* (1995–2001).

*Polonia w Niemczech* (1995) Warsaw: Elipsa.

Portes, A. (1999) 'Conclusion: toward a new world. The origins and effects of transnational activities', *Ethnic and Racial Studies* 22, 2: 463–77.

Rajkiewicz, A. (2000) *Zewnętrzne Migracje Zarobkowe we Wspolczesnej Polsce*, Wloclawek: Wyzsza Szkola Humanistyczno-Ekonomiczna.

Rauzinski, R. (2000) 'Wspolczesne wyjazdy zarobkowe z wojewodztwa opolskiego do Republiki Federalnej Niemiec', in A. Rajczak (ed.) *Zewnetrzne Migracje zarobkowe we Wspolczesnej Polsce*, Wloclawek: Wyzsza Szkola Humanistyczno-Ekonomiczna.

Rea, A. (1998) (ed.) *Immigration et racism en Europe*, Brusselles: Editions Complex.

Robertson, R. (1992) *Globalization: Social Theory and Global Culture*, London: Sage.

Roller, K. (1993) 'Neue Zuwanderung-z.B. aus Polen', in '. . . *da sind wir keine Auslander mehr' Eingewanderte ArbeiterInnen in Berlin, 1961–1993*, Berlin: Herausegegeben von der Berliner Geschichtswerkstatt e.V.

Rouse, R. (1992) 'Making sense of settlement: class, transformation, cultural struggle, and transnationalism among Mexican migrants in the United States', *Annals of the New York Academy of Sciences* 645: 25–51.

Sakson, A. (2000) 'Uczestnictwo w Zyciu Spolecznym', in A. Wolff-Poweska and E. Schultz (eds) *Byc Polakiem w Niemczech*, Poznan: Instytut Zachodni.

Schenk, W. (1993) 'Grenzgegerinnen', *Beitrage zur Feministische Theorie und Praxis* 34: 70–78.

Scheven, D. (2000) 'Kontakty z Wladzami', in A. Wolff-Poweska and E. Schultz (eds) *Byc Polakiem w Niemczech*, Poznan: Instytut Zachodni.

Schmidt, J. (2000) 'Wysiedlency Miedzy Polska a Niemcami', in A. Wolff-Poweska and E. Schultz (eds) *Byc Polakiem w Niemczech*, Poznan: Instytut Zachodni.

Schmidtke, O. (2001) 'Symbolische Gewalt im offentlichen Diskurs', unpublished manuscript.

Smith, R. (1997) 'Transnational Migration, Assimilation, and Political Economy', in M. Crahan and A. Vourvoulias-Bush (eds) *The City and the World: New York City in Global Context*, New York: Council on Foreign Relations.

Smith, R. and Guarnizo, L. (eds) (1998) *Transnationalism from Below*, New Brunswick: Transaction Publishers.

Stach, A. (1998) *Das polnische Berlin–Polski Berlin*, Berlin: Die Auslanderbeauftragte des Senats, pp. 48–52.

Staniszkis, J. (1999) *Post-Communism: The Emerging Enigma*, Warsaw: IPS PAN.

Swidler, A. (1986) 'Culture in action: symbols and strategies', *Annual Review of Sociology* 51: 273–86.

Thomas, W. I. and Znaniecki, F. (1918–20) *The Polish Peasant in Europe and America*, Boston: G. Badger.

Trzcielinska-Polus, A. (2000) 'Polacy w Niemczech Wschodnich', in A. Wolff-Poweska and E. Schultz (eds) *Byc Polakiem w Niemczech*, Poznan: Instytut Zachodni.

Vertovec, S. and Cohen, R. (1999) *Migration, Diasporas, and Transnationalism*, Cheltenham: Elgar Reference Collection.

Walicki, A. (1981) *Philosophy and Romantic Nationalism: The Case of Poland*, Oxford: Oxford University Press.

Waters, M. (1999) *Black Identities: West Indian Dreams and American Realities*, New York: Russell Sage.

Wilpert, C. (1998) 'The new migration and the informal labour market in Germany', unpublished manuscript.

Wolff-Poweska, A. and Schultz, E. (eds) (2000) *Byc Polakiem w Niemczech*, Poznan: Instytut Zachodni.

Woycicki, K. (2000) 'Poczucie Tozsamosci i Wiez Grupowa Osob Polsko-jezycznych', in A. Wolff-Poweska and E. Schultz (eds) *Byc Polakiem w Niemczech*, Poznan: Instytut Zachodni.

Wrzesinski, W. (1995) 'Niemiec w stereotypach polskich XIX i XX wieku', in T. Wlas (ed.) *Narody i Stereotypy*, Krakow: Miedzynradowe Centrum Kultury.

Zietkiewicz, G. (1995) *Polen in Berlin-Polacy w Berlinie*, Berlin: Die Auslanderbeauftragte des Senats.

# 11 Changing rhetoric and narratives

## German trade unions and Polish migrant workers

*Norbert Cyrus*

## Europeanisation and intermediary organisations

Europeanisation – defined as 'the emergence of new institutions, new types of social and political actions, and new forms of culture beyond or across national boundaries' – evidently 'challenges bounded notions of state sovereignty; of state control over social process; and of state legitimacy over political membership and participation' (Favell 1998: 1). In the processes of Europeanisation the EU turns out to be both cause and effect of itself, a result of a 'set of explosive and indeterminate effects of late-twentieth century social and political processes. These effects are fundamentally reorganising territoriality and peoplehood, the two principles that have shaped modern European borders' (Borneman and Fowler 1997: 489). The hitherto nationally bounded construction and maintenance of boundaries of belonging withers away. Some research has been done on the construction of new European institutions and symbols (for a social anthropological review see Borneman and Fowler 1997) with a focus on the transnational policy arena and the impact of great actors. But European integration is not only a structural top-down re-arrangement of the institutional framework and national juridical provision. In the age of Europeanisation, actors have to adapt to the changing cultural landscape which comes along with the institutional, political, social and cultural re-arrangements from top-down. Surveys such as those by EUROSTAT report trends in the national public perception of European issues in member states but cannot supply insights as to how bottom-up adaptation is working. Until now, the social and cultural *process* of bottom-up adaptation of Europe has been widely neglected.

Following Knill and Lehmkuhl (1999) three ideal types of modes of Europeanisation can be distinguished: *positive integration* means the imposition of concrete institutional requirements with which member states must comply. *Negative integration* means that European legislation may affect the domestic arrangements by altering the domestic rules of the game, but do not prescribe any distinctive institutional model of how the new institutional equilibrium should actually look. *Framing integration* affects domestic arrangements more indirectly, namely by altering the beliefs and expectations of domestic actors. The changes in domestic beliefs may in turn affect the strategies and preferences of domestic actors, potentially leading to corresponding institutional adaptations. In other words: framing integration, perceived as locally or nationally rooted processes of bottom-up response to and adaptation of Europe, is a salient aspect of Europeanisation. According to Knill and Lehmkuhl the domestic impact of European policies is primarily based on cognitive logic. In this view, Europeanisation means in the first place a fundamental cultural transformation from top-down as well as from bottom-up.

This chapter studies the modification of the beliefs and expectations of domestic actors. Beliefs and expectations, i.e. meaning, is not created in a cultural vacuum but localised in a cultural landscape of institutionalised knowledge and tradition (Berger and Luckmann 1967). In the modern world, the stock of knowledge is characterised by fragmentation in particular areas of meaning, uneven distribution, day by day increase and constant flux (Hannerz 1992). Much of the taken-for-granted everyday knowledge is coined by institutions, who 'classify for the people' (Douglas 1986). In the era of late modernity a vast number of cultural apparatuses deliberately generate knowledge and meaning: competing professionals in science, media, policy and civil society produce (competing) proposals on how to perceive and interpret the world. The production of knowledge and meaning by cultural apparatuses is characterised by a high degree of strategic and reflexive pursuit of interests. To act successfully, member organisations have to go on from the everyday knowledge and beliefs of people (Strauss 1968). By this, *member organisations* as cultural apparatuses play an important *intermediary* role in the cultural transformation, creation and shaping of a European horizon and identity. Within the European multi-level framework, intermediary collective actors rooted in the everyday life of people play a crucial role as transmitters and translators of top-down projects as well as bottom-up responses. The focus of this essay is on the cultural adaptation strategies of German trade unions vis-à-vis EU-Eastern enlargement. I concentrate on trade union endeavours to transmit and translate the dramatic re-shaping of categories of belonging and territoriality in the course of Europeanisation to its members with particular attention to the significance and function of the negative stereotype of Poles in the German debate on Eastern enlargement. For reasons of stringency and clarity, the study focuses on the case of the German construction trade union which became one of the key actors in the German debate on Eastern enlargement.[1]

## German trade unions in the age of Europeanisation

In order to examine how German trade unions try to sustain solidarity and adherence of members in the process of European integration, I focus on the German construction trade union IG BAU[2] for two main reasons: (1) in Germany, trade union membership is settled at the level of sectoral organisations. The German umbrella trade union organisation, DGB, is only an alliance of sectoral trade unions without direct responsibility for looking after members. In order to examine the efforts at persuasion it is therefore appropriate to study one of the sectoral trade unions. (2) Among the eight organisations the construction trade union IG BAU played and continues to play a key role in the trade union debate on Europeanisation. The reason for this is simply that IG BAU represents those sectors which are most affected by European integration: in industries such as car production, jobs can be transferred abroad. But in construction, agriculture and facility management, jobs are territorially bounded (Lubanski 1999). In these sectors the reliance on the free movement of workers and services across Europe leads to the physical presence of foreign workers in the national territory. Due to this constellation, the transformation in these sectors is a sensitive and highly politicised process (Däubler 1995). Several trends have contributed in the last two decades to a dramatic transformation process in the construction sector:

1    Since the mid-1970s, the shadow economy has increased in Germany (Schneider and Ernste 2000). The growth of the shadow economy indicates that the Fordist and neo-corporatist social arrangements are breaking down. The macroeconomic orientation is replaced by an operational economic orientation that favours short-term arrangements and irregular or illegal employment. According to surveys, half of the German population have no reservations about personally participating in the shadow economy as a seller or buyer, if the opportunity arose (Lamnek *et al.* 2000). Today, moonlighting and illegal employment is widespread among the native population. Even if illegal employment of foreign workers contributes to the shadow economy, it is neither the cause nor the central aspect (Cyrus 2001a). In construction, the change in the production structure has facilitated the increase of illegal employment.

2    Stretching back as far as the mid-1980s, the production structure in the construction industry experienced significant transformation. Huge construction enterprises proceeded to conclude contracts not with their own employees, but with subcontractors if required (cf. Cremers 1998; Hochstadt *et al.* 1999: 124). In 1975 the ratio of subcontracting to contracts of employment in the entire German construction industry was 13 per cent, and that within the large firms was nearly 24 per cent. In 1996 it was 24 per cent for the entire industry and 41 per cent for the large firms. Meanwhile, all large firms and a good number of medium and small ones simultaneously acted as general contractors or as 'turnkey contractors' (Syben 1998: 17). Subcontracting is a widespread option in construction, and contracts may pass through eight or more subcontractors. In the end the work is often carried out by small 'sport-shoes enterprises' employing workers under informal or illegal conditions (Nienhüser 1999).

3    During a period in which the German market attracted a growing number of foreign enterprises and workers, employers reckoned that the presence of foreign enterprises operating with lower costs would make it possible to lower German standards: 'A number of firms cancelled their membership of the employers' association, while regional associations withdrew from the national organisations, in both cases with a view to avoiding commitments to the standards laid down in the collective agreements' (Lubanski 1999: 285; see also Treichler 1998: 230ff).

4    After the collapse of the GDR and the re-unification, the domestic supply of construction workers increased significantly. Due to the lower productivity in

the GDR, the number of construction workers was above the Western average. After 1990, the East German construction industry grew by 125 per cent up to 1995, and by 1998, it formed 15 per cent of the total Gross National Product of East Germany (which is three times as much as in West Germany and indicates both the volume of investment in construction and the weakness of other industries in the eastern part of the country). Employment had grown by 43 per cent (Syben 1998: 14). One reason for rising unemployment in the second half of the 1990s thus derived from a previous oversupply of labour (Treichler 1998: 234).

5  Additionally, the influx of immigrants (ethnic Germans, foreigners, asylum seekers) contributed to the increase in labour supply and unemployment in this sector. A disproportionate number of those with rights of access to the German labour markets look for employment in construction. While in 1987, about 20 per cent of all those who became unemployed from the construction industry had not worked in Germany before, the share grew to 37 per cent in 1992. The increase in unemployment mirrors not so much the replacement of already-employed resident workers, but an increased presence of immigrants to the unemployment rolls: 'By no means the contract for services workers can be blamed for this increase' (IW 1993: 21).

6  The German government has since 1989 signed bi-lateral agreements with twelve Central and East European (CEE) countries on the employment of East European contract workers. These inter-governmental agreements gave large German enterprises the opportunity to cooperate with subcontractors from CEE-countries (Rudolph 1996). Within a fixed limit of initially nearly 100,000 workers, East European contract enterprises gained access to German labour markets. The CEE-firms competed for work with the German small- and medium-sized enterprises. The foreign sending-firm was under a duty to pay the workers according to the German standards. However, employment took place mostly with disregard to the statutory conditions (cf. Cyrus and Helias 1993; Bundesregierung 1996; Faist *et al.* 1999). Poland holds the greatest share of the contract for services programme, with a limit of 35,170 workers (cf. Cyrus 1994, 2001b).

7  With the completion of the European Single Market in 1993, providing for free movement of workers and service enterprises within the EU, construction firms and workers from other EU member states gained free access to the German construction market. Consequently the number of EU enterprises and the number of workers from other EU member states increased. Sending enter- prises from EU member states signed subcontracts with German construction enterprises and thus competed with the CEE-contract firms and the German small- and medium-sized firms. The numbers of EU contract workers quickly amounted to an estimated 200,000 workers (Köbele and Leuschner 1995). In a speech to a trade union conference, the Minister for Labour and Social Order, Norbert Blüm (1995) underlined that, in spite of an economic boom in construction, 134,000 resident construction workers were unemployed, while at the same time, 150,000 legal EU workers were employed (Blüm 1995: 129).

8    Another trend deeply influencing trade union policy in the construction sector was the economic performance of the construction industry. In the aftermath of the collapse of the GDR and the relocation of the German capital from Bonn to Berlin, the need for construction services increased in the 1990s to an unprecedented degree. Initially, the demand for labour increased and, until 1994, the use of migrant workers was complementary to resident employment. The number of workers employed by domestic firms increased from about 100,000 to 1.08 million employees from 1991 to 1994. The replacement of domestic labour began only in 1995, when the numbers of workers liable to social insurance fell (between 1995 and 1998, there were about 245,000 fewer) but the amount of migrant workers nevertheless increased (Bosch *et al.* 2000: 676). According to this account, since 1996, a substitution of resident construction workers can be observed. The number of employed resident workers liable to social insurance fell from 1.1 million in 1994, to 800,000 in 1998 (Hochstadt *et al.* 1999: 201ff).

9    The political volatility of this situation was exacerbated by the fact that the replacement of resident workers was unevenly distributed. Besides the disadvantaged areas of East Germany, the urban agglomerations with a number of construction sites which were difficult to control were also affected. The most dramatic locus of this development was Berlin. Here, the amount of construction activities increased between 1992 and 1995 by about 40 per cent, with a nearly constant level of employed resident construction workers liable to social insurance. Since 1996, construction activities and employment have decreased. At the end of the 1990s, the number of construction workers in Berlin was equal to the number of construction workers in the West Berlin of 1990. In view of the amount of construction activities in 1998, about 88,000 construction workers are required. However, only 28,000 resident workers are employed: 'The missing 60,000 employees either come from other regions of Germany (because of the advantages in the wage level, most likely from adjacent East Germany) or legal and illegal foreign workers from abroad or resident "moonlighters"' (Bosch *et al.* 2000: 676).

10   The already relatively low rate of unionisation, estimated at 30–5 per cent, is still falling, which places the unions in a weaker position when presenting their arguments (Lubanski 1999: 284). The number of IG BAU members decreased from 653,000 in 1994 to 539,744 in 2000.[3] Taking into account that IG BAU had gained 80,000 new members by merging with a small trade union, the loss of members is even more dramatic (see Streeck and Visser 1998).

As a result of these independent, but overlapping and mutually reinforcing developments, the labour market situation and the bargaining power of trade unions in the construction sector was eroded. According to an observer one can

> imagine that these are hard times for the German construction union IG BAU. Its strong bargaining power, which had successfully survived the crisis of the construction industry in the 1970s and in the 1980s, has now been upset. It is

in particular the crisis in the East-German labour market, which has weakened the union's position.

(Syben 1998: 14)

In the last decade, the position of trade unions was undermined by a dramatic deteriorating employment situation, in spite of an economic boom. This development signals an erosion of the traditional model of nationally bounded neo-corporatism. The erosion of the neo-corporatist national arrangements have an impact on the trade unions' framing of *categories of belonging* and *fields of activity*. Like other collective actors, trade unions have to adapt to the changing legal framework and the institutional setting of labour market regulation. At least in the labour-migration attracting countries such as Germany, the introduction of the Single Market compelled the previously nationally bounded trade unions to redefine the categorisation of domestic and foreign workers. However, some scholars expect that trade unions will not be able to manage the situation. The change of production structure, economic informalisation and the dissolution of intra-European boundaries contribute to the creation of an open space with a more flexible and liberal social order that will result in the decline of trade unions. According to Richard Münch two principles conflict in the course of European integration: the old moral of justice as social compensation, characteristic of industrial nation-states, and a new moral of justice as fairness, prospectively characteristic of the emerging Europe.

> Justice as social compensation is bounded to cohesion and needs a greater closeness. The high effect of equality of results can be achieved only on the basis of strong closure to outside and minimal chances for foreigners to get in. The interior ethics of brotherhood among comrades is accompanied by exterior ethics of rejecting brotherhood against strangers.
>
> (Münch 2001: 227)

The old, 'mechanic solidarity' characterised by strong demarcation against the outside, internal homogeneity, centralised administration and redistribution by government authorities will be replaced by a border-crossing, 'organic solidarity' of individual relations of exchange:

> Organic solidarity consists of a lot of several dependencies, which extend beyond national collectives and cause internal differentiation within the collective. External articulation and internal differentiation characterise this kind of solidarity.
>
> (Münch 2001: 275)

The European network structures will be abstract and will make a formal frame of heterogeneous, widespread and neatly differentiated networks of more or less durable loyalty connections (Münch 2001: 230). In the process of European integration the relationship between citizens of member states changes.

> The differentiation into a multitude of groups and environments cross-cutting national boundaries means that German, French, Italian or Danish people increasingly meet each other [but] not as representatives of national collectives.
>
> (Münch 2001: 291)

In the frame of these network structures, the strong collective solidarities, identities and cultures will be replaced by a pluralism of heterogeneous and widely branched associations and cultural patterns. The representation of huge masses of workers by large trade unions will be replaced by the individual representation of interests (Münch 2001: 223). In the long run nation-states with nationally based solidarities and cultures will not be obstacles on the way to integration, because they will in any event, diminish in significance:

> The Europe of the future will be not a Europe of one's native country and national culture but the Europe of individuals acting self-responsibly and of a plurality of self-reflexive biographies no longer bounded to a national frame of reference.
>
> (Münch 2001: 230)

Within such a framework, individuals inevitably have to and will adapt to the new circumstances only by adapting quickly, as the only protection from insolvency and unemployment (Münch 2001: 274). But is this simple dichotomic outline of the prospective European development correct? Not only individual but also collective actors have the capacity and the will to learn and to adapt to the changing framework. As with individuals, collective actors have to learn to cope with the increasing importance of Europe. Already in the early 1950s, German trade unions had supported the *idea* of European integration for historical reasons: European integration was principally supported as a forward-looking project to establish welfare, employment and peace. Trade unions criticised the primarily economic character of European integration, which was taking place at the expense of the social dimension. But as long as Europe remained a more abstract and far away phenomenon without a concrete impact on the domain of national trade union interests, they were not really engaged at the European level. To summarise a long and intricate story: German trade unions supported the *idea* of European integration but ignored the process of European integration as long as organisational interests were not affected (Streeck 1996; Dølvik 1997; Martin and Ross 1998).

Trade unions started to concern themselves with European affairs only when they realised that decisions made in the European arena increasingly affected the domestic situation. European directives and legislation increasingly interfered with the structuring of industrial relations, which had hitherto been the exclusive domain of national institutions and actors. The creation of the single labour market following from the Treaty of Rome reduced the discretion to regulate industrial relations according to the needs of nationally bounded actors. In Germany, legal barriers preventing the employment of foreign workers from abroad – the 1973 recruitment stop – were undermined by the right of workers from other European member states to take up employment. Even more important, the granting of the free movement for services enabled enterprises with a seat in another EU member state to provide a service in Germany with its own workers, employed on the conditions of pay and social protection of the sending country. The social and tariff standards of the hitherto closed labour market were no longer protected against competition from other European member states with lower standards of wages and social protection. At least in the member states attracting labour immigration, the presence of service enterprises from other member states contributed to the transnationalisation of the labour market. The challenge is to cope with a new situation of fragmentation and erosion of social rights of workers (Faist 1996). European integration included the transformation of hitherto nationally regulated industrial relations, with the general tendency towards more liberal arrangements, which was difficult for trade unions to accept. Moreover, on the eve of the European Eastern enlargement, German trade unions have to develop an organisational identity more appropriate to the new situation of unrestricted movement of European workers. Trade unions in Europe had to learn to take into account the European level and to re-define their position in, and their relationship to, Europe (Streeck 1996: 8).

One of the major features of German trade union policy is to maintain a positive and supportive attitude towards European integration in spite of the challenges and problems to which trade unions are exposed. In order to influence Europeanisation, trade unions began to participate in the European policy arena. Since the mid-1980s, trade unions in Europe began to intensify activities beyond the national arena and to build up cross-border channels to resist, to influence or to cope with European decision-making.

1   The first channel relies on the already established relationship with the national government. In Germany the trade union is not only a constitutive part of the neo-corporatist system of regulating industrial relations but also of the general political system: trade union representatives are integrated on supervising boards of a number of public institutions (the Federal employment service; public broadcasting) and in the political decision-making process are heard as influential and important collective actors. Considering the involvement of trade unions in the national policy arena, the lobbying of national governments to represent German trade union interests in the European arena is an important and viable channel (Streeck 1996).

2   The second channel relies on participation in the European Trade Union Confederation (ETUC) in order to counterbalance the lobbying of employers' associations. However, the channel is difficult to handle since the alliance of trade unions with differing interests reduces the likelihood of realising the goals of one particular national interest. Because of its diversity, the ETUC tends to take a lowest common denominator position in representing union interests in the European Union (Marks and McAdam 1996: 107; Streeck and Schmitter 1998: 135).

3   Most of all, sector-bounded trade unions felt uncomfortable with the ETUC-representation and founded separate alliances to lobby more effectively for the common trade union needs and demands in particular sectors. One of the sector-specific European Industry Committees in the EU is the European Federation of Building and Woodworkers (EFBWW) founded in 1958. The IG BAU is an important member of this confederation and is represented on the executive board. The significance of the confederation is, however, restricted because bargaining with employers is not undertaken at the European level (Marks and McAdam 1996: 107).

4   The bi-lateral cooperation of national trade unions is another means to overcome national isolation. After some delay, IG BAU started to sign cooperation agreements with counterparts from Portugal (1996), Italy (1998), Poland (1999), Belgium and the Netherlands (2000). With cooperation agreements, trade unions declare that they will give mutual support during industrial action and prevent all forms of strike-breaking through the use by companies of workers from another country.

5   The fifth channel to deal with the new situation of a single market consists of bi- or multi-lateral cooperation of national trade unions in particular areas of concern, such as the initiative of Doorn. Such transnational coordination focuses on particular regions within the European Union (see Weinert 2001) and is also used by IG BAU (Cremers 1998: 25ff). In particular, the creation of cross-border channels shows that trade unions are 'Europeanising'.

Trade unions are also seized by a process of Europeanisation, which resembles a development similar to the one the governments of EEC/EC/EU countries have experienced since the early 1950s. Trade unions are part of this process, they are passing through a very cautious process of development. The contemporary level corresponds roughly to the governmental integration in about 1958 . . . , when the European Commission held a more coordinating function. The liberalisation of the markets compels trade unions to go beyond nationally closed options in order to act. This opening is necessary since the institutions of the nation-state are losing relevance and the EU institutions gaining in significance. A central result of the self-organisational European policy of national trade unions is the construction of structures for transnational coordination. By this process the national trade unions will gradually increase their supra-national competencies. This process is lengthy and involves also a longer process of the reduction of organisation–cultural otherness between the trade unions.

(Weinert 2001: 335)

According to this statement organisational Europeanisation leads to the reduction of the cultural distance between national trade unions or, in other words: the re-shaping of taken-for-granted concepts of self and other.

The success of such cognitive organisational development depends as already noted on the acceptance of the members. As organisations based on voluntary membership, trade unions in Europe have to take into account the morale of their members who finance the organisation through their membership fee and provide the basis for political influence. The efficiency and success of interest representation in each of the policy channels depend on the organisational ability to mobilise the members for political action (strikes on the shop floor level, public manifestations) (Erne 2001). If members do not go along with the policy and strategy, the organisation will get into trouble. To persuade members that the organisation can act successfully in the interests of its clients is an elementary task of every organisation based on voluntary membership. Like every membership organisation, the cognitive horizon of members is the starting point of activities and forms the cultural opportunity space. In order to follow interests, trade unions have to take into account two constraints: the increasingly European shaped political opportunity structure and the still nationally rooted cultural opportunity structure.

Trade unions are reflexive organisations and their officials are aware of the tightrope they must walk between changing political opportunities whilst cultural convictions lag behind. As early as the early 1990s, trade union officials had pointed to the national frame of reference that affect the room for manoeuvre:

> Trade unions' migration policy had to operate in an extremely narrow opportunity space. On the one hand the policy was determined by the federal stipulation which was impossible for trade unions to change. On the other side, the trade unions' policy depended on the consent of the native majority of members, who showed more or less willingness to make concessions and often showed more understanding of a restrictive immigration state-policy than for the own organisation, which had the programmematic claim to represent foreign workers equally alongside the inland majority of members.
>
> (Kühne *et al.* 1994: 19)

The deep transformations since the end of the 1980s challenged the taken-for-granted interpretation the cultural apparatus used to offer its members during neo-corporatist national isolation. The increasing presence of workers from abroad accompanied by rising unemployment of domestic workers called for new and intensified cognitive efforts to keep the support of members. IG BAU also consciously took into account the constraints of the cultural opportunity structure. This becomes clear in an statement by two trade union officials who outline a 'double strategy':

> Inevitably the IG BAU will be confronted with the question who is the clientele the organisation will have to organise and if it is possible that all interests can be represented by one national trade union. In the absence of an overriding principle, the increasing competition for jobs will leave no space for solidarity. Therefore a speedy concentration of interests on binding collective regulations is necessary. The IG BAU will have to follow a double strategy: on the one hand it is necessary to present the organisation to all workers from the whole of Europe as a strong and reliable organisation with attractive services. Simultaneously the

demands of our existing members for safe jobs and reliable regulations have to be realised. Otherwise there will be no approval for joint action.

(Adams and Wiesehügel 1995: 123)

The two high ranked IG officials – one later became president of IG BAU and a member of the federal Parliament – underline that the beliefs and perceptions of members are the starting point for activities. The preference for German over foreign nationality is a rational aspect of organisational logic. 'Strategic decisions depends primarily on both the *interests* and the *available power resources* of an organisation' (Erne 2001). The trade union officials are aware of this.

In the rest of the chapter, I will examine the efforts at persuading the national members over the process of European integration. How did trade unions frame and interpret the interference and impact of European integration for their members? And did the repertoire of cognitive patterns change over the course of time? What is the impact and interaction of the political and cultural opportunity structure? The best source from which to gain insights into the trade union's efforts at persuasion is an examination of communications via the monthly membership magazine.

## Inclusive and exclusive interpretations

In order to unearth the interpretations IG BAU offered to its members, in its role as cultural commentator, I studied eight volumes of the monthly membership magazine, *Foundation Stone* (*Der Grundstein*) from 1990 until 1997. As shown in the previous section, this period witnessed deep transformations: national borders became porous in the aftermath of the collapse of the socialist states; the traditional distinction between domestic and foreign workers dissolved in the process of European integration; and the informalisation of industrial relations undermined the basis of neo-corporatist arrangements.

At the beginning of the 1990s, IG BAU still obviously believed in the possibility of continuing with the neo-corporatist framework of closed national labour markets. In expectation of an economic boom in the construction sector, with positive effects on employment and wages, IG BAU entered the tariff negotiations in 1991 with the demand for a 10.2 per cent wage increase (*Foundation Stone* 91/2: 3). However, events in the 1990s went, as already indicated, in the opposite direction. To explain the situation and to indicate a solution IG BAU – a constituent part of the weakened but still existing neo-corporatist arrangements – relied on the main argument that the problems were caused by disruptive forces from outside. In the 1990s, IG BAU named several categories of outside 'interlopers' who were blamed for the deplorable state of affairs.

### East German workers as interlopers

The first category of outside interlopers were highlighted in 1989–90. IG BAU noticed that in consequence of the collapse of the German Democratic Republic, construction workers from East Germany were threatening the standards of work and pay: 'Together with a growing permeability of the borders, irregular contract work and illegal employment are increasing. For both states considerable problems arise' (*Foundation Stone* 90/2: 8). The membership magazine published the statement of the Berlin section of IG BAU complaining that employees of GDR-based enterprises were accepting jobs with poor conditions.

> In Berlin in particular, the local enterprises are just waiting to use the cheap subcontractors from the GDR and to reduce their permanent workforce. We Berlin construction workers can and will not compete with the 'cheap-pay' [*Billiglohn* – a term with a pejorative undertone] in the GDR. This will be a competition between unequals. The local workers will not stand for the selling out of social and tariff protection. . . . The IG BAU therefore demands the restriction of the announced measures [i.e. the liberalisation of movement] on the free movement of goods only and to postpone the free movement of services until the framework [in East and West] has adjusted.
>
> (*Foundation Stone* 90/2: 8)

With this statement, workers from the East, in this case citizens of the GDR, were classified as interlopers, lumped together with irregular contract workers or illegal workers, and stereotyped as unfair competitors. The claim of the Berlin section of IG BAU to maintain the legal barriers against citizens of the GDR in order to protect the workers in the West, was published without further editorial comment, although this very clearly formulated exclusionist attitude against compatriots had no legal basis. In the course of the political events of re-unification, the issue of the construction workers from East Germany received a new framing: in June 1990 the federal executive board of IG BAU explained that the trade union would expand into East Germany in order to integrate East German workers into the organisation (*Foundation Stone* 90/5: 5). In some of the following issues, reports were published of East German workers accepting pay under the level of the tariff. But from now on, employers were held responsible for such occurrences.

> Employers and clients massively abuse the workers from the new federal Länder as price-reducers and 'cheap-paid'. Public clients are no exception in this respect. . . . We make this demand: equal pay for equal work on Western German construction sites.
>
> (*Foundation Stone* 92/2)

After an initial exclusionist reflex, perceiving East German workers as outside interlopers, they were quickly accepted as a category which was difficult to integrate but impossible to exclude. The frame of reference shifted from rejection to solidarity.

### CEE contract workers as interlopers

As expected, the construction industry enjoyed a boom period and the employ-ment situation improved. However, simultaneously, the number of foreign workers from East European countries increased as a result of the bilateral agreements on the employment of workers on 'contracts for services'. The main sending country for contract workers was Poland (Cyrus 1994, 2001b; Hönekopp *et al.* 2001). It is interesting to consider the context of the first usage of East European contract workers.

> The demand to end the recruitment stop is the wrong signal. . . . There are signs of a lack of trained personnel because of a strong climate for construction work, but it is short-sighted to fill the gaps with enforced recruitment. This is only an attempt to make the illegal sub-contracting of workers from East Europe subsequently legal. From past experience, we know that mistakes on construction sites are likely from less qualified workers and will harm the image of the construction industry in the long run. The lack of trained workers will continue – and this when the construction sector will have a stable basis for the next years. Therefore the chairman of the federal trade union demanded from the organisations of the construction industry a qualification campaign in the GDR. . . . It makes no sense to let thousands of workers in the GDR fall into unemployment when there is enough work within the construction industry.
>
> (*Foundation Stone* 90/8: 4)

This early commentary already exhibited basic elements of the main exclusionist framing of the category of the East European contract workers, which the IG BAU reproduced later on, on several occasions: the level of qualification of the individual workers was questioned, their performance was associated with bad work. The competitive relationship between domestic workers and workers from outside was stressed. Finally the placement and employment of East European workers was connected with illegality. Until a time when the employment of resident workers was unproblematic, the temporary and complementary employment of East European workers was rejected on principle; the temporary employment of East European workers was viewed negatively. The East received a new frame of reference: East European contract workers were confronted with the domestic workers, now including former GDR workers. The diffusion of this interpretation was intensified when the number of native unemployed did not diminish. In a number of subsequent reports and articles the readers of *Foundation Stone* were informed about the employment of East European contract workers with a focus on Polish workers.

In his inaugural speech in October 1991, the new chairman of IG BAU declared that it was not acceptable for Europe to become the locus for criminal activities on construction sites. He demanded legal regulation of the contracting procedure in construction. The local standards for pay and working conditions ought to be fixed as minimum standards for the employment of foreign workers, to restrict wild-west methods. This legal regulation also ought to operate in an Eastward direction: the chairman argued that the opening of the borders had brought new possibilities for dubious profiteers. He mentioned Albanians hired for hunger wages of four marks, and Poles and Czechs working for six marks and did not hesitate to compare the employment of these workers to a disease: 'The irregular contract work spreads like an epidemic' (*Foundation Stone* 10/91: 7). In May 1993 IG BAU demanded, in a joint declaration with the employers' association, the abolition of the contract for services system, with an immediate limit on the numbers of East European workers with German employers. At that time IG BAU was in accordance with the proposal of the social democratic party that the contract for services system should be changed into a new guestworker programme:

> IG BAU joined the campaign to replace the contract for services employment with an immediate temporary limited employment with German employers and a flexible granting of work permits according to the labour market situation. The decisive argument for IG BAU was the employment of foreign experts according to the conditions of the German social and employment stipulations. IG BAU believed that this could be guaranteed only by the pattern of individual employment.
>
> (Faist *et al.* 1999: 153)

This position now advocated in the membership magazine shows that the foremost attitude of trade unions is more protectionist than exclusionist. But the subsequent refusal of the federal government to terminate the contract for services agreements, or at least to turn them into a new guest worker programme, led to the following statement:

> But the problems remain unsolved. Many ten of thousands of German construction workers are without a job and meanwhile about 70,000 contract workers are working in their place, on the basis of intergovernmental agreements. And it is well known that in the wake of the intergovernmental agreements some thousands work illegally on construction sites. Low wage workers and criminal gangs of human smugglers will proceed to profit. In the near future loyal enterprises will be ruined with cheap tariff offers in front of our very eyes.
>
> (*Foundation Stone* 8/93: 6)

Such quotes stress that IG BAU marked the employment of East European contract for services workers as an illegitimate intrusion. As a result of a fierce trade union campaign against the employment of East European contract workers, the limits were reduced and controls were tightened (cf. Treichler 1998; Faist *et al.* 1999). However, the employment of East European workers remained a permanent issue on the agenda of IG BAU. Towards this category of interlopers, the trade union retained an openly exclusionist position.

### Posted EU workers as interlopers

At a time when the trade union was still campaigning to restrict and to abolish the contract for services agreements with CEE-countries, the completion of the Single European Market, with the full realisation of the free movement of capital, services, goods and labour, had already changed the situation. From 1 January 1993, the number of contract workers from other European Union member states rose and within a short time exceeded the number of the East European contract workers. The share of migrant workers in construction was 10.5 per cent in 1992, 11.5 per cent in 1994 and 17.2 per cent in 1997. Of those, 1.2 per cent in 1992, 8.9 per cent in 1994 and 15.7 per cent in 1997 were EU workers, while 9.3 per cent in 1992, 2.6 per cent in 1994 and 1.5 per cent in 1997 were East European contract workers (Bosch *et al.* 2000). The significance of East European contract workers since 1994 has been small compared to European Union posted workers. But the trade union still concentrated its attack on the bilateral agreements with East European countries. However, the trade union began to deal with the issue of free movement of workers from other EU member states. For the first time, in October 1994, the increasing competition with contract workers from other EU member states, such as Italy or Portugal and self-employed workers from the UK was indicated in the columns of *Foundation Stone*. In distinction to the contract workers from CEE the workers from EU countries were labelled 'posted workers' (*entsandte Arbeitnehmer*). Thus, a semantic distinction was introduced to distinguish between workers from EU member states and from non-member states. The semantic distinction mirrored the juridical constellation that the political opportunity structure strictly denied the exclusion of European posted workers. In February 1995 under the heading 'Does the European Single market endanger the national social and tariff policy in the construction industry?' the trade union informed its members for first time about the concrete situation on the construction sites in Germany. IG BAU began to demand the introduction of a 'European posting of workers directive' (Sörries 1997; Eichhorst 1999; Faist *et al.* 1999) in order to cope with the no longer restricted influx of workers from EU member states:

> At the moment there are subcontractors working on many construction sites. According to estimates from the employers' associations, construction enterprises from member states employ about 100,000 to 200,000 workers on our construction sites. They are sent by the firms of their home country. The posted workers receive low pay, much lower than the German tariff wages. This is a unprecedented but still legal social dumping. . . . We cannot do without German tariff wages and the inclusion of the foreign enterprises in the insurance system. We support a worker's Europe. But whoever wishes to prevent hostility against Europe and nationalism has to prevent social dumping in the European Union by the means of a 'posting of workers directive'.
>
> (*Foundation Stone* 95/2: 2)

The demand to integrate EU posted workers into the systems of social protection and wage negotiation was added to the previously expressed general demand to deny foreign workers from abroad access to labour markets. With respect to this proposal, a joint declaration by the German trade union confederation (DGB) and an employer's handicraft association is quoted: 'A low wage competition can be observed most of all in the construction industry. This leads to an unacceptable distortion of competition and disadvantages for small- and medium-sized enterprises.' Consequently the passing of a European 'Posting of Workers directive' was demanded (*Foundation Stone* 94/10: 2). With regard to the requested directive, it was argued that a responsible European policy for the economy and the workers of one's own country cannot mean opening borders and handing over the labour market to market forces; in particular when other member states secure their labour markets with regulation of minimum standards (*Foundation Stone* 94/11: 2). A month later, a report was published about a federal conference of works councils. At this gathering, the chairman of the construction trade union again touched on the problem: 'With the opening of European labour markets since 1 January 1993, we face a situation that creates a need for reforms in the area of the protection of the social flank of labour' (*Foundation Stone* 94/12). In March 1995 the German construction trade union organised a European conference in Bonn, devoted to the situation in the construction industry and the regulation of the mobility of labour (cf. Köbele and Leuschner 1995). Here, on the one hand, trade unions repeated the call to close the border to foreign contract workers from CEE-countries. On the other hand, the enactment of the European directive or comparable protection clauses at national levels were demanded with respect to the European posted workers. When the enactment of the European directive was delayed, the IG BAU returned to the national arena and finally reached an agreement that statutory levels of pay and employment would be stipulated by a national law, which would come into force in 1997 (Worthmann 1998).

## Workers from CEE-accession states as interlopers

In spite of the fact that the employment of both categories – CEE as well as EU workers – caused comparable problems, the coping strategy was different. Exclusive in the one direction and inclusive in the other. The difference in treatment cannot be derived from differences in the situation on the construction site. Reports by trade unions and official authorities substantiate the claim that statutory conditions of pay and work were not being met by East European or by EU-sending enterprises (BMAS 1997). The different rhetoric vis-à-vis East European workers can be explained only with reference to the overarching legal frame, which permitted the preferred strategy of exclusion only with regard to the citizens of non-EU member states. With regard to the workers from EU member states, exclusion had no legal basis. IG BAU was forced to develop new strategies to defend its members' interests. The only possible way to act in accordance with the European political opportunity structure was to attempt to include EU workers as much as possible in the German social and tariff order, in order to reduce the gap in labour costs. With the demand for the integration of posted workers into the system of social protection, the boundaries between domestic and foreign workers were significantly re-shaped. Following official provisions, posted workers from EU member states were no longer treated as a category of foreign workers exposed to open exclusionist claims.

With the national regulations providing equal pay and working conditions for all workers regardless of nationality coming into force in 1997, a measure was enacted that enabled the social regulation of the mobility of workers in transnational labour markets. The statutory minimum standards covered foreign workers from East Europe as well as from EU member states and German workers. But when the negotiations on EU enlargement became more concrete, an exclusionist position against East European workers returned, in spite of the existence of national minimum standards. In a press release, the IG BAU president lumped together the threat of illegal employment with Eastern enlargement. He warned against 'Mafia on construction sites', noted a growing influence of Mafia organisations from Italy, Russia, Albania and Romania and turned to the subject of Eastern enlargement:

> With regard to the Eastern enlargement of the European Union, Wiesehügel demanded an interim period of minimum of ten years, before an accession candidate receive full membership. A quicker introduction of free movement for services and workers would have a disastrous impact on the German political economy, but also on the political economies of the acceding countries, said the trade union chairman. In Poland, for example, the majority of peasants and a significant share of industrial jobs would fall victim to a brutal structural change. Also, the German labour market would not cope with the immediate introduction of free movement of workers, proceeded Wiesehügel. The results would be an even more merciless and predatory competition, more bankruptcy than today, higher unemployment and 'starvation wages within one of the wealthiest countries of the world'.
>
> (IG BAU press release, 11 December 1999)

In the trade union argumentation, the reference to the situation in Poland used to be important: it was stated that the transformation in the Polish agriculture in the course of European integration would lead to an increased influx of legal and illegal workers from Poland. Contrary to the expert views of most scientific observers making predictions about Eastern enlargement (DIW 1997 and 2000; Hönekopp and Werner 2000) IG BAU operated from the perception that the immediate grant of free movement to workers would result in an uncontrollable influx of Polish workers. In April 2001 the membership magazine published an article entitled: 'Hot issue: Eastern Enlargement. How Europe scares'. The reader is informed about the situation in East Germany: decreasing wages and increasing unemployment characterise the social reality. With an allusion to German re-unification, it is said that the last enlargement the people experienced is still hard to digest. A trade union official is quoted: 'The people are afraid of the Eastern Enlargement and you cannot gloss over this fact. To relieve people from this fear is the most important task of policy. This is yet not realised' (*Foundation Stone* 2001/4: 10).

To relieve people from fear, the trade unions demanded a restriction on the free moment from candidate countries for an interim time limit of ten years. IG BAU, as the sectoral trade union responsible for the subject of Eastern enlargement, launched intensive activities in order to guarantee the postponement of the free movement of workers from East European candidate states. The lobbying activities concentrated on the national level. Since the 1998 election, the chairman of the IG

BAU had become a social democratic member of the federal parliament. The hotline between officials from the trade union and the governing party contributed to the fact that the issue of granting free movement for the candidate states became a top priority. Chancellor Schröder personally supported the trade unions' claims and spoke in favour of postponing the free movement of workers. In March 2001 the German government proposed a regulation scheme that finally became the position of the European Commission in the accession negotiations with the candidate states: the free movement of workers from accession states is granted as a rule, but every old member state has the right to declare reservations and to postpone free movement for up to seven years within its own national territory. After three and five years the restrictions have to be reviewed and may be abolished or prolonged up to a maximum of seven years. IG BAU declared the decision to postpone free movement as a direct outcome of IG BAU lobbying:

> The IG BAU prevailed against the Federal government: the temporary arrangements to restrict the free movement of workers and services was extended to seven years. The Federal government succeeded, in that the EU Commission basically changed its negotiation position.
>
> (*Foundation Stone* 2000/7–8: 9)

IG BAU presented itself as a successful political actor effectively representing its members' interests. But with the end of the debate on Eastern enlargement the problems remained unsolved and the question remained how to cope with the existing bad situation.

### *Illegally employed foreigners as interlopers*

Currently, IG BAU is intensifying its efforts to direct attention to illegal employment in the construction industry. The earlier account already revealed that the criticism of irregular or illegal employment had been a constant issue, raised for each of the mentioned categories of interlopers from outside. This thread is contemporarily resumed and intensified. The cover story of the *Foundation Stone* for June 2001 published the message of 'Construction site as scene of the crime: 300,000 illegals'. According to this report German construction sites are characterised by a Mafia-like situation. The report opened with the description of a police action against a criminal network of 112 enterprises which used to exploit Portuguese workers with a tax and social contribution fraud of 17 million euro. The report continues:

> According to estimations by IG BAU, 300,000 illegals work on German construction sites. Of those about 150,000 come from East Europe, mainly Poland. 75,000 come from Portugal and 25,000 from ex-Yugoslavia and Turkey respectively. In February 2001 the number of statistically registered construction workers in Germany lay under one million for the first time. The Mafiosi pay the 300,000 illegals starvation wages of 6 euro. They do not pay social contributions at all, no taxes, no pension contributions. . . . A Western German skilled worker therefore costs five or ten times more than an illegal.

He really cannot live in luxury. But the profiteers see the chance to make a profit by social dumping. The huge enterprises more and more restrict themselves to the calculation and management of projects. The dirty work is left for sub-sub-sub-enterprises who finally employ the illegals. With a clean record and sharp forefinger the principals then point to the black sheep at the bottom with the attitude: 'We' have nothing to do with this. But the illegals are only an element of the major system of wage reduction.

*(Foundation Stone* 2001/6: 13)

According to this portrayal, the principal enterprises use foreign workers in order to gain a criminal profit. The consistent implication of this situational definition is the claim for increasingly tightened controls and sanctions. At the moment IG BAU is struggling to introduce regulations making the principal enterprises responsible for wage and tax fraud on their work sites. This is a consequent development taking into account that the trade union explained to its members that the prospective threat of Eastern enlargement is now likely to be under control.

However, the juridical category of irregular and illegal employment is ascribed mainly to interlopers from outside. It is suggested that the Mafia could not proceed with criminal activities without these foreign workers. The source of danger is still located beyond national boundaries. The image of illegal employment is connected with foreign workers.

Obviously the construction and maintenance of boundaries of belonging is not stable and fixed but relational and flexible. In the last decade the boundaries had to be re-negotiated: for the first time when the GDR collapsed, the second in the context of the re-definition of the relationship and neighbourhood with the Eastern states, the third time when the freedom of movement within the EU was realised, the fourth in the context of the accession process and already the fifth will be the re-shaping of boundaries in the process of EU Eastern enlargement.

In the course of time, IG BAU presented several categories of interlopers: citizens of the GDR were preferred over Polish contract workers, and posted EU workers over East European accession workers. With regard to the categories of workers portrayed as interlopers, IG BAU developed two distinct attitudes: the first and main attitude is exclusionist. IG BAU used to demand closed borders in order to protect the social regulation of the domestic labour market. The exclusionist claims encompassed the exemption of free movement of services in the case of GDR enterprises, the abolition or at least the quantitative reduction of East European contract workers and the postponement of the free movement of workers from accession states.

The account of the efforts at persuasion in the columns of the *Foundation Stone* revealed a typical pattern: the German labour market is portrayed as a strong and orderly economic system threatened from outside. IG BAU argues that problems are imported from outside by interlopers. In order to keep fairness within the labour market and welfare for workers, the boundaries have to be protected. The most important goal of IG BAU is the maintenance of the system of tariffs and social protection for all workers employed in Germany, including resident foreign workers.

With regard to this universal attitude, the organisational 'because motive' is thus not a xenophobic or an exclusionist, but a protectionist one. The claim for exclusionist practices and the use of xenophobic images among its own members is a more derived 'in-order-to motive'.

The political opportunity structure, however, restricted and prevented for particular constellations the realisation of strict exclusionist strategies. In the case of the East European contract workers, the German government could not cancel the intergovernmental agreements for diplomatic and foreign policy reasons. In this situation, IG BAU demanded alternatively the reduction of limits set by the intergovernmental agreements and the tightening of controls. In the case of the free movement of workers from accession states, IG BAU demanded as an alternative to the impossible exclusionist measure, the postponement of free entry. IG BAU turned to inclusive measures only in constellations which lacked exclusionist options. In the case of GDR workers, the organisation expanded to the accession area and integrated the construction workers from East Germany. In the case of posted EU workers, IG BAU demanded from the beginning the integration of temporarily employed workers in the German system of social protection.

## Continuation of traditional stereotypical argumentation

The above account has revealed that the undoubtedly existing difficulties within the German construction labour market are framed by IG BAU persuasion efforts as problems caused by outside interlopers. The categories of interlopers examined are differently evaluated: the influx from other EU member states is reluctantly accepted (in the law-abiding form). But interlopers from East Europe – with a particular stress on workers from Poland – were principally rejected. In the German discourse on the employment of East European contract workers as well as on the Eastern enlargement and the illegal employment, an outstanding role is ascribed to the Polish nationality: a good indicator for this constellation was the use of the term 'Polish prices' covering the cheaper bargain tender offered by foreign enterprises (Faist *et al.* 1999). Two reasons probably may have caused the prominent perception of the Polish nationality: Poland was and is the most important of the East European sending countries and holds in all categories the greatest share of temporary migrant labour in Germany (Cyrus 1994 and 2001b; Hönekopp *et al.* 2001). To explain particular attention to Poland, it is insufficient to refer to empirical facts. The perception and interpretation of facts or situations is guided by the cultural embedding. The meaning which social actors attach to social reality and situations depends on the social and cultural context. In the case of labour migration from Poland, the cultural embedding is framed by a far-reaching historical experience of Polish labour migration to Germany (Bade 2001). In Poland the contemporary use of old fashioned terms like 'going to Saxony' or 'going to the Reich' signal that the perception of the contemporary labour migration is still framed by the historical experiences (Morawska 1998; Korczynska 2001). On the other side, in Germany the image of Polish labour immigration is deeply rooted as well in the national collective memory: beginning with the immigration of Polish workers in the second half of the nineteenth century, German nationalistic interest groups created and propagated the image of the less-civilised Polish 'job thieves'. When the developing German agriculture and industry needed cheap labour, Poland became the main important country of origin. On the one hand, Polish workers were recruited because they were cheap and diligent, but on the other hand they were perceived to drive out German workers and to undermine German culture (Herbert 1986). According to perceptions once propagated by German interest groups, which are over a hundred years old, Poles represent disorder, they drive German workers out of their jobs, have a bad work performance, and accept lower wages because of lower standards of living and civilisation. Historically rooted terms like the 'Polenflut' (Polish flood) or 'Polnische Wirtschaft' (Polish economy) still have a strong negative connotation in Germany (Orlowski 1996; Kurcz 1999). The fact that the first introduction of laws regulating the entry and stay of foreigners in Germany was initially restricted to Poles from abroad (while other foreigners such as Italians were not affected) underlines the significance the Polish 'other' had to play in the process of German state and nation formation (Wippermann 1992; Gosewinkel 1997).

According to commentators, the mutual stereotypes are still relevant in the German–Polish relationship in general and in the debate on the Polish accession to the EU in particular. The Polish Secretary of Foreign Affairs, Wlodimierz Cimociewiec recently estimated that the German perception of Poland relies on negative prejudices from the past and many people do not know much about Poland. According to Cimociewiec the fear of Eastern enlargement often uttered in both countries stems from mutual ignorance (*Tagesspiegel* 21.1.2002). The Polish sociologist Zdislaw Krasnodebski, now teaching in Bremen, detects an increasing public interest in the subject of Polish immigration:

> In view of the approaching accession of Poland to the EU, worry and fear increase that a huge, uncontrolled immigration from Poland will take place. In a particular sense this is a new version of the old fear of the competition of the 'cheap hands' and the 'Slavic flood'.
>
> (Krasnodębski 2001: 13)

The critique that the stereotypical perception of Polish workers is reproduced in the debate on Eastern enlargement is shared by German observers too. The Commissioner of affairs of foreigners of the *Land* Bremen sees a 'Poland-debate':

> Since Poland stands on the threshold to the European Union, the question of the granting of free movement to Polish workers connected with the accession is used not infrequently in a populist manner in order to predicate 'us' against a Polish infiltration, a migration of peoples with decreasing wages, and to cause a competition scare against Polish workers and – to put it cautiously – to produce rejective attitudes against 'the' Poles, even against those who have lived here for many years.
>
> (Lill 2001)

It is illuminating that observers from both sides of the border, in order to describe the most striking aspect of the recent debate of the Polish–German relationship, refer to the subject of free movement of workers within the accession process. This indicates, first, that the political interest representation of the IG BAU was efficient and became an aspect of the discourse which was impossible to ignore. Second, the statements illustrate that the lobbying of IG BAU is perceived to appeal to stereotypes. The earlier account of the persuasion efforts disseminated through the membership magazine supports this estimation: IG BAU proceeded from traditional stereotypical images which were once created in the context of the labour immigration from Poland to Germany. Portrayals of the situation use allusions to the traditional images of Polish labour immigrants: as in the case a hundred years ago, the work of Polish labour immigrants is characterised as being of lower quality and causing unemployment.

For this attitude, IG BAU, as the key actor in representing the trade union positions in the treatment of immigrant labour, became the target of harsh criticism. Immigrant organisations complained that IG BAU shows no interest in supporting Polish contract workers asking for assistance (Meister 1995). Responding to an open letter by a local trade union official in Berlin, a DGB-working group on, Trade Union activists Against Racism and Fascism, accused IG BAU of racism:

> workers, most of all from East Europe, are offended to be described as a 'cancer abscess' and 'parasites'. Those workers with the worst conditions of work, pay and social protection are excluded [from protection]. The demand that the authorities intensify their actions against the employed workers is official policy of IG BAU. With this, in the first place, people are affected who are coerced to sell their labour cheaply because of the miserable economic performance or political situation. These people are made illegal by the German aliens law. We demand that IG BAU represents the interests of all those employed in construction work. We demand that IG BAU . . . [does] not rely on bad racist propaganda.
>
> (Trade Unionists Against Racism and Fascism,
> Open letter 12 April 1996; see *tageszeitung* (*taz*), 16 April 1996)

IG BAU repudiated such a criticism. The trade union would neither put forth, nor propagate nor tolerate racism and xenophobia. IG BAU justified its own position with reference to a number of facts. As already shown, for about two decades several independent, but overlapping trends led to a transformation of the constitution of the labour market. The previous account indicates, however, that the influx of Polish and East European workers is one among several factors contributing to the crisis in construction industry. The increasing use of temporary employment of migrant workers is the result rather than the cause of the transformation (Faist *et al.* 1999: 227).

According to its self-presentation, IG BAU tried hard to prevent xenophobic reaction among German construction workers. The claim was made that since 1992 'government and Parliament had to quickly initiate activities in order to meet the increasing xenophobia among our workers' (IG BSE o. J., quoted in Treichler 1998: 224). To extinguish xenophobic attitudes among its members, IG BAU proposed restricting access to German labour markets. The logic behind this argument is as follows: 'xenophobic anxieties about immigrants serve to justify a policy of restricting migration, and that policy is then expected to preserve the population from anti-foreigner ideologies' (Blaschke 1998: 25).

The more important aspect here is that IG BAU, in order to achieve its organisational goals, exploits not only the stereotype of foreign workers but also of its own members. The stereotype of a 'racist German construction worker' was accepted and used as an argument in order to strengthen its own position. IG BAU used the argument of xenophobia as a threatening means. The point of interest according to Treichler (1998: 224) is that xenophobia was discovered as a matter of fact by the organisation only in a situation when the competition with foreign workers from Poland and other CEE-countries raised the threat that domestic workers would be replaced. Xenophobia was however not the subject of intra-organisational dispute, but was

> politically used by the sectoral trade union as a threatening factor in order to mobilise against the inter-governmental agreements. To give one example, the deputy chairman of IG BAU, Ernst Ludwig Laux, mentioned with regard to the impact of the contract agreements with CEE countries on the German construction labour market in September 1992: 'Whoever adds fuel to the fire with such approaches (i.e. the intergovernmental agreements) and undermines the tariff order will in due course be surprised by the echo'.
>
> (Treichler 1998: 225)

This argument was repeated with respect to the contract workers and the European posted workers as well (Sahl 1997). The organisation portrays its members as susceptible to or even affected by xenophobia, and itself as an organisation trying to pacify them. But Faist *et al.* in their study (1999) reject the claim that xenophobia is a characteristic of construction workers:

> According to all information available, Polish contract workers explained that they have no problems with German colleagues, however they often criticised the degrading attitude of employees of German-controlled authorities against foreigners. However, in the course of the deterioration of the labour market situation in the construction sector, most of all in developments since the mid-1990s, activities could be observed that increasingly raised the media interest: bigger construction sites with a high share of foreign workers from the so-called cheap paid countries were occupied or blockaded by German workers. The impetus for such actions may have come from the increasing political visibility of the subject – with xenophobia running along – by trade unions and sectoral employers' associations, who had pointed to the high amount of employment of foreigners.
>
> (Faist *et al.* 1999: 221)

The trade union operates with stereotypes rooted in the cultural tradition of capitalism (the unstable crowd) and nationalism (the dangerous foreign other). This may explain why Polish workers became the prominent scapegoat. The mobilisation was effective because it could agree with images rooted in the collective memory. Such allusions would not work to the same effect in the European policy arena. IG BAU consciously followed the *cultural opportunity structure*. But this was playing with the fire. While IG BAU officials argued in public that the trade union had some difficulties coping with the existing hostility against East Europeans, IG BAU contributed to the emergence of hostility and xenophobia: the members were mobilised for demonstrations, rallies and even the encircling of construction sites where East European contract workers were present (Faist *et al.* 1999: 221ff). In his seminal study of 'labour migration and trade unions' Andreas Treichler (1998) recognised that this strategy had explosive effects because it supported and strengthened latent xenophobic attitudes.

> The problem of xenophobic attitudes and patterns of action against particular groups of labour migrants could not be perceived to be – as described in 1995 by the IG BAU chairman Klaus Wiesehügel – exclusively a problem inherent in the nature of trade unions. . . . It is more appropriate to grasp the xenophobic attitudes and patterns of actions against immigrants of foreign origin as an outcome of the interaction between the nature of trade unions, and their organisation.
>
> (Treichler 1998: 226)

The findings contradict the simple statement that 'Europe is a matter of the ruling elite, the nation a matter of endangered marginalised social stratas' and that 'transnational integration pressed ahead by a modernity elite will consequently cause the erosion of national collective solidarity' (Münch 2001: 294). This case study reveals that elites still strategically play the national card in order to be successful. It is impossible to decide how far individual trade union officials or members have internalised and share xenophobic attitudes. Informal discussions with the author revealed that some trade union officials see xenophobic tendencies within some of their colleagues. On the other hand these officials expressed high awareness of the sensitive topic and some distance from the trade union policy.

## Re-negotiation of categories of belonging

Some indicators support the estimation that the reliance on stereotypes is more a conscious, organisational strategy. For German trade unions, the maintenance of the social order characterised by the neo-corporatist arrangement is the main issue of concern. This goal can be reached only in cooperation with employers and the state. Trade union policy thus has to take into account the interests of these other components of the neo-corporatist compromise. When I asked a high-ranking IG BAU official in an informal discussion in 1995 why the organisation did not demand measures to protect Polish contract workers, he agreed that more inclusive strategies would fit the trade union tradition better. But he pointed out that the trade union had to act hand in hand with the employers' association, which would not agree with measures granting more rights to foreign workers. In cooperation with the social partners, only restrictive measures could be realised. The social partners agreed on a national compromise that outside interlopers were mainly made responsible for the bad situation.

By pointing at outside interlopers the organisation was able to translate the intricate situation with a whole complex of transformation causes into a straight argument indicating concrete guidance for action. Consequently, the enormous efforts to restrict or at least to postpone the freedom of movement signalled to the members that the organisation was able to represent their interests powerfully. The demonstration of interest representation became more important than the result. The content was rather *actionism*, but with xenophobic tendencies. Such a conclusion is supported by the observation that the subject of Eastern EU enlargement disappeared from the trade union agenda when the decision on the postponement of freedom of movement was finally reached. While IG BAU discussed the issue extensively on its website in the spring of 2001, the subject had completely disappeared by the spring of 2002, after the decision to postpone free movement was made. If the campaign against the introduction of free movement had been caused by anti-Polish stereotypes, the subject would still be relevant on the website.

With the postponement of free movement finally agreed, the hot issue lost relevance without any improvement to the situation. The economic performance and the labour market situation in the construction sector is still poor. In this situation exclusionist arguments returned to the rhetorical arsenal of the trade union. Today, illegal employment in general and the illegal employment of foreigners are on top of the agenda. But Polish workers are no longer presented as the most dangerous other. Some IG BAU officials meanwhile state that Polish workers are no longer the main problem. A slight re-shaping of boundaries has taken place. It is interesting to see how the boundary construction of categories of belonging changed: from a territorial-political concept excluding all workers not belonging to the German and later to the EU territory (including resident foreigners) to the preference of a juridical-territorial concept excluding workers coming from outside Germany and employed irregularly or illegally. Thus the re-framing of boundaries takes into consideration the political re-framing of the territory: Poles are meanwhile no longer excluded on the basis of territorial belonging alone. The new lines of exclusive rhetoric stress the juridical concept of illegal employment and in so doing, place Portuguese workers on the same level with Polish workers. It depends on one's perspective whether this development is interpreted as an improvement in the perception of Polish workers or as a deterioration in the perception of Portuguese workers. In any event, the new rhetoric indicates the factual orientation within the European political opportunity space that definitely includes the final completion of free movement of Polish workers. Meanwhile, IG BAU has already developed inclusive strategies towards East European workers from candidate states. These inclusive elements form the other side of the above-mentioned 'double strategy' and are part of the union's organisational endeavours to extend activities beyond the national policy arena.

The earlier examination indicated that the national policy arena used to be the most important level. IG BAU concentrated on the national policy arena in order to lobby for the maintenance of neo-corporatist national arrangements and tried to revive alliances with the national employers' associations. But increasingly, the additional European channels of policy influence were used too. IG BAU participates actively in the EFBWW and is represented on its executive board.

Furthermore, IG BAU makes use of the channel of bi-lateral cooperation with construction trade unions from other countries. In October 1999 IG BAU signed an agreement with the Polish construction trade unions, Solidarity and OPZZ, on the mutual acceptance of membership. Members of Polish trade unions enjoy the legal protection offered by the German trade union (IG BAU Circular Letter No B 38/1999). In May 2001 IG BAU even opened a contact office in Warsaw in order to intensify the cooperation between the German and the Polish trade unions (*Foundation Stone* 2001/6–7: 8). However, for several reasons this endeavour turned out to be difficult. German trade union officials complain that the Polish side does not show much engagement (cf. Treichler 1998: 235ff). Because of the dominant structure of shop floor organisation, the willingness to represent the interests of Polish labour emigrants employed in Germany is not strongly developed. The representatives of Polish trade unions were more orientated towards the interests of Polish enterprises which they perceived to be of national interest, than towards the interest of individual Polish workers (Marek 2000). Moreover, Polish workers employed in Germany were perceived to be privileged when working for wages at the German level (Golinowska 1999; Golinowska *et al.* 2001). Thus, the cooperation turned out to be difficult and ineffective (Hantke 2001).

On the other hand, the fact that self-interest motivates IG BAU activities in Poland may contribute to its weak performance. An important function of the IG BAU information office in Warsaw is to disseminate information on the conditions of work and pay in Germany and to support Polish workers to claim their rights in Poland. That the intention to open the office is connected with the situation in Germany became obvious considering the statement of the IG BAU president made on the occasion of the opening of the Warsaw office and published in the membership magazine: 'On German construction sites, enterprises with addresses in Poland are engaged in work, but they are completely unknown here in Poland' (*Foundation Stone* 2001/7–8: 8). The report signals to its members: your organisation will represent your interests even in Poland.

However, a fundamental turn took place: in the meantime, IG BAU had begun to deal with Polish workers in an inclusive modus in rhetorical and practical terms. In the June–July 2001 issue of the *Foundation Stone*, a short note informs of attempts by German trade union representatives to get into contact with Polish seasonal workers and to discuss their rights. Altogether there are some signs that the reshaping of boundary construction is taking place: the January 2002 issue of the *Foundation Stone* noted that in Hamburg the construction trade union had offered six Bulgarian workers legal protection when they refused to sign a receipt for receiving 7 euro while in reality they had only received between 1 and 2 euro. Only a few days later, Polish contract workers got in touch with the trade union in a similar case (*Foundation Stone* 2002/1: 9–12). In this report, the foreign workers are portrayed in the first place as workers and the attribute of otherness is played down. This may indicate an expansion of the repertoire of interpretation schemata, it may also indicate a more fundamental re-shaping of boundary construction.

## Conclusion

The debate in the introduction on the free movement of workers from the candidate states offers insightful material on the mode of Europeanisation. Following Knill and Lehmkuhl it can be stated that EU enlargement was designed as positive Europeanisation: the European Commission favoured the establishment of a liberal integration modus obligatory upon all member states. However, responding to the pressure expressed by trade unions, Germany and Austria resisted this modus and ensured that the modus of negative Europeanisation (at least on an interim basis) was arranged, providing the opportunity to postpone the free movement of workers from candidate states. Thus the gap between the European pretension and the cultural reality shows the importance of the dimension of the framing Europeanisation. The case study indicates that framing integration will and has to be accomplished by intermediary collective actors such as trade unions. As membership organisations, they have to take into account the cognitive and mental attitudes of their members and to mediate between the overarching political project of Europeanisation – to which they see no alternative – and their members.

With its activities, IG BAU took the lead among Euro-sceptics. The diffuse objection to Eastern enlargement received a concrete expression in a form open to argument. Having succeeded in limiting the free of movement of persons following EU Eastern enlargements, the wind was taken out of the sails of the German Euro-sceptics. The fear was channelled and neutralised with reference to the technical solution. Perhaps this constellation may even be called a trick of European reason? From this point of view, German trade union officials became the agents of European integration just because self-interest played a crucial aspect in their agency. In spite of, or even because, it was most deeply affected negatively by the Eastern enlargement, IG BAU tried to shape and slow down Eastern enlargement. By this it contributed to the process of framing integration and was *nolens volens* enabled to find a solution to organise EU Eastern enlargement. Trade unions who are responsible for the modus of integration now take the role of translators and transmitters.

Following on from this analysis, it may be stated that trade unions strategically take into account the opportunities of the national, and increasingly cross-border and transnational channels of influence. At the same time, IG BAU intensified efforts to realise inclusive strategies towards the contemporary Polish labour migration. In so doing, the process of re-shaping the categorial ascription of workers from Poland and other candidate countries is already underway. With the pragmatic orientation within the European opportunity structure, the Europeanising national trade unions contribute to the re-shaping of cultural landscapes which are currently nationally bounded.

## Notes

1 The national differences in the organisation of industrial relations are significant between the member states of EU. The tendencies of disorganisation described differ from member state to member state according to the national structure of industrial relations (Müller-Jentsch 1995; Hyman 1996, Lubanski 1999). Therefore, the description of the situation is restricted to Germany.

2 The abbreviation IG BAU stands for Industriegewerkschaft Bauen-Agrar-Umwelt (Industrial trade union Construction–Agriculture–Environment). In this chapter the term IG BAU will be used exclusively, and includes the period when the trade union used the name IG BSE, i.e. IG-BAU–Steine–Erden (Industrial trade union Construction–Stones–Earth).

3 See www.dgb.de/wir/statistik/statistik.index.htm.

## References

Adams, W. and Wiesehügel, K. (1995) 'Gewerkschaftspolitische Konsequenzen aus der Wanderung von Bauunternehmern in Europa', in B. Köbele and G. Leuschner (eds) *Dokumentation der Konferenz 'Europäischer Arbeitsmarkt: Grenzenlos mobil?'*, Baden-Baden: Nomos.

Bade, K.J. (2001) *Europa in Bewegung: Migration vom späten 18. Jahrhundert bis zur Gegenwart*, Munich: Beck.

Berger, P. and Luckmann, T. (1967) *The Social Construction of Reality*, London: Allen Lane.

Blaschke, J. (1998) 'The case of Germany: addressing the employment of migrants in an irregular situation', paper presented at the Technical Symposium on International Migration and development, The Hague, Netherlands, 29 June–3. July 1998. UN-Working Group on International Migration Paper No. V/2, Geneva.

Blüm, N. (1995) 'Standpunkt der Bundesregierung', in B. Köbele and G. Leuschner (eds) *Dokumentation der Konferenz 'Europäischer Arbeitsmarkt: Grenzenlos mobil?'*, Baden-Baden: Nomos.

BMAS (Bundesministerium für Arbeit und Sozialordnung) (1997) Bericht über erste Erfahrungen zur Umsetzung des Arbeitnehmer-Entsendegesetzes, unpublished manuscript, Bonn.

Borneman, J. and Fowler, N. (1997) 'Europeanisation', *Annual Review of Anthropology* 26: 487–514.

Bosch, G., Worthmann, G. and Zühlke-Robinet, K. (2000) 'Die Entstehung von "Freihandelszonen" im Arbeitsmarkt: die Transnationalisierung des deutschen Bauarbeitsmarktes', *WSI-Mitteilungen* 10/2000, 671–680.

Bundesregierung (1996) Achter Bericht der Bundesregierung über Erfahrungen bei der Anwendung des Arbeitnehmerüberlassungsgesetzes – AÜG – sowie die über die Auswirkungen des Gesetzes zur Bekämpfung der illegalen Beschäftigung – BillBG, *Deutscher Bundestag – Drucksache* 13/5498, 6 June 1996, Bonn.

Cremers, J. (1998) 'Building blocks for Europeanisation of our industrial relations', *CLR-News* 4, 18–30.

Cyrus, N. (1994) 'Flexible work for fragmented labour markets: the significance of the new labour migration regime in the Federal Republic of Germany', *Migration* 6, 26: 97–124.

—— (2001a) 'Schattenwirtschaft und Migration: ethnologische Annäherungen an ein offenes Geheimnis', in F. Gesemann (ed.) *Migration und Integration in Berlin*, Wissenschaftliche Analysen und politische Perspektiven, Leverkusen: Leske und Budrich.

—— (2001b) 'Die befristete Beschäftigung von Arbeitsmigranten aus Polen', in J. Blaschke (ed.) *Ost-West-Migration: Perspektiven der Migrationspolitik in Europa*, Berlin: Edition Parabolis.

Cyrus, N. and Helias, E. (1993) 'Wir haben keine andere Wahl: zur Situation polnischer Werkvertragsarbeitnehmer in Berlin (We have no choice: on the situation of Polish contract workers in Berlin)', working paper, Arbeitsheft des Berliner Institut für Vergleichende Sozialforschung, Berlin.

Däubler, W. (1995) 'Arbeitsrechtliche Aspekte bei der Umsetzung des Gemeinsamen Marktes', in B. Köbele and G. Leuschner (eds) *Dokumentation der Konferenz 'Europäischer Arbeitsmarkt. Grenzenlos mobil?'*, Baden-Baden: Nomos.

DIW (1997) 'Europäische Union: Osterweiterung und Arbeitskräftemigration', *DIW-Wochenbericht* 5/97: 89–96.

—— (2000) 'EU-Osterweiterung: Keine massive Zuwanderung zu erwarten', *DIW-Wochenbericht* 21/2000: 315–326.

Dølvik, J.E. (1997) 'Redrawing boundaries of solidarity? ETUC, social dialogue and the Europeanisation of trade unions in the 1990s', Arena Report, No. 5/97, Oslo.

Douglas, M. (1986) *How Institutions Think*, Syracuse, NY: Syracuse University Press.

Eichhorst, W. (1999) 'Europäische marktgestaltende Politik zwischen Supranationalität und nationaler Autonomie: Das Beispiel der Entsenderichtlinie', *Industrielle Beziehungen* 3: 340–59.

Erne, R. (2001) 'Organised Labour – An Actor of Euro-democratisation, Euro-technocracy or (re-nationalisation)', 6th European Congress of the International Industrial Relations Association, Oslo, 25–9 June 2001, available at <www.iira2001.org/Documents/Papers/181%20Erne.doc>.

Faist, T. (1996) 'Migration in transnationalen Arbeitsmärkten: Zur Kollektivierung und Fragmentierung sozialer Rechte in Europa', *Zeitschrift für Sozialreform* 41/1995: 36–47 and 42/1996: 108–22.

Faist, T., Sieveking, K., Reim, U. and Sandbrink, S. (1999) *Ausland im Inland. Die Beschäftigung von Werkvertragsarbeitnehmern in der Bundesrepublik Deutschland: Rechtliche Regulierung und politische Konflikte*, Baden-Baden: Nomos.

Favell, A. (1998) 'The Europeanisation of immigration politics', European Integration online papers (EioP) 2, 10 <http://eiop.or.at/eiop/texte/1998-010a.htm>.

Golinowska, S. (1999) 'Die Beschäftigung polnischer Arbeitnehmer in der Bundesrepublik Deutschland im Rahmen von Werkverträgen und Migrationsprozessen in den Neunziger Jahren', in T. Faist, K. Sieveking, U. Reim and S. Sandbrink (eds) *Ausland im Inland. Die Beschäftigung von Werkvertragsarbeitnehmern in der Bundesrepublik Deutschland: Rechtliche Regulierung und politische Konflikte*, Baden-Baden: Nomos.

Golinowska, S., Marek, E. and Rajkiewicz, A. (2001) 'Migration processes in Poland 1990–1996 – Research Summary', in E. Hönekopp, S. Golinowska and M. Horalek (eds) *Economic and Labour Market Development and International Migration – Czech Republic, Poland, Germany*, Beiträge zur Arbeitsmarkt und Berufsforschung 244, Nürnberg: Bundesanstalt für Arbeit.

Gosewinkel, D. (1997) 'Staatsangehörigkeit und Einbürgerung in Deutschland während des 19. und 20. Jarhunderts: Ein Abriß', in B. Danckwortt and C. Lepp (eds) *Von Grenzen und Ausgrenzung*, Marburg: Schüren.

Hannerz, U. (1992) *Cultural Complexity: Studies in the Social Organization of Meaning*, New York: Columbia University Press.

Hantke, F. (2001) 'DGB – Solidarność – OPZZ: Zusammenarbeit der deutschen und polnsichen Gewerkschaften', *Dialog* 57: 28–30.

Herbert, U. (1986) *Geschichte der Ausländerbeschäftigung in Deutschland 1880 bis 1980: Saisonarbeiter, Zwangsarbeiter, Gastarbeiter*, Bonn: Dietz.

Hochstadt, S., Laux, E.L. and Sandbrink, S. (1999) 'Die Bauwirtschaft auf der Suche nach neuen Konzepten', *WSI-Mitteilungen* 2: 119–31.

Hönekopp, E. and Werner, H. (2000) 'Is the EU's labour market threatened by a wave of immigration?', *Intereconomics*, January/February 2000: 3–8.

Hönekopp, E., Golinowska, S. and Horalek, M. (2001) (eds) *Economic and Labour Market Development and International Migration – Czech Republic, Poland, Germany*, Beiträge zur Arbeitsmarkt und Berufsforschung 244, Nürnberg: Bundesanstalt für Arbeit.

Hyman, R. (1996) 'Die Geometrie des Gewerkschaftsverhaltens: Eine vergleichende Anlayse von Identitäten und Ideologien', *Industrielle Beziehungen* 1: 5–35.

IW (Institut der deutschen Wirtschaft) (1993) *Die wirtschaftlichen Implikationen der Werkvertragsabkommen für die Bundesrepublik Deutschland und die Reformstaaten Mittel- und Osteuropas. Guterachterliche Untersuchung im Auftrag des Bundesministeriums für Arbeit und Sozialordnung*, Bonn: Bundesministerium für Arbeit und Sozialordnung.

Knill, C. and Lehmkuhl, D. (1999) 'How Europe matters: different mechanisms of Europeanization', European Integration online papers (EioP) 3, 7 <http://eiop.or.at/eiop/texte/1999-007a.htm>.

Köbele, G. and Leuschner, G. (1995) (eds.) *Dokumentation der Konferenz 'Europäischer Arbeitsmarkt. Grenzenlos mobil?'*, Baden-Baden: Nomos.

Korczynska, J. (2001) 'Individuelle Kosten und Nutzen der Saisonarbeit der Polen in Deutschland: Analyse und Ergebnisse einer empirischen Untersuchung 1999/2000,' in C. Pallaske (ed.) *Die Migration von Polen nach Deutschland*, Baden-Baden: Nomos.

Krasnodębski, Z (2001) 'Die Polnische Minderheit in Deutschland als Forschungsobjekt', in Z. Krasnodębski and N. Krampen (eds) *Pole in Bremen: Eine unsichtbare Minderheit?*, Bremen: Kooperation Universität-Arbeitskammer Bremen.

Kühne, P., Öztürk, N. and West, K.W. (1994) (eds) *Gewerkschaften und Einwanderung. Eine kritische Zwischenbilanz*, Cologne: BUND.

Kurcz, Z. (1999) 'Pogranisze Polsko-Niemieckie a "Polnische Wirtschaft"', in L. Gołdyka (ed.) *Transgraniczność w perspektywie socjologicznej – kontynuacje*, Zielona Góra: Lubuskie Towarzystwo Naukowe.

Lamnek, S. Olbrich, G. and Schäfer, Wolfgang, J. (2000) *Tatort Sozialstaat: Schwarzarbeit, Leistungsmißbrauch, Steuerhinterziehung und ihre (Hinter-) Gründe*, Opladen: Leske and Budrich.

Lill, D. (2001) 'Vorwort', in Z. Krasnodębski and N. Krampen (eds) *Polen in Bremen: Eine unsichtbare Minderheit?*, Bremen: Kooperation Universität–Arbeitnehmerkammer.

Lubanski, N. (1999) 'The impact of Europeanisation on the construction industry – a comparative analysis of developments in Germany, Sweden and Denmark', *Industrielle Beziehungen* 3: 268–91.

Marek, E. (2000), 'Zatrudnienie Polskich pracowników przy relizacji umów o dzieło w Republice Federalnej Niemiec', in A. Rajkiewicz (ed.) *Zewnętrzne migracje zrobkowej we wspólczesnej Polsce: Wybrane zagadnienia, Włocwałek: Wyższa Szkoła Humanistyczno-Ekonomiczna*.

*Marks, G. and McAdam, D. (1996) 'Social movements and the changing structure of political opportunity in the European Union', in G. Marks, F.W. Scharpf, P.C. Schmitter and W. Streeck (eds)* Governance in Europe, London: Sage.

Martin, A. and Ross, G. (1998) 'Die europäische Integration und die Europäisierung der Gewerkschaften', in R. Hoffmann and E. Gabaglio (eds) *Ein offener Prozeß. Elf Versuche über den Europäischen Gewerkschaftsbund*, Münster: Westfälisches Dampfboot.

Meister, H.-P. (1995) 'Anlaufstellen für ausländische Beschäftigte stärken Konfliktfähigkeit und Rechtssicherheit', *Transodra* 14/15: 63–6.

Morawska, E. (1998) 'Structuring migration in a historical perspective: the case of traveling East Europeans', EUI-Working Papers, Florence: EUI.

Müller-Jentsch, W. (1995) 'Auf dem Prüfstand: Das deutsche Modell der industriellen Beziehungen', *Industrielle Beziehungen* 2: 10–24.

Münch, R. (2001) *Offene Räume. Soziale Integration diesseits und jenseits des Nationalstaats*, Frankfurt am Main: Suhrkamp.

Nienhüser, W. (1999) '"Legal, Illegal . . ." – Die Nutzung und Ausgestaltung von Arbeitskräftestrategien in der Bauwirtschaft?', *Industrielle Beziehungen* 6, 3: 292–319.

Orłowski, H. (1996) *'Polnische Wirtschaft'. Zum deutschen Polendiskurs der Neuzeit*, Wiesbaden: Harrassowitz.

Rudolph, H. (1996) 'The New *Gastarbeiter* System in Germany', *New Community* 22, 2: 287–300.

Sahl, K.-H. (1997) 'Die politische Brisanz der Entsendeprobleme im Baugewerbe', in Industriegewerkschaft Bauen-Agrar-Umwelt (ed.) *Dokumentation der Praktikerseminare 'Das Arbeitnehmer-Entsendegesetz – vom Anspruch zur Wirklichkeit'*, Frankfurt am Main: IG BAU.

Schneider, F. and Ernste, D. (2000) *Schattenwirtschaft und Schwarzarbeit. Umfang, Ursachen, Wirkungen und wirtschaftspolitische Empfehlungen*, Munich: Oldenbourg.

Sörries, B. (1997) 'Die Entsenderichtlinie: Entscheidungsprozeß und Rückkopplungen im Mehrebenensystem', *Industrielle Beziehungen* 4, 2: 125–49.

Strauss, A. (1968) *Spiegel und Masken: Die Suche nach Identität* (Mirrors and Masks: The Search for Identity), Frankfurt am Main: Suhrkamp.

Streeck, W. (1996) 'Gewerkschaften zwischen Nationalstaat und Europäischer Union', MPIfG Working Paper 96/1, Cologne: Max-Planck-Institut für Gesellschaftsforschung.

Streeck, W. and Schmitter, P.C. (1998) 'Vom nationalen Korporatismus zum transnationalen Pluralismus: Die organisierten Interesenvertretungen im europäischen Binnenmarkt', in R. Hoffmann and E. Gabaglio (eds) *Ein offener Prozeß: Elf Versuche über den Europäischen Gewerkschaftsbund*, Münster: Westfälisches Dampfboot.

Streeck, W. and Visser, J. (1998) 'An evolutionary dynamic of trade union systems', MPIfG Discussion Paper 98/4, Cologne: Max-Planck-Institut für Gesellschaftsforschung.

Syben, G. (1998) 'Winners and losers of the crisis in the German construction industry', *CLR-News* 3/1998: 13–17.

Treichler, A. (1998) *Arbeitsmigration und Gewerkschaften*, Münster: Lit.

Weinert, R. (2001) Zwangs-Europäisierung europäischer Nationalgewerkschaften', *Soziale Welt* 52: 323–40.

Wippermann, W. (1992) *Geschichte der deutsch–polnischen Beziehungen: Darstellung und Dokumente*, Berlin: Nachdruck.

Worthmann, G. (1998) 'Der Baumarkt unter Veränderungsdruck: Kontrolldefizite in Folge der Transnationalisierung?', *Jahrbuch 1997/98 des Institut Arbeit und Technik*, Institut Arbeit und Technik im Wissenschaftszentrum Nordrhein-Westfalen, Gelsenkirchen: IAT, 86–101.

# 12 Joining an EU identity

Integration of Hungary or
the Hungarians?

*Judit Tóth and Endre Sik*

Hungary is similar to its fellow Central European countries in relation to its migratory movements and migration policy in general, namely, the number of immigrants has risen whilst the number of emigrants has declined. The immigrants originate mostly from the Eastern neighbour countries; the major groups of people entering Hungary are either migrant workers, small-scale traders or asylum seekers, refugees and transit migrants trying to get further West, and last but not least, Hungary is as attractive to both legal and illegal entrepreneurs engaged in various forms of legal and illegal economic activity as are other countries in the 'buffer zone' (Wallace *et al.* 1996; Wallace 2001).

However, there is one special feature of the Hungarian migratory situation and migration politics – a strong form of Diaspora-politics both within and across the Hungarian borders. This is a consequence of having a large ethnic Hungarian community on the other side of the Hungarian border. To give a rough estimate for those who are not familiar with this situation one should try to imagine that a diaspora of about one fourth to one third of the total population of the motherland lives next door to it.

The aims of this chapter are, first, to discuss some aspects of the previously characterised special Diasporic (Clifford 1994) situation, and, second, to describe the peculiarities of such a situation by briefly introducing ten characteristics in respect of those socioeconomic aspects of migration and migration politics (such as ethnicity, national identity, Diaspora policy, etc.) which might have strong effects on the process of integration of Hungary into the European Union (EU).

## On the diasporic nature of the hungarian ethnic community across the border and its migrant community in Hungary

With roots traceable to classical Greek, the term 'Diaspora' means dispersal. It was originally applied to the Jews and to Jewish Christians but in the sociological literature of recent times the Diaspora covers a migrant population, which

- differs in its ethnicity from that of the host country;
- exists as a minority in the host country;

- cherishes a strong nostalgia for and/or active ties with its country of origin;
- constantly prepares to return, but never actually does.

Our analysis of the sociological characteristics of Diaspora is grounded in the work of Bonacich (and its 'corollaries,' Bonacich and Turner 1980; Light and Bonacich 1988). The most profitable aspect of this approach for our analysis is that in explaining the sojourner mentality of the migrant entrepreneur, it describes a sociological behaviour highly characteristic of a Diasporic existence. This pattern is sustained by three factors:

(a)  an ambivalent but powerful emotional relationship with the country of origin (migrants maintain their connections, they keep planning to return while being aware that they will never in fact do so, an awareness which they hide from themselves and in part (over)compensate, but which makes their sojourn in the host country emotionally conceivable only as something temporary);

(b)  an ambivalent relationship with the host country and its majority population (the loyalty of alien settlers is conditional, something that is economically advantageous for migrant and majority population alike and yet continually reproduces mutual suspicions, etc.);

(c)  the intrinsic traits of the migrant existence (a strong and often introverted community in which personal ties are maintained, an (over)developed awareness of 'us', economic isolation, cultural (religious, ethnic, economic) self-defence and the dominance of highly liquid investments, etc.).

The applicability of this model has its obvious limitations as Diasporas are not exclusively made up of small entrepreneurs; further, Bonacich's approach does not consider every feature of a Diasporic existence (for example its political dimension), and ignores factors that may, on occasion, be relevant to a sociological analysis of Diasporas (such as segregation in housing or the historical, political and cultural relations between the sending and the host countries).

It is therefore appropriate to consider – using Bonacich's model as our basis – the inclusion among the characteristics of Diasporic existence (and of the relationship of the Diaspora with the sending and the host countries) the following:[1]

(a)  the majority population of the host country regard the Diaspora as an alien or, assuming a dual loyalty on the part of the Diaspora, even a hostile (scapegoat) community;

(b)  a Diaspora has its life cycles much as an individual has, and the sociological features characterising emergent, strengthened and disintegrating Diasporas greatly differ from each other;

(c)  the nature of the relationship of a Diaspora with the host country may vary according to the relative size and sociological make-up of the former and the cultural, historical and political characteristics of the latter;

(d)  the same country of origin may send out more than one Diasporas, which may communicate with each other, and this communication may result in the emergence of a 'world-wide' community of economic, cultural, and political Diaspora (which may have its own effect on the sociological features characterising the Diaspora's relations with the sending and the host countries).

World-wide trends resulting in new forms and meanings of Diaspora also suggest a more dynamic and relaxed application of the Diaspora-concept. This also implies that, in addition to the sociological features surveyed above, in the analysis of the Diasporas in today's world one has to consider elements that were not characteristic of traditional Diasporas.

It is mentioned by several sources as a characteristic feature of today's Diasporas – a feature often identified as the most important reason why the phenomenon has been brought into increasing salience in recent times – that new and inexpensive technologies used in communication (such as public transport, the telephone, the television, e-mail, postal and banking services) have made possible the (re)organisation of Diasporas in the form of transnational communities.

The multiple forms of communication, together with easier and cheaper travel, have enabled members of the Diaspora wishing to be present in the sending and the host countries simultaneously, to achieve their aspiration. This opportunity reduces the mythical attraction and emotional strain related to the past departure and the present distance from the country of origin while improving the conditions of reciprocal economic transactions and political activities. Members of this modern transnational Diaspora are no longer obliged to choose between assimilation and the maintenance of the values of the ethnic minority; instead, they can be participants on both sides (as shown by the Russian community the world over, Doomernik 1997, or illegal Polish workers in Greece, Romaniszyn 1996). What was once an absurdity as an alternative for the apocryphal Mr Kohn, has thus become a self-evident subculture, a feasible economic and political behaviour, for certain groups of the Diaspora.[2]

It is not only the widespread familiarity with technological innovations that is often mentioned among the reasons for the burgeoning of transnational Diasporas, but other political and cultural aspects of globalisation, too. Such is the postulate of the weakening of nation-states (Demetriou 1999) or of the increasing power exerted by international organisations together with the behavioural patterns and legal expectations promoted by these bodies. A not inconsiderable factor is the influence of Diasporas on the process of policy-making, in that the money raised for specific purposes by them can change forms of government, drastically increase the 'elbow-room' of political trends, or influence sets of cultural values (Shain and Sherman 1999). Neither should we forget such cultural and political influences of global consequence such as multiculturality (and its corollary, the awakening conscious-ness of Diasporas as well as their perception of themselves as constant, although continually changing, entities (Hall 1990)), or the expansion of multinational companies and the spreading of consumption patterns, providing models and standards that facilitate the survival and integration of Diasporas in their host countries (Sheffer 1999).

At this point it seems appropriate to quote, at some length, a seminal work on modern Diaspora, which can provide an apt summary of our tentative argument.

The quoted passage presents, in miniature, all the difficulties that we have come across in grappling with the Diaspora concept; however, the extract has also reinforced our conviction that what we are dealing with is a phenomenon which is both important and amenable to analysis from a peculiarly Hungarian viewpoint:

> An unruly crowd of descriptive/interpretive terms now jostle and converse in an effort to characterise the contact zones of nations, cultures, and regions: terms such as 'border', 'travel', 'creolization', 'transculturation', 'hybridity' and 'Diasporas' (as well as the looser 'diasporic'). Important new journals, such as *Public Cultures*, and *Diaspora* (or the revived *Transition*), are devoted to the history and current production of transnational cultures. In his editorial preface to the first issue of *Diaspora*, Kachig Tölölian writes, 'Diasporas are the exemplary communities of the transnational moment . . . the term that once described Jewish, Greek, and Armenian dispersion now shares meanings with a large semantic domain that includes words like immigrant, expatriate, refugee, guest-worker, exile community, overseas community, ethnic community'.

Safran . . . defines Diasporas as follows:

> expatriate minority communities (1) that are dispersed from an original 'centre' to at least two 'peripheral' places, (2) maintain a 'memory, vision, or myth about their original homeland', (3) that believe they are not – and perhaps cannot be – fully accepted by their host country, (4) that see the ancestral home as a place of eventual return, when the time is right, (5) that are committed to the maintenance and or restoration of this homeland, and (6) whose consciousness and solidarity as a group are 'importantly defined' by this continuing relationship with the homeland.
>
> (Safran 1991)

. . .

> Safran is right to focus attention on defining Diaspora. What is the range of experiences covered by the term? Where does it begin to lose definition? . . . Whatever the working list of diasporic features, no society can be expected to qualify on all accounts, throughout its history. And the discourse of Diaspora will necessarily be modified as it is translated and adopted. . . . Different diasporic maps of displacement and connection can be compared on the basis of family resemblance, of shared elements, no subset of which is defined as essential to the discourse.
>
> (Clifford 1994)

### Ethnic Hungarians living outside the borders of present-day Hungary as a Diaspora?[3]

The dominant view regarding the classification of extraterritorial ethnic Hungarians as a Diaspora is that, while Hungarians living in Western countries form Diaspora, as the emergence of their community is the result of migration, the formation of a Hungarian population in the Carpathian Basin is not (characteristically) related to migration.

> I would not by any means call the Hungarian ethnicity of Transylvania Diaspora. This term is used in different senses in the Hungarian and in the Rumanian languages. What we mean by Diaspora is a group of dispersed pockets of small ethnic communities scattered over a given area. Rumanians use the same term to cover all Rumanians living abroad. Our Diaspora is made up of Hungarians living in Western countries.

> I think the word Diaspora reflects the wrong attitude, which is alien to Hungarian traditions. It is a symptom of an emergent truncated Hungarian self-perception, which does not see anything that lies beyond the territory between Hegyeshalom and Ártánd [the furthest two villages in the West and East in contemporary Hungary]. What this truncated Hungarian self-perception means is that there are us, Hungarians, citizens of Hungary, and then there are those what-you-may-call-'em's speaking Hungarian, who might be some kind of relatives, but in any case are second-class Hungarians, just like those East-Germans who were also relegated to the status of as second-rate Germans.

Particular mention should be made of the issue of ethnic Hungarians in Transylvania (Romania), where both identity and the political question are unique and weighty matters:

> Transylvanian Hungarians have always been Transylvanian Hungarians. A Hungarian living in Transylvania is part of the Hungarian nation but he or she is a person with a autonomous identity, an autonomous value.

> I would define the Hungarian ethnic community of Transylvania as a core of the Hungarian nation at large where traditions and customs are healthy and cohesion is strong. I feel that from this point of view the Hungarians of Transylvania have much to offer to Hungary's native citizens. The Hungarian population of Transylvania should be preserved as it has ever been. That is how it can be of use both to their ancient country and to Romania.

In the application of the term Diaspora, those holding an alternative opinion make a distinction between Hungarians living in blocks and those forming dispersed pockets, which latter they regard as Diaspora even within the Carpathian Basin.

> It is a small, somewhat coherent community living among an overwhelming majority, such as Hungarians living in dispersal abroad. That is why I regard Hungarians in the West and right across the borders as Diaspora. Transylvanian Hungarians living in large blocks are not at all a Diaspora.

The understanding of dispersion (as it is deducible from dispersal, the sense of the classic notion of Diaspora) as Diaspora is of particular interest, as in that case what is to be determined is the interpretation of dispersion. Compared to the ten-million strong population of Hungary, even the ethnic Hungarian blocks of Transylvania should be seen as living in dispersion.

> Diaspora is nothing but dispersion. Therefore I regard the block of the Székely community, even though you can travel for six hours in their midst without hearing a word of Rumanian spoken anywhere; however, because of the great distance and isolation from Hungary, this is a Diaspora. I am not here using the notion of Diaspora in its religious sense as it is used in phrases like 'the dispersal of the Jewish Diaspora,' neither in the sense of migration. That sense is applicable to Hungarians in the West. That is, those who emigrate from Hungary and settle down somewhere between Austria and Canada, form *one Diaspora*. But regarding the *Hungarian Diaspora* I consider dispersal in a general sense, meaning that political boundaries do not coincide with the boundaries of language and culture. Viewed from Transylvania, the Székely community is no Diaspora, the block of Hungarians in Partium is no Diaspora, but those living in Transylvania Interior or the Banat are. Viewed from Budapest, however, the Székely – in spite of their population of 600–700 thousand – are by all means a Diaspora. The whole issue depends on where you look at it from.

> What I mean by Diaspora is dispersion. The Hungarians of Sub-Carpathia I do not regard as Diaspora, as they do not live in dispersion. After all, the Hungarians of Sub-Carpathia live in one large block.

In sum, it can be concluded that the whole of the Hungarian population living within the Carpathian Basin is not regarded as Hungary's Diaspora by the actors of Diaspora-politics. However, a number of empirical arguments available may provide us with a sufficient basis to recommend that the nature of the connection of ethnic Hungarians across the borders and in the Carpathian Basin with Hungary (a native country that they have never left) should be considered as one possibly displaying Diasporic features.

For example according to recent sociological and anthropological findings:

- the symbol of Hungarian statehood (honouring the national flag) is just as important for the ethnic Hungarians of Transylvania as the statehood of Romania is for the Romanian population of Transylvania (Szakáts 1996);
- for Transylvanian Hungarians living in Hungary, Hungary is 'home away from home' (Kántor, undated), and this dual loyalty to home survives decades (Szakáts 1996);
- Hungary (although to a lesser degree, but even today) is 'home turf' for the ethnic Hungarians of Transylvania (Bíró 1998).

### Ethnic Hungarians from abroad living in Hungary as a Diaspora?

The opinion of those involved in the Hungarian Diaspora politics is contradictory:

> Hungarians having immigrated from Rumania form a real Diaspora. They are characterised by strong networking and group formation, they are efficient lobbyists, and they are tied together by a powerful sense of mutual help and group solidarity. Further, they are regarded – as are Jews – with prejudices by the 'outside world' (the shiftless native citizens of Hungary).

> I do not regard as Diaspora even the Hungarians immigrating from Sub-Carpathia, although they do form a peculiar group compared to native citizens of Hungary in that they can organise themselves. I do not think that these immigrants are driven to Hungary by a yearning to return to some mythical homeland. They come here because the material conditions of life are better and also because they stand a better chance to make good in the long run, too. People in my environment have in any case come over on such considerations, which is why I do not regard them Diaspora. These immigrants have no nostalgic reasons for coming here, and if they form a group and have their own organisations is due to the fact that the society of Hungary does not welcome those who arrive from elsewhere. And it does not matter much whether the arrivals come from just across the border or Africa.

Sociological and anthropological data prove the existence of Diasporic mentality among ethnic Hungarians migrating to Hungary from across the borders. For example:

(a)  Their strong sense of being Hungarian, reinforced by their Transylvanian identity, results in a disdainful attitude to the sense of Hungarian nationhood they encounter in the host country on the one hand, and in an increasing, identity-shaping appreciation for the culture and community that they left behind in the country of origin on the other.

(b)  The above-mentioned Transylvanian identity is made up of such elements as pride felt over the historical success of the Transylvanian principality, religious tolerance, a cultural supremacy over the native Hungarian population of Hungary, the dignity of resisting Romanian oppression, and a sense of superiority to Romanians.

(c)  There are opinions in which the perception of 'Transylvanianhood' as a general element of identity only exists among those living in Hungary, while 'back home' identity is a function of smaller units instead.[4] What is meant by this is not simply the fact that each historically distinct region, town and village has its own, more or less distinct, identity, but also that constantly emerging old–new local identities can exist side by side.

The identities of Hungarians from Transylvania settled in Hungary is shaped in the interaction of individual decisions, governmental Diaspora-policies and domestic minority-policies. That there is room for rational considerations as well as emotional elements in this process is exemplified by a wittily bitter proposition made by the Association of Transylvanian Hungarians (an organisation of Transylvanian intellectuals living in Hungary, which was founded in 1989). The mock-suggestion, which concerns the politics of identity, would advise Transylvanian-born Hungarians to choose another identity for themselves because their associations could receive considerable support from the country's minority-policies, unfriendly towards a Transylvanian identity, as organisations of Romanian, Armenian or Gypsy communities.

Needless to say, the identity-politics of the Diaspora are greatly affected by the public perception of the given community in the host country. With regards the Diaspora of Romanian-born Hungarians in Hungary, such attitudes were favourable for a while. This support did not last long, however, and although Transylvanian-born Hungarians have been treated with more hospitality than any other ethnic community in this country, opinion polls have registered a steady deterioration in attitudes to them (see Figure 12.1).

Complaints by young Transylvanians that 'Hungary is the only country in the world where Hungarians from Transylvania are not Hungarians' cannot be dismissed as wholly groundless. Nor can the recurrent complaint be dismissed as unfounded, according to which those who have lived in Hungary since 1989 are called Romanians.

As part of the Diaspora-consciousness, a nostalgic yearning for the 'homeland' in Transylvania has not disappeared in a decade spent in Hungary; another aspect

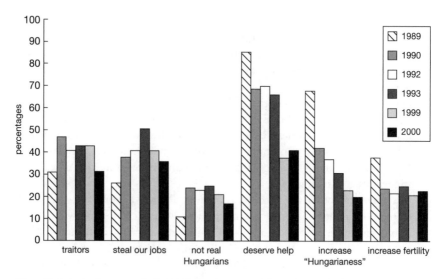

*Figure 12.1* Attitudes toward ethnic Hungarians from Transylvania (1989–2000) (%).
Source: Csepeli and Sik (1995) and TÁRKI, *Omnibus*, 1999 and 2000.

of the sociological concept of Diaspora is the fact that maintaining ties with those left home is an integral part of the life of Transylvanians in Hungary. There are several examples to support the claim that the Diaspora of Transylvanians in this country forms a 'transnational-community-in-miniature' living now here, now in Romania, thus reaping the economic and cultural benefits of its transitional position (Bíró *et al.* 1996; Bíró 1996; Grajczjar undated).

In sum, we can establish that there is no consensus of expert opinion concerning the question whether or not ethnic Hungarians migrating to Hungary from abroad can be regarded as a Diaspora, but there is no such powerful resistance against this proposition as seen in connection with the previous issue. In terms of its socio-logical features, this community can be regarded as a Diaspora. No doubt, this is a unique kind of Diaspora, because of its closeness to the host community, on the one hand, and the peculiarities of the historical, political and economic relations between the sending and the host countries, such as the peculiar legislative mechanisms regulating migration to Hungary in the country of origin (Bíró 1996), or the changes in identity-policies induced by the relocation of borders and the intermeshed networks of informal economic connections (Grajczjar undated).

## The peculiarities of migration and migration politics in contemporary Hungary

Closely related (both as cause and effect) to the strength and large volume of the ethnic Hungarian community with Diasporic features across the borders and to their paradoxical Diaspora living in Hungary, in the following we conceptualise certain peculiarities of contemporary Hungarian migration patterns and migration politics.

### *Migrating population or borders?*

Between 1881 and 1990 due to historical reasons (political suppression, economic crisis, racial persecution, ethnical intolerance), the influxes into Hungary from the neighbouring regions were significant in many cases. This is not to mention the population movements related to the changing state borders – at least four times in the twentieth century (Figure 12.2).

Despite the absence of registered data on aliens residing in Hungary, their stock and outflow as well as on migrating citizens from Hungary, it is estimated that since 1990 the net migration has been positive (Hárs *et al.* 2001). Although there are only fragmented statistics on immigration to Hungary, the overwhelming rate of ethnic Hungarians inside of each group of immigrating aliens cannot be ignored.

It is questionable whether the changing borders of a migrating state can turn a receiving country into a sending one, but according to available data net migration is positive in contemporary Hungary. As is the case with the other Central European countries, Hungary has also been considered a new receiving country, not only for those in transit, but also Hungary-bound ethnic migrants. Immigrants who were in transit came to improve their standards of living. The arrival of ethnic migrants,

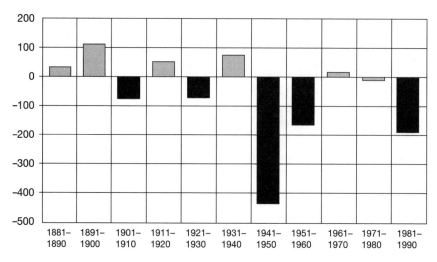

*Figure 12.2* Migration differences between the national censuses (1881–1991).
Source: Tóth, P.P. 2000 (Central Statistical Office, Institute of Demographic Studies).

however, is related to the consequence of state borders changing, which is an important and defining aspect of Hungary's role in issues of migration.

### Rich migration experiences and low acceptance of migrants

Although Hungarians have rich experiences in emigration and immigration they have not contributed to a higher level of acceptance or the increased sensitivity of migration policy. The level of tolerance toward aliens, in particular refugees (Figure 12.3), and cultural diversity has declined as migratory movements have become visible in recent decades.

### Exclusion of foreigners and/or strangers?

One might say that by definition the growing number of immigrants means the increase of foreigners provoking stronger conflicts or frictions in a receiving society. But in the case of Hungary the picture is more colourful. Immigrants are aliens by law but not necessary strangers culturally because the overwhelming majority of migrants (and almost all of those who ask for residence permits) are ethnic Hungarians coming from surrounding countries. This fact, however, does not prevent the rise of prejudice toward immigrants belonging to the same ethnic group. As surveys prove (Figure 12.1) the ethnic Hungarians have been considered as non-Hungarians or 'betrayers of the Hungarian community across the border', and they may endanger jobs in Hungary at a growing rate.

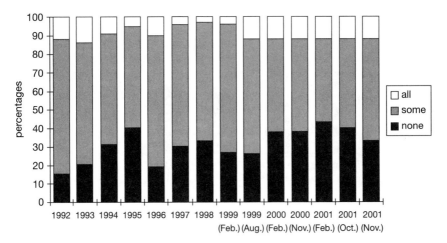

*Figure 12.3* Would you agree that Hungary should accept all refugees, or none of them, or some of them? (%).
Source: TÁRKI, *Omnibus*, 1992–2001.

## Controversies of the sovereignty of Hungary

Integration into NATO and into the EU has an impact on the feeling of sovereignty and may have a negative influence on the feeling of national pride if the nation is defined as a cultural or primordial community instead of being a political community (Csepeli 1996). Hungary seems to be in an in-between position, which is partly related to external impacts of new European architecture, partly to the lack of transparency in the European integration policy in Hungary, and partly to the influence of the ethnic Hungarian Diasporic community around and within Hungary.

In other words, the interpretation of sovereignty and its subjects would require public debates which answered questions of ethnic survival and movements, European integration, globalisation, modernisation of the post-communist country and national independence simultaneously. Due to a strongly centralised policy of accession and the ambivalent attitudes toward migration and migrants (being of non-ethnic Hungarians), there are suspicions regarding the social impact of EU-related migration (Figure 12.4).

## Instruments of exclusion of migrants

Hungary, as have other states in the region, has rapidly imported the exclusionary techniques from the EU (member states) as to how the application of asylum-seekers or non-desirable migrants can be reduced. Moreover, it has been combined with the rhetoric of combating illegal migration and harmonisation of laws. The 'safe country' principle, the rapid and simplified determination procedure in case of manifestly unfounded requests, detention of asylum seekers, readmission

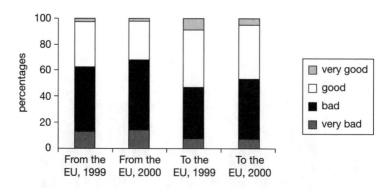

*Figure 12.4* The expectation regarding the social effects of migration in the course of EU accession (%).
Source: TÁRKI, *Omnibus*, 1999, 2000.

agreements and visa restrictions, have been introduced, consecutively or in parallel, precisely over a period in which the numbers of irregular migrants are fluctuating and those of asylum applicants are stable. It means that there is no statistical or economic evidence during the 1990s which could directly justify these restrictions against aliens, that characterise all migrants as probable enemies or potential criminals or at least abusive persons (Tóth 2001a).

In this context the restrictive elements of legal and institutional control over border crossings, preconditions of entry and residence of all foreigners have been regulated as follows:

- refoulement, the detention of aliens denied the right to enter or to reside in the country;
- stringent rules on residence authorisation and expulsion;
- a set of readmission agreements that provide for chain-deportation;
- asylum procedures and the detention of illegal migrants as applicants utilising the procedure in the case of manifestly unfounded requests, adoption of the 'safe country' principle;
- introduction of 'tolerated migrant' and 'temporary protection' categories;
- restrictions on the acquisition of citizenship;
- reduced stability of settled migrants (withdrawal of 'green card', their expulsion).

All of these devices to combat clandestine migration and applicants abusing the system were imported and did not come from the public law tradition of Hungary (Tóth 2001b). Moreover, citizens of Hungary, considered as third country nationals in European Community law, have been subjected to almost all of these restrictive and preventive legal and administrative instruments, while Hungary has introduced the same measures in parallel against foreigners arriving from and out of its own region.

These factors have a double impact. On the one hand, they obviously and rapidly opened new fields of international cooperation on such matters that traditionally belonged to the state sovereignty. On the other hand, these overlapping changes of transition and external effects contribute to the noticeable growth of xenophobia and anti-European sentiments, in spite of the original aims.

### Admit only 'self-made men'

The previously mentioned sense of emergency and suspicious attitude towards migrants, strongly reduced the moves towards family unification and integration of lawful foreign residents (recognised refugees, protected persons and settled migrants) into the local community, labour market and society in general. Although there are no notices attached to the border-crossing points to the effect that 'Hungary admits only self-made men' the migration policy has been based on this principle. It means that the harsh selective (exclusive) entry policy is not paired with a set of support mechanisms in order to integrate the foreigners into the society as smoothly as possible, preventing further social, cultural and political tensions. The logic is the opposite: the major aim is to frighten aliens, and those who remain are ethnic Hungarians. Why do they want integration programmes and assistance? The others who are non-Hungarians form an easily ignored small group that can manage the transition period alone, surviving the labyrinth of alien policing and refugee administration (Tóth 1995). This policy has led to a relatively high rate of transit, re-migration and irregular migration, which seems to support the government's unwillingness to develop an integration policy. Further, the ethnic preference in reception policy jeopardises the impartial implementation of human right obligations (Fullerton 1997) and produces dysfunctions in immigration law (Tóth 1997).

### Controversies in foreign affairs doctrine

There is a triple priority system within foreign policy, outlined by the first democratic government in 1990, which has been gradually developed and re-interpreted by all ruling coalitions since. Originally, this policy had three equally important components: (1) Hungary intends to integrate into the Euro-Atlantic alliance and organisations; (2) the country commits itself to establishing a good neighbourhood and friendly relations in the region; (3) as the mother country, it has responsibilities for ethnic Hungarians living across the border.

> The Hungarian Republic feels responsible for the lot of Hungarians living outside her borders and promotes their relations with Hungary.

The amendment of the Constitution[5] to include this sentence significantly changed the policy of the democratic Hungarian government and legislation related to the Diaspora. Since 1989 the expressions most frequently used were national minorities, nationalities, parts of the nation, Hungarians abroad, Diaspora or Hungarians beyond the borders but terminological diversity has remained up to now strongly linked to the controversial nature of the policies and their legal obscurity (Tóth 2000a).

Members of the nation can be legally classified into three simple categories. First, and the great part of them, the citizens of the Hungarian Republic. Second, several million ethnic Hungarians, who are foreign citizens. Finally, the family relationships of the two previous groups have created a great number of ethnic Hungarians in possession of multiple citizenship. Attachment on the basis of citizenship is just one aspect, the other being that of registered, lawful residence. In accordance with the latter, a differentiation is made between Hungarian citizens living in Hungary, Hungarian citizens living abroad, and foreign citizens residing in Hungary or living abroad but belonging to the Hungarian nation. These simple elements of classification may only be used if it can be legally determined what belonging to the Hungarian ethnicity means, and what the requirements of living somewhere include.

Although the number of domestic and international legal sources covering the various legal aspects of Diaspora is increasing – it amounted to over 150 sources in force in 2000 – the Diaspora law has been subjected to changing political priorities, but has not established a coherent structure. Further, the Diaspora policy is based on the basis of myths or common belief on the part of ethnic Hungarian communities. For instance, Hungarians beyond the borders are always referred to as a community of three million in the surrounding states, and two million emigrants all over the world (Tóth 2000). While the first group is considered the innocent victims of migrating state borders, the emigrants are stigmatised. The Hungarian community in the neighbouring states is regarded as a depository of genuine ethnical identity, but the assimilated emigrants are regarded as 'second-class patriots' who left voluntarily for a better life, despite the fact that the Holocaust exchanges of population in 1945–6, the Communist suppression and the revolution in 1956 produced thousands of expatriated nationals. Social surveys on various patterns of all socialisation to the environment in each majoritarian society and statistics on composition of Diaspora groups have never been required in order to establish informed Diaspora policies or regulation. The European integration of the mother country inspires the birth of new myths (Bárdi 2000) as well as new stereotypes of Hungarians across the borders.

Needless to say, these priorities of foreign affairs doctrine have never been equal. Frequently they are in competition, and the government in power has to make choices in concrete political situations. Meanwhile, public opinion can feel reassured (Tóth 2000b).

### Do not panic over Schengen – stay at home!

The 'imported' instruments of exclusion during the efforts towards accession to the EU have been implemented against migrants, of which about two thirds belong to the nation. Besides the fact that the public administration is overworked, the implementation of these restrictive alien-policing provisions has been laden with controversy. In the near future, the existing conflicts between the written law, the aims of regulation and its implementation may be more complex, due to increased friction. Apart from Diaspora policy, Hungary as the mother country has not welcomed the ethnic Hungarians coming with the intention to settle in the country. It is said that Hungary must not encourage emigration from the homeland and relinquish the historical living space and settlement of ethnic Hungarians. Thus the immigration to Hungary has been gradually limited, in parallel with the European tendency towards stricter migration regulation (Tóth 2001a). The Governmental message on staying at home will be in accordance with European Community law, too. At the same time, transit migration of ethnic Hungarians coming from the surrounding states for short term visits (visitors, irregular traders, labourers, students or tourists) as a form of migratory movement has been more fully endorsed through laser border control and the visa-free system. But it would be endangered by the adaptation of the 'Schengen regime' which requires the imposition of entry conditions on all third country nationals, on the basis of unified provisions within European Community law on all candidate/ newly acceded member states. 'The development of a Schengen type cooperation in the immediate future does not coincide with the Hungarian interests, in other words, the slower they are realised, the better it is for Hungary' (Kovács 2000).

## Nation-building as compensation

Compensating for the negative impact of speedy European integration and the increased harmonisation of law, Hungary has developed new instruments of nation-building, although they exclude certain parts of the Diaspora (ethnic Hungarians living out of the Carpathian Basin) from these institutions.

The Office for Hungarians Across the Border Affairs was established to carry out government policy in 1992 at first located within the Prime Minister's Office,[6] and in 1998 integrated into the Ministry of Foreign Affairs. The institutionalisation of Diaspora policy has gradually taken place, from 1990. The Standing Hungarian Conference as an institution of dialogue among the representatives of the Government, the parties in the Parliament and Hungarian communities of the Diaspora was set up in 1999.[7] This body includes numerous sub-committees and plays a vague role: the Parliament only 'welcomes its establishment' and calls upon the Government 'to give a yearly report on its operation and execution of the political proposals of the Conference concerning Hungarians across the border'. Thus the Government has a wide room for manoeuvre to exchange views, to reconcile divergent opinions, to find political consensus or to maintain the veneer officially. According to the Government's interpretation,[8] the main national task is to develop the connection between the Hungarians living beyond the borders and the mother country, in the fields of education, culture, economy, health care, welfare, local governmental and regional relations in order to 'remain resident in the homeland, yet preserve national identity'. For these reasons, working committees of the Conference were also formed on citizenship and European integration issues. The state secretary (deputy secretary) of the competent ministry chairs all of the committees, while expert members are appointed by the Office for Hungarians Across the Border Affairs. Parties in the Parliament, representative organisations of Hungarian communities across the border and the World Alliance of Hungarians as an NGO, may delegate the other members of the committees. This organ produces proposals but their relevance, the decision-making procedure and publicity has not been defined. In this way, the Conference may be considered as a shadow or a substitute body of genuine negotiation, discourse or compromise-making. However it is enough to legitimise the actual Diaspora policy.

The Bill on Hungarians living beyond the border or as ordinary people call it the 'Bill on status law' was the result of about three years of preparatory work. It was finally submitted to the Parliament in March 2001, and the Parliament passed the Act on Hungarians Living in the Neighbouring States in late June 2001.[9] In order to advance national cohesion and identity, the Act provides rather symbolic services, assistance and finance for ethnic Hungarians who live permanently in Croatia, Yugoslavia, Slovenia, Slovakia, Romania and Ukraine but it excludes the other ethnic Hungarians (in the Czech Republic, Russia, Baltic States, CIS countries or in the West) from the nation building. Why? They may have a strong national identity, or none at all, or be able to afford to buy services for maintaining their own ethnic identity, or live far from the new frontiers now emerging on the Hungarian borders due to the Schengen visa system and its system of control. The new Act, together with numerous executive decrees, intensifies disputes not only between the government and its political opponents, but also internationally, such as those inside the Council of Europe (the Venice Committee) and the EU, as well as between Hungary and its neighbours.

### Lobbying for the whole but fragmented nation

Hungary hopes to be integrated into the EU as a state but is lobbying on behalf of the whole nation that has remained fragmented in various senses, such as to be excluded from Diaspora law and policy or EU or both. This lobbying includes efforts to remove Romania[10] from the list of states whose nationals must be in possession of a visa for entry into the territory of the EU, to ensure that Slovakia accedes to the EU together with Hungary, and to implement the Schengen/EU border control regime in a flexible manner. On the other side, these possible developments may contribute to regional stability, better economic links in the region, and pro-European feelings. Thus the failure of lobbying may have a negative effect in these fields.

## Conclusion

The practical effects of a one-sided accession and enlargement policy can have unintended consequences, both on the enlargement process and beyond. The potential frictions can be summarised as follows.

The enlargement of the European Union will move the present external Schengen border to the East, in a manner which will be more restrictive for the movement of persons in Central and Eastern Europe, and which has seen the arrival of a new era of freedom of movement of persons.

There are several highly sensitive border regions, which could be adversely affected. In fact these are found virtually all the way round the EU's future external frontier. For instance, the frontiers between Ukraine and its EU candidate neighbours (Poland, Hungary, Slovakia and Romania) currently witness very large movements across these borders for purposes of trade and personal connections; or the borders of South-East Europe, where there is an outer ring of visa-free states (Croatia, Slovenia, Hungary, Romania, Bulgaria and Greece) surrounding by an inner core subject to visa requirements (Bosnia, Macedonia, Federal Republic of Yugoslavia and Albania).

The priority of the EU is to ensure that the new member states will be able to implement the existing Schengen rules, including the new visa requirements. The priority of the applicant states is to clear the way for accession to the EU as soon as possible. Neither side has therefore yet given sufficient attention to the need to make the new external Schengen frontiers of the EU as friendly as possible for the new borderland neighbours. The EU has not yet developed a positive, pro-active approach to minimising these problems. Many ways exist which could alleviate undesirable restrictive effects of the Schengen regime on the movement of honest citizens in and out of the EU, without prejudice to the security objectives of the EU. Examples include (1) *provision of adequate consular services* for people living in frontier regions as well as capital cities, (2) *upgrading of border facilities* to provide for the rapid passage of large numbers without the long queues which are often experienced today, (3) *special bilateral agreements for border regions*, such as long-term multi-entry national visas at low or zero charge, very short-term visas for one or two days to facilitate local family contacts, tourism and small scale commerce, and (outside the Schengen jurisdiction) permanent resident permits; (4) *customer-friendly border services*, with training of personnel to eliminate the undignified interrogation styles, cut visa queues and delays, and make application forms available by post or from Internet sites; (5) *planning in neighbouring states for visa-free status*, with help from the EU to prepare action programmes for approaching the conditions under which visa requirements may be lifted; (6) *development of Euro-region programmes* to boost cooperative regional development across the EU's new external frontier, with revision of segmented EU aid programmes to make them a more border-region friendly; (7) *clarification of the rights of movement, residence and employment in the EU of stateless persons*, (8) *sequencing in the introduction of Schengen*, taking care in managing the inevitably progressive application of the full Schengen regime so as to minimise frictions between candidate and third countries; (9) *possible easing of immigration policy by EU member states (or later, by the EU)*.

This process should be launched by a Political Declaration from leaders of the European Union, in favour of a 'Friendly Schengen Border Policy' (FSBP)[11] giving due weight to the external policy objective of the European Union. It may avoid new dividing lines on the EU's Eastern frontiers, alongside its internal policy priority to achieve security objectives, social cohesion and solidarity.

On the other hand, the Diaspora discourse with all its controversies and consequences has remained the organic part of the Hungarian foreign and domestic policy. The newly adopted Act on Hungarians Living in Neighbouring States, as a major pillar of institutionalised Diaspora politics, cannot provide a satisfactory remedy for the painful fact: Hungary as a state can gain access to the EU, but the nation is, at the same time, unable to unite under the same roof. The mental or spiritual unification of the nation would be developed but not through legal instruments or political rivalry prior to the coming general elections. The ambivalent attitudes of people toward foreign citizens as members of the Diaspora can be related partly to new security measures and stringent police control of aliens as features of enlargement, and partly to jealousy over economic, social or political advantages in the transition period. The Act provides numerous benefits for the Diaspora living in the Carpathian Basin in respect of cultural relations, education, public travel, labour market and community life, but their implementation will depend on the central budget and the variable level of prejudice within public opinion. The Act has had a noticeable impact on subsequent legislation, such that about two dozen governmental and ministerial decrees were passed during 2001–2. The offices issuing the 'Certificate for Ethnic Hungarians' are under siege, especially in poor regions, from those who wish to obtain the benefits as soon as possible. For them the Certificate may provide evidence of national identity, although this new document cannot replace either full emancipation, citizenship rights or equal opportunities in the home country, nor can it replace entry visas, financial support for entry, international insurance[12] or the lack of solidarity in Hungary.

In additional, the government has underlined how the new Act is greatly inclusive. For example, upon request, the state secretary confirmed that Gypsies living in the neighbouring states could enjoy the benefits of the Act on the basis of free self-declaration of identity.

> The draft legislation – the parliamentary debate on which is currently underway – is of an inclusive nature: it says he is Hungarian who describes himself as being Hungarian.
>
> Those who wish to avail themselves of the benefits and assistance provided by the Act should have the so-called 'Hungarian Certificate', which will be issued on the basis of the recommendation of an organization operating in a neighbouring state and recognized by the Hungarian Government. According to the plans, for the recommendation to be issued, one will have to provide a written declaration stating that he belongs to the Hungarian nation, an application for the recommendation, with a knowledge of the Hungarian language as another prerequisite. Provided certain supplementary conditions are present, an exemption may be granted from this latter condition. If the applicant meets these criteria, the recommendation must be granted regardless of origin, religion or political affiliation.[13]

The inclusive approach adopted toward the most frequent victims of discrimination and racism in our region, together with non-practical benefits, are likely to reduce the enthusiasm of Diaspora and their supporters in Hungary; thus disappointed voters may endanger the success of the ruling party at the elections.

The members of the Diaspora who do not benefit, sceptics in the mother society as well as the majority societies in neighbouring countries, have taken into consideration the opinion of the Venice Commission from the earliest days. The Commission endorses the tripartite system involving the representatives of minorities, the mother country and the home country in the preparation of legal instruments. If the Diaspora (minority) is part of the nation-building process, the states have to adopt measures in accordance with international legal obligations, human rights, sovereignty of parties and political commitments. It means that unilateral regulation by the mother state in favour of the Diaspora living in another country may inspire further regional conflicts instead of a durable solution for national minority protection.

> Responsibility for minority protection lies primarily with the home-states. The Commission notes that kin-states also play a role in the protection and preservation of their kin-minorities, aiming at ensuring that their genuine linguistic and cultural links remain strong. Europe has developed as a cultural unity based on a diversity of interconnected languages and cultural traditions; cultural diversity constitutes a richness, and acceptance of this diversity is a precondition to peace and stability in Europe.
>
> The Commission considers, however, that respect for the existing framework of minority protection must be held as a priority. In this field, multilateral and bilateral treaties have been stipulated under the umbrella of European initiatives. The effectiveness of the treaty approach could be undermined, if these treaties were not interpreted and implemented in good faith in the light of the principle of good neighbourly relations between States.[14]

To conclude, national identity and cultural unity cannot precede security and sovereignty, while the symbolic and spiritual nation-building should not interfere with European integration. It is the level of science and art of governance that determines the extent of migration control, the desire for security, the commitment to Europeanisation and the strengthening of national identity. For Hungarians the Diaspora policy or politics means this test will be confronted in future.

## Notes

1 This model was adopted by Szántó (1984) when, in his discussion of the Hungarian Diaspora – without actually mentioning the term 'Diaspora' – in the West, he employs a typology that addresses conjointly the tripartite relationship of the given community with Hungary, with the host country and the ethnic population living there.

2 What we have in mind here is a joke from the 1960s, which has Mr Kohn emigrate to Israel only to return soon after to Hungary. When he applies for an emigrant passport a second time, the Hungarian policeman asks him why he does not make up his mind where he likes it best: in Israel or in Hungary. Mr Kohn's answer is: 'On the plane'.

3 This section is based on Sik (2000). The interview excerpts are from in-depth case

    studies with politicians (both in Hungary and in the ethnic Hungarian community across the Hungarian border) deeply involved with Diaspora politics.

4　Similarly, a Chinese identity is the only characteristic of the Chinese Diaspora, whereas the Chinese of China will far sooner identify with a particular province. The power of a 'Pan-Chinese' identity stems partly form the 'lowest common denominator' and partly a product of China's Diaspora-policies (Nyiri 2001). Further, this is the identity-element which is meaningful for the foreigner, which is why it provides the individual living in Diaspora with a 'usable' identity.

5　Constitution, para 6 (3), enacted by Act XXXI of 1989, para 2, in force as of 23 October 1989.

6　Government Decree No. 90/1992, 29 May 1992, replacing the Secretariat of Hungarians Across the Borders inside the Prime Minister's Office.

7　Parliamentary Resolution No. 26 of 1999, 26 March.

8　Government Resolution No. 1079 of 1999, 7 July.

9　Act No. LXII of 2001, which entered into force on 1 January 2002.

10　The frontier along the Hungarian–Romanian border depends on how and when Romania could be removed from the common list of countries requiring a visa, in accordance with the EU's requirements (500PC0027 document of the Commission, issued on 28 February 2000).

11　See the Conference report with recommendations on the reshaping of Europe's borders: Challenges for EU and External Policy (Centre for European Policy Studies – Sitra Foundation and Stefan Bathory Foundation, Brussels, 6/7 July 2001: New European Borders and Security Cooperation – Promoting Trust in an Enlarged Union).

12　'The Republic of Hungary, in order to ensure the maintenance of permanent contacts, provide for the accessibility of benefits and supports defined in this Act, ensure undisturbed cultural, economic and family relations, ensure the free movement of persons and the free flow of ideas, and taking into account her international legal obligations, shall provide for the most benefited [favoured] treatment in the given circumstances that are possible with regard to the entry and stay on its territory for the persons falling within the scope of this Act' (Article 3).

13　Letter exchange between Mr Zsolt Német and Mr Joszef Krasznai (Deputy leader of the Roma Parliament) Annex No. 3 to Paper Containing the Position of the Hungarian Government in relation to the Act on Hungarians Living in Neighbouring Countries (Budapest, 2001).

14　European Commission for Democracy Through Law (Venice Commission), Strasbourg, 22 October 2001 (CDL-INF (2001) 19) 'Report on the preferential treatment of national minorities by their kin-state' adopted by the Venice Commission at its 48th Plenary Meeting (Venice, 19/20 October 2001).

# References

Bárdi, N. (2000) 'Cleavages in cross-border Magyar minority politics 1989–1998', *Regio (Minorities, Politics, Society)*, Budapest: Teleki L. Institute, Centre of Central European Studies, 3–36.

Béla, B. K. (1999) 'Válasszunk magunknak új identitást', *Erdélyi Hívogató*, 2, 1: 1–2.

Bíró, A. Z. (1992) 'A regionális identitáskialakításának néhány vonásáról', *Régió* 3, 4: 61–71.

—— (1994) 'Adalékok a vándorló ember ikonográfiájához', in E. Sik and J. Tóth (eds) *Jönnek?Mennek?Maradnak?*, Budapest: MTA PTI.

—— (1996) 'Egyéni és kollektív identitás a kilépési gyakorlatban', in J. Bodó (ed.) *Elvándorlók? Vendégmunka és életforma a Székelyföldön*, Csíkszereda: KAM, Pro-Print Kiadó.

—— (1998) *Stratégiák vagy kényszerpályák?*, Csíkszereda: KAM, Pro-Print Kiadó.

Bíró, A.Z., Bodó, J., Gagyi, J., Oláh, S. and Túrós, E. (1996) 'Vándormunka – otthonról nézve', in J. Bodó (ed.) *Elvándorlók? Vendégmunka és életforma a Székelyföldön*, Csíkszereda: KAM, Pro-Print Kiadó.

Bonacich, E. (1973) 'A theory of middlemen minorities', *American Sociological Review* 38: 583–94.

Bonacich, E. and Turner, J. H. (1980) 'Toward a composite theory of middlemam minorities', *Ethnicity* 7:144–158.

Clifford, J (1994) 'Diasporas', *Cultural Anthropology* 9, 3: 302–38.

Csepeli, G (1996) 'Nem tudják, de érzik: A nemzeti szuverenitás reprezentációja a mai magyar társadalomban', in E. Hankiss (ed.) *A szuverenitás káprázata*, Budapest: Korridor.

Csepeli, G. and Sik, E. (1995) 'Changing content of political xenophobia in Hungary – is the growth of xenophobia inevitable?' in M. Fullerton, E. Sik and J. Tóth (eds) *Refugees and Migrants: Hungary at a Crossroads*, Budapest: MTA PTI.

Demetriou, M. (1999) 'Beyond the nation state? Diasporic identities, loyalty and transnational politics', paper presented at the conference on 'Diasporas and Ethnic Migration in 20th Century Europe', 20–3 May, Berlin.

Doomernik, J. (1997) 'A society without borders? "Russian" transnational communities in Western Europe', paper presented at the conference on 'Central and Eastern Europe New Migration Space', 11–13 December, Pultusk.

Fullerton, M (1997) 'Hungary, refugees, and the law of return' in M. Fullerton, E. Sik and J. Tóth (eds) *From Improvisation toward Awareness? Contemporary Migration Politics in Hungary*, Yearbook of the Research Group on International Migration, Institute for Political Science, HAS.

Grajczjar, I. (undated) 'Külföldiek a Moszkva-téri emberpiacon', unpublished manuscript, Budapest.

Hall, S. (1990) 'Cultural identity and diaspora', in J. Rutherford (ed.) *Identity, Community, Cultural Difference*, London: Lawrence and Wishart.

Hárs, Á., Sik, E. and Tóth, J. (2001) 'Hungary' in C. Wallace and D. Stola (eds) *Patterns of Migration in Central Europe*, New York: Palgrave.

Kántor, Z. (undated) 'Jövőelképzelés és kivándorlás', unpublished manuscript, Budapest.

Kovács, P. (2000) 'Co-operation in the spirit of the Schengen Agreement – the Hungarians beyond the borders', *Minorities Research (A collection of studies by Hungarian authors)* No. 3, Budapest: Lucidus.

Light, I. and Bonacich, E. (1988) *Immigrant Entrepreneurs*, Berkeley: University of California Press.

Nyri, P. (2001) 'Expatriating is patriotic?' in P. Nyri, J. Tóth and M. Fullerton (eds) *Diasporas and Politics*, Budapest: Centre for Migration and Refugee Studies.

Oláh, S. (1996) 'A kilépés társadalmi feltételei a Székelyföldön', in J. Bodó (ed.) *Elvándorlók? Vendégmunka és életforma a Székelyföldön*, Csíkszereda: KAM, Pro-Print Kiadó.

Romaniszyn, K. (1996) 'The invisible community: undocumented Polish workers in Athens', *New Community* 22, 2: 321–33.

Shain, Y. and Sherman, M. (1999) 'Diasporic transnational financial flows and their impact on national identity', paper presented at the conference on 'Diasporas and Ethnic Migration in 20th Century Europe', May 20–3, Berlin.

Sheffer, G: (1999) 'From Diasporas to migrants, from migrants to Diasporas', paper presented at the conference on 'Diasporas and Ethnic Migration in 20th Century Europe', May 20–3, Berlin.

Sik, E. (1999) *Idegenellenesség Magyarországon 1999-ben*, Budapest: Európai Összehasonlító Kisebbségkutatási Alapítvány.

—— (2000) 'Diaspora: tentative observation and applicability in Hungary' in I. Kiss and C. MacGovern (eds) *New Diasporas in Hungary, Russia, and Ukraine: Legal Regulations and Current Politics*, Budapest: COLPI.

Szakáts, M. E. (1996) 'Az Erdélyből áttelepült magyarok otthonképe', in E. Sik and J. Tóth (eds) *Táborlakók, diaszpórák, politikák*, Budapest: MTA PTI.

Szántó, M. (1984) *Magyarok Amerikában*, Budapest: Gondolat.

TÁRKI, *Omnibus* (1992–2001) Budapest, Hungary.

Tóth, J. (1995) 'Who are the desirable immigrants in Hungary under the newly adopted laws?' in M. Fullerton, E. Sik and J. Tóth (eds) *Refugees and Migrants: Hungary at a Crossroads*, Yearbook of the Research Group on the International Migration, Budapest: Institute for Political Science, HAS.

—— (1997) 'Choices offered by the migration policy menu', in M. Fullerton, E. Sik and J. Tóth (eds) *From Improvisation toward Awareness? Contemporary Migration Politics in Hungary*, Yearbook of the Research Group on International Migration, Budapest: Institute for Political Science, HAS.

—— (2000a) 'Diaspora in legal regulations: 1989–1999, in I. Kiss and C. McGovern (eds) *New Diasporas in Hungary, Russia and Ukraine: Legal Regulations and Current Politics*, Budapest: Open Society Institute/COLPI, pp. 42–95.

—— (2000b) 'Diaspora politics: programs and prospects' in I. Kiss and C. McGovern (eds) *New Diasporas in Hungary, Russia and Ukraine: Legal Regulations and Current Politics*, Budapest: Open Society Institute/COLPI.

—— (2001a) 'The impact of the EU migration policies on Central-Eastern European countries', *Refugee Survey Quarterly* 20, 2: 102–14.

—— (2001b) 'Security of residence and expulsion: protection of aliens in Hungary', in E. Guild and P. Minderhoud (eds) *Security of Residence and Expulsion: Protection of Aliens in Europe, Immigration and Asylum Law and Policy in Europe, Vol.1*, The Hague: Kluwer Law International.

Tóth, P.P. (2000) 'Contributions to the forming of Hungarian political strategy concerning the emigrants', *Minorities Research (A collection of studies by Hungarian authors)* No. 3, Budapest: Lucidus.

Wallace, C. (2001) 'Conceptual challenges from the new migration space' in C. Wallace and D. Stola (eds) *Patterns of Migration in Central Europe*, New York: Palgrave.

Wallace, C., Sidorenko, E. and Chmouliar, O. (1996) 'The Eastern frontier of Western Europe: mobility in the buffer zone', *New Community* 22, 2: 259–86.

# Index